RECURRENT EDUCATION AND LIFELONG LEARNING

WORLD YEARBOOK OF EDUCATION 1979

RECURRENT EDUCATION AND LIFELONG LEARNING

Edited by

TOM SCHULLER and JACQUETTA MEGARRY

LONDON AND NEW YORK

First published in 1979 by Kogan Page Ltd
This edition first published in 2006 by
Routledge
2 Park Square, Milton Park, Abingdon, Oxon, OX14 4RN

711 Third Avenue, New York, NY 10017

Routledge is an imprint of the Taylor & Francis Group, an informa business

First issued in paperback 2012

© 1979 Kogan Page and Named Contributors

All rights reserved. No part of this book may be reprinted or reproduced or utilized in any form or by any electronic, mechanical, or other means, now known or hereafter invented, including photocopying and recording, or in any information storage or retrieval system, without permission in writing from the publishers.

The publishers have made every effort to contact authors and copyright holders of the works reprinted in the *World Yearbook of Education* series. This has not been possible in every case, however, and we would welcome correspondence from those individuals or organisations we have been unable to trace.

These reprints are taken from original copies of each book. In many cases the condition of these originals is not perfect. The publisher has gone to great lengths to ensure the quality of these reprints, but wishes to point out that certain characteristics of the original copies will, of necessity, be apparent in reprints thereof.

British Library Cataloguing in Publication Data
A CIP catalogue record for this book
is available from the British Library

Recurrent Education and Lifelong Learning

ISBN13: 978-0-415-39295-2 (hbk)
ISBN13: 978-0-415-50235-1 (pbk)
ISBN13: 978-0-415-38605-0 (set)

World Yearbook of Education

World Yearbook of Education 1979
Recurrent Education and Lifelong Learning

Edited by **Tom Schuller** *(Subject Editor)*
and **Jacquetta Megarry** *(Series Editor)*

UK Consultant Editor **Gerry Fowler**
US Consultant Editor **Myron Atkin**

Kogan Page, London/Nichols Publishing Company, New York

Previously published under the title *Year Book of Education* from 1932 to 1964 and then as *World Year Book of Education* from 1965 to 1974 by Evans Brothers Ltd

First published as *World Yearbook of Education* in Great Britain in 1979 by Kogan Page Limited

Copyright © 1979 Kogan Page Ltd and contributors
All rights reserved
ISBN 0 85038 166 5
ISSN 0084-2508

First published in the United States of America in 1979 by Nichols Publishing Company, PO Box 96, New York, NY 10024
ISBN 0-89397-058-1
LC Catalog Card No 32-18413

Printed in Great Britain by McCorquodale (Newton) Ltd.

Contents

List of Contributors   7

Preface *Jacquetta Megarry*   9

Part 1: Orientation

1. The work/leisure/education life cycle *Jarl Bengtsson*   17
2. Changes in western society: educational implications *Tom Stonier*   31
3. Recurrent education and lifelong learning: definitions and distinctions *Denis Kallen*   45

Part 2: Major Issues

4. Research insights into adult learning *Alan B Knox*   57
5. The need for diversity of provision *Geoffrey Hubbard*   80
6. Recurrent education: tackling the financial implications *Maurice Peston*   86
7. The democratization of work: educational implications *Tom Schuller*   97

Part 3: International Developments

8. Lifelong learning in the United States *J Roby Kidd*   113
9. Paid educational leave in France *Pierre Caspar*   128
10. Recent legislation and the Norwegian pattern of adult education *Øyvind Skard*   137
11. Strategic planning on a recurrent basis *Hans-Erik Östlund*   146
12. West German experience of 'popular' higher education *Helmuth Dolff*   159
13. Lifelong education policies in western and eastern Europe: similarities and differences *Ettore Gelpi*   167
14. Lifelong basic education for the 'absolute poor' in Africa *Marjorie Mbilinyi*   176
15. Education in China: a lifelong process *Peter Mauger*   193

16. Asia and the South Pacific: the exchange of ideas with 209
    Australia *Chris Duke*

Part 4: Trends in Britain

17. Recurrent education: perceptions, problems and priorities 227
    Frank Molyneux
18. A comprehensive system of education for adults 244
    Naomi McIntosh
19. Co-ordinating vocational education for adults *Ron Johnson* 257
20. The Open University and the future of continuing 271
    education *Peter Venables*

Part 5

Signposts *Gerry Fowler* 287

Part 6: Bibliography and Biographical Notes

Bibliography 301
Biographical notes on contributors and editors 312

Index 319

List of Contributors

Dr Jarl Bengtsson, Counsellor, Centre for Educational Research and Innovation, OECD, Paris	Chapter 1
Pierre Caspar, Chairman of the Board of Quaternaire Education, Paris	Chapter 9
Helmuth Dolff, Director, Deutscher Volkshochschul-Verband, Bonn	Chapter 12
Dr Chris Duke, Director, Centre for Continuing Education, Australian National University, Canberra	Chapter 16
Professor Gerry Fowler, MP from 1974-79, formerly Minister of State for Higher Education, Professor Associate, Brunel University, London	Part 5
Ettore Gelpi, Chief, Lifelong Education Unit, UNESCO, Paris	Chapter 13
Geoffrey Hubbard, Director, Council for Educational Technology for the United Kingdom, London	Chapter 5
Dr Ron Johnson, Director of Training, Manpower Services Commission, Training Services Division and Visiting Professor, Department of Adult Education, University of Surrey	Chapter 19
Professor Denis Kallen, Institute of Education, European Cultural Foundation, Paris	Chapter 3
Professor J Roby Kidd, Professor of Adult Education, Ontario Institute for Studies in Education and Secretary-General, International Council for Adult Education	Chapter 8
Dr Alan B Knox, Professor of Continuing Education, University of Illinois at Urbana-Champaign	Chapter 4
Professor Naomi E McIntosh, Professor of Applied Social Research, Open University, and member of the Advisory Council for Adult and Continuing Education	Chapter 18
Peter Mauger, free-lance writer and lecturer on Chinese Education	Chapter 15
Dr Marjorie Mbilinyi, Assistant Professor in Education, University of Dar Es Salaam	Chapter 14
Dr Frank Molyneux, School of Education, University of Nottingham and Association for Recurrent Education	Chapter 17
Hans-Erik Östlund, Head of the Budget and Planning Secretariat, Ministry of Education, Stockholm	Chapter 11
Professor Maurice Peston, Department of Economics, Queen Mary College, University of London	Chapter 6
Tom Schuller, Research Director, Centre for Research in Industrial Democracy and Participation, University of Glasgow	Chapter 7
Dr Øyvind Skard, Director, Norwegian Employers' Confederation and Chairman of the Board of the Norwegian Institute for Adult Education	Chapter 10
Dr Tom Stonier, Professor and Chairman, School of Science and Society, University of Bradford	Chapter 2

Sir Peter Venables, Chairman of the Open University
    Planning Committee 1967-69 and Pro-Chancellor and Chairman
    of Council 1969-74

Chapter 20

Where affiliations are given above, they do not imply identification with the views expressed by the authors, who are writing as individuals.

Preface

The return of the *World Yearbook of Education* after an absence of five years calls for comment. Faithful readers with long memories may know that this series was first published in 1932 as the *Year Book of Education*. Its founder was the then Chairman of its publishers, Sir Robert Evans, and except during 1941-7 Evans Brothers published it until 1974. In the period 1932-40 the *Year Book* was concerned with educational issues in the UK, the Commonwealth and elsewhere and provided large amounts of statistical information. Later, in the post-war years, a thematic emphasis displaced the statistical sections and in 1965 the title was changed to *World Year Book of Education* in recognition of its increasingly international coverage. Up to 1970 (*Education in Cities*) it was published annually; afterwards it was biennial. The last issue to be published by Evans Brothers was the 1974 WYBE *Education and Rural Development*. It contained explanations of the termination of the series (or suspension, as it has subsequently turned out to be). The purpose of this preface is to assert afresh the rationale for the WYBE; to identify its distinctive features; to outline the aspirations and intentions of the new series; and to introduce this particular volume.

In the preface to the last volume (WYBE 1974:xv) the editors gave several reasons for discontinuing the project. For example, they pointed to the 'major proliferation of educational research journals', the fact that 'the field of comparative studies has itself become more specialized and infinitely more complex' and the 'almost inevitable trend' that scholars 'prefer to publish their research and findings within more specialized periodicals' and concluded that 'the pool of potential contributors to the *Year Book* has declined.' While in no way underestimating the development of the comparative education field, nor in any way denigrating the specialised periodicals, we entirely reject this line of reasoning. The WYBE should never be a mere juxtaposition of articles which, had they not appeared together, might otherwise have been scattered in a variety of periodicals. For one thing, there should be a consistency of style and an integration of approach consequent on the way in which each volume is planned.

Moreover, the intended readership is quite different. The WYBE series has been used in the past by teachers, lecturers, students, administrators, researchers, politicians — and parents. Its contributors must address themselves to an intelligent lay audience; that is, they must write simply and intelligibly and without making unrealistic assumptions of detailed background knowledge in their readership. They must eschew the academic convention of peppering each assertion with references which disturb the flow of the reader's thoughts. This requires a different style and, in many ways, a tougher discipline of authorship than the art of writing for one's peers and colleagues. However — and this is the hallmark of what will distinguish a good WYBE from a mediocre popularization — there must be no trace of 'talking down' to the audience, no suggestion of glossing over conceptual difficulties, no expectation of readers accepting 'on faith'.

More fundamentally still, the whole purpose of the comparative perspective in a WYBE context is *not* the accumulation of information about various different countries. There is no *intrinsic* value in 'notching up' as many countries as possible. What is valuable in reading about other countries' educational systems, their problems, and the solutions they have attempted, is the fresh perspective it gives us on our own problems. To help us transfer the ideas and apply them to other contexts, we need authors who can paint on a broad canvas; they must select and concentrate on a significant trend, a keynote issue, a recurrent problem, and examine it in such a way that the discussion is relevant to readers from a variety of countries, including those not represented in the volume. Above all, they must avoid getting bogged down in details about their own countries, systems or individual research interests, though they must be authoritative and knowledgeable on their themes.

The last WYBE contains a lengthy and fascinating postscript by Brian Holmes; it combines the roles of retrospect, valediction and post-mortem. He explains the aims of the series, the origin of the thematic approach and the international perspective, and offers an analysis of its demise. He also contemplates ways in which it might have been saved:

> What might have been attempted with success would have been to collect each year a relatively small number of high quality, previously published articles on a worldwide problem. (WYBE 1974:405)

Enough has been said in the previous paragraphs to explain why we did not give this expedient serious consideration: WYBE chapters must be purpose-written. (And Holmes himself remarks that 'Nobody was prepared to allow the WYBE to become a textbook of readings however scholarly.') Nor did we contemplate the other course of action the London board considered 'of reducing or omitting the comparative element'; it seemed that a World Year Book without the comparative perspective would be a contradiction in terms.

Perhaps the difference between the present editorial team and the previous is merely one of confidence; we may just have the faith and hope born of inexperience. If so, however, it does not stem from confidence in ourselves, but in the reputation of the series and the professional dedication of the potential authors. To take a related issue, there are several references in Holmes' postscript to the lack of resources for the WYBE and the need for official backing; he mentions, perhaps with regret, the possible effect of the bold policy of opening up new ground and encouraging controversy in making it 'difficult for the *World Year Book* in the long run to receive substantial official support from national or international sources.' Elsewhere he speaks with regret of the 'lack of resources' and with apparent envy of research units with 'sufficient funds to provide for adequate research assistance and secretarial help'. He contrasts their ability 'to pay participants a professional fee' with the fact that WYBE authors 'were paid a nominal sum as an honorarium and consequently the editors had to rely on the goodwill of scholars throughout the world . . . It says much for the reputation of the editors and the prestige of the sponsoring institutions . . . and the name of the publishers, that so many distinguished scholars wrote for the *World Year Book*'.

However, we attribute the splendid response we have had from authors not to our publisher, not to our institutions (least of all to ourselves) but to the reputation of the series and their respect for its long tradition. True, the logistics of modern publishing prevent payment of a 'professional fee'. But authors with the qualities outlined earlier cannot be bought. They are *amateur* authors in the original sense of the word; they will do the task, if at all, because they want to — for the intrinsic interest, because of the challenge it presents — or, the cynic may say, because of the prestige of the series. Either way, it makes little difference to the unattractiveness of the idea of official support, with all its connotations of possible censorship, bureaucracy and, above all, delays. Let the WYBE remain independent if it is to survive.

Apart from the lack of resources, other purely logistic problems were emphasized in Holmes' postscript. One was the burden on the editors in always having three volumes on three different themes 'on the go' at once. This is no more worrying than the 'problem' that Foster and Sheffield identified in their preface that no one can now claim 'omnicompetence' in the field of comparative education. If each volume has a different theme, then it will require one or more subject specialists to work in conjunction with the Series Editor. The present volume has had the benefit of two Consultant Editors and the Subject Editor, Tom Schuller. They not only 'supply the competence', they also spread the load. In any event, all the authors and editors are busy people; but it is busy people who get things done. Usually the things they do first are those that they see as valuable, important and professionally satisfying. So far, it seems that the WYBE comes in this category for everyone who has been connected with it.

We are conscious of our tradition; in some ways we have followed it. For example, the departure from anonymity (both of authors and of editors) has been taken a stage further by the inclusion of biographical notes. We have also tried to increase still further the assistance provided to readers by supplying summaries with each chapter, a map of future signposts (by Gerry Fowler), and a separate bibliography (which subsumes and supplements the more important references provided with each chapter).

In other ways, we are conscious of minor breaks with tradition. In no way is this the 'English publication' that the WYBE 'has always been' (WYBE 1974:390); nor, with the two principal editors located in Glasgow, could it remain 'London-centred'! More important, we have not even attempted to follow the 'working rule' applied in the 60s that 'one third of the articles each year would come from Britain and the Commonwealth, one third from the USA and one third from the rest of the world.' We do not believe that 'balance' is to be achieved by simple geographical quotas and we were influenced in our choice of authors more by the quality, style and breadth of their intellectual vision than by the country in which they happened to live and work. Naturally, since editors can only choose among known quantities, the result is that British authors are the largest minority. In any event the revived WYBE, like its predecessor, is at heart a British publication and for this we make no apology. We are also proud of our link with the United States, embodied in the US Consultant Editor, Myron Atkin. Given time this should become stronger and result not only in more American contributions but also in American influence on the choice of themes.

A comment on the present and future themes is perhaps in order. Worldwide interest in lifelong learning and recurrent education has become evident in the 70s. The five years since the last WYBE have seen major growth in this field. Reasons are not difficult to identify. The traditional approach assumed that education preceded life, taking place in youth and adolescence, prior to full-time employment in adulthood. If a society required more education, the tendency was to increase the period of compulsory full-time schooling. This model rested on a number of questionable assumptions. It presupposed that youth is the best time for learning, and has been associated with the assumption that schools are the best place. Sociological studies of adolescence (reinforced by manifest student unrest) in the 60s underlined the folly of these assumptions. It reminded us of what we should never have forgotten; that with sufficient motivation, almost anyone can learn almost anything — and that compulsion destroys motivation. The minor handicap of the adult learner in *capacity* to learn is more than outweighed by his or her advantage over the reluctant adolescent in *willingness* to learn.

Learning was never confined to schooling in any event; we learn many things only in adulthood. We have to make decisions about what job to seek, which way to vote, where to live, whether and how to bring up children, whether and which trade union to join. We also often need to learn new skills — to drive a car, to handle money, to negotiate with employers, to use committees effectively, to handle bureaucrats and officials, to deal with 'professionals' (medical and legal); some people, sad to admit, still have to learn to read in adulthood. Yet in most countries, until recently, the formal education system has largely ignored these problems.

The broader sweep of social and demographic change has in any case demanded attention to lifelong learning for more pressing reasons. It has been said that education is a socially acceptable form of unemployment. Moreover, the difference between 'leisure' and 'unemployment' is fundamentally one of compulsion, not affluence. The speed of technological change has raised the spectre of large-scale compulsory unemployment whose devastating social and personal effects cannot be counteracted by calling it 'leisure' or paying higher levels of unemployment benefit. This has forced the developed countries to reassess their assumptions about the working week, the working year and the working life. The combination of greater longevity, a reduction in the demand for unskilled labour, the increased participation of women in the workforce and the need for training in new skills to increase employability — all these point to a major impetus for lifelong learning. Interest has thus grown in recurrent education — either as an integral part of each living day, or as discrete periods interspersed throughout the working life — as the strategy for achieving the lifelong learning demanded by our rapidly developing society.

Technology has not only affected our patterns of employment and industry, however. The revolution in microelectronics is having a major impact on the methods by which we learn and are entertained — and is helping to blur the distinction between the two. It is too soon to say whether the major trend will be towards complete home computers — the logical extension of the electronic videogames which are already commonplace on both sides of the Atlantic — or whether the limited storage of such devices will give the balance of advantage to broadcast and telephonic viewdata links between central mainframe computers and the user's television receiver. Either way, it is unquestionable that the potential for variety in media for learning at a distance has never been greater. And for many people who are not mobile, who live in remote areas, or who are for whatever reason housebound, lifelong learning necessarily involves distance learning. True, the Open University has breathed new life into the public image of correspondence texts (compared with which the role of broadcasting in their courses is relatively marginal). Courses like Jordanhill's own CNAA Diploma in Educational Technology have demonstrated the scope and variety which are possible with cheap software (spiral-bound text, audio cassette and filmstrip). But we have not yet begun to exploit the potential of the sophisticated, compact and cheap hardware for enhancing lifelong learning at a distance.

Thus the choice of the 1979 *theme* was not a difficult one — though the different nuances and connotations of the terms 'lifelong learning', 'recurrent education' and 'continuing education' (see Chapter 3) made the choice of a *title* problematic. The book was planned in June 1978 but the exact title was not resolved until December.

Thoughts are now turning to the future. Planning for the 1980 WYBE *Professional Development of Teachers* (co-editor Eric Hoyle, Bristol

University) is well advanced, and themes for 1981 are already being debated. The challenge, throughout the series, will be to respect the tradition of the past but to respond to the signposts towards the future. The aim of the WYBE series is to be a forum for the discussion of practical educational problems illuminated by comparative perspectives, by the fruits of research and by the wisdom of good minds.

Jacquetta Megarry
WYBE Series Editor
February 1979

Part 1: Orientation

1. The work/leisure/education life cycle

Jarl Bengtsson

Summary: The economic climate and educational context have changed considerably since OECD/CERI adopted recurrent education as a strategy in the late 60s; this has promoted a fresh look at the concept, against the backdrop of current demographic trends, altered demand patterns and new challenges of employment and unemployment. The idea that educational opportunities should be distributed more evenly over the individual's life cycle is receiving fresh impetus from the changing patterns of distribution of work and non-work. Three possibilities for the future of employment (identified by Johnston) are outlined ('technology/consumption', 'full employment' and 'multiwork') and their educational implications considered.

Trends and predictions for work and non-work time are examined critically; the decline in the working week and working year has been slower recently than is often assumed, and it has benefited various categories of workers differently. Nevertheless, the combination of longer life expectancy with shorter working lives lends greater significance to the educational needs of those at or near retirement. This is especially true of women, who are also participating more in the workforce earlier in their lives.

Apart from the possibility that a greater proportion of the non-work time will be used for education, these changes have wider implications for lifelong learning. One promising trend is the development of paid leave of absence. More generally there will be a redefinition of the relationship between work and leisure, with changing patterns of family life a major factor in this redefinition.

Introduction

For most people the dominant life pattern is still education, work and retirement. The somewhat Utopian vision of breaking up this model of the life cycle, replacing it with a more flexible one in which the three main phases of life would be intermingled, has remained on the whole a dream – or a threat. The reasons for this are many but the basic ones are certainly a combination of constraints laid down by the productive system and persisting attitudes towards what a life cycle should be. However, it has become increasingly clear during the 1970s that this traditional life-cycle model is in need of change and that one of the possible strategies for changing it is recurrent education.

When in particular CERI (the Centre for Educational Research and

Innovation) and OECD member countries started work on recurrent education in the late 60s (OECD, 1973), the general economic and educational situation was very different from that of today. Continued economic growth was taken for granted even if several critics made their doubts known. The educational system was expanding at all levels, and in some countries the interest in recurrent education could actually be seen as a way of taking the pressure off the traditional system. In nearly all countries the belief in education as a powerful instrument to redress inequalities was strong, and the arguments for recurrent education tended to reinforce this assumption.

When looking at education today in an overall perspective, one sees something of a paradox. On the one hand, confidence in education is wavering in a number of countries, and pessimism about future expansion is being expressed in many quarters. Yet — and this is the paradox — there is in a growing number of countries an optimistic, new and fresh way of looking at the future of education in the context of recurrent and lifelong learning. How then will this paradox be resolved for recurrent education in the changing economic and political climate? It is possible to identify several new social forces which are likely to have an impact on future developments.

Demographic factors are becoming increasingly important for educational policy-makers. Demographic projections have often proved to be notoriously unreliable, but at the moment they point clearly towards a declining proportion of young people in the total population over the next ten years (OECD, 1978b). This means first of all that much of the capacity of the educational system, which was dramatically expanded to cope with the post-war baby boom and increase in demand, is surplus to the current needs of young people. Moreover, the population bulge which caused the initial expansion demands, as children become adults, much greater access to educational facilities of all kinds. This creates the opportunity to expand recurrent education facilities.

Demand trends therefore constitute a second factor. First, there is the growth of demand on the part of older people for formal and non-formal facilities, a corollary of their higher initial level of education. But the other way in which demand trends favour a shift to recurrent education is in a sense a negative one: the growth of post-secondary enrolment rates has slackened off very sharply in this decade in most major OECD countries except Germany and Austria. Although a decline in absolute numbers is as yet rare, the institutions which historically relied upon a steady flow of students directly from secondary school are now beginning to feel obliged actively to recruit other students.

Employment trends have probably been the most important single factor in broadening support for recurrent education. In the first place, the traumatic changes which have taken place in the world economy have given fresh impetus to the arguments for retraining for different occupational groups at various points in their lives, and for conceiving this not as a luxury but as a necessity. Secondly, and somewhat ironically, high unemployment has meant that governments have been forced to devote large sums of money to manpower schemes. Thus the opportunity cost of expanding education has rarely been lower. It has also prompted unions and employers to bring pressure to bear on governments to develop further training capacity. In several countries the flow of funds has switched from education to the manpower authorities, provoking the former into rethinking their priorities.

Apart from these recent changes, however, it can be argued that in arriving at a better understanding of the future perspectives for recurrent education and lifelong learning, it is necessary to look at the more global changes taking place and likely to develop further in relation to the individual's work and non-work life seen in the perspective of his or her whole life cycle.

Education and an emergent new mixture of work and non-work time

The perspectives and problems for the development of education in the 1980s are obviously closely related to the kind of economic development the leading industrial countries will face during the coming decade. The links between education and employment were relatively clear and unproblematic during the 1960s when both the economy and education systems were expanding. During the 1970s these links seem to have been blurred for an increasing number of individuals in terms of an increased mismatch between educational qualifications and employment prospects. This situation will probably be aggravated during the 1980s. Such a perspective poses some very basic questions for the future of education. First, there is the question whether the 'notion' of an over-production in education will alter in a significant way people's attitudes towards education in terms of its instrumental values for status and job career. Secondly, there is the question of whether the situation of a possible continuation of high unemployment will equally and significantly change people's attitudes towards work. And consequently, will there be an increased concern for sharing a limited number of available jobs and the possibility of a different mixture of work and non-work time for the individual?

The educational policy responses towards these new economic and social factors vary from a concern for a return to traditional educational values and standards to a concern for starting to analyse and plan another way of providing education other than within the traditional life-cycle model — education/work/retirement.

While many countries have witnessed a significant concern during the 1970s that educational opportunities should be distributed over the life cycle in a more flexible way and that education should alternate with work and leisure, it is nevertheless true that this concern has had very little concrete impact on the majority of people. It can be argued, however, that this concern will become much more relevant in relation to one of the most important emerging questions for the 1980s; namely, the distribution and changes in work and non-work time for the individual over his whole life cycle. Most developed countries have experienced a gradual decline in the working week, much more marked increases in holidays and vacations and, perhaps most significantly, changes in the length of working lives and the balance of work to other activities during the life cycle. People enter the labour force later, retirement policies are changing and life expectancy has increased during this century — with the possibility of still greater life expectancy in the future. Moreover, the time spent in work activities has been increasingly concentrated into the middle years while non-work has been concentrated in the early and late years of life (Best and Stern, 1977).

Another major component of non-work time is now unemployment which raises the question of how work and non-work should be distributed for different groups in society, provided we are entering the 1980s with high unemployment as a permanent feature for a number of countries. Certainly, education is only one among several institutions that will have to respond creatively to these emerging new social and economic forces, but its responses could be of vital importance in terms of making educational opportunities available over the individual's whole life cycle and during his increased non-work time.

While recurrent education is obviously crucial to such global concerns, and in particular the notion of increased non-work time during adult life, there is also a need to concentrate more on some possible alternatives to the future of work. Firstly, a large amount of research experience and forecasting exists dealing with the meaning and scope of work. For instance, when the meaning of work is looked at, one finds that the views range from the assertion that work will continue to provide the central focus for personal satisfaction and status achievement to the argument that the traditional work ethic is rapidly disappearing and being replaced by an increased concern for personal development unrelated to work (Freedman, 1978).

Secondly, on the number of jobs available in the future, views range from the belief that the economy will soon recover and full employment will be re-established, to the view that even with modest economic growth and inflation under control, there will still not be a sufficient number of jobs for all those who want to work.

Thirdly, there is the question of what kinds of jobs will be available. Are we moving towards the service economy of the 'post-industrial society' or towards the 'self-service economy' with a declining number of jobs in the public service sector? (Gershuny, 1978).

Given these different opinions reflecting an uncertain economic future, it becomes hazardous to speculate on the main features of an emerging new mixture of work/non-work time. Any such forecasting may encounter the fate of a bull in a china shop. Nevertheless, in order to provide a framework on this issue, it is possible to spell out some alternatives concerning the future of work.

In an article called 'The future of work: three possible alternatives' (Johnston, 1972), three different possibilities for the future of work were outlined. The first, which could be called the 'technology/consumption' alternative, is based on the postulate that the displacement of workers, both blue- and white-collar, will increase sharply in favour of automated production processes.

Concern for economic security or for material goods is no longer a significant motivation for the expenditure of work effort, since the supply of these goods is ensured by increasingly automated processes, and their distribution among the members of society is ensured by a variety of social mechanisms. Such a scenario also implies a separation between work and rewards, and society would evolve into a two-class system, comprising a small *élite* of highly trained people and a growing majority of people whose primary relationship to the economy would be limited to consumption.

It is likely that the life-styles of this majority would be oriented towards highly diversified forms of non-work activities of which education could be an important activity

(a) as a means for the few to have access to a limited number of jobs; and,

(b) as a means for the many to have access to education as a consumption good.

The second possibility can be called the 'full employment alternative'. The main characteristic here is that full employment, as defined before the 1973-4 recession, be re-established. Two basic assumptions differentiate this alternative from the first one. First, the pace and direction of technological change are modified and channelled by the introduction of measures which ensure a sustained high level of demand for workers. Second, this demand is matched by a supply of appropriately trained persons willing to work. In other words education and training related to this alternative would continue to be basically linked to the individual's positions and activities in working life.

The third possibility, which can be called the 'multiwork alternative', assumes continued improvement and application of automated machinery and related technological advances in meeting the growing needs of society. However, it differs from the first alternative in terms of the life-styles which are seen to accompany the technological advances. In this setting economic growth, traditionally defined, is generated and maintained by an increasingly sophisticated technology and accompanied by a sustained demand for work in four major areas

1. A core of highly trained technicians and engineers needed to maintain and improve the machinery of production and distribution, supplemented by a growing corps of ombudsmen to provide the feedback information needed to direct this machinery in accordance with public wishes and agreed social values.

2. A growing number of workers in the fields of public and personal services.
3. A growing number of craftsmen and artisans whose handiwork continues to be valued because of its individualistic, non-machine characteristics and stylistic qualities.
4. A major expansion of employment in a blending of recreational and educational opportunities packaged to appeal to the interests of an increasingly affluent and educated population enjoying greater amounts of leisure time.

The role of education in this setting would have to be multi-purpose as well. Education would have to prepare individuals for the different kinds of work activities and could also be envisaged in an important role in recurrent education for the individuals who would change from one work area to another during a lifetime.

The three scenarios briefly described above, and actually developed in 1972 before the present economic recession, hardly represent the actual situation in any of the industrialized countries in the western world, even if aspects of alternatives one and two can be found in several countries. It should be noted that in none of the three possibilities has the potential for a breakthrough in industrial democracy been discussed. On the other hand, both alternatives one and two reflect directly and indirectly a major policy concern in a number of countries, namely, what to do if high unemployment continues to be a permanent feature of our economies during the 1980s. In other words, what kind of work/non-work activities will be available to and should be stimulated for an increasing number of persons who will not find a job in the traditional private and public sectors? The responses and strategies most often discussed in dealing with this problem fall basically into four categories

1. A policy of subsidizing employment in the manufacturing industries. This is certainly an important and in many cases a necessary social measure in the short-term perspective. However, it may well be counter-productive in the long term, if the competitive strength in the international market of a country's manufacturing products is to be based increasingly on capital-intensive rather than labour-intensive production.
2. A second category of proposals relates to the creation of further employment in the service sector and, in particular, the public service. However, if the observation made by Gershuny is correct (that there is a diminishing demand for public service coupled with anti-inflationary policies in terms of cutting back on public expenditure), then this option may be less appealing.
3. A third category tends to focus on different forms and styles of reducing work time. Their responses include part-time work, job-sharing, shortening of the working day, week, year or active life, less systematic overtime, longer holidays and even sabbaticals for everybody.

4. The fourth category is perhaps the least clear and the most contentious. It is based on two assumptions: firstly, that even a growing economy will not be able to provide jobs (as traditionally defined) for everybody, and secondly, such a situation can give rise to the possibility of a 'dual' economy.

> The 'dual economy' strategy would not seek to discourage the continuing drive for efficiency, with accompanying unemployment, in the formal sector. Instead it would seek to improve the quality of both work and leisure in the informal sector: indeed, since in this sector production and consumption activities are based on the same social unit, the distinction between work and leisure might itself become less clear-cut. As a result of this strategy the complex of activities including recreation, education, housework and other production activities, which might in the future be transferred to the informal sector, might become a viable alternative to employment in the formal sector. (Gershuny, 1978:150)

The links between the perspectives and the issues above and a possible new mixture of work and non-work time are far from clear, but it can be argued that it is important to bring in this overall perspective in relation to any analysis of work and non-work time. It can also be argued that, relatively speaking, less attention has so far been given to what kind of non-work activity a reduction in working time would lead to.

Obviously, it must be basically up to the individual to decide about the way he wants to use his increased non-work time but if education is considered as a 'non-work activity', any decrease or change in the individual's work-time would pose new challenges and conditions for educational policy-making and practice.

What therefore is needed is a better understanding of what is actually happening in this field of work and non-work and in what direction the main trends are pointing. What follows below is an attempt to present some of the facts and the trends on this issue.

Trends and changes in work and non-work time

In 1965 Fourastie predicted in his 'les 4000 heures' that in 1985 man will work for only one-third of his life, leaving two-thirds to be spent on studies, leisure and retirement; the length of the working week would not be more than 30 hours and an average of 12 weeks of holidays would be available per year. Consequently one of the crucial problems in the 'post-industrial society' would be to create sufficient and adequate education and cultural facilities to cope with the problem of a growing amount of non-work time.

Today, with 1985 only six years ahead of us, we are still far from a 30-hour working week and 12 weeks of holidays. What has happened is that although cross-occupational and cross-national data support the hypothesis that with increasing Gross National Product and real incomes one can expect a decline in working hours, data on time series from the 1960s and 1970s as analysed by, for instance, Wilensky (1964) and Linder

(1970) do not confirm their expectations. Instead, their analyses indicate that the length of working hours in most industrial societies fluctuates only within a small range rather than declining in overall terms. An actual levelling off in hours of work seems to have taken place during the last 30 years; this is in sharp contrast to a steady decline in working hours during the 50 to 60 years before World War II.

Owen (1976) has shown that in the United States there was an overall decline in working hours from 58.4 hours a week in 1901 to 42 hours in 1948 and little or no change since. If this trend in the reduction of working time had continued during the post-war period one would have had the 30-hour working week in 1985 that Fourastie predicted. The explanation behind this levelling off in the reduction of working time is to be found in the simple fact that the post-war period followed 15 years of depression and war. During the post-war period the economies were booming; people were catching up on purchases and consumer goods. There was relatively little demand and 'time' for reduction in working hours. Furthermore, a combination of the baby boom and the 'educational revolution' increased the costs of child-rearing in the post-war period, making a loss in earnings due to reduction of working time less attractive. To this can also be added a general increase in overtime work during the whole post-war period.

Therefore, diminutions in the working week during the post-war period have been relatively modest on the whole. But apart from differences over time, it is also important to look at the way changes in working time affect different social groups. It is possible to identify a rough U-shaped distribution where manual workers work longer than those in offices and are much more likely to do overtime or be on shiftwork, and those at the top of the status hierarchy — top management and professionals — tend to work comparatively much longer hours (Wilensky, 1964).

Holidays are longer and new groups of workers are now entitled to them. What used to be a privilege of white-collar and office workers is common today for most manual workers as well. Again, one must be careful not to exaggerate the universality of these facts nor to ignore their impact on different groups. Those who are employed for short periods or on a part-time basis are less likely to be entitled to holidays than those in poorly organized occupational sectors. Some occupational groups — farmers and the self-employed are notable examples — often do not take holidays at all. Moreover, there may be a big difference between holiday entitlement and its actual take-up.

Yet, while there may have been exaggerated claims in recent years about the increased non-working time available in the week, that available in the year as a whole has become greater and more widely distributed. Even more significant, perhaps, has been the changing duration of people's working lives and the ratio of working to non-working years during the life cycle. Life expectancy is now much greater than it was at the beginning of the century, and in some countries one need only go back a much shorter period to see very marked increases. Part of this is, of course, attributable to the strides made in reducing infant mortality, but people also stay on in education for considerably longer periods before entering the workforce, especially with the expansion of education in the 1960s, and the activity rates and retirement ages of older workers have almost universally been declining. Active working life has been compressed and more people now have a significant spell of retirement at the end of their working lives. Moreover, as the age structure of the population alters with declining birth-rate and greater life expectancy, this group becomes proportionally more significant. Again one must be careful not to ignore the differences contained within these overall patterns — women, for instance, live longer than men and the gap is widening. Furthermore, the educational experiences, the retirement possibilities and life expectancies of workers in different parts of the class structure are markedly different, producing a distinct portioning of work and non-work over the life cycle of these social groups (Economies et Statistiques, 1973; Fullerton and Byrne, 1976).

One often thinks of changes in working time in terms of the week or the year or even the lifespan for those who are working — especially full-time workers. But equally relevant to the question of work and non-work time are the patterns of participation in the labour force and the increase of phenomena such as part-time work and shiftwork (Maurice, 1975).

First, one must take account of the far greater participation of women in paid work — a trend which has been evident in some countries much more than others, but which has been in most places very marked indeed (OECD, 1975). Whereas most of the other changes described here have been mainly towards a diminution of working time, this (one could say) is working in the opposite direction especially as women still dominate that major form of unpaid work — housework.

Second, over the last few years, the post-war tranquillity of relatively full employment has been broken and high unemployment is becoming more and more a permanent feature in many countries. Unemployment tends also to be concentrated among certain vulnerable members of the labour force — for instance, the young and the unskilled. It is therefore becoming a significant lump sum of non-working time and one which affects some groups much more than others (OECD, 1978d).

Third, whether out of choice or necessity, there appears to be greater flexibility and diversity among people's working patterns. More people drop out of the labour force for periods during their working lives and phenomena such as multiple job holding and black market work are far from insignificant. It may well be getting more difficult, therefore, to talk of typical working and non-working patterns. What does seem clear, however, is that the balance between work and non-working time is changing and that these changes are not evenly distributed over different social groups.

Towards new life cycles for the individual and groups

We have discussed the increase in non-working time but shown that the reduction of working hours per week has been less spectacular than is often thought. On the other hand, significant changes are taking place in the relationship between work and non-work time seen over the individual's whole life cycle in terms of increased education, earlier retirement, longer holidays, etc. It has also been made clear that these changes affect social groups according to their hierarchical position in working life, as well as the way their work is being scheduled, ie full-time, part-time, shiftwork, long spells of employment, etc.

The claim is not that more non-work time is or will be used for education, although that certainly remains a strong possibility. Rather it is that to look at recurrent education from this perspective provides a very useful point of departure for placing it in the broader context of emerging new life-styles and life cycles. Most likely, the crucial factors behind changes in the individual's life-cycle pattern will be the economic and employment conditions that the industrialized countries will face during coming years.

It is being argued by more and more people that even an optimistic economic growth prospect will not lead to the resumption of full employment as traditionally conceived. It is also being argued, given the expected increase in the labour force (youth, women, elderly) and the continuous process of automation, that the amount of work necessary to maintain the economic process cannot employ all the people eligible and willing — at least not to the present extent — unless a large number of new jobs are created either in the public or private sector.

This situation has stimulated an intensive policy debate about job-sharing, part-time work and the further reduction of working hours. Some favour early retirement; others argue for a prolongation of compulsory schooling which is more relevant to working life. Such suggestions would, of course, mean a further reduction of working life either at the entry or at the exit stage of the working process. But while overall working time by such measures would be reduced by one or more years, the traditional life cycle (education/work/retirement) would not be affected. However, other proposals exist that would break up the traditional three-block patterns by providing for a more flexible workplace. For instance, instead of, or in addition to, a reduction of the working period at its beginning or end, there could be provision for one or more periods of leave within that phase which could considerably exceed the time of educational leave of absence as it is at present granted in several countries (OECD, 1976; OECD, 1977a). Thus the concept of the 'sabbatical year', which is in many countries granted to those working within the university system, would be extended to a much wider range of people in the labour force.

These more far-reaching proposals call for a more flexible and changing mixture of work and non-work time. For university teachers, the term 'sabbatical leave' means a period of leave granted for study which may or may not be related to the professional field. Were this universally available, such paid leave need not necessarily mean recurrent education but could encompass other leisure activities chosen by the individual. But the basic idea is that part or all of the additional leisure time should be used for educational purposes, at least for workers who have not had the chance to enjoy a satisfactory education or who did not use it at the time. Some kind of financial incentive could help motivate them to use part or all of this non-work time for education. Such an approach would give a new dimension and a different thrust to the development of educational leave. Whereas previously it had been seen mainly as a vehicle for job-related training or general, civic or trade union education, it now has the potential for becoming an important instrument of a new full employment policy which would result in a more equal sharing of a limited number of jobs. For instance, the present problem of finding jobs for young people may be partially solved if sabbatical leave is granted to a large number of older workers. Of course, in order to use a sabbatical system in this way, a number of requirements have to be met, like the guarantee of re-entry for employees into their previous (or comparable) positions, as well as the retention of social security and pension rights.

Even if such a scheme does not materialize in the near future, it is probable that there will soon be pressures for a more equal distribution of labour and leisure for all adults, and that consequently there will have to be education which is suited to the needs of people who are alternating it with periods of work. The basic argument here is for a redefinition of the relationship between work and leisure. This poses a challenge to education which will be even more important if economic growth continues to be slow.

However, if one is going to see recurrent education in relation to increased non-work time and how free time is spent, then this requires an analysis of what leisure generally means for people, how it varies for different groups, and some of the major factors which influence it. It therefore seems less strange that, for example, working-class groups consistently participate in education less than the middle classes, when one sees also that they less often attend museums, cinemas, theatres, read less and are much less likely to be involved in organizations or community affairs. What might be described as active and social pastimes which take place outside the home are more the habit of the middle classes (Burdge, 1969; Willmott and Young, 1973). Moreover, with greater affluence, with the consumption of goods in the home, and changes in communities (and people's relationship to their communities), the development of what might be called 'home-centred' life-styles is of great importance to recurrent education. It suggests that to respond merely by increasing the supply of education is bound to meet with only limited success.

Nonetheless if one is to look at the supply of education and the provision of facilities, one can place it in the wider context of community amenities generally and see how these vary by geographical areas with different socio-economic profiles. Therefore another set of 'living patterns' of importance is how communities are differentiated according to social groups — affluent middle-class areas, suburban communities, immigrant areas, working-class housing estates, areas with many elderly people — and what sorts of provision are available in these localities.

'Home-centred' life-styles are one aspect of people's non-working lives whose features and causes are worthy of examination if we are to understand better why people do or do not see education as having potential for them. In addition, observers are increasingly interested in the part which different types of work play in determining these 'living patterns'. Levels of discretion and autonomy at work, fatigue and stress in one's job, the importance of money alone in deriving meaning from work — these are all factors which have been identified as important (Gardell, 1976). Partly, of course, the reasons are cultural and the cultural assumptions and appearance of education are frequently at odds with the involvement of certain social groups in education. But also the above discussion has suggested that age differences, sex differences and differences in family status and situation have numerous implications for all aspects of people's working and non-working lives. Therefore, it is worth a brief examination of some changes in the family which have been evident in recent years.

In some respects we may be moving away from a small number of typical 'living patterns' here too.

> From 1950 to 1965 a certain type of family made its appearance in most OECD countries: more early marriages, rapid birth of two children, followed by a slowing down or halt in family building. Since 1965 this alignment on the pattern of the early family with two children has begun to change and in every component: larger number of families with no children or an only child, longer intervals between, later age at marriage and a reduction in its frequency, more illegitimate births and divorces. It would seem ridiculous to deduce from this that the family is in danger but it seems that new models are being set up and that they are not identical in every country ... The only common point is the trend of the disappearance of large families. (OECD, 1979)

At the upper end of the age scale, the greater longevity of women is now increasingly differentiating the marital status and social situation of older people. 1976 US data shows a pattern repeated elsewhere: whereas 79 per cent of men over 65 years old were married, only 39 per cent of women over this age were (OECD, 1978c). These patterns could be elaborated in order to draw up profiles of groups of people in different family situations and their respective sizes. From this, a better understanding of the possibilities of participating in education would be facilitated. One could then ask about the possibilities of the single mother or the elderly widow, for instance, going back to study? What of the manual worker with a family, in his 30s, who does shiftwork in order to enjoy a certain standard of living? Or the housewife with a part-time job and a home and children to look after? Again this brings us back to identifying certain groups, differentiated by age, by family situation, and by their working and non-working experiences, as a strategy for better understanding the reality and potential of recurrent education in their lives.

The main trends and issues described above point clearly to the fact that changes in work and non-work time have different effects and meaning for different social groups. Consequently, to be effective, the educational response to a general increase in non-work time and/or changes in the way work is being scheduled will have to be based on a deeper understanding of the specific work/non-work mixture that different groups of people are experiencing and experimenting with. Any attempt to identify such target groups is a hazardous task and can be criticized on many grounds ranging from purely technical to normative arguments. However, the main justification for trying to identify such groups in order to provide them with adequate recurrent education opportunities can be summarized as follows

(a) The belief that education continues to be of vital importance to the personal development of the individual over his whole life cycle as well as to the democratic development of the society.
(b) The belief that increased non-work time in the future should provide more opportunities for education.
(c) The belief that the current provision of education does not reflect the changing living and working patterns of an increasing number of people.

References

Best, F and Stern, B (1977) Education, work and leisure: must they come in that order? *Monthly Labour Review* 100 7:3

Burdge, R J (1969) Levels of occupational prestige and leisure activity *Journal of Leisure Research* 1 3

Economies et Statistiques (1973)

Freedman, D H (1978) *The Contemporary Work Ethic in Industrialised Market Economy Countries* Working Employment Programme Research Working Papers, International Labour Organisation (ILO): Geneva

Fullerton, H N Jnr and Byrne, J J (1976) Length of working life for men and women 1970 *Monthly Labour Review* 99 2:31

Gardell, B (1976) Reactions at work and their influence on non-work activities: an analysis of a socio-political problem in affluent societies *Human Relations* 29 9

Gershuny, J (1978) *After Industrial Society: The Emerging Self-Service Economy* Macmillan:London

Johnston, D F (1972) The future of work: three possible alternatives *Monthly Labour Review* 95 5:3

Linder, S B (1970) *The Harried Leisure Class* Columbia University Press: New York

Maurice, M (1975) *Shiftwork* ILO: Geneva

OECD/CERI (1973) *Recurrent Education: A Strategy for Lifelong Learning* OECD: Paris

OECD (1975) *The Role of Women in the Economy* OECD: Paris

OECD/CERI (1976) *Developments in Educational Leave of Absence* OECD: Paris

OECD (1978a) *Alternation between Work and Education A Study of Educational Leave of Absence at Enterprise Level* OECD: Paris

OECD (1978b) *Demographic Trends: Their Labour Market and Social Implications* OECD: Paris

OECD (1978c) *A Medium-term Strategy for Employment and Manpower Policies* OECD: Paris
OECD (1978d) *Youth Unemployment Vols I-II* OECD: Paris
OECD (1979) *The Child and the Family in Statistics of the Developed Countries* OECD: Paris
Owen, J D (1976) Work weeks and leisure: an analysis of trends 1948-1975 *Monthly Labour Review* August 1976
Smigel, E O (ed) (1964) *Work and Leisure* College and University Press: New Haven, Connecticut
Wilensky, H (1964) The uneven distribution of leisure: the impact of economic growth on free time *in* Smigel, 1964
Willmott, P and Young, M (1973) *The Symmetrical Family* Pelican: London

Note

The author would like to emphasize that the views expressed in this article are his own, and not necessarily those of the Organisation for Economic Co-operation and Development.

He would also like to acknowledge the contribution made by Mr David Istance.

2. Changes in western society: educational implications

Tom Stonier

Summary: Western society has undergone a series of profound changes as a consequence of the electronic technology revolution. Coming hard upon the heels of this revolution is a second one – the computer-based information revolution. As a result, western society is rapidly moving into a post-industrial economy in which knowledge industries are superseding manufacturing industries. By early in the next century, education will have emerged as the principal employer.

The electronic information technologies are displacing the printed word as the primary repository of information. This means that home television sets will have unprecedented information resources at their command. Home-based education will become increasingly important, particularly for teaching children the traditional skills. At the other end of the age spectrum, there will be an increase in community-based education. Cradle-to-grave education will become the norm as a rapidly changing society with rapidly altering economic requirements will require the continuous information recycling of most individuals.

I. Our changing society

Western society is experiencing a series of technological revolutions which is changing our societies and economies as profoundly as did the industrial revolution, and is possibly as basic as the neolithic revolution when hunter/gatherers became farmers.

The industrial revolution involved the invention of devices which extended the human musculature. The electronic revolution, in contrast, extended the human nervous system. The most profound, and of the greatest interest to educators, is the development of television and the computer. Television acts as an extension of our eyes and ears, transporting them across time and space. The computer is an extension of our brain.

Under the impact of the new technology, the technologically advanced sectors of global society have moved into a new era. It is not the purpose of this article to describe this new 'communicative era' in detail. Suffice it to say that every major cultural institution is being affected: religion, marriage, sex mores, the family, the city, the state, etc. Any one of these has implications for the educational institutions. However, this article will confine its attention to two aspects: 1. the emerging post-industrial economy and 2. the emerging information revolution.

The post-industrial economy. This term is not meant to imply that industry will no longer be an important component of the economy. Just as an industrial society needs a strong, though not dominant, agriculture, so a post-industrial society needs highly efficient manufacturing and primary industries (including agriculture). Manufacturing industry, however, has been displaced by the knowledge industry both in terms of labour requirements and value output. The phenomenon is viewed with as much incredulity and lack of comprehension by most economists today as the shift from an agrarian to an industrial economy was viewed by the 'physiocrats' two centuries ago. The manipulation of information and the creation of knowledge are rapidly becoming the dominant form of economic activity.

Technology — the application of knowledge to solving human problems — is responsible for creating new resources and new wealth. It is crucial that educators understand that education, coupled with research and development, constitutes the most important form of investment a society can make. They must also understand that over the last two centuries the bulk of the labour force has shifted from farm operatives, to machine operatives, to information operatives. Among the last the shift has been from clerical, to managerial, to professional-technical, reflecting the need for increasingly sophisticated (educated) information operatives.

The information revolution. This is based on the emerging information machine technology. These information machines, usually referred to as computers because they were initially used for mathematical computations, have evolved at an almost incredible pace. The first non-mechanical computers were based on electronic valves. These were displaced by transistors, then integrated circuits, and now microprocessors. This latest step makes information machines so cheap that they will be coupled to most other forms of machinery. As such, microprocessors comprise a new 'meta-technology'.

A meta-technology is a technology which affects a large sector of existing technology. The classic example is the steam engine. Initially designed to pump water out of mines, it subsequently gave rise to a class of power machines which could be coupled to most other existing mechanical devices. The computer, initially designed to carry out mathematical calculations, will now be coupled to all forms of power machinery, creating 'intelligent' machines capable of 'learning' the operations currently carried out by their human machine operatives.

Industrial robots perform their tasks faster and more accurately, are able to work 365 days a year (limited only by the supply of electricity and normal wear and tear) and can be designed to carry out any and all routine manual or decision-making tasks.

Robots can be made to monitor and control their mechanical brethren, monitor an entire assembly line, test the final product, keep track of materials consumption, maintain optimum stocks of supplies, keep track of sales and orders and adjust production accordingly, devise optimum cashflow strategies, and communicate all relevant information to suppliers, customers, and top-line management. Early in the next century it will require no more than 10 per cent of the labour force to provide us with all our material needs — food, textiles, furniture, appliances, housing, etc.

II. Educational implications

The post-industrial economy is characterized by the following

1. It is primarily a service economy rather than a manufacturing one, with the knowledge industry predominating.
2. It is a credit-based economy characterized by a flow of credit information rather than cash transactions.
3. It is primarily trans-national rather than national.
4. Changes are taking place at an exponential rate rather than linearly.

A French report entitled 'L'Informatisation de la Societé' (written in 1978 mainly by Simon Nora) points out that the cheap microprocessors, combined with satellite technology, broadcasting and telecommunications, will bring about such gains in productivity that the heavy industries and large corporations will decline and be replaced on the one hand by numerous small, but viable, entrepreneurial organizations, and, on the other, by non-profit organizations.

The main task of western governments in the late 1970s and early 1980s is to effect the orderly transfer of labour from employment in the manufacturing industries to employment in the knowledge industries. The most economic way to do this is to enter into a massive expansion of the education system. Such an expansion will do three things

1. Education, when done properly, is labour-intensive and will provide substantial employment.
2. An effective education system will encourage young people to remain in education, and attract older people back into it, thereby keeping a significant percentage of the potential workforce off the labour market.
3. An expanded and improved education system will produce a more versatile labour force of more skilled information operatives which, when coupled with research and development, will produce new knowledge, new technology, new industries, and in consequence new wealth.

Just as the British government is now collecting revenues from North Sea oil, so could an expanded technology generate income from wave-powered electricity, oil and other cheap chemicals from coal (after the oil runs out), single-cell protein for cattle feed, coastal fish farming, deep ocean minerals, etc. The importance of knowledge (organized information) as the critical input into modern primary and manufacturing industries has been discussed elsewhere. Suffice it to state here that an expansion of education, coupled with R & D, constitutes an investment in the future which, if made properly, will pay the government back many times over.

It becomes the major task of educators to understand the economic reasons for expanding education massively, to support such expansion, and to prepare for it. Education will eventually become the principal industry, but what sort of education do we want?

A. New objectives

If we are moving into a society in which most physical work is going to be done by robots — a society in which a mere fraction of the workforce can produce all our material wants and goods, then education for employment, although still a part, would become only one of the several objectives of the new education order. At least as important will be 'education for life', 'education for the world', 'education for self-development', 'education for pleasure'.

Education for employment. It is clear that society is going to need an increasingly versatile labour force, able to respond to the needs of a rapidly changing economy, and a rapidly changing society. Students of today are likely to undergo two or three careers in their lifetime. Some of the most important things we can teach are certain categories of organizational skills which allow individuals to develop entrepreneurial self-reliance to hunt skilfully for new areas of employment, or even start up their own business.

Education for life. The primary emphasis of the new educational order must involve a shift in objective from making a living to learning how to live. There are two major aspects of learning how to face life in the twenty-first (or any other) century. The first involves understanding the world, the second involves understanding oneself.

Education for the world. It is not possible to understand the world if we do not understand the impact science and technology have on all aspects of society. Government, commerce and industry can no longer be run by *technological illiterates.* At the same time, we need to avoid training scientists, engineers and other specialists who do not understand the impact their efforts are making on the social system. That is, we can also no longer afford a society whose progress depends on technologists who are *humanistic illiterates.*

Understanding the world requires not only exposure to traditional disciplines — ranging from the natural sciences to the social sciences and the arts — which allow students to understand the natural and social world in which they live, but also a more global focus. We are all members of the human race living on an isolated planet, floating in a hostile space. We need education for environmental responsibility and, what is even more crucial now, education for developing harmonious relationships within and between societies. This means a playing down of ethnocentric and nationalistic values and an expansion of a more humanistic, anthropological approach. Young people must learn to enjoy and accept cultural diversity.

Apart from improving relationships within the immediate community, the major problem confronting this generation is to close the gap between the rich and poor nations of the world. If that cannot be accomplished within a reasonable period, it must presage international conflict. Improvement in third-world productivity will come, partly through the transfer of capital, but largely as a result of the transfer of information, leading to productive technology. Our students, as well as the educational establishment as a whole, must become increasingly involved. We need to expand the exchange of students and academic experts to provide practical solutions to problems confronting those parts of the world desperately struggling against poverty — a poverty not of their own making.

At the more individual level, we need to teach a whole series of skills on how to survive in this world. Most of these are either not taught at all or relegated to a minor position in the curriculum: how to deal with government bureaucrats, how to get the most out of interviews with physicians, how to be successful teenagers, how to be good lovers, how to be effective parents, how to grow old gracefully, how to face death. Most of the really important decisions made in life are not based on information acquired during formal education. Why not?

Even decisions central to education itself, such as which university to attend, or which career to pursue, are left largely to chance, or to last-minute advice from teachers who have no training for the task, and who are not compensated either for the task or the training. As for coping with the physical aspects of life — how to shop for food wisely, repair the plumbing, drive a car safely and maintain it mechanically (basic information necessary for survival in a technological society) — that is generally left out of the education of most. The author can only applaud the efforts of some educators to institute 'wRoughting'* as the fourth R, to be coupled with Reading, wRiting and aRithmetic.

Education for self-development. It has always been the dream of educators to develop critical faculties so that students are able to understand concepts and develop them on their own. This should be expanded, however, not only to foster more creative imagination, but also artistic, physical and social skills. Particularly important among the latter are communicative and organizational skills. It is one of the sad features of the present education system that it gives the students very little chance to organize things themselves or to prepare for real-life situations. In the real world it is not only what you know that counts, but also how fast you can find out new things. Furthermore, the major activities of the real world involve interacting with *people*. Social development, by contrast with intellectual development, has always been part of the hidden curriculum. Such skills need to be fostered in a more conscious and systematic fashion.

Education for pleasure. First, we must educate for the constructive use of leisure time. Since the early nineteenth century the work week has been cut by half, and this trend will accelerate. Second, education itself must

---

* A neologism for 'making with the hands' (as in 'wrought iron') — Editor.

become a pleasurable activity. There has long been a hidden puritanical tradition in much of the curriculum which can be summed up by the attitude that 'it doesn't matter what you teach them so long as they don't like it.' The new attitude must involve the thought that if students are going to live in an information explosion and be happy, they must pick out of that mushrooming growth of new information what they consider interesting and enjoyable. Otherwise, the richness of the new information environment could lead to a sort of neurological indigestion — possibly leading to serious psychological disturbances.

There is another more vital aspect: in the future, obtaining and organizing information will become the dominant life activity for most people. What one enjoys learning most, one learns best. Enjoyment contributes substantially to the cost-effectiveness of time spent learning.

B. New technology and the new patterns of education

To a large extent, the changes in both objectives and approach will be a product of the new technology. The major impact will involve the displacement of printed information storage and retrieval systems by electronic ones. This will result in an almost unbelievable increase in the quantity of information available to the average home. These features coupled to an accelerating information explosion will lead to a cradle-to-grave education system with less emphasis on the existing centralized, institutional form of education and a development of home-based education, at one end, with an expansion of community-based education at the other.

Electronic education. The use of radio and television for information communication, reorganization and storage, and the use of computers for information processing and storage and retrieval, represent new technological developments as important as the invention of the printing press. Education television at the pre-school and primary school level has come far in the last two decades. In the USA the Children's Television Workshop's *Sesame Street* and *The Electric Company* have built up an impressive record of research and practical experience. In Britain the experience has moved well beyond the experimental to the routine, not only with the government-sponsored programmes of the BBC, but also with independent broadcasting, such as Thames Television. The increasing sophistication of TV aimed at children reflects the increasing sophistication of adult 'entertainment' including such programmes as *Panorama, Horizon, The World About Us*, etc whose educational value cannot be overestimated. Nor should educators underestimate the value of historical drama, travel, and other documentaries. The experience and utility of formal courses involving television, such as those put on by the Open University, will be greatly expanded as cable television comes on line allowing for simultaneous broadcasts via telephone or other cable links, and as home video-recording equipment becomes less expensive. Combined with other systems, eg the Post Office's Prestel, BBC's Ceefax, etc, that colourful box in our living room will become an information screen displacing telephone directories, travel agents, estate agents, encyclopedias, and even our daily newspaper.

The use of computer-assisted learning is also developing rapidly. It is most easily adapted to, and most needed in, teaching mathematical skills at all levels. An example of the extensive use of computer-assisted mathematics instruction is found in the system developed in northern Ontario: the project began in the late 1960s under the sponsorship of the Ontario Institute for Studies in Education and a number of community colleges, particularly Seneca College in Toronto. Tens of thousands of students have gone through the programme since then with some of the following advantages emerging: students complete a course in roughly one-third of the time required for a standard course, with teacher intervention involving less than 10 per cent of the time. The cost per student is approximately one-third. Most students like it: student drop-outs in remedial maths were reduced by 80 per cent and one girl commented: 'it's the first maths teacher that never yelled at me.'

The advantages of computer-assisted teaching are several: a computer can give individual attention which the average teacher in the classroom situation cannot hope to give. Computers have infinite patience, never put down a student, and rely on positive reinforcement. They can monitor a student's progress more accurately than any other means so far devised, and are getting cheaper all the time. The main resistance will come from the educators themselves who do not understand the new technology and are frightened by it. Such educators, in their ignorance, disparage TV and the computer, and create a generation gap between themselves and the electronic teaching professionals on the one hand, and their students on the other.

Home-based education for the young. The major shift in technology, then, is the emergence of the electronic home-based education capability using the television screen and the new communications systems which allow a tie-in via telephone, air waves, or local cable television to the local education authorities, a second tie-in to national and international computer network systems and, finally, a tie-in to the global library archives. As these networks expand, the home television set will have available to it information which vastly exceeds the largest city library and which makes owning a mere encyclopedia seem as primitive as owning a Victorian slate to scratch on. There is a second, enormously important feature about this new technology: in addition to being a much greater source of information, television also provides a form which is more easily assimilated. Our brain was designed to cope most efficiently with visual images, the major sensory input of primates. The development of language in our proto-human ancestors involved the evolution of a translating mechanism which could translate visual images into abstract sound patterns. Reading involves a 'second order' visual abstraction of audible abstractions of visual images. Although it may be true that we cannot do much abstract thinking without words, as far as memory storage is concerned, it is much more efficient to use visual images.

Thus traditional reading, writing and arithmetic — the sciences, geography, history, etc — can all be learned either by playing 'games' with a home computer, by playing 'games' with friends (on the computer), or by looking at live programmes, films or video-tapes which deal with geographical, anthropological, historical, etc subjects. Coupling computer-based learning to educational TV in the home means that tailor-made, child-oriented education will be able to replace the much less adaptable, mass classroom-based education currently foisted on all children in western countries save those whose parents have the financial resources to afford individual tutoring.

Finally, we must add to the home-based education system one other ingredient. It is not enough to provide highly sophisticated and advanced electronic teaching devices. There much be a human touch. That touch should be provided by the western world's most under-used resource: its mature citizens. There is reason to believe that the human species evolved post-reproductive females (an anomaly according to classical evolutionary theory) in order to facilitate the transfer of information across the generations. That is to say, grandmothers were humanity's first information storage and retrieval system. (This is not to exclude grandfathers, although in the old days they were probably killed hunting giraffes.) Using older people to provide the cultural heritage and the personal touch would be of enormous benefit to both the young and the old. Each mature person could be assigned to a group of two or three children for a period of perhaps ten or more years. Parents moving from one locality to another might consider leaving their children in the care of the surrogate grandparent in order not to interrupt their education. This may become perfectly feasible as travel becomes increasingly more efficient and cheap.

The upshot of evolving such a system is that young children as they begin to learn to speak — the most important thing they must ever learn in their lives — become progressively immersed in an information environment which is enormously rich and pleasurable. They will learn most traditional skills on their own or within small groups of neighbourhood children. The efficiency, flexibility and depth of learning will be considerable.

School-based education. During the first decade of a child's life, most of its learning will involve education in its own or a neighbour's home. However, children need to play with other children to facilitate their own emotional growth and to acquire social skills. Such play may take place in 'nurseries', as is the practice today, or it may involve play centres in a neighbour's home (rented by the government). Periods of play alternating with home-based learning also provide rest periods for the grandparent.

As the children grow older, groups of friends will go to school to avail themselves of facilities such as gymnasium, sports, laboratory, dramatics, etc, while at the same time beginning to interact with large peer groups. However, school experiences should not be structured strictly in terms of age groups, except where that is appropriate (eg certain kinds of team sports). Learning how to handle laboratory equipment, learning how to swim or how to play chess, may best be handled by mixing ages. The idea of peer teaching will be discussed later on.

One of the primary functions of the traditional school is that of an institutional device for educating for community interaction. School is also a place (and stage) where one begins to encourage the children to develop organizational skills and to prepare them to assimilate a more systematic body of information. That is, the schools can now begin to consolidate a child's information base in a more formal, uniform way – at least where it is necessary to have such uniformity. As discussed later, in general, the new objective of education will not be to educate for uniformity, but rather for versatility and diversity. Nevertheless, it may be necessary to achieve a common data base, and to socialize the children into certain accepted group values.

Community service for teenagers. As the children approach their teens, a profound shift in interests occurs. Partly as a consequence of shifting hormonal patterns, the interests begin to shift to members of the opposite sex and to an enlarging awareness of the community in which they live. Part of the emerging interests relate to the desire to enter the adult world and share some of its responsibility and be accorded some of its status. In the western world university education is sometimes interspersed with work experiences. There is no reason why that principle should not be enlarged at the university level and brought down to the teenage period. Teenagers are not only eager to accept certain job responsibilities, but very much look forward to the financial rewards which give them a measure of independence. In a way, teenagers constitute an ideal underclass: all the mucky jobs in our society tend to be done now by ethnic minorities who stand very little chance of moving beyond those jobs. It usually takes them several generations to move up. In the process they are subjected to serious deprivation (often denigration) in holding down those jobs.

Consider, on the other hand, having teenagers do all the nasty jobs which society still needs. It is understood that this is part of their service to humanity and it is understood that as they grow up, they move into the better jobs. The use of a teenage labour force should also be coupled, perhaps somewhat later, with a period of 'community service' – a form of national service which is not militarily oriented, although it may be appropriate to exercise a fair amount of discipline. *(See also Chapter 15.)* Certain units, for example, might be used for land reclamation, community work and work overseas. Some youngsters might stay on for further training for a career in the police, fire, ambulance corps, coastguard, etc which will continue to be an important career sector. Others may become involved in digging irrigation ditches in the Sahel, or planting trees in the denuded tundras in order to improve global productivity. The emphasis should be on global, rather than national, service. In other instances, the work would be done in the local community. The main objectives of such a programme would be to break the school routine, to mature the students by introducing attitudes of discipline, group integration, and community service. Provision should be made for students who for reasons of conscience or talent would be excused from such service. In general, however, young people are ideally suited to become involved in service activity which would become their cultural passport to adulthood.

Community-based education. Following the teenage schooling and the community service phase, students would advance into higher education. They might do so only after a period of several years of paid employment or, alternatively, after a substantial period of leisure. Higher education will be a mix of traditional university, coupled to electronic data media, based at home or in a similar environment. Much of the university education of the future will involve students moving around from one institution to another. This trend is developing in the USA, where the credit system allows students to spend one or two years at one institution then shift to finish off at another institution, perhaps even to go through three or four. This makes for a much better education because, first, moving among communities is in itself an education and, second, different institutions have different strengths and weaknesses which can be exploited by a mobile student force. Increasingly, as higher education becomes mixed with appropriate work experiences and with practical applications outside the university classroom, the majority of the population will attain by their mid-thirties perhaps 20 years of schooling. A very substantial minority will have gone on to the equivalent of doctorate degrees.

Information recycling. This process has already begun, as witnessed by the marked rise in adult and further education. In many instances it is spearheaded by middle-class housewives who have time on their hands. It also increasingly involves people who for reasons of finance, social background, or some other lack of opportunity were unable to move into higher education earlier in life. Many universities in North America and an increasing number in the UK are starting to cater for mature, part-time and extramural students. An increasing number of commercial and industrial companies are also sending their employees and managers on to courses or are organizing series of in-house seminars.

Among the most exciting of experiments in western education is the UK's Open University. The use of electronic facilities in the student's own home represents one of the major patterns for future community-based education. One should not, however, overlook one of the most popular aspects of the Open University courses, which is the gathering of students at some particular place during the summer.

A different paradigm in community education is offered by the New School for Social Research in New York City, where the vast bulk of its student body involves adults taking evening courses. The importance of the New School is not only that it acts as an intellectual centre, but it also acts as a centre facilitating social intercourse. Adult education is an important facilitator of personal interactions.

Lastly, with the continued expansion of global transportation systems, organized travel will become as much a part of the educational scene as will the traditional classroom. Moving groups of people to different sites to satisfy different kinds of interest will be a major new industry coupling education with tourism.

C. New attitudes and approaches

Exploring knowledge. The traditional authoritarian approach which provided immutable 'facts' served industrial society well. It provided not only the 'facts' necessary for operating in a simpler society, it also provided the socialization for national, industrial conformity. However, the authoritarian approach will be negated by the need for a more versatile, self-reliant population. Furthermore, the practice of information recycling will make apparent the relativistic nature of much knowledge. Another reason for shifting from a central authoritarian to an exploratory mode is to exploit the student's own interests. Interest is probably the most important single correlate of the efficiency of information transfer.

The expanding information environment will make it increasingly difficult for teachers to keep up with new developments. At the same time it will allow students to become 'experts' at a much earlier age. As a result of the decentralization and democratization of education, there will be increasing reliance on peer teaching (ie students teaching students), and teaching across age groups — at times in reverse (ie students teaching teachers). The common effort of exploring new knowledge can be extremely rewarding, and is probably very much more efficient as a method of effective learning than the traditional hierarchical one-way approach which is the basis of contemporary education.

Interdisciplinarity. Knowledge may be defined as organized information. In the past two centuries a whole host of new disciplines have proliferated. These tend to organize knowledge in what might be called a vertical fashion. What is desperately needed now is the emergence of professional generalists (in contrast to professional specialists) capable of organizing knowledge along horizontal lines. Such integrators of knowledge are still few and far between in present educational circles. Professionalism is associated with specialization, and attracts a degree of snobbish appeal (bred by ignorance about the nature of knowledge). The difference between a professional and a lay person is that the professional is able to understand relationships which escape the lay person. It is as professionally challenging and difficult to establish relationships *across* disciplines as it is to establish them *within* specialisms. In fact, the case could be made that it is more difficult and therefore requires a higher degree of professionalism to be a generalist.

Interdisciplinary courses are beginning to appear in a number of western universities. Vital to interdisciplinary courses is the recognition that either they are oriented toward a broad problem, eg the attainment of peace, or they are created on a very broad knowledge base, such as the interaction of science, technology and society. The Science and Society course at the University of Bradford illustrates a number of the points considered above. For example, the first year, although highly structured, does not develop knowledge along disciplinary lines. Instead students learn about major technologies such as energy, materials, food and medicine. In the process they obtain and assimilate information from traditional disciplines such as physics, chemistry, engineering and biology. In addition they are also introduced to economic, historical and sociological aspects. Another feature of the course is that, because the students coming into it have a very varied academic background, increasing efforts have been made to allow the students to learn on their own by means of computer-assisted or audio-visual assisted materials, coupled to peer teaching. That is, students whose background is strong in one subject teach those who are weak in it. The peer teaching is greatly strengthened by having both the traditional literary and the more modern electronic information back-ups, eg lecture notes, textbooks, tape-slide sequences, video-taped lectures, and programmed computers.

The world is going to need specialists — doctors, engineers, architects, lawyers. However, in the future society will increasingly require professional *generalists* able to integrate the mass of new and rapidly expanding information. It is much easier (when it is done properly) to convert a generalist into a specialist than the other way around. A specialist, in spite of the popular myth to the contrary, can experience enormous difficulties in shifting from a paradigm appropriate to one area, to another in a second area. This is not true for a generalist who has been rigorously trained.

Use of information. Again it must be emphasized that the authoritarian mode of handing down information, using the carrot of academic rewards, and the stick of economic and physical deprivations, will be displaced by a greater reliance on self-motivation. If the education system is properly structured, it is the student who perceives the need for information and searches for it. Among the most important skills to be taught is the technique for obtaining information, organizing, and applying it. This skill of acquiring 'meta-information', ie information about information, is greatly facilitated by engaging students in project work, either by themselves or with colleagues. Such projects should be designed, wherever possible, to be productive, ie to solve real problems, rather than merely to be sterile repetition of previous student exercises. This will shift the educational process from passive to active learning and will be greatly facilitated by the availability of electronically based information which bypasses the intellectual limitations of individual teachers.

The Science and Society course already referred to may serve as an example. Students are required to engage in a variety of activities during the first two years designed to help acquire communication and organizational skills. These involve, in addition to the more traditional essays and class reports, etc, team projects, class debates, simulated public hearings, simulation games, and audio-visual reports. The use of projects in the second and fourth year is designed to help students acquire meta-information, ie how one goes about obtaining, applying, and storing information. Projects also allow the students to develop a specialist base in accordance with their own interests. In addition, the projects (which comprise a third of their formal university time) generate new information. Such new information becomes a part of the learning experience, not only for the students but for the staff as well. Furthermore, in the earlier more formative years of the course, the evolution of the course involved a very significant input from the students themselves. Such innovations and modifications were always subjected to rigorous examination by staff.

Future orientation. The only way to learn to live with rapid change is to be educated for it. As Alvin Toffler has pointed out, the only insurance against future shock is to educate for the *changing* future. Increasingly we must teach students the techniques of forecasting, and where we teach about the past it is to help us understand the future. History can no longer be used merely as a series of facts relating to some sort of a time context. History must become an important tool for testing social theories and the realities of the world in which we live. Just as evolutionary theory allowed biologists to predict the existence of creatures never seen (and subsequently discovered), so must historical analysis allow us to predict certain features of society, including how to move into a future shaped by human needs and desires.

A systematic examination of the future is slowly beginning at several universities. The core of the fourth year of the Science and Society course at Bradford University is centred on future studies. Postgraduate programmes are emerging such as the one at Houston (Clear Lake City) in Texas. Such courses explore methods of forecasting, future scenarios, and how one distinguishes between likely and unlikely scenarios. Equally important is the effort to include normative as well as objective analyses.

It will not do to continue a morbid preoccupation with the past ... with the inequities which have manifested themselves throughout human society — slavery, famine, torture, war, economic injustice ... what is more important now is to create the conditions for moving into a new social order in which the material wants of society are easily satisfied with almost no physical effort on our part, and where the major economic and social preoccupations will be to satisfy human — primarily psychological — needs. This, then, is the challenge to education: to understand what is now happening to our society, and to respond to it imaginatively and, most important, effectively.

References

Advisory Council for Applied Research and Development (ACARD) (1978) *The Application of Semiconductor Technology* Cabinet Office, HMSO: London

Gosling, W (1978) *Microcircuits, Society and Education* Council for Educational Technology for the United Kingdom, Occasional Paper 8: London

Hooper, R (1977) *The National Development Programme in Computer Assisted Learning: Final Report of the Director* Council for Educational Technology: London

McHale, J (1976) *The Changing Information Environment* Westview Press: Boulder, Col

Stonier, T (1976) The natural history of humanity: past, present and future Inaugural Lecture, University of Bradford: Bradford, UK

Stonier, T (1978) The social impact of the information technology *Eurocomp 78* Proceedings of the European Computing Congress, Online Conferences Ltd: Uxbridge, UK

3. Recurrent education and lifelong learning: definitions and distinctions

Denis Kallen

Summary: Recurrent education and the affiliated policy concepts of *éducation permanente* and lifelong education are now coming of age. They have been presented as remedies for all the shortcomings and ailments of education, but beyond that they have also been welcomed as policies that would make an end to the isolation of schools and universities from socio-cultural and economic life, and to their poor responsiveness to people's real needs.

Over time, the original concepts have undergone change and interpretation. They were all initiated by international organizations. Depending upon the degree of homogeneity and heterogeneity in their member countries' philosophies they were formulated in more general or in more specific terms and later elaborated in lesser or more general policy terms: the UNESCO concept of 'lifelong education' has remained a Pandora's box in which every country discovers policy implications that suit its own philosophy. The 'recurrent education' concept of the OECD has been divested of its radical overtones and has become one of the preferential policy instruments for combating the economic and social crisis that the OECD member countries are facing. The Council of Europe concept of *éducation permanente* has, in line with this organization's vocation, been translated in terms of a coherent socio-cultural policy concept in which education in the larger sense of the word is given a pivotal function.

Recurrent education and its affiliated concepts have, since the beginning of the present decade, been the most debated educational issues. They have been presented as the panacea for all the ills of ailing educational systems and been written off as simple face-lifts of old ideas. Recurrent education has been called 'the first new idea in education this century' (Houghton, 1974) but it has also been said that the only new thing about recurrent education is its recurrence.

The purpose of this introductory contribution is to clarify the discussion around recurrent education and the related concepts of lifelong learning, *éducation permanente* and continuing education.

Two major risks have to be avoided in writing on 'definitions and distinctions' in this field. The first relates to the temptation to see distinctions and differences where there are none or where they are irrelevant. Much of the literature about the issue ignores the distinctions between recurrent, permanent and lifelong education and even treats the terms as interchangeable. This may indicate that whatever the fundamental differences between the various concepts may be, their protagonists have not succeeded in conveying them to the non-initiated. The term 'relevant' begs comment in the context of the educational debate. It refers in the mind of the present author to educational policy and practice. Conceptual differences that have no consequences for educational policy and practice are considered as being irrelevant in the perspective of the debate that is the object of this contribution.

The second risk that must be avoided is that of reconstructing history. Every major idea can with some goodwill and much artisanship be traced back to antiquity. There is great merit in this *démarche*, as it allows us to see the continuity in human needs and in human thinking. But as long as ideas do not become the focal points of policy and action, their political relevance is not obvious. In order to play this role, ideas need to be developed into models that can serve as the basis for policy-making. Our purpose is not to trace the origin of the ideas that underlie recurrent education but the evolution of the practice.

It has been said that recurrent education is 'a chameleon, its appearance changing with every observer' (Blaug and Mace, 1977). The analogy is useful. There is indeed a striking lack of consistency in the use of the term over time and between different spokesmen, not only in terms of the indiscriminate use of the various concepts 'recurrent', 'permanent', 'lifelong', but also in the use of the same concept. The seeming inconsistency may, however, derive not so much from the confusion in the minds of the protagonists as from the fact that connotations have indeed changed. These changes, as will be seen below, can be clearly demonstrated for the terms 'recurrent' and 'permanent' education.

There are several explanations of the changes in connotation. The foremost lies in the complexity of the concepts in question and more particularly in the complexity of their implications. Another explanation lies in the role perception of the instances that promoted these concepts, ie three major international organizations: the primary task of UNESCO, the OECD and the Council of Europe is neither to develop and promote entirely new ideas and concepts of their own making, nor to translate policy concepts into concrete proposals for educational policy-making or educational practice. As far as the first constraint is concerned – the initiation of ideas and concepts – they have to navigate between the extremes of mere jumping on obsolete and run-down bandwagons and losing contact with the mainstream of thinking in their member countries. On the second constraint, they must avoid remaining at too abstract a level, as well as avoid developing models for policy and action that leave no room for alternative decisions at the national level.

As a result of this none too comfortable position – and of often conflicting expectations about their role – the ideas that they develop evolve over time in line with the reception that is given to them in member countries.

The result may be that concepts and ideas become clearer, but more often they lose in clarity and seem to become more and more 'chameleonic'. Another way of appreciating this evolution would be to consider it as the inevitable, if not desirable, conversion of theoretical concepts into policy concepts that require consensus and compromise and that gain in acceptability what they may lose in conceptual clarity.

Recurrent education: the evolution of an idea

Already in 1968 the concept of 'recurrent education' had been launched as an alternative strategy, first by Olof Palme, at that time Swedish Minister of Education, in his address to the Conference of European Ministers of Education held at Versailles in 1968, later in many OECD reports. Thus in the General Report of the OECD Conference on Policies for Educational Growth held in 1970, Palme's successor, Ingvar Carlsson, pleads in favour of recurrent education on a variety of grounds: first in order to achieve a more equitable distribution of educational resources between the younger and the older generations; second in order to reduce the gap between theory and practice and between workers and students. An additional benefit would consist in the moderation of the educational demand from the younger generations.

Whereas it is stressed again and again that planning for recurrent education will take much study and time and that the structure, the financing, the curricula and other educational aspects of the new policy can only be elaborated after the principal economic, social and financial implications have been explored, the OECD seemed at the time to favour a recurrent education system that differed little from the existing formal systems of education. 'Recurrent education is formal, and preferably full-time education for adults who want to resume their education, interrupted earlier for a variety of reasons (OECD, 1971).

Thus it could appear as if recurrent education was a replica of youth education, its main novelty being the age of the students. The reason for this preference for full-time and formal education is to be found in the priority given to equality. An unpublished discussion paper from 1971 says 'Priority will have to be given for a long time to come to those adults who have not completed a secondary or even a primary education course . . . This implies that in the first decade or so, a great deal of the resources for recurrent education will have to be spent on basic education courses.'

In the policy report on recurrent education that was written under my auspices (OECD/CERI, 1973), the OECD position is developed. It stresses that the 'essence of the recurrent education proposition . . . is the distribution of education over the lifespan of the individual in a *recurring* way.' In terms of the structure of recurrent education the report takes a more differentiated view than the previous OECD writings. According to the report, students must be able to take up and leave study throughout their lives. This implies that courses should include full- and part-time variants of equal standing and quality. The existing post-compulsory education system and adult education must become part of an integrated recurrent education system. Recurrence should start at the level of the upper secondary school, ie in the years following the completion of compulsory schooling whose task it is to lay the foundations for the later recurrence. The task of compulsory schooling is to provide basic education, but it is made clear that recurrent education embraces all education and hence also compulsory schooling.

Contrary to the impression created by earlier reports, the 1973 text stresses that

> it is not implied in the recurrent education proposals that the institutionalised type of schooling that characterises the contemporary formal educational system be imposed upon adults. It would be absurd to reproduce elsewhere the shortcomings of the conventional system . . . It is obvious that this implies a certain amount and type of 'deschooling' and that other learning situations may be more appropriate for attaining this objective than the institutionalised school . . . Part-time study will probably be an essential part of a system of recurrent education. It will require educational facilities close to the place of residence, and reinforce the need for a well-distributed and decentralised system. (op cit: 25)

The report is less explicit about the priority to be given to specific target groups and to specific objectives than some of the earlier texts, in which a clear preference could be discerned in favour of under-privileged groups: people with little basic education, immigrant workers and women. The reasons lie in a gradual shift that had taken place in the OECD thinking about the nature and role of the recurrent education proposal. In the earlier writings it was primarily treated as a specific policy with its own objectives and target groups. Certainly, it was recognized from the beginning that the principle as such was universal, ie concerning all citizens and affecting educational and social policy at large. But at the same time the equality objective was given preference.

In the 1973 policy report recurrent education is presented as an organizational principle, leading to a complete change of system. It is a 'long-term planning strategy' and not a specific policy with a specific objective, such as policies for compensatory education or for the introduction of comprehensive schools. Eventually a wide spectrum of objectives is assigned to recurrent education. It is not seen as a contradiction that these objectives seem at first hand incompatible and that recurrent education as a planning strategy is 'neutral' towards them.

On closer reading, however, matters are less simple. It is emphasized that 'there is a close interaction between the media used and the objectives being effectively pursued' (op cit:61): 'the choice of the medium inevitably implies that a certain type of candidate is most easily attracted and reached, and that a certain learning target is attained.' On the other hand, there is no total freedom in the choice of media. The market determines to a large extent what is available and, furthermore, media can be used for other purposes than those for which they were created. What is true for the media is also true for curricula, admissions criteria and in fact for every aspect of recurrent education. The 'neutral' planning strategy therefore loses its neutrality as soon as it is translated into policy decisions and put to the test of practice.

But there is a second line of argument that attenuates the apparent neutrality of the recurrent education strategy. The main objectives assigned to recurrent education are grouped under the headings 'individual development', 'equality of opportunity', 'the world of work', 'education and knowledge' and, finally, 'the larger context'. In fact, these do not differ from the global objectives of present educational policies. In the elaboration of the five headings, however, a certain (although not too outspoken) preference appears for the achievement of objectives that serve the advent of a more equitable society, ie a society in which the citizens are entitled to develop fully their abilities and follow their genuine interests (ie not determined by social background, but deriving from their own experiences). Equality of educational and social opportunity is, however, given priority over considerations of productivity and efficiency, and full scope is to be given to active and creative participation in shaping society in all its sectors of activity. The report considers recurrent education in view of these targets as 'a more emancipatory strategy' than present education and assumes that it 'has the potential to facilitate a shift towards such an emancipatory strategy in each of the goal areas mentioned above'. But it immediately warns that 'the credibility of this optimistic assumption is based on the nature and scope of the proposed policy instruments.'

These policy instruments fall into two categories: educational and non-educational. The educational strategies are to some extent elaborated. It is stressed that

> the introduction of recurrent education . . . must be part of a wider policy for educational change in which all types and levels are carefully coordinated . . . Recurrent education will necessitate reforms in curricula and structure, both at the compulsory and post-compulsory level. It also implies bringing upper secondary and post-secondary education together into one flexible and integrated system. (op cit:51-2)

The non-educational measures include financing policies, educational leave and measures on the labour market and inside industry, but transport, housing, medical care and culture will also be affected.

The OECD approach is thus characterized by two main points:

1. The insistence on the necessity of a comprehensive policy for all post-compulsory education and for adaptation of compulsory schooling to the recurrent education policy. The latter is no longer to be a mere exercise in providing knowledge, skills and attitudes for life, but 'to provide all young people with the basic knowledge, attitudes and skills that will allow them to profit fully from the possibilities for educational, professional and personal development offered to them on leaving compulsory schooling' (op cit:53). In the 1973 OECD report it is implied — although not made sufficiently explicit — that these possibilities for educational, personal and professional development are offered through recurrent education. Hence one should not conclude from the OECD report that compulsory education is sufficient for anyone: the recurrent complement

is necessary for everybody.

The most far-reaching implication for compulsory education is the need to set minimum standards of achievement every youngster should have reached on completing compulsory schooling and before being allowed to set out on a lifelong recurrence or alternation scheme. Absolute priority should therefore be given to attaining this objective. This 'implies that the target of developing individual talent through diversified curricula must be given a lower priority at this stage'.

2. The insistence on the necessity to change 'the world of work', not only by educational leave facilities, but also by changes in career structures, remuneration systems, and participation in decision-making. Recurrent education aims not only at achieving a better match between education and the labour market, but is also meant 'to emancipate the individual from socio-economic constraints' and to provide the individual 'with the capacity and the tools to change society'. And society includes the place of work and the production system.

It was perhaps unavoidable that, coming as it did from an economic organization that includes most of the world's richest countries, such a daring message was ignored. Inevitably, perhaps, in OECD's further work on recurrent education the full conclusions of this far-reaching goal were not always drawn. Neither have the full consequences been realized in terms of the educational policies to be adopted. Thus, the need to revise the goals of compulsory education has not been recognized, although increasing concern is voiced about the inadequacies of basic schooling. There is a growing awareness of the fact that a high percentage of youngsters leave school badly equipped and poorly motivated for further study. Little progress has been made in devising a coherent policy for all post-compulsory education in order to attain the objective of availability of educational opportunity on a recurrent basis during the whole life cycle. Little has been done to integrate higher education into such a policy. On the whole, adult education and open universities operate parallel to, not in conjunction with, higher education.

This is not to say that no progress has been made towards the implementation of recurrent education. Many examples of such progress are given in the second OECD publication (OECD/CERI, 1975). But the aim of formulating a comprehensive educational policy has not been met and opportunities for adults to return to education are on the whole created alongside the formal educational system.

The frequent question 'What is new about recurrent education?' must be answered in terms of its originality as an organizational principle for all education. As far as the institutional and curriculum arrangements that have been developed are concerned, it must be admitted that these are on the whole further developments and extensions of the already existing systems of post-compulsory education or of adult education. Neither at the policy-making level, nor in practice, have the two systems come much closer to each other.

Education Permanente and lifelong learning

The history of *éducation permanente* and that of 'lifelong learning' is somewhat longer than that of recurrent education. Both in the Council of Europe — where the *éducation permanente* idea has mainly been fostered — and in UNESCO — the home base of lifelong learning — the necessity of spreading educational opportunities over a lifetime had been recognized in the late 60s. In several UNESCO and Council of Europe reports of the late 1960s, the concepts of *éducation permanente* and of lifelong learning had been developed.

In both organizations the roots of the new concept are to be found in existing adult education, while its justification lies in the insufficiencies of the educational system. There are, however, differences in stress and in argumentation between both organizations. In the Council of Europe *éducation permanente* originated in the organization's ideas about the role of cultural policy in changing society. Permanent education was seen as a 'strategy of social action', but with little reference to the economic dimension. Cultural policy was rather considered on its own merits. This is understandable in an organization in which long-standing ideas and traditions of the European cultural heritage are strongly embodied. Permanent education was considered as a means of preserving and renewing this heritage, and at the same time as a strategy for promoting European cultural integration. In the practice and the orientations of adult education much could be found that was in accordance with the aims of permanent education. It looked as if permanent education could be grafted on to adult education and that what was mainly needed was to give adult education a new purpose and codify the disparate adult education programmes, without sacrificing their diversity of methods and contents. At the same time, however, the idea of a comprehensive educational policy for all education from childhood through adulthood was promoted. Already at an early stage, around 1970, the inadequacy of youth education for the needs and expectations of many, if not most, young people was stressed, and it was advocated that the school should scale down its pretensions and leave post-school education to complete the tasks it had started to perform. A further notion that has been stressed from the beginning in the Council of Europe's thinking is the need to decentralize and to entrust to the community the responsibility to formulate its own objectives and organize its own permanent education. In one of the earliest Council of Europe reports 'community' is defined as 'a group of persons with common interests and sufficient motivation to follow a joint course of instruction' (Council of Europe, 1970).

The UNESCO report *Learning to Be* (UNESCO, 1972) is the leading policy document on lifelong education. It had been preceded by many other statements and publications in which the concept of providing educational opportunities over the whole life cycle of the individual had already been put forward. In *Learning to Be* for the first time a coherent philosophy was developed about man, education and society to which the idea of lifelong learning was related. *Learning to Be* adopts an optimistic view about human nature and about the power of education to change society. Eagerness to learn, *libido sciendi*, is deeply rooted in human nature and once external obstacles are removed, it will provide the necessary motivation for lifelong learning. The society of the future will be a 'learning society', the culture of future society will be 'scientific humanism'. The report argues that lifelong education, if properly organised, is capable of making every citizen participate fully in this scientific humanism and thus enable him to play a creative role in the future scientific-technological revolution. Lifelong education is to be democratic education. It is a condition for democratic society. It is recognized that there is a long way to go before this ideal state is reached, but it is suggested that the ideal can be reached provided the right policies and strategies are adopted.

Unlike the OECD and the Council of Europe reports, the UNESCO report is not very explicit about the necessary adaptation of youth education to a system of lifelong learning. Nor is it very outspoken about the social and economic changes that will be needed. As to the educational policy, the report formulates a set of principles and recommendations, but provides no clear indications as to the structure of the future lifelong education system. The report is a goldmine of ideas and suggestions for change. It is, however, less coherent than the OECD and the Council of Europe thinking on the educational and non-educational strategies to be adopted in order to attain these objectives. Its greatest weakness is, perhaps, that it is too optimistic about the possibility of avoiding incompatibilities and conflicts between objectives and priorities. With much goodwill these can, it is suggested, be solved. It will be possible to integrate both the existing formal educational system and existing adult education schemes in the future system of lifelong learning.

Ten years later

It is now almost ten years since the new paradigms of recurrent, permanent and lifelong education were launched almost simultaneously all over the world and forcefully propagated by the world's major international organizations. It would be tempting to make up the balance of what has hitherto been achieved and to confront these developments with the concepts that were formulated ten years ago. A few brief comments may give an impression of the way in which the original ideas have evolved over time.

In the OECD, recurrent education has been elaborated extensively in terms of its implications for the labour market. It is stressed that both sectors must be closely interconnected and that this requires new types of consultation and co-ordination between the several administrations involved and between these and the educational and social partners. Much importance is attached to paid educational leave and to the principle that leave must be granted for vocational as well as for general education. The interconnection between work and education must also be embodied in conditions for access, ie in the recognition of work experience, and in the organization, content and methods of recurrent education.

Much less progress has been made in the OECD on the promotion of a comprehensive educational policy of the recurrent type. Higher education and adult education in particular are on the whole still considered as educational sectors in their own right, to which recurrent education is added as a third sector and with which it may enter into competition for resources.

The OECD position reflects the modest progress made in the OECD member countries. In the educational sector, recurrent education has not taken deep root, except where it could be exploited to the advantage of existing types of education. New initiatives in the field of higher education or adult education that incorporated one or the other aspect of the recurrent education policy package were baptized 'recurrent education' and greeted as the first steps towards a recurrent education system. It was often not recognized that without a clear long-term planning strategy, such new ventures risk being incorporated in the existing patterns and lose their innovative characteristics. Progress in adopting such long-term planning strategies towards a comprehensive recurrent education policy has been greatest in the Scandinavian countries (Nordic Council of Ministers, 1977) whereas in the Anglo-Saxon OECD member countries (Canada, Australia, the United Kingdom and New Zealand) the situation is much more complex because of the existence and the growing strength of extramural schemes, further education, and the like.

In the Council of Europe the concept of *éducation permanente* has been extensively elaborated in terms of its methods and content and its implications in the field of social and cultural policy. The concept's full political implications and the contradictions and conflicts are spelled out more than in the other international organizations. The three principles or 'fundamentals' adopted in 1971 (equalization, participation and globalization) have been tested out in pilot schemes in the member countries and on the basis of an evaluation of these schemes the 'fundamentals' have been reformulated (Council of Europe, 1978). The result is a conceptual framework that is more coherent and more in accordance with the original conception than the ones developed in the OECD and UNESCO contexts. On the other hand, the Council of Europe's direct influence on the member states' policies is probably weaker and its policy conclusions and recommendations for the time being less binding than those of the other two organizations. This could explain why a politically daring policy concept could be developed. For example, the principle of participation has been interpreted as meaning direct democracy of the self-management type. Permanent education is thus directly linked to industrial democracy, to consumer democracy and to straight political democracy as distinct from representative democracy. The community, ie the group, must have nearly complete autonomy over its own permanent education programme. The notion of the educational district is fully elaborated as the place where education and environment (cultural, social and economic) can be much better co-ordinated and articulated than at the central or regional levels. Ultimately, the Council of Europe's concept of *éducation permanente* rests upon the concept of cultural democracy and the democratization of culture. Adult education is a privileged instrument for achieving these objectives. Its tradition and organization make it much more suitable to embody the permanent education philosophy and approach than the formal education system. In the Council of Europe's view, adult education is to become the privileged sector in which permanent education objectives are to be pursued. Permanent education has been declared the central policy principle towards which all education activities of the organization are to be geared. The UNESCO position (UNESCO, 1972) comes very close to the one developed over the years within the Council of Europe. But, unlike the latter, UNESCO has not made a consistent further elaboration of the original concept, in spite of the fact that a policy for lifelong learning has been given top priority in the UNESCO philosophy and in its medium and long-term programming. Nevertheless, the ideas and suggestions for policy and practice of *Learning to Be* have permeated the organization's programmes and have found their way into the policies of many of UNESCO's member states. This is more true, however, in some developing countries than in the developed world, where the OECD and the Council of Europe's thinking have had more influence.

References

Blaug, M and Mace, J (1977) Recurrent education: the new Jerusalem *Higher Education* 6:3
Council of Europe (1970) *Permanent Education: A Compendium of Studies* Council of Europe: Strasbourg
Council of Europe (1978) *Permanent Education: Final Report* Council of Europe: Strasbourg
Houghton, V (1974) *Recurrent Education — An Alternative Future?* The Open University: Milton Keynes
Nordic Council of Ministers (1977) *Recurrent Education in the Nordic Countries*
OECD (1971) *Equal Educational Opportunity: A Statement of the Problem with Special Reference to Recurrent Education* OECD: Paris
OECD/CERI (1973) *Recurrent Education: A Strategy for Lifelong Learning* OECD: Paris
OECD/CERI (1975) *Recurrent Education: Trends and Issues* OECD: Paris
UNESCO (1972) *Learning to Be* (The Faure Report) UNESCO: Paris

Part 2: Major Issues

4. Research insights into adult learning

Alan B Knox

Summary: Insights from North American research about the continuing education of adults can help North American practitioners (teachers, administrators, policy-makers) increase their effectiveness, and can suggest similar developments for practitioners in other nations. The discussion is arranged under four headings — adults as learners, programme development, administration, and the field of continuing education.

Adult development and learning includes attention to developmental trends and adjustments regarding performance in family, work, community, and education; change events; personality; learning ability and dynamics; physical condition; and societal expectations.

Programme development includes attention to analysis of setting, assessment of needs, establishment of educational objectives, selection and organization of learning activities, and programme evaluation. Both planning and implementation are included.

Administration includes at least six general components in addition to programme development and agency functioning. They are personal qualities, attraction and retention of participants, acquisition and allocation of resources, staff selection and development, leadership and using research.

An understanding of the field of continuing education contributes to continuity, a sense of direction, constructive relationships with other providers, recognition of societal influences, and resource identification.

Each section concludes with suggestions for research, and the article itself concludes with suggestions regarding future directions with implications for research and policy. The references embrace most of the research on continuing education of adults that has been conducted in the United States and Canada.

Lifelong learning during adulthood is very widespread. Recent research studies on educative activities by North American adults have produced fairly consistent findings regarding participation rates. Each year about three-quarters of American adults engage in at least one learning project, of which less than one-third are formal continuing education programmes provided by an agency (Tough, 1978; Johnstone and Rivera, 1965; Boaz, 1978).

The term continuing education refers to all forms of systematic learning on all topics by all categories of adult learners, except for students engaged in full-time post-secondary education. The term continuing education thus includes self-directed study and systematic information-seeking from the media and from experts, along with participation in informal discussion with self-help groups, as well as participation in formal part-time or short-term educational programmes for adults on a credit or non-credit basis sponsored by a wide range of educational and other organizations.

As continuing education programmes for adults are planned and co-ordinated, important decisions are made by learners, teachers, administrators, and policy-makers. Adults recognize gaps between current and desired proficiencies and thus decide to engage in continuing education activities. Teachers select instructional methods and materials designed to help adults learn and encourage participant persistence. Administrators decide on programme priorities and resource allocations to achieve agency objectives. Policy-makers set policies for continuing education when they appropriate government funds to support educational programmes for adults, and when they establish policies for continuing education activities as members of governing boards of parent organizations of which continuing education agencies are a part.

Types of parent organizations include schools, community colleges, universities, libraries, employers (business, industry, military, government), labour unions, religious institutions, hospitals, professional associations, social agencies, museums, and voluntary associations. Most organizations have an organizational unit or agency that co-ordinates the provision of continuing education programmes.

Most of this decision-making and policy setting regarding the continuing education of adults is based on the local experience of those involved. However, with the growing public interest in lifelong learning during adulthood and the expanding volume of research related to continuing education, there has been increased attention to the available tested knowledge from research that is available as practitioners and policy-makers make decisions.

The purpose of this chapter is to provide an overview of research findings that are available to continuing education practitioners and policy-makers. Because of the broad scope of the decisions to be made, only a summary of the main conclusions from research can be provided. The focus is on North American experience and research in the United States and Canada. Although I am familiar with continuing education research in other parts of the world, such familiarity is fragmentary in contrast to a fairly comprehensive understanding of the research literature in North America. Friends and acquaintances engaged in research and evaluation related to continuing education in various parts of the world have exchanged research reports which have helped to supplement published sources (especially colleagues from the United Kingdom, Sweden, France, Germany, Yugoslavia, Israel, and India). However, in addition to confirming some cross-national similarities in findings, this exchange has contributed to a recognition of how much continuing education research findings are related to the societal context in which they occur and how cautious practitioners should be in generalizing from one national setting to another. Therefore, this article provides a case example of the types of tested knowledge available to North American practitioners.

Although nations vary in the extent and emphasis of the relevant research and evaluation that is available, each nation has some tested knowledge that can be used by teachers and policy-makers (Lowe, 1975). This article may suggest unused local sources or topics for new research and evaluation.

The overview is organized around four broad themes — adults as learners, programme development, administration, and an understanding of the field of continuing education and the societal context in which it occurs. It does not, of course, deal with research on the subject matter that teachers of adults present, but is restricted to the process by which practitioners and policy-makers plan and conduct effective educational programmes for adults. The article concludes with brief suggestions regarding future directions (Knox, 1977b).

Adults as learners

The amount of research on adult development and learning conducted in North America has increased rapidly during the past two decades so that there is now a substantial body of tested knowledge on adult learning, personality, performance, condition and context that has implications for practitioners who help adults learn (Knox, 1977a). A major source of this research literature has been studies of ageing and gerontology which have included middle-aged as well as older adults (Binstock and Shanas, 1976; Birren and Shaie, 1977; Eisdorfer and Lawton, 1973). An understanding of adults as learners is of critical importance to teachers, counsellors, administrators and policy-makers as they make decisions about programme purposes and procedures. An understanding of adults as learners includes participation in educative activity and dynamics of learning.

Adult development

There are many aspects of adult development that have implications for continuing education practitioners. Practitioners are typically interested in developmental generalizations regarding performance or personality in order to predict and explain successful participation in educative activity. Such participation declines somewhat with age but increases greatly with educational level. This reflects a more general relationship between educational level and adult information-seeking. Adults with less formal education seldom engage in instrumental information-seeking from print and electronic media or from impersonal experts, but instead rely mainly on conversations with family and friends.

Adult life-cycle trends in performance in family, occupational, and community roles suggest ways in which continuing education participation might facilitate adaptation and growth related to each role area. Regarding family role, as adolescents leave home, parents lose satisfaction from active parenting but gain freedom to pursue personal interests (Hill *et al*, 1970).

Regarding occupational role, young workers tend to excel in tasks that use speed, strength, memory and production of novel solutions, in contrast to older workers who tend to excel in tasks that use experience, steadiness, attendance, patience, and conscientiousness. Regarding community roles in recreation, organizations, political affairs and religious organizations, although the extent of social participation is stable during most of adulthood, the mix of types of activities shifts from active in young adulthood to interpersonal in middle age to introspective in old age.

From time to time, the stability of adulthood is punctuated by role change events such as the birth of the first child, a move to another community, or retirement. Some adaptation is inescapable, but problems of adjustment can be moderated by satisfactory social participation and warm human relationships. Such change events typically produce heightened readiness to learn which, if recognized, can contribute to the effectiveness of marketing and instructional activities. Such major role changes can also be associated with personality development which continues throughout life. The impetus for change may come from the individual or from society, and constructive change is more likely when facilitated by both personal striving and societal encouragement. Both gradual trends and role changes contribute to adult life-cycle shifts in values and interests. The outlook of many young adults is characterized by expansiveness and high expectations, in contrast with efforts towards self-limitation and reduction of frustration which are more widespread during middle age.

Early research on performance mainly gave attention to family life and occupation, but seldom included analyses of developmental process or implications for continuing education. The provocative monograph by Havighurst and Orr (1956) illustrated how to study developmental tasks with direct implications for continuing education, but only a few similar research studies on adult role changes have resulted (Lowenthal *et al*, 1975). More research is needed on the relationship between role changes and educative activity during adulthood. For example, what are the main developmental processes that adults use to adapt to major role change events in family, occupation, and community? And to what extent do adults with various characteristics experience heightened readiness to learn before, during and after major role change events?

An important aspect of adult development is personality. From adolescence through middle age, a person's self-concept tends to become more positive. Self-concept and performance interact. During adolescence many young people develop dreams of who they want to become that sometimes sustain them during the striving of young adulthood. During mid-life reassessments, such abstract commitments tend to wane and, in the process of becoming their own person, many adults conclude that the future is now and the years remaining become more important than the years spent. Although being self-directed instead of dependent is part of the concept of maturity and adulthood, some adults are concerned about being too reactive. Self-directedness entails assertiveness and a sense of direction.

Early research on personality variables related to continuing education focused on attitudes associated with educational participation, and on ego development and developmental tasks. Recent compilations of research findings related to adult personality indicate the great variability in adult personality patterns as well as suggesting developmental trends during adulthood that have implications for practitioners (Neugarten et al, 1964; Maddi, 1972; Baltes and Schaie, 1973; Eisdorfer and Lawton, 1973). Some studies have dealt with the developmental interweaving of personality and performance variables during adulthood (Lowenthal et al, 1975; Maas and Kuypers, 1974). Some studies have examined the impact of college experience on student personality development (Feldman and Newcomb, 1969; Trent and Medsker, 1968). Some have focused on personality stability and change in relation to adjustments during adulthood (Gould, 1978; Levinson et al, 1978; Vaillant, 1977; White, 1961; Williams and Wirths, 1965). Self-concept during adulthood has been increasingly studied during the past decade (Fitts, 1972). There are a number of promising research questions related to adult personality that should be studied. To what extent can adults with various characteristics become more self-directed and creative? What are the major shifts in self-concept that typically occur during adulthood, and what are the implications for systematic learning activities?

Adult learning

Generalizations about adult learning abilities and dynamics are especially important for those who help adults learn, but such generalizations are also useful for those who select, supervise, and evaluate instructional personnel and programmes (Gagné, 1972). Effective practitioners typically understand that almost every adult is able to learn almost any subject given sufficient time and attention. Furthermore, adults vary in learning ability, but for the individual person learning ability is quite stable during most of adulthood.

Effective adult learning is an active search for meaning. Adults seldom learn, remember, and use answers for which they do not already have the question. Practitioners who understand this point seek to involve participants actively in objective settings to increase relevance, in selection and organization of learning activities to fit preferred learning style, and in evaluation to increase responsiveness and use of increased proficiency. The general goal is helping adults learn how to learn.

Adjustment to the social environment of the learning activity is very important to some adults. A participant who feels estranged by social relationships or threatened by the educational expectations typically has difficulty in learning and withdraws. Practitioners who understand this concept seek to create a setting for learning that helps participants achieve important and relevant educational objectives, and in addition encourages them to feel welcome, reassures them against fear of failure, encourages group support and sharing, and provides freedom to explore within democratic limits achievement of educational objectives and discovery of additional desirable objectives.

Most adult learners perform well below their capacity, and underestimate their learning ability by overemphasizing their early school experience and underemphasizing their recent informal learning experiences. Social class differences in verbal behaviour compound this situation. Practitioners who recognize this can provide newcomers with attractive learning tasks in which they will readily succeed so that they gain realistic estimates of their learning abilities. Evaluation feedback during learning activities can further contribute to effective learning.

Adults learn most effectively when they proceed at their own pace. With age, adults become more cautious in learning tasks, and because they accumulate more experience and information (some of which can interfere with the learning task) have to engage in a wider search when trying to remember.

Since early longitudinal studies demonstrated the stability and even growth in learning ability during much of adulthood, research interest has shifted from describing trends in learning ability to analysing dynamics of the learning process. Major contributions have been made by educational psychologists interested in adult development and learning (Botwinick, 1967). Communications researchers have helped to broaden attention to include less formal means of adult information-seeking. The finding that the extent of prior participation in continuing education was associated with learning effectiveness has encouraged greater attention to adult learning strategies (Sjogren *et al*, 1968). One useful focus of learning is as a component of problem-solving under conditions of uncertainty.

There are several promising research questions related to learning strategies. What are the major learning strategies which adults typically use and which learning strategies tend to be most effective? How stable is an adult's learning strategy across a variety of learning tasks, and with what characteristics are learning strategies associated?

There has been very little research on the impact of physical conditions on adult learning in continuing education activities. There have been some studies of condition and learning by older adults who are increasingly likely to experience physical deficits that can interfere with learning. The compilations of tested knowledge about developmental physiology during adulthood by Timiras (1972) and by Finch and Hayflick (1977) contain many generalizations about physical functioning that can be analysed in relation to adult learning performance. Atypical adults for whom special education is needed constitute a specialized target market about whom very little research is available (Long, 1973). The few major studies and reviews on this topic that have been conducted deal mainly with adult mental retardation (Baller *et al*, 1967). It would be useful for researchers to study the typical impact of various deficits in physical condition on adult learning.

There has also been very little research on the impact of the societal context of family, work or community on purposeful learning by adults.

Such studies have occurred for full-time college students (Feldman and Newcomb, 1969). Living in a housing complex for older adults is associated with more information-seeking, but less so with younger people. In work settings, a higher proportion of employees who were optimistic about promotion chances were more likely to participate in continuing education than those who were pessimistic (London *et al*, 1963). Moreover, in communities with an abundance of continuing education opportunities there are higher participation rates than in communities with fewer opportunities (Johnstone and Rivera, 1965). Procedures for studying the quality of community life have been developed and refined in recent years (Barker and Schoggen, 1973).

Promising research questions include: how do the type of urban community and neighbourhood and educational and income levels affect the attitude of adults to lifelong learning? How much and what type of variability in interest and participation in purposeful learning activities occurs between employees whose employers actively encourage personnel development, and similar employees and employers where such encouragement does not occur?

Programme development

Programme development tends to be the concern of everyone associated with a continuing education agency, but it is a core concern of programme administrators (Pennington and Green, 1976). They deal with five basic components of programme development as they work with planning committees, relate to potential participants and to resource persons, prepare materials, and orient those who conduct continuing education programmes. Two components that relate to the origination of ideas for new programmes are needs assessment and analysis of resources and influences in the societal setting. The other components are selection of high priority objectives, selection and organization of learning activities, and programme evaluation.

About one-third of continuing education research in North America over the years has dealt with aspects of programme development which include both planning and conducting educational activities for adults. Research related to programme development has focused on programme planning and evaluation procedures, instructional methods and materials, and needs of special client groups including ways to adapt continuing education programmes to their circumstances. Basic books on continuing education programme development approaches and procedures usually include research findings (Houle, 1972; Knowles, 1970). Havelock's (1969) comprehensive review and synthesis of research findings on procedures to facilitate the dissemination and use of knowledge contains many research-based generalizations that have relevance for continuing education procedures.

Setting

Most continuing education programmes are planned and conducted within a context of the providing agency, along with the organizational or community context in which participants function. This context includes influences on the clientele that encourage or discourage them regarding participating in continuing education activities and applying what they learn (Hackman *et al*, 1975). The context also contains resources that can be used to plan and conduct programmes. Included are the purposes and resources of the providing agency (Craig, 1976; Lindquist, 1978; Nakamoto and Verner, 1973). Proficient programme administrators are able to inventory these resources and influences, and to reflect them in the continuing education activities that are conducted.

Unfortunately there is very little research on specific ways in which the characteristics of providing agencies and co-sponsoring groups influence programme priorities and objectives. For example, what is the current pattern of use of resources located in the geographic service area (facilities, materials, instructors) by agencies that provide educational programmes for adults, and how might more desirable use be achieved?

Needs

Information about educational needs is a major source of ideas for the creation or modification of programmes. Most practitioners draw ideas for new programmes from local personal experience (Pennington and Green, 1976). Proficient practitioners use somewhat more formal procedures for needs assessment, which entail use of several methods of obtaining information about educational needs (Monette, 1977). The types of information include: expressed preferences by potential participants, demonstrated willingness to respond to the programmes when offered, conclusions of experts regarding educational needs of a category of adults, evidence from those who are affected by the proficiency level of a category of adults (such as patients regarding educational needs of nurses), and proficiency level as compared with similar adults. Among the sources of information about educational needs of adults are historical, philosophical, and operational traditions (Knowles, 1977; Smith *et al*, 1970), societal and agency context (Mezirow *et al*, 1975), emerging social, political and economic trends (Freire, 1970), an exploration of likely and desirable future alternatives, (Ziegler, 1970), and an understanding of adult development (Knox, 1977). A promising question for research concerns the relative effectiveness of various procedures for educational needs assessment for adults.

Objectives

The origin of a programme idea typically yields more potential objectives than can be accommodated feasibly in a single continuing education course or workshop. Objective setting consists of screening potential objectives for desirability and feasibility, and establishing a clear and realistic set of educational objectives to which both potential participants and resource persons are committed. In best practice the objective setting process includes a programme administrator, resource persons or teachers with content competence, and some representatives of potential participants. Although objectives are sometimes stated in terms of instructor purposes or institutional goals, it is more useful for programme planning and marketing to state objectives to reflect intended participant knowledge, skills and attitudes along with subject matter content. Effective procedures for objective setting typically provide opportunities for participants to help modify the objectives, if required, as the activity progresses (Knowles, 1970).

Although there is some descriptive literature on policy boards and advisory councils, there has been very little research on the process of objective setting. Relevant studies have dealt with such topics as teacher-learner goal expectations, contributions of knowledge of objectives to learner achievement (Blaney and McKie, 1969), and relative attention within the field to various types of objectives, such as civic education (Stubblefield, 1974).

Within broad programme areas, research is needed on the major perceptions of high priority objectives for continuing education programmes for adults. Also, it would be helpful to improve our understanding of the relative effectiveness of various procedures for exploring the range of potential continuing education objectives, and for gaining consensus on high priority objectives.

Activities

There are dozens of learning activities that have been used in continuing education programmes, each with distinctive instructional methods and materials (Miller, 1964; Klevins, 1972). Proficient programme administrators select from this range those activities that are most appropriate for the objectives and participants, and organize the activities so that they are effective in presenting and pacing the total programme (Houle, 1972). Five criteria for selection of learning activities are: appropriateness to the objectives and content, suitability for the students, effectiveness in relation to the stage of a programme, pacing and variety and compatibility with teaching style (Knox, 1974; Travers, 1973; Joyce and Weil, 1972).

Some research studies and many evaluation reports deal with the teaching-learning transaction, including procedures for selecting and organizing learning activities. Teaching methods tend to be very similar to each other in effectiveness for those adults who persist, so a major criterion for programme design is attraction and retention of participants. Some of the most useful studies of the continuing education teaching-learning transaction have analysed interrelations among teaching style, learning style, and types of objectives (Bradford *et al*, 1964; Hill, 1960; Solomon *et al*, 1963). If ever people are to become self-directed learners it seems likely to occur during adulthood. The studies by Houle (1961) and Tough (1967, 1971) have stimulated additional studies of self-directed learning by adults (Tough, 1978). A recent overview of the topic contains additional generalizations and guidelines for learners (Knowles, 1975).

Descriptions and evaluations of innovative learning activities and educational programmes, such as the Metroplex Assembly for civic education, can be very valuable for other practitioners and researchers as well (Johnson, 1965). The basic question regarding learning activities, which continues to need research, is what is the relationship between teaching style, adult learning style, and learner achievement?

Evaluation

Proficient practitioners use formal programme evaluation procedures to supplement the informal evaluation that always occurs (Stake, 1967; Worthen and Sanders, 1973). Programme evaluation is a process of making judgements, based on evidence, regarding programme worth and effectiveness, in ways that encourage persons associated with the programme to use the conclusions for improvement and justification. Evaluation activities include planning, selecting, describing, judging, and reporting (Grotelueschen *et al*, 1976). A feasible evaluation project is typically smaller than the wide range of evaluation purposes and components that might be included, so focusing is required. The emphasis might be on internal formative evaluation which encourages persons associated with the programme to use findings for programme improvement that is largely within their control. By contrast, external evaluation emphasizes impartial judgements about outcomes, the achievement of objectives, and unintended consequences, for purposes of justification and accountability (Belasco and Trice, 1969; Miles, 1965). Many of the most effective programme evaluations combine both internal and external evaluation.

In addition to the use of evaluation findings to improve understanding of aspects of continuing education, research can be conducted regarding the programme evaluation process. Some research reports relate to evaluation procedures and the validation of evaluation instruments (Knox *et al*, 1968). Recent research on evaluation procedures has dealt with such topics as non-cognitive measures, materials improvement, and evaluation of short-term programmes. Perhaps the greatest need for research related to evaluation procedures is for validation studies to develop feasible outcome measures for continuing education programmes that have a demonstrated relationship to application. An illustrative research question is, to what extent does continuing education participation contribute to occupational advancement and relocation?

Administration

Research findings related to agency function and administration tend to be of particular interest to full-time continuing education practitioners because most of those who are employed full-time in the field are directors and programme administrators. Most teachers of adults do so on a part-time basis.

There is a small but steady amount of continuing education research on various aspects of administration each year. A much larger amount of relevant research is reported from related fields, such as business administration and public administration that also deal with administration and organizational behaviour. Continuing education programme administrators tend to be interested in generalizations about adults as learners and programme development procedures as they select, supervise, and evaluate those who teach and counsel adult participants, and conduct in-service staff development programmes for them. In addition, continuing education research findings are of interest to administrators in relation to the major tasks they perform. Included are marketing, counselling, staffing, dealing with finance and facilities, understanding organizational dynamics, and providing organizational leadership in relation to administrative, instructional and support staff (secretarial, custodial) in the agency, as well as in relation to the parent organization, co-sponsors, and community. There are few comprehensive reviews of research findings related to continuing education administration but there are several handbooks for continuing education administrators (Knox, in press, Smith *et al*, 1970).

Effective continuing education administrators share some basic administrative functions with administrators in all fields. It is important to work with others to achieve agreement on important goals, encouraging them to make contributions to the achievement of those goals. Administrative leadership also entails dealing with organizational stability and change within the context of the continuing education agency, parent organization, and community.

Continuing education administration is an art based on a science. The art of administration entails concern for responsiveness, interpersonal relations, and humanistic values that should guide professional practice. Effective practice is based on science because it draws upon research-based generalizations. Administration includes at least six general components in addition to programme development. They are personal qualities, attraction and retention of participants, acquisition and allocation of resources, staff selection and development, leadership including planning and co-ordination, and using research (Knox, 1979).

Most continuing education agencies are dependent units of parent organizations whose main purpose is not the part-time or short-term continuing education of adults. For example, the main purpose of a business in which an education and training department is located is to produce goods and services, and the main purpose of a school system in which an adult education division is located is to educate children and young people who typically attend full-time. Most experienced practitioners recognize that relationships between the continuing education agency and the rest of the parent organization greatly affect agency performance (Knox, 1975).

A few major studies have been conducted over the years regarding organizational functioning of the continuing education agency, both internally and in relation to the parent institution and community (Clark, 1956; Carey, 1963; Mezirow et al, 1975). In addition, national studies of external degrees (Houle, 1973) and of continuing higher education generally (Knowles, 1969) contain both reference to tested knowledge regarding organizational relationships and generalizations to be tested by future research.

Promising research questions include: what characteristics of the organizational units that sponsor continuing education programmes are generic to all types of sponsors? Which are distinctive for those associated with each type of parent organization (school, employer, association, university)? Which are idiosyncratic? Also, in what ways do participant numbers, characteristics, objectives and performance influence the character and direction of continuing education agencies?

Personal qualities

There is both research and anecdotal evidence that getting along with people is crucial for effective practice in continuing education. Continuing education administrators typically function in positions lacking power; lack of support for policy causes them to provide a type of human cement that holds many continuing education agencies together. This, along with delegation, supervision, co-ordination, and a concern for staffing and resource acquisition, places a premium on effective interpersonal relations. The ability to win co-operation especially from experts and those who control resources is repeatedly exemplified by the most effective practitioners in the field.

The voluntary nature of continuing education participation also places a premium on effective interpersonal relations by continuing education teachers and counsellors. Concern and respect for adults with varied backgrounds, a sense of humour along with responsiveness and flexibility while helping adults learn are qualities that have emerged frequently as desirable characteristics of effective continuing education teachers and counsellors (Spear, 1976; Knox and Farmer, 1977). A concern for interpersonal effectiveness is probably even more crucial for personnel selection than for personnel development. The part-time arrangements for most continuing education teachers allow administrators the opportunity to find out how well a teacher relates to adult students and to continue to employ only those teachers who do so well. This practice is widespread.

Another personal quality is the general approach that the practitioner makes to the improvement of professional performance. This issue has been explored for professional development generally and for continuing education practitioners in particular (Argyris and Schön, 1976; Schein, 1978). A continuing education administrator is also well served by several seemingly contrasting personal qualities such as creativity and planfulness.

Participation

Marketing and counselling practices to attract and retain continuing education participants are intended to focus and accelerate an adult's information-seeking and adoption of practices (Rogers and Shoemaker, 1971). Participation rates increase with the level of formal education (Johnstone and Rivera, 1965; Boaz, 1978). Especially for reaching underserved adults, marketing efforts are more likely to be effective if they have targets. An understanding of specific major influences on continuing education participation helps to define the adult's prejudices and apprehensions that administrators seek to overcome with their marketing and counselling services (Miller, 1967).

Personal characteristics (such as educational level) and situational characteristics (such as accessibility of information) have been identified as important influences (Knox and Farmer, 1977). Other major influences include encouragement by friends and acquaintances and co-sponsorship by organizations to which potential participants belong (Booth and Knox, 1967). Reasons for adult participation in continuing education vary with people and activities, and multiple reasons are typical. The most usual reason is to be able to use what is learned to achieve goals in work, family, or community. Other major reasons are interest in the content and enjoyment of association with other participants (Boshier, 1976; Burgess, 1971; Houle, 1961).

Concepts and procedures for the marketing of services for non-profit organizations apply fairly well to continuing education (Kotler, 1974). Marketing is basically a responsive client-orientation which emphasizes a mutually beneficial exchange between the agency and its public. For continuing education this includes potential participants, potential resource persons (such as teachers), and policy-makers. In addition, continuing education counselling services can contribute to continued participation (Farmer, 1971), such as by provision of information about educational and career opportunities, assessment of interests and abilities, assistance in planning sequences of courses, discussion about personal problems and possible solutions, referral, and advocacy on behalf of clients. Although there are some professional counsellors who assist current and potential continuing education participants, most of the counselling function is provided by programme administrators and teachers as a small part of their roles (Knox and Farmer, 1977).

There has been a substantial number of continuing education persistence and withdrawal studies (Knox and Sjogren, 1964; Truesdell, 1975) but little attention to the counselling function to encourage persistence.

Some research questions include: what are the major personal and contextual correlates of an adult's decisions to participate in systematic learning activities? What are the main reasons for non-participation in lifelong learning during the adult years by various categories of learners? What can be done to reduce barriers to participation?

Staffing

One of the most important components of administration is the attraction, selection and development of staff — including teachers, counsellors, administrators, and support staff. Included in the process is enrichment of talent pools, preparation of position descriptions, creation of positions that are attractive in terms of the work itself and related benefits, and selection procedures to screen and select applicants (Flippo, 1976). Staff and organization development includes activities aimed at individual performance (Harris and Bessent, 1969) and at agency effectiveness (Bennis, 1969). Participation in staff and organization development activities appears to be associated with extent of professionalization and effectiveness of continuing education administrators (Mezirow *et al*, 1975).

Although staff selection and development is a crucial administrative function, there has been relatively little research on continuing education staffing. To what extent are accepted principles of continuing education generally reflected in educational programmes for continuing education staff? What are the implications for the strengthening of agency staff and organization development activities?

Resources

In addition to recruitment of participants and acquisition of staff, continuing education agencies acquire various financial and physical resources, along with contributed facilities and services. Resources include income (from participant fees, tax support, external grant funds) and subsidy by the parent organization or co-sponsors in the form of the free provision of facilities, equipment, materials, and volunteer services (Kidd, 1962). Some resources such as facilities and materials may also be acquired by the use of continuing education funds, or may be rented. Legislation also provides appropriation of tax funds to support some continuing education programmes (Dorland, 1969).

Resource acquisition procedures include preparation of a budget request within the parent organization, fees paid by participants, financial assistance and vouchers for participants, and preparation of proposals for external grants. A continuing concern for very effective administrators is the allocation of resources to achieve agency objectives. This is aided by including those who administer budgets in the budget-making process. Accounting concepts and procedures can also help an administrator to monitor and influence staff performance, expenditures, and inventories (Hentschke, 1975). There is a tendency for tasks related to resource acquisition and allocation to take up so much of the administrator's time and energy that little is left for programme development. As a result many continuing education agencies are not very innovative.

There has been a scattering of research related to continuing education resources, including topics such as conference centres (Alford, 1968), financial assistance to participants (Kurland, 1977), staff accountability and economic return to participants. A promising research question is, what arrangements for the acquisition of resources by an agency are most responsive to attracting and serving under-served adults?

Leadership

In addition to proficient performance of the foregoing administrative functions, leadership entails co-ordination so that in concert the individual programmes are well conducted and the total agency achieves its objectives and runs smoothly. Effective leadership reflects an understanding of organizational behaviour, programme productivity, priority setting, and administrative strategies (Drucker, 1966). The core of administration is decision-making that takes into account both organizational productivity and individual satisfaction. Decision-making is only partly a formal rational process. It also reflects legal requirements along with political and bureaucratic influences.

Because most practitioners enter the field of continuing education with little specific preparation, they may lack concern for past and future trends. However, this is at least partly made up for in their intense concern for current results. A type of missionary spirit attracts many practitioners to the field and contributes to a commitment to responsive programming. When this is combined with effective programme development procedures, continuing education programmes that are educationally sound and have impact can result.

There has been a scattering of studies of administrative practices and role expectations but very few analyses of time use and administrative styles. Statements on issues that continuing education administrators confront suggest dynamic topics for research on leadership (Knox, 1975). One administrative function is to initiate new projects and facilitate innovation. Some of the procedures that are especially conducive to such efforts have been identified (Darkenwald, 1977; Farmer and Knox, 1977). The professional competence of the director of continuing education tends to be crucial. Some studies have identified potential relationships with graduate programmes that prepare continuing education administrators (Campbell, 1977; Knox, in press). A fundamental research question on this topic is, what are the main functional and dysfunctional relationships between the organizational units or agencies that provide continuing education for adults, and the remainder of the parent organization of which they are a part?

Use of research

Two decades ago, a review of research related to education of adults revealed few important studies that specifically dealt with aspects of continuing education but quite a few studies from other fields that contributed useful generalizations (Brunner *et al*, 1959). Today the amount of useful research-based generalizations related to education of adults has increased enormously (Niemi *et al*, 1976). Very little of this research has been produced by practitioners in the field who tend to be very action-oriented. Most of it has been produced by continuing education professors and their graduate students, and by researchers in related fields (Campbell, 1977; Jensen *et al*, 1964; Knox, 1973). However, continuing education administrators are in a central position regarding the production and especially the use of findings from research and evaluation.

Field

Research regarding history, philosophy, trends, and issues contributes to a sense of the unity and continuity of the field of the continuing education of adults. This includes experience in other parts of the world as well as in North America. A modest amount of continuing education research deals with the historical development and current scope of the field, and this research is important to the sense of perspective and continuity that practitioners have of adult and continuing education (Berrol, 1976; Penfield, 1975).

Studies that contribute to a broad perspective on the field include historical research on leaders, individual agencies, types of agencies, professional associations and the entire field of continuing education. Also included are comparative studies that contribute to a cross-national perspective that can place domestic experience in its societal context. A small but growing number of such studies is conducted each year. Analysis of issues and traditions that confront practitioners and policy-makers can also produce findings that contribute to the sense of coherence and continuity that spans agency sponsorship, time, and place (Knowles, 1977). Such statements include philosophical perspectives on educational goals as well as comments on future directions (Christoffel, 1978; Irish, 1975; Lloyd, 1972; Merriam, 1977).

The coherence of the field stems from the common function of helping adults learn. The fragmentation of the field stems from the wide variety of agencies that do so. Most efforts to define the scope and structure of the field focus on the categories of provider agencies (Knowles, 1977). The distinction is usually made between continuing education agencies that are part of educational institutions (schools, community colleges, universities) that have educational resources (teachers, books, facilities) and that seek participants; and continuing education agencies that are parts of all types of other organizations (employers, labour unions, religious institutions, associations) that have members who need increased proficiency and who seek educational resources. A practitioner with even a year's experience in the field typically gains some understanding of his or her agency, and perhaps a comparative perspective on other provider agencies associated with the same type of parent organization, that enables a practitioner to recognize alternatives and to learn from the experience of others. Similar benefits regarding sharing and innovation can result from familiarity with agencies and practitioners from other segments of the broad field of continuing education.

Continuing education agencies have been greatly influenced by their societal context. Within the agency's service area, community problems (such as employment and health), available resources (such as money, participants, and qualified people), national and international trends (such as federal funding for adult basic education or for continuing education for the health professions), and the offerings of other providers can have a major and sometimes sudden impact on programme size and emphasis. A subtle but important proficiency of practitioners with a sense of direction is a broad perspective on trends and issues based on familiarity with the history of the field (Grattan, 1971; Knowles, 1977), recurrent policy issues (Blakely and Lappin, 1969; Knowles, 1969), social change (Bennis et al, 1976), community power structure, and recent legislation, as well as emerging issues for topics on which continuing education programmes are focused (Broschart, 1977).

A promising research question is, what have been the trends regarding various types of agency sponsors of part-time educational programmes for adults over the years, and what have been the main influences?

Another benefit of having a broad perspective on the field is an awareness of resources that other practitioners might overlook. Some resources are in the form of professional literature that contains concepts which might be useful, for example, in developing a rationale for investment in continuing education. Awareness of a basic bibliography might be valuable. Other resources include the people who could contribute to programme planning or implementation. The practitioner's task is to match needs and resources, and this is aided by an awareness of relevant resources and a strategy for proposal preparation. Information about relevant resources is available from various sources, eg general directories (Niemi and Jessen, 1976).

Future directions

In an applied field such as the continuing education of adults, future directions for research are closely tied to the major emerging policy issues in the field. The following are some of the major issues and trends that call for the use of available tested knowledge regarding the continuing education of adults as well as the creation of new knowledge. As in the preceding review, the focus is on North America, but these recommendations may suggest themes that might be explored in other national settings.

The rising average level of formal education in the adult population, combined with the need for personal adjustments precipitated by social change, makes it likely that adult participation in continuing education will become even more widespread in the coming decades. During the past decade or two there have been major strides in the advent of an educative society in which various social institutions encourage and contribute to lifelong learning. Policy research is needed to explore future alternatives and educational programmes are needed to help people explore which of these are most desirable, and ways to move in the chosen directions.

The general public is becoming more aware that adulthood is not just stability and decline, but includes major positive changes and difficult adjustments. Practitioners concerned with lifelong learning can work with journalists to help people gain a more comprehensive and developmental understanding of adulthood. Continuing education practitioners can use such generalizations to generate new programme ideas, develop relevant instructional materials, attract participants, and provide counselling services.

Generalizations about adult learning now enable practitioners to design more effective learning activities than usually occur. A major challenge to continuing educationists and leading theorists is to help teachers cf adults become more effective, and a crucial area of research is in adult learning strategies.

Programme development procedures are at the core of continuing education practice. Effective practices for setting objectives, or organizing learning activities, or programme evaluation occur in one segment of the field (such as public school adult basic education or industrial training) but are unfamiliar in other segments. More concerted effort is needed to exchange programme development practices across various segments of the field.

As lifelong learning is becoming more generally accepted, it is increasingly important that those involved in continuing education develop more collaborative approaches to practice. The day seems to be over when the staff of a continuing education division of a school or university can function in isolation from the remainder of the parent organization. Regardless of the benefits that may have been associated with benign neglect, those in preparatory education increasingly want to serve adult part-time students. Collaborative approaches to the continuing education function within the parent organization can harness this interest and retain a vital role for practitioners in continuing education divisions. Collaborative approaches outside the parent organization can enable practitioners from several agencies to co-sponsor programmes when such co-operation seems desirable. However, it should be recognized that the pluralistic system of multiple providers has many advantages and the distinctive contributions of various agencies should be preserved.

One benefit of multiple providers is the impetus to reach under-served adults. This partly reflects the response to competition in which each agency seeks to attract more of the type of adult who constitutes their main clientele. Research and programming efforts are needed to demonstrate delivery systems for continuing education that fit the life-styles of the main target markets of adults. Reaching more of the types who are under-represented in current programmes, (such as older adults and those with low levels of formal education) is also likely to entail selective public tax support.

Because continuing education programmes have not been very institutionalized, and because many practitioners enter the field with a missionary spirit to help the less advantaged, the quality of leadership of continuing education practitioners has been very influential in programme growth and effectiveness. It seems likely that in the coming decades the quality of leadership will be affected somewhat by research findings, graduate study, and professional associations.

As lifelong learning concepts are being accepted by society generally, there is increasing attention to application of concepts and practices from continuing education of adults to preparatory education of children and youth. Some practitioners are assuming leadership in this effort but more assistance is needed.

In general, effective continuing education practitioners have a sense of direction. In addition to proficiency in administration and programme development, such a sense of direction arises from a commitment to lifelong learning and an understanding of the field. Familiarity with continuing education in other national settings can contribute to this sense of the field (Lowe, 1975). One of the greatest opportunities of the coming decades is to arrange for greater international exchange of continuing education practitioners and scholars;

References

Alford, J (1968) *Continuing Education in Action* John Wiley & Sons: New York

Argyris, C and Schön, D A (1976) *Theory in Practice: Increasing Professional Effectiveness* Jossey-Bass: San Francisco

Baller, W R, Charles, D C and Miller, E L (1967) Mid-life attainment of the mentally retarded: a longitudinal study *Genetic Psychology Monographs* 75: 235-329

Baltes, P B and Schaie, K W (eds) (1973) *Life-Span Developmental Psychology: Personality and Socialization* Academic Press: New York

Barker, R G and Schoggen, P (1973) *Qualities of Community Life* Jossey-Bass: San Francisco

Belasco, J A and Trice, H M (1969) *The Assessment of Change in Training and Therapy* McGraw-Hill: New York

Bennis, W G (1969) *Organization Development: Its Nature, Origins, and Prospects* Addison-Wesley: Reading, Mass

Bennis, W G, Benne, K D, Chin, R and Corey, K E (1976) *The Planning of Change* Holt, Rinehart, and Winston: New York

Berrol, S C (1976) From compensatory education to adult education: the New York evening schools, 1825-1935 *Adult Education* 26 4:298-325

Binstock, R H and Shanas, E (eds) (1976) *The Handbook of Aging and Social Sciences* Van Nostrand Reinhold: New York

Birren, J E and Schaie, K W (eds) (1977) *Handbook of the Psychology of Aging* Van Nostrand Reinhold: New York

Blakely, R J and Lappin, I M (1969) *Knowledge is Power to Control Power* (notes and essays on education for adults, no 63) Syracuse University Publications in Continuing Education: Syracuse, NY

Blaney, P and McKie (1969) Knowledge of conference objectives and effect upon learning *Adult Education* 19 2: 98-105

Boaz, R L (1978) Participation in Adult Education: Final Report 1975 DHEW, National Center for Education Statistics, US Government Printing Office: Washington, DC

Booth, A and Knox, A (1967) Participation in adult education agencies and personal influence *Sociology of Education* 40 3: 275-7

Boshier, R (1976) Factor analysis at large: a critical review of the motivational orientation literature *Adult Education* 27 1: 25-47

Botwinick, J (1967) *Cognitive Processes in Maturity and Old Age* Springer: New York

Bradford, L P, Gibb, J R, and Benne, K D (eds) (1964) *T-Group Theory and Laboratory Method* John Wiley and Sons: New York

Broschart, J R (1977) *Lifelong Learning in the Nation's Third Century* United States Office of Education, DHEW (publication no OE 76-09102) US Government Printing Office: Washington, DC

Brunner, E DeS et al (1959) *An Overview of Adult Education Research* Adult Education Association of the USA: Chicago

Burgess, P (1971) Reasons for adult participation in group education activities *Adult Education* 22 1:3-29

Campbell, D D (1977) *Adult Education as a Field of Study and Practice* University of British Columbia, the Centre for Continuing Education: Vancouver

Carey, J (1963) *Forms and Forces in University Adult Education* Center for the Study of Liberal Education of Adults: Chicago. (Available from Syracuse University, Publications in Continuing Education: Syracuse, NY)

Christoffel, P H (1978) Future federal funding of lifelong learning *Lifelong Learning: The Adult Years* 1 10:17-24

Clark, B R (1956) *Adult Education in Transition* University of California Press: Berkeley, Ca

Craig, R L (ed) (1976) *Training and Development Handbook* (2nd edition) McGraw-Hill: New York

Darkenwald, G G (1977) Innovation in adult education: an organizational analysis *Adult Education* 27 3:156-172

Dorland, J R (1969) The impact of legislation on adult education Chapter 6 in N C Shaw (ed) *Administration of Continuing Education* National Association for Public School Adult Education: Washington

Drucker, P F (1966) *The Effective Executive* Harper and Row: New York

Eisdorfer, C and Lawton, M P (1973) *The Psychology of Adult Development and Aging* American Psychological Association: Washington, DC

Farmer, J A, Jr and Knox, A B (1977) *Alternative Patterns for Strengthening Community Service Programs in Institutions of Higher Education* University of Illinois, Office for the Study of Continuing Professional Education: Urbana, Il

Farmer, M L (1971) *Counseling Services for Adults in Higher Education* Scarecrow Press: Metuchen, NJ

Feldman, K A and Newcomb, T M (1969) *The Impact of College on Students* Jossey-Bass: San Francisco

Finch, C B and Hayflick, L (eds) (1977) *Handbook of the Biology of Aging* Van Nostrand Reinhold: New York

Fitts, W H (1972) *The Self Concept and Performance* Dede Wallace Center: Nashville, Tenn

Flippo, E B (1976) *Principles of Personnel Management* (4th edition) McGraw-Hill: New York

Freire, P (1970) The adult literacy process and cultural action for freedom *Harvard Educational Review* 40 2:205-25

Gagné, R M (1972) *The Conditions of Learning* (revised edition) Holt, Rinehart, and Winston: New York

Gould, R (1978) *Transformations* Simon and Schuster: New York

Grattan, C H (1971) *In Quest of Knowledge: A Historical Perspective on Adult Education* (reprint) Arno Press and the *New York Times*: New York

Grotelueschen, A D, Gooler, D D and Knox, A B (1976) *Evaluation in Adult Basic Education: How and Why* Interstate: Danville, Il
Hackman, J R, Oldham, G R, Janson, R and Purdy, K (1975) A new strategy for job enrichment *California Management Review* 17 4: 57-71
Harris, B M and Bessent, W (1969) *In-Service Education* Prentice-Hall: Englewood Cliffs, NJ
Havelock, R G (1969) *Planning for Innovation* Institute for Social Research: University of Michigan, Ann Arbor
Havighurst, R J and Orr, B (1956) *Adult Education and Adult Needs* Center for the Study of Liberal Education for Adults: Chicago. (Available from Syracuse University, Publications in Continuing Education: Syracuse, NY)
Hentschke, G C (1975) *Management Operations in Education* McCutchan Publishing Corporation: Berkeley, Ca
Hill, R J (1960) *A Comparative Study of Lecture and Discussion Methods* The Fund for Adult Education: New York
Hill, R, Foote, N, Aldous, J, Carlson, R and MacDonald, R (1970) *Family Development in Three Generations* Schenkman: Cambridge, Mass
Houle, C O (1961) *The Inquiring Mind* University of Wisconsin Press: Madison
Houle, C O (1972) *The Design of Education* Jossey-Bass: San Francisco
Houle, C O (1973) *The External Degree* Jossey-Bass: San Francisco
Irish, G H (1975) Reflection on means and ends in adult basic education *Adult Education* 25 2:125-130
Jensen, G, Liveright, A A and Hallenbeck, W (eds) (1964) *Adult Education: Outlines of an Emerging Field of University Study* Adult Education Association of the USA: Washington, DC
Johnson, E (1965) *Metroplex Assembly: An Experiment in Community Education* Center for the Study of Liberal Education for Adults: Boston, Mass. (Available from Syracuse University, Publications in Continuing Education: Syracuse, NY)
Johnstone, J W C and Rivera, R J (1965) *Volunteers for Learning* Aldine: Chicago
Joyce, B and Weil, M (1972) *Models of Teaching* Prentice-Hall: Englewood Cliffs, NJ
Kidd, J R (1962) *Financing Continuing Education* Scarecrow Press: New York
Klevins, C (ed) (1972) *Materials and Methods in Adult Education* Klevens Publications: New York
Knowles, M S (1969) *Higher Adult Education in the United States* American Council on Education: Washington, DC
Knowles, M S (1970) *The Modern Practice of Adult Education* Association Press: New York
Knowles, M S (1975) *Self Directed Learning* Association Press: New York
Knowles, M S (1977) *A History of the Adult Education Movement in the United States* (revised edition) Krieger: Huntington, NY
Knox, A B (1973) *Development of Adult Education Graduate Programs* Commission of the Professors of Adult Education, Adult Education Association of the USA: Washington, DC
Knox, A B (1974) Life-long self-directed education Chapter 2 in R J Blakely (ed) *Fostering the Growing Need to Learn* Division of Regional Medical Programs, Bureau of Health Resources Development: Rockville, Md
Knox, A B (1975) New realities in the administration of continuing higher education *The NUEA Spectator* 39 22:6-9
Knox, A B (1977a) *Adult Development and Learning* Jossey-Bass: San Francisco
Knox, A B (1977b) *Current Research Needs Related to Systematic Learning by Adults* (occasional paper no 4) University of Illinois, Office for the Study of Continuing Professional Education: Urbana, Il
Knox, A B (1979) *Enhancing Proficiencies of Continuing Educators* New Directions for Continuing Education, Quarterly Sourcebooks, Vol 1, Jossey-Bass: San Francisco, Ca
Knox, A B (ed) (in press) *Adult Education Program Development and Administration* Jossey-Bass: San Francisco

Knox, A B and Farmer, H S (1977) Overview of counseling and information services for adult learners *International Review of Education* 23 4: 387-414

Knox, A B, Grotelueschen, A D and Sjogren, D D (1968) Adult intelligence and learning ability *Adult Education* 18 3: 188-96

Knox, A B and Sjogren, D D (1964) Achievement and withdrawal in university adult education classes *Adult Education* 15 2:74-88

Kotler, P (1974) *Marketing for Non-Profit Organizations* Prentice-Hall: Englewood Cliffs, NJ

Kurland, N D (ed) (1977) *Entitlement Studies* (NIE Papers in Education and Work — No 4) US Department of HEW, National Institute of Education: Washington, DC

Levinson, D J et al (1978) *The Seasons of a Man's Life* Knopf: New York

Lindquist, J (1978) *Strategies for Change* Pacific Soundings Press: Berkeley, Ca

Lloyd, A S (1972) Freire, Conscientization and Adult Education *Adult Education* 23 1:3-20

London, J, Wenkert, R and Hagstrom, W O (1963) *Adult Education and Social Class* (Cooperative Research Project No 1017, USOE) University of California Survey Research Center: Berkeley, Ca

Long, H B (1973) *The Education of the Mentally Retarded Adult* Adult Education Association and ERIC Clearinghouse on Adult Education: Washington, DC

Lowe, J (1975) *The Education of Adults: A World Perspective* UNESCO: Paris

Lowenthal, M F, Thurnher, M, Chiriboga, D, Beeson, D, Giay, L, Lurie, E, Pierce, R, Spencer, D, and Weiss, L (1975) *Four Stages of Life: A Comparative Study of Women and Men Facing Transitions* Jossey-Bass: San Francisco

Maas, H S and Kuypers, J A (1974) *From Thirty to Seventy* Jossey-Bass: San Francisco

Maddi, S R (1972) *Personality Theories: A Comparative Analysis* (revised edition) Dorsey Press: Homewood, Il

Merriam, S (1977) Philosophical perspectives on adult education: a critical review of the literature *Adult Education* 27 4: 195-208

Mezirow, J, Darkenwald, G and Knox, A B (1975) *Last Gamble on Education* Adult Education Association of the USA: Washington, DC

Miles, M B (1965) Changes during and following laboratory training: a clinical-experimental study *The Journal of Applied Behavioral Science* 1 3:215-42

Miller, H L (1964) *Teaching and Learning in Adult Education* Macmillan: New York

Miller, H L (1967) *Participation of Adults in Education: A Force Field Analysis* Center for the Study of Liberal Education of Adults: Chicago. (Available from Syracuse University, Publications in Continuing Education: Syracuse, NY

Monette, M L (1977) The concept of educational need *Adult Education* 27 2: 116-27

Nakamoto, J and Verner, C (1973) *Continuing Education in the Health Professions: A Review of the Literature, 1960-1970* ERIC Clearinghouse on Adult Education: Syracuse, NY

Neugarten, B S et al (eds) (1964) *Personality in Middle and Late Life* Atherton: New York

Niemi, J A, Grabowski, S M and Kuusisto, E A (eds) (1976) *Research and Investigation in Adult Education* (1976 Annual Register) Northern Illinois University, ERIC Clearinghouse in Career Education, DeKalb, Il

Niemi, J A and Jessen, D C (1976) *Directory of Resources in Adult Education* Adult Education Association (and ERIC Clearinghouse in Career Education at Northern Illinois University): Washington, DC

Penfield, K R (1975) Public service vs redeeming values: university extension in conflict *Adult Education* 25 2: 107-24

Pennington, F and Green, J (1976) Comparative analysis of program development processes in six professions *Adult Education* 27 1: 13-23

Rogers, E M and Shoemaker, F F (1971) *Communication of Innovations* Free Press: New York

Schein, E H (1978) *Career Dynamics: Matching Individual and Organizational Needs* Addison-Wesley: Reading, Mass

Sjogren, D D, Knox, A B and Grotelueschen, A D (1968) Adult learning in relation to prior adult education participation *Adult Education* 19 1:3-10

Smith, R M, Aker, G F and Kidd, J R (eds) (1970) *Handbook of Adult Education* Macmillan: New York

Solomon, D, Bezdek, W E and Rosenberg, L (1963) *Teaching Styles and Learning* Center for the Study of Liberal Education for Adults: Chicago. (Available from Syracuse University, Publications in Continuing Education: Syracuse, NY

Spear, G E (ed) (1976) *Adult Education Staff Development: Selected Issues, Alternatives, and Implications* University of Missouri-Kansas City, Center for Resource Development in Adult Education: Kansas City, Mo

Stake, R E (1967) The countenance of educational evaluation *Teachers College Record* 68 523-40

Stubblefield, H W (1974) Adult civic education in the post World War II period *Adult Education* 24 3:227-37

Timiras, P S (1972) *Developmental Physiology and Aging* Macmillan: New York

Tough, A (1967) *Learning Without a Teacher* (Educational Research Series No 3) Ontario Institute for Studies in Education: Toronto

Tough, A (1971) *The Adult's Learning Projects* (Research in Education Series 1) Ontario Institute for Studies in Education: Toronto

Tough, A (1978) Major learning efforts: recent research and future directions *Adult Education* 28 4:250-63

Travers, R M W (ed) (1973) *Second Handbook of Research on Teaching* American Educational Research Association, Rand McNally: Chicago

Trent, J W and Medsker, L B (1968) *Beyond High School* Jossey-Bass: San Francisco

Truesdell, L R (1975) Persisters and dropouts in the Canada Manpower Training Program *Adult Education* 25 3: 149-60

Vaillant, G (1977) *Adaptation to Life* Little, Brown: Boston

White, R W (1961) *Lives in Progress* Holt, Rinehart, and Winston: New York

Williams, R H and Wirths, C G (1965) *Lives Through the Years* Atherton Press: New York

Worthen, B R and Sanders, J R (1973) *Educational Evaluation: Theory and Practice* Wadsworth: Belmont, Ca

Ziegler, W L (ed) (1970) *Essays on the Future of Continuing Education* (notes and essays on education for adults, no 66) Syracuse University Publications in Continuing Education: Syracuse, NY

5. The need for diversity of provision

Geoffrey Hubbard

> **Summary:** This chapter surveys the likely pressures on the educational system, particularly in relation to lifelong education and training, as a consequence of the pressure of technological change in our society.
>
> It then considers some of the ways in which more flexible and diverse provision can be made, through open learning, flexible study arrangements, the bringing together of education, training, advice and consultancy, and the closer linking of educational institutions, communications networks and libraries.

I start from the premise that the need for lifelong learning stems from the changes facing the developed countries in particular. Other chapters in this World Yearbook have described those changes in more detail; here it is enough to indicate that the impact of advanced technologies based on microelectronics is likely to require us to change our pattern of life, in particular by spending less of it on work. By the nature of the change, the work that will disappear, taken over by automated devices of one sort or another, will be dull, boring work on which sentient human beings should not be required to waste their time. But we have a society in which most people are required to do just such work and are conditioned not only to accept it, but to find in it a major justification for their existence and the principal support of their self-esteem.

So my starting point is that work of this sort may not be available in sufficient quantity to fill the greater part of the waking hours of the bulk of the adult population, and that this situation will be combined with a high level of output of material goods and services; the world of the idle rich rather than the undeserving poor. Other types of work will be plentiful; there will be work for the highly qualified, and socially beneficial activity of one sort or another for all. The significant questions which I cannot answer are how our society will ultimately adapt to these changes, how long it will take and what sort of intermediate phases we may pass through on the way. It seems fairly certain, however, that the developed countries will tread this road; the first steps have already been taken and such is the interdependence of our world that no one country will be able to contract out. Whatever the initial impact, the ultimate outcome must be a pattern of life for everyone that is satisfying and fulfilling, for the alternative — a rich, full life for the employed *élite* and unemployment benefit at subsistence level for the rest — is a formula for social and political disaster.

It is in this context that I see the need for lifelong education. It is not a simple requirement, easily met by the extension of existing provision. There are a number of different needs to be met, often in highly unpredictable circumstances. The need for training and retraining, for providing people with new vocational skills, is relatively straightforward. The somewhat frenzied recent discussion in Britain has tended to concentrate on microelectronics, on the design and programming of the chips themselves. It is true that there is a need for these very sophisticated talents, and that our economic position may depend crucially on their availability, but the actual numbers involved are relatively small. It is the next stage in the chain that makes a numerically significant demand, the stage at which products which use microelectronics are designed, built, installed, operated and maintained. This is not a radically new requirement; it calls for the designers and skilled workers industry has always needed, only retrained to appreciate the potential of the new technology. It is, however, unfortunately the case that this need has hardly been adequately met in the past; our education system has always been a little weak on producing those who make as opposed to those who think. So, if we need more engineers and technologists, more designers, more production engineers, more skilled technicians and, moreover, we need them all reoriented towards the new technologies, we have a fairly substantial task on our hands and few ideas on how to attack it.

There is also the need to provide education as a contribution to the wise use of increased leisure. This leisure may sometimes be involuntary, if we do not have the wit to share the work out; it may come either at odd hours or in concentrated periods. Education has to help those with unaccustomed leisure to pursue their interests and to discover new ones. If one adds to the range of formal post-school education the activities of the less formal adult educators and the broadcasters, working up to the frontier where 'education' borders on 'entertainment', it is difficult to think of any legal and socially accepted leisure activity that is not included within the current range of educational provision.

The most difficult requirement for lifelong education is, however, in the area of attitude formation. Most people will have to change their perceptions, to see work as the curse of Adam and be glad to be called on to do less of it. They will have to define work as doing what you do not like and play as doing what you enjoy, rather than making the distinction between what earns money and what costs money. They will need to base their evaluation of themselves on what they are and what they have discovered themselves to be, rather than on the status conferred by their job.

They are also going to have to rediscover somehow the value of service to others. I am not very confident about the educational process as a way of modifying attitudes. I recognize that education does modify attitudes, but looking at the difference between our intentions and our achievements suggests that we have got our wires crossed somewhere. Nevertheless, however difficult it may be, many attitudes are going to need changing, not least the attitudes of those of us concerned with education.

There is, of course, an alternative view which sees much of the contemporary concern over the impact of microelectronics as exaggerated. It is argued that microelectronics is merely another in a long sequence of new technologies, the social and economic consequences of which will be easily absorbed, particularly if the essential adaptability of the market economy is allowed full scope. Some industries may be eliminated but new ones will spring up to take their place. There may be a further shift of employment from manufacturing industry to computer-related or information-based industries, but this no more implies large-scale permanent structural unemployment than did the corresponding run-down of the agricultural labour force over the first half of the century which, it should be noted, was accompanied by a substantial increase in the total numbers employed. Thus the reduction, if any, in the total labour demand can easily be met by a modest contraction of the average working week.

From this standpoint, there is certainly no desperate social need for lifelong education as a counter to the destructive effects of unemployment. On the other hand, it does imply a more imperative need for vocational retraining, if the labour force is going to be able to switch jobs to newly created industries at the sort of rate envisaged. Moreover, if the first model is one of a wealthy society, this one, in which all are busily engaged in creating wealth at the higher productivity rates associated with new industries, must surely be rich beyond the dreams of avarice. But it might be beyond not only the dreams of avarice, but also the limits of growth. We are still constrained by availability of energy and natural resources. We may yet have to reject a high-growth economy and find ways of distributing purchasing power that are not related to the production and distribution of ever-increasing quantities of consumer goods.

This alternative view, therefore, also requires a developed system of vocational training and retraining. It also implies availability of resources which would make possible a wide-ranging system of lifelong education. And since the immemorial cry has been that such a system is eminently desirable, that our masters would love to make such a system a reality but that, alas, in the present economic conditions . . . , we should perhaps put the prospect fairly categorically:

a) The likely consequences of the impact of microelectronics will in any event require extensive provision for vocational training and retraining.
b) It may also require the provision of opportunities for lifelong education as an essential counter to the adverse social effect of structural unemployment.
c) If the adverse social effects do not occur, then there will be the resources to provide an adequate system of lifelong education.

However, it is a little too glib to talk of a 'system' of lifelong education. It suggests one overall pattern, centrally designed and imposed, and that is not the way change occurs in education. Moreover, in this context particularly, it is not the way things should be done, for we have discerned several different requirements, even in the very broad terms of the preceding analysis, and different requirements are likely to require different provisions.

In fact, the provision of education and training for adults at intervals throughout their lives really needs to be approached from the standpoint of the adult requiring the education and training rather than (as has traditionally been the case) from the standpoint of the teacher or the institution offering it. (*See also Chapter 4.*) Let us try to set out the characteristics which are likely to distinguish adult learners

a) They are not susceptible to coercion.
b) They have obligations limiting their freedom of movement and making inescapable demands on their time. (These demands may not be predictable; thus, it may not be possible to commit oneself to availability at a certain time.)
c) They know what they are interested in, and what they want to achieve. (They may be prepared to modify their perceptions; but equally they usually have fairly clear ideas of what they are *not* interested in and what they do *not* want to achieve.)

These characteristics indeed highlight the inappropriateness of almost all current education and training provisions, which require the recipient to set aside a specified time (usually predetermined and at regular intervals), which require attendance at a particular place, and which offer a predetermined amount of education or training which the student must accept as a whole. Even the more informal offerings — adult education broadcast series designed in collaboration with other agencies — tend to make these demands.

This is where we need to provide diversity. Not as a cafeteria, a pick-and-mix counter where the student can find the particular learning approach which suits his style, for I doubt whether there is much to be gained by offering adult students the same content in different presentational forms. Indeed, the more proper thought that goes into designing the educational process offered to the student, the more the presentational form in which the content is offered will be of secondary importance. The important issue is likely to be the mode in which the student operates, as an individualized learner, in a peer group and so on, rather than the choice of medium for conveying instructional content. The strongest argument for diversity of presentation is when it helps to motivate unmotivated students, or to avoid boredom in reluctant students, and the adult learner will not be unmotivated or bored; given either of these conditions he or she is somewhere else. Diversity is needed in the arrangements for offering education and training. Diversity and flexibility must be incorporated so that the opportunities offered match the conditions of the potential student.

In no respect does this require the removal or replacement of existing arrangements. In the United Kingdom, the Open University offers opportunities for degree studies to those unable to attend a conventional university; it augments but does not replace that provision. Similarly, the development of open learning systems in non-graduate further and higher education augments, but does not replace, present provision. There are courses available at various institutions for a wide range of qualifications, wherever there is a fortunate coincidence of staff and student availability. Arrangements can be devised to make courses available wherever there is student demand, however few and scattered the students (Coffey, 1978; Davies, 1977).

Another aspect of flexibility which often goes with an open learning approach, but which is not necessarily so linked, is the availability of instruction at whatever time the student wishes. This is provided, for example, in the various 'learning by appointment' and flexible study schemes. (See Davies, [1977], Appendices 1 and 4, on flexible study schemes. Learning by Appointment Centres are located at Bath College of Technology, Napier College of Technology and Bradford College of Higher Education.)

We have, however, as yet made little progress in breaking up the predetermined course and offering the student the right to choose what he will learn. There are certain 'design your own degree' arrangements but the student still has to take a full degree course. More beneficial would be a merging of the 'advisory and consultancy' and the 'education and training' functions. I envisage an arrangement whereby a client can bring a problem to a service point, can be helped to define the problem and to find a solution to it. The assistance he receives may be partly in terms of advice and consultancy, partly in terms of education and training. The boundary between the two should not be all that precise.

In describing this possibility I use the phrase 'service point'; this is not a particularly elegant term, but the term 'educational institution' is almost certainly inappropriate. Indeed, the most likely point of service under present arrangements is the public library, and this leads to a consideration of the relative places in a system of lifelong education of the public library, the communications networks and the educational and training institutions.

At this stage, one cannot go beyond broad generalizations. Radio, television and the telephone reach into the home. In the developed countries, the public library system is an immense resource with many points of contact with the general public. The education and training institutions have the capacity to teach and train, but will need to develop in ways which will make their skills more available to recipients whose needs cannot be met within the existing educational structure or through regular attendance at a particular place. This surely points to a need to improve the links between these three aspects.

We live in a period of rapid change and we may, if we wish, use the inherent conservatism of the educational system to slow down and inhibit change (and it is right that it should be inherently conservative, for it conserves the values of our culture). But the pressures on us are too insistent: the challenge of our time requires us to take positive steps to build on what we have that is worthwhile and to do so in ways that will make those merits more widely accessible.

References

Coffey, J (1978) *Development of an Open Learning System for Further Education* Council for Educational Technology Working Paper 15 CET: London

Davies, T C (1977) *Open Learning Systems for Mature Students* CET Working Paper 14 CET: London

6. Recurrent education: tackling the financial implications

Maurice Peston

Summary: This article considers recent trends and possible developments in the economy, especially in connection with technological change. It argues that a likely scenario is one in which the overall demand for labour falls. It then follows that the costs of financing recurrent education will fall. Indeed, if the economic system is slow to adjust, these costs will become zero or negative. Thus the main problems of recurrent education in the future will not be financial in the ordinary sense but social, political and educational.

It is customary to regard recurrent education as the latest fad in what is altogether a rather faddy activity. Education is a process which normally occupies a fixed period at the beginning of a person's life. For the disadvantaged and below-average, the period lasts ten to 12 years up to the age of about 16 (eg in Britain). For some of the population, it may extend up to another ten years but, except in peculiar circumstances, no one will be a full-time pupil or student beyond their mid-twenties. Of course, it is sometimes said that a person's education continues throughout his life, but that is meant to be an aphorism rather than a description of a formal and structured process. There is also something called adult education, but that is not really education but recreation. And then some employed people, notably management, go on courses, but that too is not education but training. Thus although it is possible to show that adult education and training have existed for a long time and currently absorb considerable sums of money, none of that counts in any discussion of recurrent education. That is designated as futuristic, airy-fairy, or Utopian.

It may now need to be taken more seriously, because of certain developments taking place in technology and as people, especially in the industrialized nations, become satiated with goods. But, with a bit of luck they may be persuaded to demand more and more cars, freezers, houses, furniture, and other durables. If not, the developing world will become the target of mass-produced consumer goods and nothing will change. Thus the 'optimists' face the future, unwilling to conceive of nil economic growth or the re-education it will necessitate.

My own view of the matter is rather different. Firstly I would argue that recurrent education is old hat. There is nothing new about it at all. But that is not to say it is uninteresting or poses no problems, particularly no financial problems, for the future. Quite the contrary, its future development already gives rise to complications of a fascinating nature which need unravelling. Secondly, it may be expected to play a major role in the future on two counts. On the one hand, there will be genuine difficulties in absorbing the available labour force, especially the part without skills or whose skills are obsolete. On the other hand, technological development will enable mankind to rethink its objectives and to confront and indeed welcome certain forms of demand satiation.

Economic and technological developments will have social and political consequences of a quite fundamental nature. Curiously enough, concentrating on problems of finance will bring many of these into focus. It may also be added that misinterpreting the financial issues will lead to needless fears and serious mistakes of policy. To state the main proposition of this chapter, if recurrent education is viewed as something costly, to be encouraged only when it can be afforded (which may well be a long way off in the future), it will not be seen as the essential part of a process of adjustment to potentially dangerous and destructive forces. In other words, the issue is one of maximizing recurrent education, creative leisure, or whatever in a way that individuals find attractive and compatible with their status as adults and free citizens. The alternative will be unemployment or useless work, coupled with consumption expenditure which will be seen as of temporary value and will be intrinsically unsatisfying.

Let me, therefore, describe a likely time path for a typical western industrialized economy, eg the UK, from now into the beginning of the next century. Largely this is merely a matter of extrapolating existing trends and giving imaginative consideration to the outcome of forces which are already operational.

The most important assumption to be made is that technological advance will occur more frequently and in more sectors in a form that is labour-saving rather than capital-saving. There will be an increase in the demand for some forms of labour, namely those which are complementary to the technology or are themselves responsible for the technical progress. But this cannot be relied upon to maintain full employment in the long term, for we are already entering the era of machines able to design and control the production of other machines.

The second key assumption is that, even where a labour input is demanded, its nature will change over a typical person's working life. Instead of a man or woman learning one basic skill which is developed over a lifetime but remains intrinsically the same thing for 40 to 50 years, in the future the adaptation required will be from one skill to a second and then on to a third, etc. Human beings will need much more flexibility, and personal adaptability will be a key capability. Once again, it may be remarked that this is already happening and the many changes that occur in the labour force should not be underestimated. The important point is the way the process will accelerate in the future.

The third assumption is that the female propensity to enter the labour force and remain in it will continue. This may continue to such a degree that female participation rates hardly differ from male ones. But, even if nothing as drastic as that happens, there will still be considerable scope within the next generation for women's propensity to enter paid work to rise.

The fourth assumption concerns competition from the Third World. Productive techniques are now easily copied, and for their routine operation do not require a highly skilled labour force, but one which is careful, well-disciplined, and, presumably, as low paid as possible. The advanced world will invent new products and produce and export them in their initial phase, but thereafter it is cheaper to take the productive equipment, western management and engineering personnel abroad and use cheaper overseas labour. Thus the advanced world must be able to make rapid technical progress merely to stand still in competitive terms. It will be able to export advanced equipment; the services of its high-level personnel will be demanded overseas; but, above all, it will sell ideas and techniques abroad. It follows that ideas and techniques must become the major home production industry.

We are entering a world where most of the labour force appears to be in excess supply, but where some high powered parts of the labour force will become more scarce. It is obviously important to transform as many as possible of the former into the latter. In other words, discovering people with the capacity to develop great skills and investing in them will, if anything, be more important than discovering and exploiting new oil reserves.

But what of the remainder of the population? There are three questions here: (a) How are they to be employed? (b) How are they to be paid? (c) How are they to occupy the time in which they are not employed? In considering these questions it is as well to be reminded of a point that is sometimes misunderstood. We are discussing economic systems which retain the capacity to grow and produce increasing quantities of goods and services. The problem is not one of a declining economy – far from it, since the system continues to retain a great potential for production. The trouble is that in doing so it is unable to find work for the whole of the labour force, or to pay them incomes which are intrinsically fair relative to society at large and which enable them to buy the goods that the productive capacity generates.

The solution to this problem is partly to reduce the extent of an individual person's working life in all of its dimensions, but to make (or rather help him/her to make) constructive use of the resulting time at his/her disposal. At the same time he/she has to be given an income which is regarded as fair and reasonable.

Before examining both these matters in more detail, it is worth taking a brief look at what has been happening in the UK to the length of the working week, working year, and working lifetime.

The number of hours worked per week by male operatives in manufactuing industry declined by 7 per cent between 1962 and 1977. In that period output per employee rose by about 60 per cent, and employees have preferred to see greater productivity transformed into purchasing power over goods and services rather than tremendously increased leisure per week.

In the 1970s, full-time male manual workers' weekly hours have fallen from just over 47 to just over 45, a decline of 4 per cent. For comparable women, the fall has been from 40 hours to just over 39, a fall of 2 per cent. Similarly, although non-manual workers work about seven hours a week less than manual workers, in the 70s the decline has been only 2 per cent, which is also the case for non-manual working women.

Manual workers now have on average just over three weeks' paid holiday a year compared with less than two in the 1950s. Similarly, non-manual workers receive about four weeks' paid holiday compared with two or three a couple of decades ago. The number of public holidays has risen from six to eight days.

Finally, on the average length of working life, for men at the beginning of the 50s it was 49 years, while today it is approximately 46 years. For unmarried women it has been about 33 years over the whole period, and for married women it has risen from 12 years to approximately 26. (In interpreting married women's employment it is vital not to misunderstand this as substituting work for leisure. What it does is substitute paid work in the office or factory for unpaid work in the home.)

The picture that emerges for men is fairly straightforward. From the early 50s to the present day the total lifetime's work input has declined by about 15 per cent for manual workers and by 10 to 12 per cent for non-manual workers. In this same period Gross National Product has risen by more than 80 per cent. This reinforces the point made earlier that the purchase of goods and services has dominated the retention of leisure in the expansion of welfare, at least as far as men are concerned.

The position of women is more complex. Unmarried women have not, according to the same calculation, increased their leisure significantly but this may, rather like the married women's case, reflect the abandonment of unpaid work (eg looking after relatives) and the breaking down of various social barriers to women's employment. As for married women, nothing about preferences for leisure can be inferred from their greater propensity to enter the labour force. Without hard figures on work in the home (which are really not available, especially for the early period), no definite conclusions can be arrived at. There is no reason to believe *a priori*, however, that women's preferences for leisure differ significantly from those of men.

Reverting to our main theme, if shortening of working life in all its dimensions is to dominate the economic and social experience of the next quarter century, this will represent a radical change compared with the previous one. Suppose, for example, our productive capacity increases by only 2.5 per cent per annum for the next quarter century. It will then be 85 per cent higher than it is now. Consider someone who expected to work 45 years and to receive a real income growing by 2.5 per cent per annum compared with his counterpart of a previous generation. His average lifetime real income would be more than three times that of his predecessor. Note that all this is predicated on the UK continuing at its post-war average growth rate of 2.5 per cent per annum and not accelerating towards the levels achieved by our more successful competitors and counterparts in Western Europe.

This provides part of the context within which to consider a decline in labour input. To take one case, assume that, instead of real income growing by 2.5 per cent per annum, it grew at 1.5 per cent per annum. This would still leave people some 40 per cent better off by the beginning of the new century. Moreover, given the new technology, it would be possible for labour input to decline by 1 to 2 per cent per annum. Thus, by the start of the next century the average worker would be required to work between 20 and 40 per cent less than he does now. In terms of hours the manual workers' working week might be reduced to something between 27 and 36 hours. Alternatively, his active working life might be reduced to between 28 and 37 years as compared with the existing 46. Combining the two effects, a possible variant would be a working week of 40 hours actually worked and a working life of 40 years on the more restrictive assumption and 30 to 36 on the more generous. For non-manual men the working life would be reduced to the same degree but hours worked per week would fall to something between 30 and 33.

What use will be made of the extra years and the extra hours? The simplest answer to this question is to reduce the retirement age and the average number of days worked per week, adding directly to a person's leisure time. The objection to this is twofold. Firstly, a large number of people already fail to make satisfactory use of the leisure time available to them. Secondly, some of the time made available needs to be used to upgrade the quality of the labour force to cope with its new circumstances.

The present model of education, training, and work assumes they occur in precisely that order. A broad base is provided in school and for some in further and higher education. Then there is more specific training for a job. Finally, there is the job itself within which experience and on-the-job training might lead to improved performance.

It is already recognized, however, that there are exceptions to this pattern. Some parts of the labour force, notably at the higher levels, are retrained. Sometimes this is on very short courses, but on other occasions absence from the point of production can be as long as a year. Moreover, not all these courses are to be regarded as training in a narrow sense. Many of them contain a much broader, educational element, especially when they are devised for medium and higher level management.

Quite separately from this, not all people regard their education as ending at the start of working life. Many continue their education in a part-time way; a few even return from work to full-time education. Indeed, there are a small but not insignificant number of people who start their further and higher education on retirement.

Thus there is nothing new in principle in suggesting that education and training need not be confined to one stage of life, but are activities relevant to the whole of a person's active existence. What may be regarded as new, even revolutionary, is that an approach to these matters, which already applies to a small minority of the population, should be applied to the whole of the employed labour force.

It might be argued that the best way of approaching this problem is to extend the time that people spend in educational institutions before they start work. It is said that their minds are more receptive then, and that the productive benefits of their extended education will last longer. Education at 16 will be useful for 50 working years; education at 26 for 20 at most.

The counter-arguments are fairly clear. Many people have had as much of school or university as they can stand at 16, 18, or 21. They have absorbed as much as they can for the time being, but this does not mean that subsequently they will be unable to take in more. Indeed, once it is accepted that returning for extra education is the norm, some of those who at the moment take the whole of their education in a single block before starting work will switch to the new basis. Moreover, just as physical capital equipment becomes obsolete, investment in human beings (ie their education and training) also becomes obsolete. Pursuing the physical capital analogy, old investments need to be replaced or at least refurbished. Just as the machine a man uses is not built to last for the whole of his working life, so his education and training will also become obsolete. These arguments for recurrent education are true *a fortiori* when account is taken of uncertainty. Even if on other grounds it was thought desirable to complete the process of education and training before starting work, in the increasingly dynamic world we are entering it will not be possible to do the whole job ahead of time.

To take an obvious example, the computer methods being taught to students today will not last for ten years, let alone 40 or 50. Even the broad general principles may change. The result is that such students will have to be retrained more than once in their lifetimes.

Economic and social necessities for once converge: less labour will be required in the productive process, but all labour will need to spend time away from the productive process to remain useful. Moreover, industry will require a highly flexible labour force which will have to be given a generalized set of skills. This is another way of saying that people will need re-education as well as retraining.

At this point it is useful to say a little more about the distinction between training and education which I, like many others, have made. Sometimes the difference is said to be that the former is relevant to production and the latter to consumption. 'Training is for work and education is for life', or 'training is for the economy, education for society'. This leads us to see training in terms of private costs and benefits and as something which the decentralized private sector can carry out satisfactorily, with some slight public sector support. It is education which is much more of a public good and suitable for government intervention, but it is then education which presents a problem of financing. Indeed, this can be made necessarily so by defining training as anything which raises the productivity of the worker so that it can always be financed out of the extra which he or she contributes to the productive process. Education then simply becomes a non-productive enterprise as a definitional residue. It can only be financed by reducing consumption or by taking resources away from some productive activity.

Now, there are problems for which this approach is useful, but in the present context it is in danger of obscuring more than it clarifies. In the first place, it actually flies in the face of what happens when a person is educated or trained. Although it is possible to distinguish the transmission of particular skills from the imbibing of general principles, and to identify such different phenomena as being able to operate and repair a machine, understanding how it was built and how it works and appreciating the theory of machines in broad terms or in detail, all of these are points on a training and education continuum and virtually all are mixtures of the two. To put the point differently, much that is recognizably educational goes on in training programmes, and there is a good deal which is clearly training to be found in educational institutions of all kinds.

A second criticism of this artificial distinction centres on the notion of what is productive. This is best seen again by example. It will surely be agreed that what workers and management actually achieve in 'the productive process' depends on attitudes, flexibility and general outlook, their ability to work as a team, and so on. In addition, the economic system as a whole requires a mobile and adaptable labour force. In the case of the British economy it might be argued that it is these general characteristics which are most lacking and, therefore, most responsible for our poor economic performance in the past three decades. Thus, without under-valuing training, it must be said that what is recognizably 'educational' undoubtedly contributes to economic efficiency, however it is defined.

My third criticism is the fundamental proposition of this chapter. It is that the production processes of firms and the operation of markets are embedded in a social system whose proper working is a prerequisite of economic success. Education is *par excellence* a social process which can make all the difference to economic performance, in particular, and social stability and progress in general. Moreover, in the context of a world with rapid labour-saving technical progress and growing conflict over the distribution of the proceeds, recurrent education will have a most important and perhaps decisive role to play.

This is especially the case when the maintenance of full employment is in doubt. If full employment is taken for granted, either because of the automatic working of the economic system or because of government intervention, recurrent education involves an economic cost, in that time away from work involves a loss of production. Of course, this may be offset by greater productivity in the future, and there is also the additional benefit of the personal pleasure and enhancement of the worker to be taken into account. Thus, even on the conventional view, it is possible to argue the case for some education during a person's working life if the individual wants it. Decisions in this matter are left to households and firms because the costs and benefits of recurrent education are assumed to be private ones, and government only involves itself if the market is imperfect, lacks appropriate information, or cannot deal with the problems (especially financial) that arise. But overall it is difficult, on the usual assumptions, to find a major role for government intervention. Post-school investment in human capital, if it is possible, will occur within the decentralized system to an optimum degree, especially if the government underwrites its financing.

What may be called the normal approach to recurrent education is based, therefore, on the following assumptions:

1. The economy usually operates in a state of full employment or can be made to do so by central governmental fiscal and monetary policy.
2. The individual normally has a continuous working life of some 40 to 50 years, a working year of 46 to 48 weeks, a working week of five days comprising 40 to 48 hours.
3. The working individual is typically a male who is the head of household and its chief income earner.
4. The labour force is divided into workers and management. Workers receive initial on-the-job training to which they add work experience, but then stay at the same level of performance and occupy the same position in the working hierarchy for the rest of their lives. Managers may receive initial training and certainly mature in the job but, in addition, they require continual re-education and retraining. Moreover, they are expected to have a career and to rise in a hierarchy, although not necessarily from the very bottom to the very top.
5. A manager is a part of the firm which is responsible for him (even if it has in due course to do without his services). Management participates in the decisions which affect its current and future position. The remainder of the labour force, the workers, are not part of the firm, but are inputs whose services are bought or not as the firm needs them. They do not participate in the process of decision-making.

Now, it is easy to say that this is a caricature and to point to counterexamples, but it is not a caricature of the classical features of the economy as economists have formulated them. While it is true to say that the economy at present is not exactly like that, there are many economists who regard its existing and likely future state as an aberration from that norm towards which we ought to return.

The purpose of this chapter has been to argue that these assumptions are not a correct account of the actual state of the economy, and are not appropriate for defining a new normal state. In addition, I take the view that they do not represent a desirable state towards which policy measures ought to guide firms and households.

Once the assumptions are varied and it is recognized not only that the economy has a propensity to behave cyclically, but also that in the future it will show a classic tendency to large-scale and persistent unemployment, the very nature of the question of recurrent education changes. In these circumstances the decentralized economic system is unable to solve the employment problem (or its speed of solution is far too slow). It then follows that the government has a permanent part to play, and one of its functions is the encouragement of recurrent education. In addition, far from finance being a constraint on action which may also involve distortions due to resource misallocation, its costs are trivially small and, therefore, not constraining relative to its benefits. Instead of the question 'can we afford some education during working life?' we must ask 'can recurrent education be mounted on sufficiently large a scale and in an effective enough way to make full use of the human resources which are available for it and need it?'

However, it will not be as easy as that. Of course, a by-product of much of the extra education will be a capacity for making better use of leisure. But it will be only a by-product and some additional effort will have to be made to enhance the quality of leisure-time activities. Furthermore, it will not be the case that those who have most leisure will also be those who are most capable of being re-educated and retrained. The figures given earlier of a possible reduction in work input are average ones. The economic argument suggests that it will be high-level manpower that gets the smallest reduction and low-level manpower the greatest. Thirdly, there is the question of the nature of the payments made to support people when they are not engaged directly in the production process.

An immediate political danger is apparent. It is easy to imagine the employment potential of average and below-average people falling through time. The result is that they spend much less of their lives actually working. A beneficent government, recognizing it is not their fault they are unwanted, may pay them an income not much less than is paid to them when they are working. Education for leisure and some retraining is made available, but these are precisely the people who make least use of these facilities and gain little from them. Instead, they extend their leisure in ways that are characteristic of the present day, namely as spectators dependent on others to amuse them. The question arises whether the emergence of such a dependent class of non-workers is conducive to democracy, or whether it is not much more likely to give rise to some form of totalitarian system of a technocratic kind. In other words, we can see clear signs of 1984 or a Brave New World.

If these people are not to become a major social and political problem, a much more imaginative approach will have to be adopted to prepare them for their greater leisure. The most sensible line to be taken is likely to be to place the educational and training institutions close to the factory or office. Instead of the present state of affairs in which the gap, physical and intellectual, between work and education and leisure is as large as possible, the tendency will be to diminish it.

There is a complication here in that technological development in audio-visual methods will change the nature of the teaching process and enable it to become more individualized and more solitary. We already possess the technical ability to record television programmes. It is possible to set up a dial-in system whereby a viewer owns no visual records himself but merely calls them up from a central library which transmits them to his own demand. Beyond that, on-line methods exist so that the student can actually dial in his questions and expect to receive his answers back on the computer. (*See also Chapter 2.*) Though well-motivated adults can make excellent use of these methods, the sort of people we are talking about will be of a different kind. They will be bewildered, may feel rejected and unneeded by society because they have no self-validating occupation, and if they have been brought up in the usual way with great emphasis placed on the work ethic, they will have no predisposition towards creative leisure. (It is worth emphasizing at this stage that the quantitative appraisal I have put forward of the decline in work needed in the next generation is quite modest. Other estimates have been much more drastic and would imply an intensification of the problems being discussed here to almost unmanageable proportions.)

To some extent this can be dealt with by emphasizing the retraining element; and many of those out of the direct productive process will be returning to it in another role. Once again, however, while this may be sufficient for the top 60 to 70 per cent of the population, there will be real difficulties for the remainder.

Another aspect of the changing relative significance of work and leisure is the changing nature of the family. The conventional picture of father at work, mother at home, and children at school is changing. In the future it is possible to envisage the alternative of mother at work, children at home, and father at school. Clearly, with greater female participation in the labour force, it will become increasingly likely that father's periods of education and retraining will not coincide with mother's. Beyond that, to the extent that the unemployment problem is not solved, children will leave school, have no desire for further training, but will be unable to find employment.

This extreme case merely serves to emphasize the tensions that may arise in family life if the possibilities are not anticipated and properly prepared for. It is not an exaggeration to warn of disruption and social unrest as the family is subject to new pressures which it may find itself unable to resist.

To the cynic these problems themselves may appear to be the solution to the greater macroeconomic problem of unemployment. What lies behind many of the developments we have pointed to is a demand for people to work in education, training, and the leisure industries. The labour released by the new technology can find employment elsewhere. But this is to miss the two central points: firstly, the sheer scale of the likely surplus of labour and, secondly, the concentration of the surplus in the vulnerable section of the population. To say that some of the remainder can find employment ministering to the needs of this latter group is not the same as actually solving their problems and giving them a proper place in society. It is, if anything, to go to the other extreme and make them still more dependent.

To summarize, it is impossible to deny that technological advance of a labour-saving kind ought to be a boon to mankind. Throughout history there has been a desire for less work and more leisure, a shorter working life and longer periods of retirement. But there are difficulties in responding to the real prospect before us, especially in the short and medium-term. Our society and political system have been based to such a great extent on the work ethic and the social and political independence provided by earned income that the new possibilities may undermine it totally. Certainly it cannot be assumed that existing institutions can survive the new technology, or that we can satisfactorily overcome these problems without the most careful planning.

7. The democratization of work: educational implications

Tom Schuller

Summary: The growth of industrial democracy in various forms poses a major educational challenge. There is a tension between the need to enable participants to learn the 'rules' of policy-making in the enterprise and the need to change those rules in accordance with the changing distribution of power. A further dilemma derives from the importance of allowing students to define their own learning needs without abandoning the responsibility for providing education in a systematic and effective fashion. The role of 'experts' such as accountants is sure to be called into question, and this may lead to a scrutiny of the whole basis of such expertise. Four broad groups of skills are identified as necessary for effective participation in decision-making: procedural, technical, micro-level policy-making and macro-level policy-making. The chapter concludes with some reflections on the implications of the democratization of work for the construction and dissemination of knowledge.

The scope of the issue

Both recurrent education and industrial democracy are terms which regularly provoke appeals for clear definition. I am assuming, however, that as far as the former is concerned the reader's definitional thirst has been adequately slaked by previous contributions, and for the purposes of this chapter I propose to operate with a relatively broad conception of industrial democracy, based essentially on the notion of a wider dissemination of decison-making powers at the place of work. This will allow me to concentrate on two central issues: the role education can play in the growth of industrial democracy, and the reciprocal impact which the further democratization of work may have on the structure and character of our educational systems.

> The term 'industrial democracy' implies a form of 'suffrage' similar to that in the political sphere. In other words, a strict usage of the term would indicate the ability of the workers to change the government in industry or directly to determine management decisions. In practice, 'industrial democracy', along with a host of associated ideas, is often used to denote far more limited forms of influence and involvement. (Batstone, 1976:10)

The key notion with which I shall operate is the equalization of power, viewing this as a process which is likely to continue without ever reaching a state of equilibrium. It is assumed that this equalization will occur predominantly through the medium of trade unions, but I do not distinguish voluntarist from legalist approaches (Sorge, 1976). Elliott's broad statement will therefore suffice: 'Industrial democracy involves workers . . . claiming rights to have a greater say over matters affecting their working lives' (Elliott, 1978:4).

'It is tiresome to hear education discussed, tiresome to educate, and tiresome to be educated' (William Lamb, 2nd Viscount Melbourne, political tutor to the young Queen Victoria). Perhaps; education has probably been oversold in the past as a social policy capable of resolving a whole range of problems, most particularly those surrounding the distribution of wealth and life chances. In many countries it is now paying the penalty, as the stubborn persistence of almost all those problems is bitterly juxtaposed against the earlier, over-optimistic claims of educationists. These now find themselves struggling to defend reforms already achieved, let alone pioneer new ones. The strategy of recurrent education was in part a response to this, in two ways: first, by nudging the common conception of education away from the 'front-end model', confined to the early years of the individual's life, and secondly, by stressing the interdependence of education with other social and economic policies (OECD/CERI, 1975).

I have argued elsewhere that to view education as a service in the literal sense of the word, a sector which helps other parts of society to change and improve, is in no way to denigrate it: 'The status of "necessary precondition" for the proper functioning of a democracy is not an unworthy one' (Schuller, 1978). This is highly apposite in the case of industrial democracy. No one would pretend that education is the cornerstone of industrial democracy, as the struggle for a more equal share of power has its roots in a much more primeval *rapport de force*. Yet workers and their representatives are doubly handicapped if the rules of the game are weighted against them in the first place and they are anyway denied access to the rule-book. It is difficult to play a good game of chess if the capacities of the pieces are explained move by move (if at all) and if your opponent's flanking manoeuvres are declared acceptable according to criteria which you have difficulty in challenging.

The game analogy is, as so often, in part misleading. Not only does it present the image of a neatly structured set-up, with two opponents facing each other squarely across the board; it also implies that there are clearly defined and objective rules, and deviance from these rules entails abandoning the game. The democratization of work, by contrast, implies precisely that the rules are to be recast with two consequences: previously disadvantaged participants are better placed and — crucially — the criteria of 'success' are altered. As Gramsci argued in the broad political sphere, education has a vital part to play in challenging the hegemony, the rule-defining capacity, of the dominant classes.

There are two fundamental aims of education for industrial democracy, and they proceed *pari passu:* redefining the management function so that it answers to employee and community interests rather than to those of shareholders, and establishing how far the practices and techniques implied in such a redefinition coincide with or conflict with current practices and techniques. To these must be added a third: the development of a capacity to initiate proposals and formulate policy. In this respect, the position of the Bullock Committee Report on industrial democracy is far too passive. 'The aim is not to turn employee representatives into experts in any of these areas, but to provide them with sufficient understanding to grasp and question proposals put to them by professional management' (Bullock, 1977:157). This gives due recognition to the need for a critical capacity but ignores the possibility of employee representatives taking the initiative themselves rather than responding to those of management. The TUC General Secretary, Len Murray, puts forward a more positive formulation:

> In the future there will be a move away from the negative veto role of resistance to unacceptable management policies, and a shift towards a more constructive approach to policy-making and the joint development of alternative strategies and proposals where existing ones seem inadequate. Workers have had enough of just being able to say what they don't want and are now seeking to have a decisive influence over what they do want.

Attitudes towards workers and their representatives participating in the running of industry are a function of both political standpoints and national origins. Is it an extension of labour rights, or a delusion? Perhaps the most striking comparison is between the French and American labour movements: diametrically opposed in broad ideological terms, they are at one in their opposition to industrial democracy as subversive of the straight oppositional role of unions. The German labour movement is, on the whole, happy to be 'incorporated'. Swedish and Norwegian unions have never hesitated to involve themselves in joint policy formulation with the management, but at the same time they do not ignore the conflict of interest between labour and capital. Perhaps the most illuminating trend, for the British observer, is in Italy: from a classic oppositional stance, the labour movement has moved over the last few years to a recognition of the need to influence policies more directly at national, regional and local level.

The evolution of industrial democracy, therefore, and the advantages and dangers it presents to both labour and capital, will naturally depend on the national context and on the way power relations shape the specific forms which are adopted. A final point, to conclude this introduction, relates to the Protean character of industrial life. The involvement of workers in new areas of decision-making both reflects and gives fresh impetus to the gradual and uneven trend towards a more equal distribution of power; it may also reveal the radical consequences of a more equal distribution of knowledge.

A pattern of alternation

It is now time to turn from these broader political considerations and focus more closely on the nature of education for industrial democracy. Much of what follows is phrased as if it were concerned only with formal modes of education ('courses', 'structure' and so on), but this is not to be understood as undervaluing the importance of informal education, and special attention is given later to the impact which experiential learning may have on the acquisition of formalized knowledge.

Our point of departure is the principle of recurrent education as representing a pattern of alternation between education and work (and other activities). It is easy to envisage a system which reproduces — albeit at a later stage in the individual's life cycle — the 'front-end model', by limiting itself to the provision of a preparatory spell of training. (It is worth remarking here that education for industrial democracy may well prove to be an unusually strong weapon for dismantling the education/training barrier; part of what is learnt will inevitably be 'technical' skills, but they should be set firmly in a broader social and cultural context which demands consideration of 'ends' — the usual criterion for 'education'.) Such a structure would have limited impact, and would ignore the need for education to be linked to problems as they arise, a need which demands regular opportunities for learning. How systematically provision along these lines can be made is a matter for exploration, and will probably vary according to the industrial context and the level of participation; the basic point is that the education should not be seen as purely preparatory.

This is particularly important for the motivation of students. Many of those with little experience of participation in decision-making will also, given the structured nature of inequality in our societies, have benefited little from their initial education and be very hesitant about 'returning to the classroom'. The evidence is, however, that appetite comes with the eating, provided that the food is cooked to order. Force-feeding on prepackaged produce leads only to the educational equivalent of *anorexia nervosa*. On the other hand, when students can see the application of what they are learning it not only makes the whole process easier and more effective, but also serves to extend their perceptions of what knowledge and what power can be acquired. In short, therefore, if it is accepted that moves towards industrial democracy should be accompanied by adequate educational provision, this must be on the basis that such provision will be available on a recurrent basis, and that it is likely to generate further demands.

Professional education and the place of 'expertise'

The ability of educational institutions within the formal sector to respond and to make provision along these lines is a matter for speculation.

Demographic trends are forcing many colleges and universities to reappraise the potential of adult working people and to revise admission policies, but it is very doubtful whether much thought has been given to the additional changes which would be needed in content and perspective. This is, of course, true as a general point, but particularly so in the case of industrial democracy, where the challenge is not only to educational standards in the sense of formal qualifications, but also to the assumptions and premises on which many disciplines and professions are based.

Take accountancy, for example. Pressure to 'open the books' is toothless unless worker representatives are able to read them; clearly then, there is a problem of learning about accounting techniques, and this is in fact one of the most common educational demands expressed by trade unionists at present. But it is not a purely educational problem, of how to put across knowledge and skills to adult students with little formal education and a mistrust of schooling. The crucial point is that the growth of industrial democracy entails a change in accounting techniques themselves. Even for an accounting illiterate, it is not difficult to point to one or two examples. Is labour always to be regarded as a 'cost' to be entered on the debit side of the ledger, or should a company's balance sheet reveal the contribution it has made to providing stable and satisfying employment for its workforce? How far should costs such as pollution effects, which companies are at present able to 'externalize' or unload on the community, be brought into the reckoning? The challenge takes various forms, ranging from the technical to the political. Methods have been suggested which are based not on profit and loss but on net value added, which would preserve financial stability but take items such as pay or community service out of the cost category and express them as the net proceeds of the enterprise (Fogarty, 1976). For a more radical and comprehensive critique see, for example, Barratt Brown, 1978. The cliché of education as a two-way process will be given fresh significance: the 'professionals' will be called upon to revise their own ideas at the same time as they impart their expertise.

Ivan Illich has pointed his dreaded finger at the credibility of the professional expert as the Achilles' heel of the industrial system (Illich, 1978), and critical analyses, preferably less nihilist than his own highly professional excoriation, need to be carried out on the way in which the professions impinge upon industrial democracy. Five such 'specialist groups' have been identified by Professor Bill Ford as particularly in need of education themselves: economists, engineers, systems analysts and marketing specialists, as well as accountants (Ford, 1977). Ford adds other groups, such as members of industrial tribunals and educators themselves, and the list could usefully be extended, but the focus of this article is more on the needs of those involved in the industry or workplace itself, and especially those coming from the shop floor.

Democracy at work has many parallels with democracy in society at large, and one issue common to both is that of participatory versus representative modes (Pateman, 1970). For the moment, however, one can safely assume that representatives will play a key part in the democratic process, without prejudging the question of how far attempts should be made to make the process a fully participatory one. Nevertheless, although reference will be mostly to workers' representatives, two factors will be discussed later which should remind us of the primacy of the rights of those who are represented: the provision of education for the rank and file, and the question of how a representative keeps up two-way communication with his/her 'constituents'. But before we turn to the content of education for industrial democracy, two paradoxes must be considered which may seem to undermine the validity of this article.

The first paradox is that it is an underlying principle of the most valuable type of education in this field that it should be student- not subject-centred, yet I shall go on to discuss a number of specific subject areas. To repeat the cliché, hoary but valid: learning must be linked to the student's experience and the problems he/she encounters, not structured according to some *a priori* system of disciplines. The answer here is that one can legitimately point to fields of knowledge which will have to be drawn upon, without implying that they must be tackled directly in a mono-disciplinary fashion. A distinction needs to be drawn between the direct analyses which one can provide of these different fields, and the way in which tutor and students approach them.

The second paradox is closely related but more problematic, and concerns the identification of 'need'. Is it not inconsistent on the one hand to preach about the importance of students defining their own needs, and on the other to proceed to discuss, in their absence as it were, the educational implications of industrial democracy? (What is less democratic than a single-author article?) The problem is logical, methodological and political at the same time. One can only hope to resolve it by putting forward ideas on the basis that they are a contribution to a continuing discussion, and not in any sense a terminal definition. Prescriptive, yet, but not insistently so. Let me linger for a moment on the methodology.

It would be doubly absurd for the provision of education for industrial democracy to be determined by 'experts', by those in a position of authority in their respective fields. In the first place, it would infringe a basic principle of adult learning, that adults should participate in the definition of their own education. This was admirably enshrined in the Norwegian Adult Education Act of 1976, which made public support conditional upon adequate involvement of the students in deciding the content of courses. *(See also Chapter 10.)* Secondly, it goes against the democratic ethos which it is supposedly promoting. The fission of power releases energies which are not always predictable and for those who are members of a dominant group and yet genuinely support a broader distribution of power, one of the hardest bullets to bite is that the process of change which they help to initiate may have consequences which are both unforeseen and unwelcome to them as individuals or as a group. It is, of course, legitimate for them to press their own values once that process is in motion, but it is the duty of education in this context to stimulate, not to control.

> The intellectuals are making up the game, and the rules for the game. The problem to be emphasized is whether, with regard to participation, the academicians are not acting and thinking too much on the basis of their own motives and abilities; perhaps these do not coincide with the motives and abilities of others. In the development of more participation by the have-nots in power, the concept of participation should be applied without restriction by those who advocate it with so much ardor. (Mulder, 1971:35)

On the other hand, it would be highly disingenuous to pretend that all potential participants are equally capable of formulating their own educational needs, and all that one has to do is give them the chance to articulate them. A blank sheet of paper is not a principled alternative to a predetermined syllabus, even if accompanied by a sympathetic amanuensis, pen poised to record the expressed demands.

The development of education for industrial democracy only makes sense if it is seen as a continual interchange amongst the various participants, linked to the changes in conditions at work. Along one dimension, this requires the matching of technical expertise to practical experience. But equally important it means giving serious attention to the fact that both the learning and the process of change within a company take place over time — a fact so banal that its implications are regularly ignored. The following observation refers specifically to the training of shop stewards in the use of financial information, but its application is valid generally:

> One emphasis of a conventional training course on the *interpretation* of financial information is often on common financial practices of companies, taking as its starting-point *the information provided by the company itself*. We propose a course on the *use* of information which starts from *the functions of a shop steward* and his or her *subsequent use of information*. The main advantage of our approach is that it is *dynamic*. Both the functions of shop stewards and the information system of a company change over time; the first approach cannot take account of these changes. (Trade Union Research Unit 1977:20)

Alan Fox, in his categorization of industrial relations, highlights the problems posed by the unpredictability of the change process.

> A shift of power from management to the managed, whether fortuitous or engineered, may enable subordinates to offer a challenge that is inspired by sentiments which they have long cherished but hitherto been unable to manifest in action. It may also, of course, stimulate wholly new aspirations and sentiments which have not previously emerged simply because no prospect existed of realising them . . . What follows the disturbance of the equilibrium depends on whether the disturbance takes a low-trust or a high-trust direction. (Fox, 1974)

Crudely summarized, the triggering of the low-trust dynamic means that divergences of interest and antagonistic behaviour are accentuated on both sides, the converse being the result in the case of the high-trust dynamic. This is relevant whether the future of industrial democracy lies mainly in the extension of collective bargaining, as many observers of the British context would see it, or more in the introduction of new institutional forms of worker representation. It underlines the fact that the 'success' or 'failure' of industrial democracy initiatives (however those terms are defined) depends in part on the timespan over which they take place and the degree of continuing commitment to them on the part of management and workers. Contrary to the naive pronouncements of some proponents, especially those of narrow job enrichment schemes, participation in itself is no guarantee of greater satisfaction for all the parties concerned, and initiatives in this direction may serve only to accentuate existing problems.

Education is very much part of the dynamic, whether high- or low-trust. Its impact will be coloured by the climate of industrial relations prevalent in the enterprise, and in particular by the degree to which the various participants see their interests as congruent or at least not incompatible. It would therefore be unrealistic even to begin with a universal set of objectives formulated independently of the industrial context to which they apply; *a fortiori* the more detailed content of the education cannot be abstracted from the variety of enterprise conditions with which the students are concerned. The inherent dangers of education, and the volatility of its interaction with the working and living conditions of the participants, must be given due recognition.

Content

Subject to all the reservations expressed in the preceding section, let me propose a number of areas as candidates for inclusion in the development of educational provision for industrial democracy. In a curious way, the content of the education which accompanies democratization constitutes a rough guide to the degree of democracy involved: if the associated courses deal only with narrowly defined questions relating to the worker's individual performance on the shop floor, one can pencil in the scheme at the 'technical' end of the spectrum; if, on the other hand, participants are encouraged to raise and answer questions of broad socio-political concern, it is prima facie an indication that a more fundamental redistribution of control is under way.

To talk of such a spectrum, spanning the range from technical to political, is simplistic and tends to disguise the way in which issues which may at first seem purely technical contain the seeds of political discussion. Nevertheless it is heuristically useful, and the following schema – and it is no more – can be loosely charted along such an axis. (See Espinosa and Zimbalist [1978] for an attempt to plot the 'magnitude' of participation along three axes: administrative-economic problems; information – consultation – determination; minority-majority representation.) However, the emphasis in each case is on *rules* and the grounds on which these are based. The guiding principle, already sketched out above, is that education should have the double aim of allowing participants to grasp the rules and at the same time to challenge the rules and change the nature of the game. The learning of rules, it should be added, is not incompatible with an essentially problem-solving approach.

There are three substantive categories: the new occupational skills entailed in a reorganization of the structure of work; policy-making skills at the company or micro level; and political competence — broadly conceived — at the macro level. But first there is a class of what might be called procedural skills, apparently banal but important competencies such as the ability to handle piles of written information, of keeping adequate records and of speaking effectively. The institutional structures introduced under the heading of industrial democracy are often unfamiliar to many of the new participants, who lack the skills required to make any bureaucratic (in the non-pejorative sense) structure function to their advantage.

Within the committee chamber itself, the possible handicaps of worker representatives have been crisply described in an account of an abortive participation scheme in Australia:

> *Education*, Company — two university trained people and probably one school certificate. Workers — three people who would be lucky to share a school certificate amongst them. Scores for being articulate, logical and confident, Company 3, Workers 0.
> *Teamwork*, Company — two people who had already made up their minds that they were not about to give a damn thing, plus one 'me too-er'. Workers — three people unsure of what they wanted and with very little idea of how to get it, Company 3, Workers 0 . . .
> *Soft lights and sweet music!* Company using its own home ground conference rooms, pleasant smiles, first names, tea and biscuits, workers overawed and overwhelmed. Game, set and match to the Company. (Work Research Centre, 1977).

Yet the category embraces more than just committee skills; it includes understanding of the variety of ways — formal and informal, rational and irrational, legitimate and illegitimate — in which decisions can be taken. The following comment refers to worker directors, but the point holds good for other levels of participation: 'Worker directors seldom find that the information provided prior to board meetings is sufficient. Further information and real debate are typically confined to informal situations and sub-committees' (Batstone, 1976:26). Mastering the techniques necessary to exploit these informal or 'para-institutional' channels is an essential aspect of this procedural category.

Two points need to be made briefly in this context. The first is that procedural rules are not immutable, and the democratization of work may entail changes in them as much as in anything else. The second is that participants from the managerial side have corresponding educational needs if they are to adjust to power-sharing. This latter point, indeed, applies to the whole issue of industrial democracy, and not only to committee forms. 'It is easy to underestimate what democracy means for managers' conventional approaches to problems and their claimed skills, particularly since these become so much a part of managers' self-identity and taken-for-granted world' (Batstone, 1978:235).

The first 'substantive' category is that of the occupational and technical skills which are called for by a reorganization of the work structure. These are inevitably highly specific to the particular context, and it is pointless to attempt to list them. Two general remarks can, however, be made. The first is that they will tend to reflect a more co-operative and group-based approach than is predominantly the case today. Secondly, it is crucial to recognize that from the point of view of motivation the individual's commitment to participate often stems initially from a development of his or her occupational skills. This raises aspirations and whets the appetite for further learning. In this sense the progress from technical to political is a sequential one, starting from narrower job-related issues and moving through to broad political, social and economic ones.

The second broad area of skills and knowledge is situated further along the technical-political axis: the components of company planning. Without prejudging the question of how corporatist or technocratic the approach is to be, there will in any case be a planning function to be discharged, and familiarity with the techniques and a critical appreciation of the premises on which they are based need to be developed. Accountancy has already been given a brief look, and other specialisms referred to. What we are talking about here is the functioning of industrial democracy at the micro level, ie within a given plant or company. Within this broad area, topics could be grouped under the following headings:

a) *The company: its status and structure*
    i) company law
    ii) ownership
    iii) its place in national economic strategy
    iv) management structure and the location of decision-making powers.

b) *Development of the company*
    i) investment policy
    ii) research and development, including the use of technology
    iii) pricing and market policies
    iv) the relevance of world trade patterns.

c) *Finance and accounting*
    i) sources of finance, budgeting techniques
    ii) analysis of financial reports
    iii) the strengths and weaknesses of existing accounting techniques and the possibility of introducing social criteria
    iv) taxation.

d) *Employment policy*
    i) recruitment, manning and productivity trends
    ii) training and internal labour markets
    iii) labour turnover
    iv) job satisfaction and work environment.

This outline is crude and summary. It is evident, moreover, that the way in which these issues are treated will reflect the political perspective of those responsible for the education; all I am suggesting is that they are strong candidates for inclusion if control over the running of the enterprise and its impact on the workforce is to be more equally shared.

The third category concerns the competencies needed to place industrial democracy in its social and political context — the macro level. The path into this may be through the question of whom the representative is answerable to, who are his or her 'constituents'? Are they simply the current members of the company's workforce? Or of the industry as a whole? What about the interests of future workers in the industry, or those on the periphery of the economy? A recent analysis of internal enterprise policy in Germany points to the problem:

> In this context [the disciplinary role of works councils] works councils act as the representative of the strong core workforce against the weak fringe groups and against deviating individuals. This makes them open to the criticism that they are more concerned with securing the privileges of the strong than with improving the lot of the weak. (Jacobs et al, 1977:94)

Nor is it only the country's employed or would-be employed who have claims. It can be argued that consumer interests are threatened by the coalition, however friable, of worker and shareholder representatives. More broadly still — and especially in the vexed case of multi-national companies — there are the pressing claims of the third and fourth worlds.

Thus the question 'who are my constituents?' leads the representative into a global jungle of problems, both tropically dense and arctic in the coldness of its climate. How can education contribute to the solution of these problems? Mainly, I would suggest, by bringing to the surface and clarifying issues which are at present perceived imperfectly, if at all. This is not to promote a covertly unitary perspective which sees all interests as happily coinciding, nor to present the hyper-rationalist view that if only arguments are stated sufficiently clearly and logically a consensus will emerge smoothly and naturally. It is to suggest that a broadening of the criteria used for making decisions at all levels is likely to raise in some general utilitarian sense the value of successive outcomes, however sharply contested the issues may be.

Two points demand renewed emphasis. The first is that the three categories overlap. Discussion of a firm's investment policy cannot occur without reference to wider concerns such as the condition of the national economy or the type of criteria to be employed, for example, in the use of capital. Secondly, a comprehensive understanding, as conveniently understood, of all the issues referred to above could only be acquired by a disturbingly hyperactive polymath. What this underscores is the importance of a problem-solving approach which is not defined by the lines of established disciplines, but recognizes the need to cut across them. The implications of this for our conception of education and the knowledge it imparts are briefly described in the next section.

I have so far identified four categories of skills: procedural, technical, micro-level and macro-level policy-making. Except for the second of these, all are geared towards the needs of the representative, rather than the constituents. At whatever level the representative is functioning, however, be it company board, local plant, or national economic sector, he or she will need to be permanently aware of the importance of communication with the rank and file. 'Employee participation in decision-making must not result in a small clique monopolising information and knowledge' (Viklund, 1977). The weakness of contact between representatives and the people they represent has already been identified as one major factor diminishing the effect of the Swedish law on board representation (Abrahamsson and Broström, 1978:127). It can be assumed that this issue and the surrounding issue of the accountability of representatives will in any case be raised in discussions of social and economic policy, but it is worth stressing the need for communication skills — and insisting that communication is a two-way process and not the simple transmission of information.

Yet if the process is to be two-way, there are implications for rank and file education. One source of frustration for trade union officials is the lack of training on the part of shop stewards (Brown and Lawson, 1973); stewards similarly complain of ignorance or apathy amongst their members, and the same is probably true for those at the other end of the hierarchy, above the full-time officials. What this underlines is the importance of spreading education more or less evenly, rather than restricting it to those who actually take up office. The promotion of paid educational leave as a general right could have a highly significant impact in this respect.

The construction of knowledge

Industrial democracy, viewed as the institutionalized equalization of decision-making powers, has major implications for the balance of power within society as a whole. The implications for educational practice of the concomitant demand for new knowledge are likely to be equally significant. Put summarily, the education of those who gain unaccustomed access to decision-making powers will pose a major challenge to existing paradigms in the Kuhnian sense. To expect participants (whether they are acting in a representative capacity or not) to become competent in economics, politics, accountancy, industrial relations and so on is absurd, if the approach to problems continues to be defined in terms of those different disciplines. Of course, some delegation of responsibility to 'experts', and the division of labour that this implies, is perfectly reasonable, especially in the short term. But the basis for the division of knowledge into these different fields may well be threatened.

As Wittgenstein said: 'the existence of experimental methods makes us think we have the means of solving the problems which trouble us; though problem and methods pass one another by.' Stronger insistence on the primacy of the problem, such as is likely to accompany the involvement of employees, will entail a major reconsideration of epistemological structure; the methodological tail may no longer have the strength to wag the substantive dog, as is the case in several fields today.

What is true for the methodology is true for its practitioners. If one links the hoary cliché that knowledge is power to the notion of industrial democracy as power-sharing, one is left with the realization that not only *knowledge,* but also control over what *counts* as knowledge will have to be shared. To lapse for a moment into the terminology of the factory, one could hazard that the new knowledge will start to come off the democratized production lines, and those producing it will for the first time be in a position to press their claims for its value.

One should not exaggerate, especially as to do so would reinforce the impression that industrial democracy represents some brave new dawn rather than the extension of social and economic egalitarianism. But it does pose questions which educational practitioners and policy-makers should be wrestling with, if they are not to find themselves bypassed by trends in the world outside.

The point is not solely epistemological, but also has a bearing on the teaching and learning process. Like other forms of worker education, training for industrial democracy is more likely to succeed if it is based on the group as the basic learning unit. Such an approach would recognize the carry-over between what happens at work and what happens in the classroom (or wherever learning takes place), and that the majority of the new students will be accustomed to operating collectively. Democratic rights so often cease at the factory gates; education should be in with the rest of those rights when they eventually march through the gates.

References

Abrahamsson, B and Broström, A (1978) Participation and the mandator role: some comments and an outline of a research project *in* Social Science Research Council (1978)

Barratt Brown, M (1978) Profits and losses and the social audit *in* Coates (1978)

Batstone, E (1976) Industrial democracy and worker representation *in* Batstone, E and Davies, P L (1976)

Batstone, E and Davies, P L (1976) *Industrial Democracy: European Experience* HMSO: London

Batstone, E (1978) Management and industrial democracy *in* Social Science Research Council (1978)

Brown, W and Lawson, M (1973) The training of trade union officers *British Journal of Industrial Relations:* 11 : 431-48

Bullock, Lord (1977) *Report of the Committee of Inquiry on Industrial Democracy* (The Bullock Report) Cmnd 6706 HMSO: London

Coates, K (1978) *The Right to Useful Work* Spokesman Books: Nottingham

Elliott, J (1978) *Conflict or Cooperation? The Growth of Industrial Democracy* Kogan Page: London

Espinosa, J and Zimbalist, A (1978) *Economic Democracy: Workers' Participation in Chilean Industry 1970-73* Academic Press: New York

Fogarty, M (1976) The place of managers in industrial democracy *British Journal of Industrial Relations* 14

Ford, W (1977) Educational implications of industrial democracy *in* Pritchard (1977)

Fox, A (1974) *Beyond Contract: Work, Power and Trust Relations* Faber and Faber: London

Illich, I (1978) *The Right to Useful Unemployment* Marion Boyars: London
Jacobs, E, Orwell, S, Paterson, P and Weltz, F (1977) *The Approach to Industrial Change* Anglo-German Foundation for the Study of Industrial Society: London
Mulder, M (1971) Power equalization through participation *Administrative Science Quarterly* 16: 31-8
OECD/CERI (1975) *Recurrent Education: Trends and Issues* OECD: Paris
Pateman, C (1970) *Participation and Democratic Theory* Cambridge University Press: Cambridge
Pritchard, R L (1977) *Industrial Democracy in Australia* CCH Australia Limited: North Ryde 2113
Schuller, T (1978) Education through life Young Fabian Pamphlet 47: London
Social Science Research Council (1978) *Industrial Democracy: International Views* Warwick University: Coventry
Sorge, A (1976) The evolution of industrial democracy in Europe *British Journal of Industrial Relations* 14: 3
Trade Union Research Unit (1977) *The Acquisition and Use of Company Information by Trade Unions* Ruskin College: Oxford
Viklund, B (1977) Education for industrial democracy *Current Sweden* 152 March
Work Research Centre (1977) *Worker Participation: Fact or Fallacy* Centre for Urban Research and Action: Melbourne

Part 3: International Developments

8. Lifelong learning in the United States

J Roby Kidd

Summary: Lifelong learning is an accepted concept in the United States, but recurrent education is not. Ideas associated with lifelong learning have been held and expressed from earliest times (eg Jefferson). Recurrent education is perceived as a European notion restricted primarily to work-oriented education supported by government policy. Continuing education is another concept receiving general acceptance in the United States, particularly that offered through universities, colleges, professional societies, and by management in both government and corporations.

While the notion of lifelong learning had been accepted and expressed in many forms before the debate at UNESCO concerning *éducation permanente*, the largest volume of scholarly writing about the concept, and about the allied notion of a *learning society*, has occurred over the past decade, spurred particularly by the passage of the Lifelong Learning Act sponsored by the former Senator, now Vice-President, Walter Mondale. The debate both before and after the passage of the Act has generated studies, reports, manifestoes and position papers of many kinds.

A typical definition of lifelong learning is 'a conceptual framework for conceiving, planning, co-ordinating and implementing activities designed to facilitate learning by all Americans throughout their lives'. While the Act has not been funded, and therefore is not fully implemented, the process of study and debate continues.

To understand the passage of the Act, it is important to review the support that had been accorded earlier to a number of measures that provided wide access to education, such as agricultural extension, educational support for veterans and government employees, support for manpower needs, for workers and for the education of management personnel.

Attention is now being directed to conditions necessary to achieve a learning society, to ways of supporting and sustaining opportunities for continuing education for all, and to financial policies (such as *educredit*) which permit and encourage persons of lower income, or low educational attainment, to participate. There are increasing numbers of studies related to the improvement of learning skills of people of all ages and of measures to encourage self-initiated learning.

A new and significant social and educational problem is the appearance, in many states, of laws requiring the re-certification of health professionals, and making the renewal of a licence to practise conditional upon certain mandatory continuing education requirements. The desirability and validity of such practices is under debate.

The sonorous words from Ecclesiastes, 'To every man there is a season and a time for every purpose under heaven', are frequently sung or chanted in

America by congregations in established churches, by new believers in revivalist meetings, by folk singers such as Pete Seeger and in the powerful rock musical, *Hair*. The celebration of the changes in status and circumstances of living that every human being will encounter has been an encouragement and sometimes a solace throughout the history of the United States. Rural folk, many of them regular church attenders, took more meaning from these words than from Shakespeare's recital of man's inevitable decline, 'sans teeth, sans eyes, sans taste, sans everything'. It was never very hard for such people, in observing the continuities of change, to associate learning with each successive stage. The notion of lifelong learning and a learning society have never been foreign to America, although nowhere have they been fully practised and continuing education is a term and a field of work of persisting significance.

Lifelong learning is an accepted concept in the United States but recurrent education is not. Most Americans have never heard the latter term and those who have associate it with alien traditions.

> The recurrent education concept, which originated in Europe, is understood primarily as the development of a national policy that would provide citizens with opportunities to alternate periods of work with periods of formal training throughout their lives. In general, the learning experiences are to be related to career goals. (Shulman, 1975)

There was one conference in Washington on recurrent education, but it has never been repeated. Occasionally one encounters the term in writing about employment or about adult education, but it has never been well understood or adopted anywhere in North America.

It is not entirely clear why that is so but one can speculate about it. When recurrent education was being advanced at the Organization for Economic Co-operation and Development and by leading educationists in Europe it seemed to fill a vacuum there. But all over North America there was competition from other concepts and programmes. This was the period of rapid expansion of community colleges, promising and delivering forms of continuing education for many people. It was a time when the term 'non-formal' education had been advanced with the authority of the World Bank, when the significance of 'self-directed learning' was becoming better understood, and when attention was being directed to several 'non-traditional' alternatives to formal institutions. These were all indigenous developments that did not face a journey across the ocean. Moreover, for many in America, learning was being directed to self-expression and self-understanding not primarily to the linkages between work and learning.

In consequence, the key terms in America have been continuing education, lifelong learning, self-directed learning and learning society. The 1970s has been a period of formal commissions studying further education and various legal enactments. There has been increasing awareness of and much vigorous expression about lifelong learning.

The concept of lifelong learning is not new in America. It is sprinkled through the literature published on adult education in the 1920s and

1930s, and in the 1950s I was the editor of a series of books on lifelong learning. When Paul Lengrand began in the 1960s to advocate the notion of *éducation permanente* at UNESCO, the first response in America was that this was simply an old and established idea and therefore not worthy of much response. Some years elapsed before the significance and substance of the notion of *éducation permanente* was appreciated. However, whereas in the 1960s many of the foremost contributors to argument on and understanding of lifelong learning resided in Europe, in the 1970s there has been an unparalleled outpouring of American ideas and proposals.

The reasons are several, but probably the most important was the preparation that led to the passage of special legislation in 1976. Innovations, fads, promises, even threats respecting adult education occur constantly. Not everyone stirs himself when a new call is sounded. The signals that are likely to command attention are those that have legislative and financial backing. For example, in the late 1960s when the World Bank indicated a willingness to support financially some programmes of 'non-formal education', that term and area of work suddenly achieved considerable prominence, leading even to the creation of special institutes in certain universities.

The Bill that has made a marked difference in study and debate is the Lifelong Learning Act (Public Law 94-482) proposed by former Senator Walter Mondale and enacted by the Congress as part of the Higher Education Act of the Educational Amendments of 1976. For some years before the passage of the Bill, Mondale and other legislators had been interested in the idea of much greater equity and accessibility to education for all adults. An account of the debate in the Senate and the House of Representatives before passage provides considerable information about the political process in the United States that is involved in obtaining support for education (See Hartle and Kutner *in* Peterson *et al*, 1978). Indeed the title itself was changed in the process; it started out as a Life*time* Learning Act in Senator Mondale's first draft. The subsequent fate of his Bill, not well funded and not yet fully implemented, provides a further case study of the difficulties and uncertainties of obtaining political support.

Whatever the future fate of the Bill, it has served to generate study and discussion in committees, commissions and institutions all over the United States and has increased both the quantity and the level of comment about lifelong learning.

The term itself and its meaning have evoked considerable discussion. Mondale said of it:

> Lifelong learning offers hope to those who are mired in stagnant or disadvantaged circumstances – the unemployed, the isolated elderly, women, minorities, youth, workers whose jobs are becoming obsolete. All of them can and should be brought into the mainstream of American life . . . Lifelong learning is a necessary step toward making the lives in all Americans more rewarding and productive. (page IV-1 *in* Peterson *et al*, 1978)

One definition that may be taken as being typical:

> Lifelong learning is a conceptual framework for conceiving, planning, coordinating and implementing activities designed to facilitate learning by all Americans throughout their lives. (page V *in* Peterson *et al*, 1978)

Lifelong learning is learning from birth to death. It is not necessarily a compulsory form of education, includes all forms of learning within and outside the formal system and it will involve the development of services directed to those hitherto poorly served. It is also a philosophy, a touchstone to test all forms of educational service, and continues to draw the fire of those who ask continuously 'how can you implement a philosophy?'

The impact of Mondale's Bill, whatever the final outcome, necessitates a review of some of its antecedents, the proposals now being debated and the means intended to achieve the goals of lifelong learning. What is different about the concept and the programme embraced by the term continuing education will be considered later.

We begin with the Bill itself:

SCOPE OF LIFELONG LEARNING

Section 132. Lifelong learning includes, but is not limited to, adult basic education, continuing education, independent study, agricultural education, business education and labour education, occupational educational and job training programs, parent education, postsecondary education, preretirement and education for older and retired people, remedial education, special educational programs for groups or for individuals with special needs, and also educational activities designed to upgrade occupational and professional skills, to assist business, public agencies, and other organizations in the use or innovation and research results, and to serve family needs and personal development.

LIFELONG LEARNING ACTIVITIES

Section 133 (a) The Assistant Secretary shall carry out, from funds appropriated pursuant to section 101 (b), a program of planning, assessing, and coordinating projects related to lifelong learning. In carrying out the provisions of this section, the Assistant Secretary shall

(1) foster improved coordination of Federal support for lifelong learning programs;

(2) act as a clearing house for information regarding lifelong learning, including the identification, collection, and dissemination to educators and the public of existing and new information regarding lifelong learning programs which are or may be carried out and supported by any department or agency of the Federal Government;

(3) review present and proposed methods of financing and administering lifelong learning, to determine
   (a) the extent to which each promotes lifelong learning,
   (b) program and administrative features of each that contribute to serving lifelong learning,
   (c) the need for additional Federal support for lifelong learning, and
   (d) procedures by which Federal assistance to lifelong learning may be better applied and coordinated to achieve the purposes of this title;

(4) review the lifelong learning opportunities provided through employers, unions, the media, libraries and museums, secondary schools, and postsecondary educational institutions, and other public and private organizations to determine means by which the enhancement of their effectiveness

and coordination may be facilitated;
(5) review existing major foreign lifelong learning programs and related programs in this country;
(6) identify existing barriers to lifelong learning and evaluate programs designed to eliminate such barriers; and
(7) to the extent practicable, seek the advice and assistance of the agencies of the Education Division (including the Office of Education, the National Institute of Education, the Fund for the Improvement of Postsecondary Education, and the National Center for Education Statistics), other agencies of the Federal Government, public advisory groups (including the National Advisory Councils on Extension and Continuing Education, Adult Education, Career Education, Community Education, and Vocational Education), Commissions (including the National Commission on Libraries and Information Sciences and the National Commission on Manpower Policy), State agencies, and such other persons or organizations as may be appropriate, in carrying out the Commissioner's responsibilities, and make the maximum use of information and studies already available.

The review required by clause (3) of this subsection shall include

(c) The Assistant Secretary is authorized, with respect to lifelong learning, to assess, evaluate the need for, demonstrate, and develop alternative methods to improve
   (1) research and development activities;
   (2) training and retraining people to become educators of adults;
   (3) development of curricula and delivery systems appropriate to the needs of any such programs;
   (4) development of techniques and systems for guidance and counselling of adults and for training and retraining of counsellors;
   (5) development and dissemination of instructional materials appropriate to adults;
   (6) assessment of the educational needs and goals of older and retired persons and their unique contributions to lifelong learning programs;
   (7) use of employer and union tuition assistance and other educational programs, educational and cultural trust funds and other similar educational benefits resulting from collective bargaining agreements, and other private funds for the support of lifelong learning;
   (8) integration of public and private educational funds which encourage participation in lifelong learning, including support of guidance and counselling of workers in order that they can make best use of the funds available to them for lifelong learning opportunities; and
   (9) coordination within communities among educators, employers, labour organizations, and other appropriate individuals and entities to assure that lifelong learning opportunities are designed to meet projected career and occupational needs of the community, after consideration of the availability of information regarding occupational and career opportunities, and the availability of appropriate educational and other resources to meet the career and occupational needs of the community.
(d) In carrying out the provisions of this section the Assistant Secretary is authorized to enter into agreements with, and to make grants to, appropriate State agencies, institutions of higher education, and public and private nonprofit organizations.

To be specially noted in the above is the expectation that many institutions other than colleges and universities would be involved, that co-operation and co-ordination of all kinds of agencies and institutions would be demanded and that assessment of performance would be funded as an essential part of the process.

This is a sweeping and complex proposal which attracted enough support for passage in both Senate and the House. That would not have been possible a decade or so earlier, nor without the previous Federal Government legislation that paved the way. Two Bills that were considered as significant precedents and had resulted in strong support for many phases of adult education for more than half a century were the Smith-Hughes Act of 1917, and the GI Bill (Public Law 78-346) of 1944. The recognition of the *entitlement* of servicemen and women to educational benefits led gradually to the extension of the idea as a right for all citizens. The Vocational Education Act of 1963 (Public Law 90-576) contributed to a further extension of that notion:

> Those in high school, those who have completed or discontinued their formal education and are preparing to enter the labor market, those who have already entered the labor market but need to upgrade their skills or learn new ones, those with special educational handicaps, and those in postsecondary schools — all will have ready access to vocational training or retraining which is of high quality, which is realistic in the light of action or anticipated opportunities for gainful employment, and which is suited to their needs, interests, and ability to benefit from such training. (page IV-8 *in* Peterson *et al*, 1978)

Amendments throughout the 1960s to three Acts (Higher Education, Elementary and Secondary Education and Adult Education) widened the concept and programmes still further. Note the wording of the 1970 Act (Public Law 8-750) amending the Adult Education Act:

> It is the purpose of this legislation to expand educational opportunity and encourage the establishment of programs of adult public education that will enable all adults to continue their education to at least the level of completion of secondary school and make available the means to secure training that will enable them to become more employable, productive, and responsible citizens. (page IV-9 *in* Peterson *et al*, 1978)

Through these successive increments in concept and programmes the ground was prepared for a more comprehensive proposal for lifelong learning.

One of the features of the Lifelong Learning Act was its reference to the various agencies of learning; some, such as universities, designed specifically for education and others, like trade unions for whom education is a secondary objective, intended to support the primary goals of the organization. It is not always recognized how broad is the range of sponsorship for adult education in the United States. Some of the significant auspices under which education is fostered in addition to libraries, museums and galleries include such organizations and programmes as:

- ☐ private industry
- ☐ professional associations
- ☐ trade unions
- ☐ state and federal government services
- ☐ state and federal manpower training programmes

- military services
- agricultural extension
- city and country recreation services
- community organizations of many kinds
- churches of many faiths and denominations
- parks and forest programmes

At the time of writing it is not known if the Lifelong Learning Bill will be substantially funded, minimally funded or not funded at all. However, even if the programme is not funded there is already an established body of federal legislation that moves a substantial way towards a lifelong learning system. Moreover, legislation has produced research, analysis and debate from which a consensus is emerging. The ferment of recent discussion will now be reviewed.

Other significant developments

In 1976 the Coalition of Adult Education Organizations (which represents a score of national agencies in the United States) held a conference following the passage of the Mondale Act to review the status of lifelong learning. The conference reached agreement that 'the appropriate role of governments at all levels regarding lifelong learning is to provide affirmation, leadership and critical support.' Several areas vital to national policy were specified.

- Adult counselling and information services should be expanded to account for the users' limited time, unique needs, and special interests
- Adult learners' needs should take priority over those of educational institutions
- Lifelong learning opportunities should be better publicized
- Financial support must have top priority
- Adult education research and development should be expanded
- More efficient use should be made of existing adult education resources – human, fiscal, programmatic
- An ongoing and mutually beneficial relationship among the federal, state and local levels of government *and* various sectors of the adult education community should be developed
- Interactions among national education groups and other interested organizations should be encouraged. (page IV-38 *in* Peterson *et al*, 1978)

Meanwhile, in Washington, supporters of lifelong learning were faced with the disappointing fact that no substantial funds had been voted for action to carry out the provisions of the Mondale Bill. In February 1977 the National Advisory Council on Extension and Continuing Education (NACEELF) made a public statement urging that funding be provided and also took their case to members of the House and the Senate as well as to the President and senior government officials. So far there has been no positive response. NACEELF had also held an important conference in January 1977 which resulted in a report 'Proceedings of the Invitational Conference on Continuing Education, Manpower Policy and Lifelong Learning'. Meanwhile within the Department of Health Education and Welfare, a small project staff were at work and wrote a report entitled 'Lifelong Learning and Public Policy' as well as a compendium of background papers.

Private and institutional activity has also been considerable. A group of representatives from universities and state governments convened in Florida in 1977 and published *State Planning for Lifelong Learning: Improving Access for all Citizens*. Perhaps the initiative that has received the greatest attention is 'Future Directions for a Learning Society Project' of the college board, financed by the Exxon Foundation. Individual institutions and individual scholars have also been at work systematically during this period and the quantity of writing and research is now considerable.

A learning society

This term learning society appears frequently; it refers to the societal conditions that support lifelong learning. Neither this term nor the broad concept is new. Political leaders such as Thomas Jefferson expressed hopes that an education well founded in good schools and embracing all of life would be the basis for a just society, a society that would be nurtured and transformed by constant learning. Utopian writers, such as Edward Bellamy (especially in his best-selling novel *Looking Backward*), held similar views which, while not fully accepted, were expressed from time to time during much of the two hundred year history of the United States. In the 1970s, proposals have been more numerous and more sharply focused. One example is the effort by the National Advisory Council on Extension and Continuing Education to obtain a bill that would adopt 'as a matter of public policy measures related to the full concept of a learning society'.

Financial measures

Much of what has been said and written is mere rhetoric and will not be considered too seriously unless and until political and financial actions are taken. Some proposals for financial support display commendable imagination but few have been formulated carefully and fewer have been tried. As noted earlier, some are founded in part on successful programmes of co-operative extension for farm families, general support for military veterans, and attempts by various states to provide a comprehensive kind of financial support to needy individuals through a system of grants and loans. Financial proposals cover three areas: i) support of the libraries, museums and the arts, ii) grants and contracts for institutions, and iii) financial assistance to individual learners. For the latter, various forms of 'recognition of basic entitlement', including vouchers and *educredit*, have been proposed for use by individuals for purposes and at times that suit their particular needs and interests. An example of the proposals under consideration is that of Norman Kurland of the Department of Education of the State of New York, who advocated that financial assistance should be provided for both career-related training and for general education. Each individual would be entitled to a Lifelong Educational Entitlement (LEE) perhaps of $200.00 a year which could be used or accumulated over several years and used when needed. Another proposed feature is a system of 'drawing rights' that would enable a learner who needed substantial funds to draw upon his future entitlement.

No one has estimated how much this or other measures might cost, and the current preoccupations of legislators with financial deficits and with paring all government expenditures have vitiated some of the most optimistic proposals. In respect to some, the principle of 'ability to pay' has been recommended through the application of income tax to recover costs, thus establishing a differential scale according to income.

In some of the states considerable progress has been achieved through providing access to college or university for older and less affluent adult students and other proposals are under consideration.

The achievement of all of the elements that must fit together before a country can be appropriately described as a 'learning society' will take time and considerable effort. Shulman emphasizes:

> It appears unlikely that long-range reform would occur in the United States because of this country's decentralized educational structure and the financial costs involved in such a major undertaking. More probable is the increase of federal and state involvement in supporting lifelong learning activities and promoting their further development.

He continues with a warning:

> If this strategy directed at the adult population were undertaken in the belief that it would serve the goals of social equity, safeguards would be needed to ensure that it did not result in segmentation of our postcompulsory educational system. Such division, by assigning greater education and social status to particular forms of postsecondary education, might actually create less equity in a credential-conscious society. (Shulman, 1975)

Attitude and performance of learners

Any discussion of lifelong learning or a learning society must be based on the realization that substantial numbers of adults must be *willing* to continue to learn and that the *quality* of their performance will be substantial. In the past two decades particularly, evidence has been accumulating to provide such assurance. *(See also Chapter 4.)* It is now generally known that for most healthy adults the threshold at which performance in learning begins to decline, in all three realms of cognitive, psychomotor and affective learning, is about the age of 75. The results of research by Professor Allen Tough in Toronto, and some scholars in the United States, indicate that the amount and quality of learning, and the numbers of persons who continue to carry learning projects under their own initiative and direction, are very substantial. Tough estimates that of all identified learning projects (with a minimum time of at least seven hours) about 80 per cent are carried on by the learner outside formal institutions and according to the learner's own plan. About 20 per cent have been instituted by colleges, universities and other institutions. Regardless of the accuracy or not of this estimate, the amount of self-initiated learning seems to be accelerating and if serious efforts were planned to improve the quality of such learning, the result might go far beyond present forecasts. A third source of information comes from studies made of what citizens express as their wishes or intentions respecting learning. Waniewicz, in a carefully constructed study based on interviews, reports that 30 per cent of adults living in the Province of Ontario were engaged in a recognized learning programme and 18 per cent had a definite plan and would enter into a programme within three months (Waniewicz, 1976). Forty per cent had no concrete plan but expressed the wish to engage in suitable programmes and only 10 per cent said that they had no intention of undertaking any educational programme. Reasons for the decisions to take part or to reject education are reported and analysed. However, assuming the reliability of the remarks of the 40 per cent who are not engaged, but say they want to be, this is a sizeable number of adults, many of whom might be encouraged to participate. A study in the United States by Abraham Carp, 'Adult Learning Interests and Experiences', confirms the size of the present and potential 'learning force' but also reports that current preferences displayed by many would-be learners might prevent them enrolling in traditional universities.

Despite the optimism about present and future participation, there is a lively concern for those who do not participate. Several studies have been made of the barriers to wide participation. Some of those reported frequently are: costs of tuition or maintenance, the need of many female potential students for home and child care, lack of time particularly for men and women between the ages of 30 and 50 whose family and job demands are heavy, and transportation problems that may frustrate rural or older adults. Ways to overcome such real or perceived barriers must be provided if the full impact of lifelong learning policies is to be achieved. Moreover, it has been observed that well-planned programmes are needed for special 'target groups' such as women, older adults, and 'veterans of the Vietnam war'.

Non-traditional studies, counselling and 'educational brokering'

Another phenomenon of the late 1960s and 1970s is the emergence of many forms of 'non-traditional studies', usually, though not always, associated with colleges and universities. External degree programmes of many kinds have been developed in most states: some national programmes for post-graduate degrees are beginning to emerge and a number of the professions are also developing non-traditional approaches to professional preparation as well as the continuing education of their personnel. In other words, many of the innovations and adaptations necessary to ensure good quality of learning experience throughout life are beginning to appear in formal institutions.

Most studies of low participation find that the adults who do not take part are poorly informed about opportunities and lack help in making selections. The provision of systematic information services in all communities, and effective counselling as a right, are often cited as essential services in any programme of lifelong learning.

During the past decade some examples of 'educational brokering' both nationally and in certain states have appeared. 'Brokering' is the name given to a set of non-instructional services that include information-giving, counselling, assessment of individual needs, interests and capabilities, aid in locating appropriate services, and referral. One such service that has been established for several years is the Regional Learning Service (RLS) of Central New York that is located in Syracuse, NY. Federal legislation supplying some funding to Educational Information Centers (EICs) will probably result in increasing the numbers of such services.

The continuing element — continuing education

As we have seen, during the past decade, interests in such concepts or programmes as lifelong learning, non-traditional studies and 'educational brokering' is genuine, widespread and sustained. However, a much larger field or sector is one that began at least a century ago, usually known as continuing education, typically meaning an extension of secondary education organized for adults, and offered by many diverse sponsors but notably by universities and colleges. As Rosalind Loring explained to a seminar on American studies for a largely European audience:

> In the USA continuing education does not take place from the cradle to the grave as in lifelong education, nor is it typically a full-time proposition as in recurrent education. The official legal definition of continuing education in the Educational Amendments (1976) to the Higher Education Act states: 'Continuing education program means postsecondary instruction designed to meet the educational needs and interests of adults, including the expansion of learning opportunities for adults who are not adequately served by current educational offerings in their communities.' (Loring, 1978)

Continuing education has many attributes:
- ☐ voluntarism is the accepted principle
- ☐ learner involvement in planning and assessment of the programme
- ☐ multiple means of organization, content, methods
- ☐ multiple auspices and providers

☐ multiple publics and kinds of participants
☐ diverse curricula
☐ financial self-support, for the most part.

It is also a very substantial enterprise. Statistics collected between 1969 and 1975 reveal that enrolment in continuing education increased 30.8 per cent while the number of adults in the population increased only 12.6 per cent. Continuing education has been referred to as a growth industry. The most conservative report about its extent and character comes from the National Center for Education Statistics. Its 1977 report, *The Condition of Education*, employs three major criteria: age 17 or older, not enrolled full-time in high school or college, and engaged in an organized instructional activity. Using these criteria, NCES reports:

Sponsoring agency	Activities		Participants	
	Number (thousands)	Per cent	Number (thousands)	Per cent
Four-year college or university	5833	21.6	3257	16.6
Two-year college or technical institute	4966	18.4	3020	15.4
Employer	3242	12.0	2605	13.3
Grade or high school	2347	8.7	1881	9.6
Community organization	2129	7.9	1784	9.1
Vocational, trade or business school	1748	6.5	1469	7.5
Government agency	1646	6.1	1367	7.0
Labour or professional group	1373	5.1	1035	5.3
Private tutor	1346	5.0	1184	6.0
Correspondence school	691	2.6	606	3.1
Other	1634	6.0	1319	6.7
Not available	93	0.3	71	0.4
Totals	27,048	100.2	19,598	100.0

(Source: NCES, 1977)

Table 1: *Sponsor of activities by number of activities and number of participants*

The NCES estimate of 27 million persons enrolled in activities and 17 million different active participants is a sizeable number. However, other estimates report that Americans engaged in active and systematic continuing education total at least 80 million a year.

One of the most significant current social problems contained within the field of continuing education, 'mandatory re-certification' and *compulsory* continuing education leading to re-licensing, affects many professions. In an effort to promote greater accountability on the part of such professional personnel as doctors, nurses, pharmacists, hospital administrators, the lawmakers in many states have passed statutes that require that such practitioners, after being permitted legally to practise for a designated number of years (sometimes ten), must apply for re-certification or be forbidden to practise. Usually the designated way to achieve renewed certification is to present oneself for so many clocked hours of continuing education. These measures have been passed in the name of 'accountability' although there is no evidence to prove that the attendance for so many class hours of instruction has any impact on improved performance. Meanwhile, there has been very little public debate about either the assumptions or the practice, nor has there been much serious search for optimal means to ensure better performance through continuing education. Both the public debate and the search for better practice will become much more important in the next decade.

Conclusion

In a situation that is somewhat fluid it is not possible to predict all that may happen with respect to lifelong learning. Over the next year or two it can be anticipated that with financial constraints of many kinds there will be cut-backs in support of various institutions and programmes serving adults, which will produce some decline in participation. However, it is now so well accepted that a basic 'floor' of educational attainments and the opportunity for learning throughout life are *rights*, not just privileges or luxuries, that even a severe set-back will probably only be a temporary phenomenon. Eventually other legislation and other provisions will be made. Moreover, many people who have developed a taste for further education will find additional ways to satisfy it — individually or in small groups or through privately financed programmes if broader schemes are lacking.

The chief questions will continue to be those of equity; how much access can be provided for the greatest numbers and, in particular, those who have not yet had much benefit from education. It is to them particularly that legislation will be directed, perhaps through a further progression of individual bills in Congress and by the states, rather than in some omnibus bill.

It is certain there will be a legally supported and broad programme of basic education and various kinds of job and career training, and the auspices under which such education and training will be provided will be as varied as at the present — governments, educational institutions and many forms of private educational enterprise. It is probable that much of the education offered will have liberal or personal development components, it will be oriented to individual growth as much as to the skills and knowledge needed for a career or participation in community life. There may be some oscillation between career and social and individual goals, but all will be considered. However, the amount of emphasis upon individual goals and attainments may distinguish American continuing education from that offered in many other countries. Considered as a whole it will be less job-oriented, less systematized in modular units than programmes of recurrent education in Europe.

A probable trend is the exploration and testing of newer forms of financing, application of *educredit*, in association with corporate and industrial taxes, various forms of union contracts, ie which financial payment is part of the bargaining contract, and various programmes to which the state, the employer and the individual will all contribute.

One additional trend is certain to continue. The median age of students in all kinds of educational institutions is increasing and many such institutions, particularly colleges and universities will not continue to be a domain primarily for the young. The numbers of elderly people in educational classes will rise dramatically, in addition to many special programmes for those over 55, who will form a substantial part of the total 'learning force'.

The relatively new issues of *imposed* re-certification and *compulsory* forms of re-education for adults may take some time and considerable public debate before they are settled. The ramifications are considerable. However, we live in a society and at a time when there are signs that governments and educational authorities are moving away from a position that all youth must be compelled by law to stay in the school room, particularly when there will be other and perhaps more appropriate learning opportunities available throughout life. In such a society, it does not seem probable that grown men and women, the chief practitioners and decision-makers in the professions, business and government can be forced, or will accept for long, rigid forms of compulsion about what and how they will study in order to continue to practise.

Will the United States become a learning society? This was the goal of Jefferson and many others of the 'founding fathers'. Perhaps never in the complete form that they had in mind. However, along with the elements that were anti-intellectual and alien to rational human growth, American society always had and now possesses some of the chief components of a learning society. What may still be needed is a more systematic framework and a generalized will.

References

Loring, R K (1978) The continuing education universe — USA: a multi-faceted picture. Paper given at session 185, Salzburg Seminar in American Studies. To be published in *Proceedings* by the WK Kellogg Foundation, Battle Creek, Michigan, in late 1977.

National Center for Education Statistics (1977) *The Condition of Education* US Government Printing Office: Washington, DC

Peterson, R E *et al* (1978) *Toward Lifelong Learning in America: A Sourcebook for Planners* Educational Testing Service: Berkeley, Ca

Shulman, C H (1975) *Premises and Programs for a Learning Society* American Association for Higher Education: Washington, DC

Waniewicz, I (1976) *Demand for Part-time Learning in Ontario* The Ontario Educational Communications Authority: Toronto

9. Paid educational leave in France

Pierre Caspar

Summary: After giving a few landmarks in the growth of the idea of a special time devoted to educational activities, this article defines the concept of educational leave in the present French context. The main regulations and the six different possible types of leave are examined. Then a preliminary evaluation is made of the use of French educational leave as established in 1971 and of the main reasons for its rather limited success: the difficulty for workers in making up a personal and individual training plan; the lack of remuneration for certain courses, especially the cultural ones, and for the various costs attached to the education process; the lack of information about educational leave for a great part of the French population, especially those most in need of information.

Describing the innovations in educational leave generated by the recent law of July 1978, this article sketches the present scope of adult education and the factors which may be important in the future in increasing the use and impact of educational leave. The conclusion is devoted to a more general reflection about the role of education in the present underemployment crisis and in the perspective of industrial democracy.

Introduction

The right to educational leave was offered in 1971 by Parliament as an important innovation full of potential change in many fields; eight years later, this specific scheme has been implemented but it does not occupy as important a place as was hoped among the various rights concerning education defined by the law of 16 July 1971.

This article will analyse the origins of French educational leave and then describe precisely its legal content, before giving a few indications about its present and possible future application.

I — A few historical landmarks

The need for a special period devoted to training activities appeared when adult education itself was first considered from an institutional point of view, that is, soon after the Revolution of 1789 when evening courses were created. Before this, a certain type of vocational training was used, mainly by *compagnonnage* (informal tutoring), and thus a certain amount of time was devoted to it; but it is interesting to note that the length of the training was not defined. Time was not important compared to the status of the trainer *(apprenti auprès du maître)*. The necessity of preserving a special time for education appeared much more recently with the industrial society and the introduction of time as a new constraint in people's lives. The golden age when education and life were intertwined ceased, and adult education for a long time took place specifically in the evenings.

For many years adult education was considered to be oriented solely towards increased personal knowledge; naturally this individual progress was to be obtained through individual effort. It would not have been fair for an adult (except for special classes of society) to gain knowledge during the time when others were working. This feeling was accepted by trade unions themselves which soon organized evening promotion courses. But it became obvious later that there was a contradiction between these practices and the desire to live a normal life, and that adult education conceived in that way could be an additional form of selection instead of a part of a large educational system open to everybody.

The period after World War II was characterized by a full inquiry into equality and democracy in the school system and thus into the possibility of giving all adults a second chance. At the same time, some trade unionists and some employers considered that adult learning was not only the result of personal effort but also a necessity, deriving from an economic evolution neither completely planned nor completely managed. So adult education appeared necessary to give everybody an equal opportunity for progress. The first concrete shape was given to these ideas in the laws of 1957 and 1961, creating non-paid educational leave for workers' education and executive training.

The law for workers' education is interesting as it takes into account the potential contradiction between the employer's wishes and power and the understandable desire of trade unions to train their members. From this point of view, non-paid leave appears as the only means by which workers can remove themselves from the employer's authority in order to be trained in a field which is, by definition, out of the employer's responsibility. When Parliament decided to give all workers the opportunity to choose training freely to improve their position, it followed the same principles, giving the right to educational leave to everybody for the first time in the law of 1966.

In France, a law has to be completed by an application bill. As nothing was done after the 1966 law, we had to wait until 1970 for this interesting idea to be given effective form. The inter-professional convention on vocational training of 9 July 1970, signed by trade unions and employers (and enlarged by new texts in 1971 and 1976), was the last step before the law of 16 July 1971 on recurrent education which settled educational leave, among other things. Finally, the recent law of 17 July 1978 enlarged and further specified its application.

II — The concept of educational leave

1) The 1971 law established two new principles: first, an obligation on employers to contribute to their employees' recurrent education, at least 1 per cent of the latter's salaries to be compulsorily devoted to educational activities (0.8 per cent in 1971). Second, it established the right of employees to take the initiative in demanding educational leave. While the inter-professional convention established a system of leave authorization still more or less subject to management decision, this law defined an autonomous right that the employee might claim when he wished. The only restriction on its use is not the subject of the required training but the length of time and its distribution over years. This innovation was necessary as the employer, according to French law, was previously completely responsible for the economic and social decisions of the firm.

The employer manages, controls, evaluates and disciplines the activities of his employees during working time. Collective rights, like union rights, modify these powers but do not transform them. So it was difficult to reconcile the pre-eminence of managerial power with a real freedom for the employee to withdraw from the economic and cultural constraints of the past. Among those constraints, the organizational structure of industry itself has to be taken into account. Thus the legislation obviously tried to give everybody a chance of escaping from their present situation:

> It is important to give everybody a second chance and sometimes a third chance, during their working life, in order that all men and women who had a slight, trifling or non-existent first chance at the beginning of their life might always have a realistic hope of personal progress.

2) As far as the law is concerned, educational leave is the opportunity given to any working person to devote a certain amount of time, during working hours, to a training period of his or her own choice. This leave is certainly not to be confused with paid holidays. The length of leave is the length of the training period, with a limitation of one year in the case of full-time studies, or 1200 hours for a part-time cycle.

All wage-earners can use this right, subject to a sufficient lapse of time since their last employment began (two years), their last diploma (three years) or their last use of educational leave: in the latter case the number of training hours divided by eight gives the number of months between two periods of educational leave, with a minimum of one year and a maximum of 12 years between two training periods. This delay between two training periods is divided by two if the initiative is taken by the firm and not by the individual.

At the same time, the employer has no right to refuse leave to anybody but does have the option of delaying it for reasons of duty, or if the number of employees absent from work at the same time for educational reasons exceeds 2 per cent for a firm with at least 200 people. For smaller firms, the total number of hours devoted to these periods of leave cannot be over 2 per cent of the total working hours.

3) One can now distinguish more precisely between six different types

of educational leave *(congé-formation):*
- leave defined by the inter-professional agreement of 1970 and 1976 and the laws of 1971 and 1978. This leave is usually unpaid, although more and more firms contribute towards costs and maintain their employees' pay during their absence. It allows the worker to follow any type of training — general, cultural or vocational — related to economic or social activities and also to prepare for an examination.
- paid educational leave, in which the employee keeps his wages or receives a grant, if the training is approved by the state or by a *commission paritaire de l'emploi,* a joint representative body of employers and trade unions. This type of leave refers both to vocational and, since the law of 1978, to personal education.
- worker educational leave *(congé d'éducation ouvrière),* mainly oriented to the needs of trade unionists wishing to follow the union's specific seminars. This leave can be paid, according to a rather complex rule.
- teaching leave *(congé-enseignement),* specially designed for preparation for full-time teaching posts in firms, schools or vocational institutes. This interesting opportunity is hardly known and rarely taken.
- youth educational leave *(congé cadre jeunesse)* which can be taken by men and women of less than 25 years, before taking responsibilities in youth organizations.
- leave for youngsters *(congé jeune)* is a short leave (no more than 200 hours) which is offered to unqualified working people of less than 20 years.

Those various forms of leave, which give a broad set of training possibilities, illustrate (as B Pasquier of Centre Inffo suggested) four different but complementary tendencies:
- educational leave is considered as a social benefit in addition to paid holidays, and thus reinforces the autonomy of the worker
- the leave is a legislative tool helping the development of the individual, especially through the new disposition of 1978 and with the *congé jeune*
- the leave can also represent a path towards a more collective form of social development if we consider the *congé d'éducation ouvrière* and the *congé cadre jeunesse*
- the government can use educational leave, in a broad educational context, as a means of improving the relationship between schools and firms, and of facilitating the development of an alternative educational system.

So, from the formal point of view, this right appears to give to working people total freedom as far as their personal educational desires are concerned. But, in fact, the use of this right is not as simple as it was hoped, as initial evaluation reveals.

III — Initial evaluation

After several years of use, what can be said about educational leave in France? Five thousand sessions and seminars were approved by the *commissions paritaires*, 27,000 persons followed training in the framework of paid educational leave in 1976 and 58,000 had the benefit of paid or unpaid leave. At the same time, 1,740,000 people were trained in French firms. Why such a difference? The studies made by Centre Inffo on this subject reveal three main causes:

1) *The difficulty which people experience in putting forward in their own firms a proposal for their own training.* Many training opportunities are offered to employees by the firm; but when somebody asks for a different, long or specific training, the hierarchy usually interprets this demand as an intention to develop new skills and leave the firm. Moreover, colleagues are not always willing to take over a share of the work of somebody leaving the firm for a while for educational purposes. To leave for a holiday is acceptable; to be ill is also acceptable, if it does not occur too frequently, but to stop work to be trained for a few weeks is heresy. Therefore, the few instances of effective educational leave are not the result of negative answers from firms but the consequence of a strong self-inhibiting force. In this crisis period, one needs a certain amount of courage to express a desire for development or retraining — that is to say a wish for mobility. It is easier and less dangerous, even if the danger is unreal, to follow correspondence courses (400,000 people) or take evening classes (250,000 people). In other words, the right to educational leave in France remains the right to ask for something abnormal.

Thus, in spite of clear regulation, the exercise of the right to educational leave is difficult compared to the opportunity for the employer to organize his own educational policy in the firm. This is the sign, in fact, of an inequality between the employer's initiative and the employee's freedom. Certain obligations about preserving workers' remuneration are incumbent upon firms which signed the Convention of July 1970, as well as on those who belong to what we call *Fonds d'Assurance Formation* (bipartite financing bodies created by agreement between employers and trade unions). But it is obvious that the worker, faced with a choice between training outside the firm and the training proposed by the firm (which is likely to influence his personal progress in the firm's hierarchy), will be tempted by the latter and will probably not take the risk of the former, except under very strong personal motivation or for a specially efficient training. This was confirmed as early as 1972 by a survey which showed that 93 per cent of training hours were organized by employers.

2) A second reason for this underuse of leave lies in the *absence of remuneration,* linked to the absence of any substantial financial fund specially attached to it. Most of the training approved by the *commission paritaire* is very similar to that organized within the firms. Why should an employee follow an unpaid training course outside the firm? And if the

training period is paid, what are the objective reasons for going outside to follow something he or she can find inside the firm? Even in the perspective of the application of the 1978 law, which approves long training periods in the main, this problem will not be solved: a long absence will still signify a tendency to leave the firm and thus represent a potential danger in many people's minds.

3) The third and last important factor strengthens the effect of the previous ones: *the lack of information* available to the average French man and woman about training opportunities offered at present by the 5000 private or public agencies. The point is that people can only give their educational ambitions concrete shape by enrolling in a specific course. That is why the present relative lack of information about training opportunities and sometimes the high fee required represents a third factor limiting the use of educational leave in France.

IV — The present and the future

Faced with this interesting and innovative right to educational leave, the regular French habit of establishing a mass of legislation to anticipate as many situations as possible resulted in a decrease in its creative power. In 1974 somebody had already counted more than 487 pages of official texts on this subject and noted that no more than three or four specialists in the whole of France are really able to give an accurate interpretation if the case is at all unusual. The legal position is so complex that it has not been possible to give more details in this short survey.

The most recent law on adult education in France was passed in July 1978. It gives a simpler and more precise formulation of the training taken into account by the government under the label of vocational recurrent education (*éducation professionnelle continue*). Speaking of 'activities' instead of only 'courses' (*stages*) and thus enlarging the scope of training, the law enumerates:

- preparatory training (*actions de préformation*) for any person without vocational qualifications for professional life
- adaptation training (*actions d'adaptation*) designed to help people get a first or a new job
- promotion training (*actions de promotion*) giving a higher qualification
- refresher training (*actions de prévention*) conceived to counter the risk of skill shortages in a time of evolution of techniques and structures
- retraining (*actions de conversion*) specially designed for people suffering an interruption in their work contract and looking for a different job
- general training (*actions d'acquisition, d'entretien ou de perfectionnement des connaissances*) giving anyone the opportunity to maintain or improve his or her knowledge, to have access to culture and to assume responsibilities in community life.

Thus the scope of recurrent education, as seen by the government, appears larger than in 1970 and 1976, in that the law explicitly includes cultural and social objectives. This difference has both positive and risky aspects: it is interesting, from the national point of view, to give a broader sense to the legal concept of education and to promote a genuine national policy of education. But, at the same time, it may be a source of conflict if neither the government nor the firms provide sufficient finance to enable people to be well-informed, and then to choose and follow non-vocational training. The answer to this will soon appear after the law comes into effect, probably during 1979.

The 1978 law also gives a broader definition of educational leave: its purpose is to allow any individual during his or her professional life to follow training activities on his or her own initiative, even to prepare for an examination. Participation in these activities is completely distinct from training organized by the employer *(plan de formation)*. Thus any worker, whether receiving wages or not, can ask for leave. This means the theoretical possibility of taking leave not only for 'ordinary' workers employed by an enterprise, but also for independent workers and for those who are unemployed. Consequently the government, as well as employers, now has obligations towards the 'worker-citizen'. Will they be transformed into true rights? The law also specified that leave can be taken during or outside working time. This measure is not innovative in that workers already had the right to use leisure time as they wished, but it opens up an interesting field: any trainee *(stagiaire de formation professionnelle)* during his educational leave can now be covered by national social insurance in case of accident out of working time. The worker, during his leave, begins to have legal status. Let us also note the broad meaning and importance given to the individual and the free choice of training attached to educational leave. In a way this choice may now be made out of the labour contract field and the company's training programme. Any training organized by the firm which workers attend voluntarily is no longer considered as leave, and so does not count towards the number of people who may be away at any one time. We should, nevertheless, remember that educational leave does not break the labour contract. But the principle of true free choice is strengthened. The next few years will teach us if this free choice will overcome the strong psychological barriers we noted above, and if the challenge posed by the government through the combined vocational and cultural education policy here proposed will be met.

A last point to analyse is the financial aspect. The principle of paid educational leave is nowadays introduced in the French labour code whatever the type of training and for any type of firm (whether more or less than ten people). Two possible sources can pay for the same course: the state or the employer. Anybody can ask for leave, under precise administrative conditions of application, until the simultaneous absences reach a certain level (usually 2 per cent of the total number of people, but for paid leave, 0.5 per cent for the workers and 0.75 per cent for higher management).

But when the chosen training has been previously covered by state agreement the leave is paid:
- if the training period is less than three months full-time (or 500 hours part-time) the employer maintains the previous remuneration for the first four weeks (or 160 hours) and the state pays for the rest
- for three- to 12-month periods (500 to 1200 hours) the employer pays for 13 weeks (16 for executive people) or 500 hours (600 hours for executives), the cost then being taken on by the state
- the opportunity is given to follow courses of more than one year. But in this case, and only for people with more than three years of professional experience, the minimum national guaranteed salary (SMIC) is given after 13 weeks or 500 hours.

In all cases, state support is given directly to the trainee or to his employer if the latter maintains his wages. In fact, the state support will be limited to a certain maximum amount (probably three to five times the SMIC). Moreover, for part-time courses, the trainee will lose the equivalent of travelling time as the remuneration will only be for training hours. Various types of grants *(primes)*, common in France, will also be lost as state help will be computed on the basis of legal working hours and not on the previous salary. Finally, the registration, scholarship and documentation fees are paid neither by the state nor by the employer if the firm did not sign the 1970 agreement. Also not taken into account are the various expenses for housing and food if the course is in a different city. This represents a very important limitation for many workers.

In conclusion the new law opens up interesting new avenues and greatly clarifies the general framework in which educational leave will now be taken. Naturally, one has to wait for various 'application texts' planned for 1979 to see if the opportunities offered by the leave become a true and general right, broadly used, or remain as previously rather limited. But at the same time the previous analysis shows that, in any case, *four main points will constitute major blocks* if they are not sufficiently taken into account. First, more approved courses must be set up giving the right to leave; second, information about educational leave must be more widely disseminated, using both the traditional educational network and the mass media; third, the desired growth in demand for a network of counselling services must be faced; and last, but not least, the financial problems of helping the less fortunate to meet the various expenses linked to any training must be solved. Dealing with these four points is now less a matter of law and more a question of collective and general will.

More generally, the real issue is the contradiction between what has been expressed about recurrent education since 1971 and the concrete reality of industrial life and values. In fact, many people associated with this legislation and involved in the development of recurrent education behave as if it were possible, in the field of education, to find technical solutions to political problems, and as if economic and social decisions could be taken without assessing contradictory social forces. Many attempts made during the 1960s to promote individual training failed because they overestimated the value of knowledge in the *rapport de forces*.

Now this illusion is disappearing but, at the same time, to place training in a merely technical context does not give full significance to the system of leave. Thus one can predict that as long as the remuneration problem remains, and as long as there is high unemployment, few people will exercise their right to educational leave, faced with the financial and employment risk they will have to take: 'what will happen to me if I leave my job for six months, or a year, for personal interest training and come back and find I am not indispensable?'

The tendency of French legislation seems to be more to clarify the employer's financial participation and less to reinforce the status of educational leave. But status is as important. Employers, as well as the state, have an important role to play in these financial and status issues. Trade unions, too, clearly have a role in the evolution of leave through more precise demands, based on more informed agreement on the part of their members. We do not know if they are on the verge of elaborating a precise policy in this rather ambiguous field of education, faced as they are with what are considered more crucial problems: unemployment and the economic crisis. So, as we said previously, reflection on the development and future of educational leave does not simply concern issues of administration and legislation. It relates to the image and status of training in workers' minds and to the structure of employment itself in the present context; and it relates also to people's mobility linked to many variables far removed from education, to the capacity of people to conceive a personal ambition, express it realistically and put it into practice. That is to say, it relates to the possibility for anybody to behave, within economic and political constraints, as a full partner in the framework of industrial democracy.

10. Recent legislation and the Norwegian pattern of adult education

Øyvind Skard

Summary: The whole educational system in Norway has been revised since the last war. The basic political principles have been to create educational equality and promote democratization.

The period of compulsory schooling has been increased from seven to nine years, and this gave adult education the task of bringing adults up to date. The secondary school system has been expanded and brings together general and vocational education. It has introduced a pattern of alternation between education and work, and also adapted itself to the education of adults and to the creation of programmes for adults.

Co-determination in industry has initiated expansive training programmes both for representatives and employees; so has the new law on worker protection and the working environment, and the different revisions of the 'Basic Agreement' between the Norwegian Employers' Confederation and the Norwegian Federation of Trade Unions.

The law on adult education is new and its effects cannot yet be evaluated. It clarifies the duties and responsibilities of adult education. It introduces democratic principles in the organizations carrying out adult education programmes and in the learning process itself. It introduces the principle of positive discrimination with regard to financial support, favouring the educationally disadvantaged groups.

In the years following the last world war Norway shared the common belief that education was one of the main sources of economic growth. For this reason numerous new laws on education were passed. The general increase in living standards led gradually to a greater demand for education. Education began to be regarded as an article of consumption.

For these reasons the entire Norwegian educational system, ranging from the pre-school level to adult education and preparation for retirement and old age, has expanded.

Some of the most important laws and reforms which have had a strong effect on the educational system are as follows:

1. Between 1960 and 1970 the years of compulsory schooling were increased from seven to nine years.
2. In 1974 a law was passed which changed the whole system of secondary education and co-ordinated general academic education with vocational education.
3. The law giving employees representation on the board of directors

in industrial companies came into force in 1973. This law has since been expanded to cover areas other than industry.
4. A law on adult education came into force in 1977.
5. A new law on worker protection and the working environment was passed in 1976 and came into force in 1977.
6. The 'Basic Agreement' between the Norwegian Employers' Confederation and the Norwegian Federation of Trade Unions was revised in 1974 and 1978 and includes paragraphs relevant to educational problems, specially adult education.

Basic principles

Certain basic political principles underlie all these different laws and reforms. The most basic principle has been to create equal educational opportunities for all. This has meant that difficulties with regard to economic, social or geographical barriers have had to be overcome.

Another basic principle has been that of equality and democratization. This meant that the gap between those who had profited most from education and those who had profited least had to be diminished. It also meant that educational opportunities for all kinds of abilities and interests had to be created.

A third principle has been to equalize academic and occupational education. One of the steps taken to achieve this has been to co-ordinate academic and occupational education in one secondary school system. Still another political principle has been to postpone occupational choice for as long as possible. This means that specialization in education must start fairly late and that transfer from one educational specialism to another must be easy.

The last principle is the principle of breaking down the isolation of school and university from the world of work.

Effect of change in the compulsory school system

The expansion of the period of compulsory schooling had immediate effects on adult education. About 75 per cent of the Norwegian population had only seven years' compulsory schooling. This meant that they were disadvantaged in relation to the youngsters coming out of the new school system as far as competence for jobs and higher studies was concerned. They were also disadvantaged as regards access to cultural benefits because of their low reading ability and their lack of familiarity with literature and the arts. Against this background both the school system and the informal educational sector started to develop programmes which would enable people with only seven years' schooling to catch up. This was for a long time regarded as one of the main tasks of adult education. Financial aid for this kind of adult education was also supplied.

The addition of two years to the old system of seven years' compulsory schooling created certain problems. One of these was that quite a number of young people became tired of a mainly theoretical education. They felt uncomfortable with prolonged schooling and had difficulties adjusting to the social situation. It was felt necessary to develop alternative forms of education for these youngsters. The result was a system which made it possible for pupils in the eighth and ninth grades to take part of their compulsory education as work experience in a company. The plan for this work experience has to be worked out between the school and the company. This represented one step out of the isolated position of the school. It also began a pattern of co-operation in education between school and working life which was important for the whole educational system, and which also influenced adult education, especially in the context of lifelong learning.

Effects of secondary school reform

The secondary school system in Norway before 1974 consisted of two separate systems. One system was the so-called 'gymnasium'. This was a theoretical school giving general education and preparation for university studies. This school system had a lot of prestige, and only 20 to 25 per cent of young people attended these schools. The other system consisted of different vocational schools, which gave practical and, to some extent, theoretical training for special occupations. They had a somewhat lower social prestige than the 'gymnasium'. The general opinion was that these schools were for young people who did not have the ability to go through the 'gymnasium'. To a very large extent social traditions also decided who should go to the 'gymnasium' and who should go to the vocational schools.

In the new secondary school system the vocational schools and the 'gymnasium' are integrated in one system. Pupils can combine vocational and general education in different ways. They can decide to take only some special branch of general education or they can decide to choose a special line of vocational education. In principle, three years in the secondary school system should give sufficient competence for university studies irrespective of educational choice. Adults from the world of work may enter this system at a stage corresponding to their competence as part of a system of recurrent education. Students may leave the system and come back to it with some work experience, making it possible to enter the system at a higher level. It is also part of the new secondary school system to develop and carry out alternative forms of education for people who do not want to follow the usual school pattern. This generally means a combination of planned occupational experience and different forms of education inside or outside the school system. These alternatives will usually be part of some form of adult education.

The equalization of general and vocational education has also had certain consequences for the admission rules for university studies. Students may enter with qualifications other than the traditional purely academic ones. In the same way, adults with no formal secondary education, but with a certain amount of occupational experience, may take part in university studies on certain conditions.

The political intentions behind the new secondary school system are that it should have some educational programme suitable for any field of interest and any level of ability, and that most young people should avail themselves of the opportunities of the secondary school system. As a consequence there has been a great increase in the number of students attending secondary school. This has had some of the same effects as the expansion of the compulsory educational system. The majority of grown-ups have not had the opportunities which the secondary school system can now offer the younger generation. This is often seen as a difficulty. In work organizations, for instance, the relationship between supervisors and employees is not made easier when the employees have a broader general educational background than their superiors. This general situation has created a demand for adult educational programmes giving the kind of education to adults which is offered by the secondary school system. Both the educational organizations and the schools are involved in such educational programmes. The schools, however, have formal responsibility for setting standards and evaluating results.

Effect of law on co-determination in industry

The Norwegian Employers' Confederation and the Norwegian Federation of Trade Unions have since 1935 had a 'Basic Agreement' regulating the general relationship between the local unions and management and between the national unions and the national employers' federations. This agreement has been revised every four years. The revisions have been characterized by changes such as giving more information and influence to employees, facilitating consultation and co-operation between management and employees, and permitting a certain amount of co-determination within specified areas. In order to make these forms of co-operation effective, both the companies and the organizations have had to carry out different training programmes, both for employees in general and especially for their representatives on committees, councils, etc. The law giving employees representation on company boards led to a great increase in these educational efforts. Both the employers' organizations and the unions introduced comprehensive training programmes for the board representatives. As the representatives change from time to time, these training efforts have become continuous. The content ranges from business economics to production planning, marketing, company law and human relations.

Both employers and unions realize that if representation of employees on the board is to have the intended effect, the representatives must have the support and understanding of those they represent. This means that co-determination necessitates a new kind of education for the ordinary employee, education going beyond the demands of his job. Both the school system, the employers' and unions' organizations and the educational organizations are gradually increasing their offers of this kind. Education for industrial democracy is not only offered in special programmes, but is influencing other programmes, being taken up as a special issue or as an underlying philosophy.

Effect of law on worker protection and work environment

This law gives the employees co-determination in the areas specified by the law. Representatives of the employees, together with representatives of the employer, have certain powers of decision. The work of developing and carrying through the necessary changes concerning safety and the working environment is to be carried out by employees in the different departments. This calls for new forms of competence. The law obliges all employers to carry out and finance comprehensive courses for all employees who are given responsibility for safety and environment under this law. As the law includes all enterprises that engage employees, irrespective of the nature of the enterprise and irrespective of whether the enterprise is private or public, these educational programmes involve an enormous number of people. (The only areas exempt from the law are shipping, hunting and fishing, aviation and agriculture.) Both management and union organizations and educational organizations have been extremely busy with these kinds of programme all over the country during the last years. As the personnel in the enterprises change from time to time, this educational activity will also be permanent.

The law embodies the intention that working groups should be established in the enterprises, analysing the safety and the environmental conditions and developing plans for improvement. This has led to special educational programmes for instructors and group leaders.

Effects of the 'Basic Agreement'

Some of the effects of the 'Basic Agreement' have already been mentioned. Norway has not yet ratified the International Labour Organisation (ILO) convention on paid educational leave. Under the present economic conditions there is little likelihood that this will be done in the near future. The Norwegian Employers' Confederation (NAF) and the Norwegian Federation of Trade Unions (LO) dealt with the same problem as part of the revision of the 'Basic Agreement' as early as 1969. This resulted in the following declaration which has become a part of the 'Basic Agreement':

> NAF and LO realize the importance of further education to the individual,

the company and society. General education, vocational training, adult education and retraining must be seen from that point of view.

The parties therefore wish to emphasize the value of employees increasing their knowledge and improving their competence, and also of the companies giving special attention to the systematic training of their employees.

If, in connection with education which is valuable to the individual and the company, it is necessary to have full or partial leave of absence, this should be allowed unless special reasons make it impossible.

Also, where other education is important to the further development of the individual, the company ought to be obliging if full or partial leave of absence is necessary, provided this can be granted with only minor inconvenience to the company.

This led in 1970 to the agreement that the two main organizations would establish a training and development fund whose aim is to initiate and support efforts to intensify the spread of information and education throughout Norwegian working life. The scope of the fund is as follows:

Scope — information and educational activities, including the use of courses and schools, which among other things shall have as their aim:
1. the training, along modern lines, of shop stewards; with special attention to rationalization, safety precautions, productivity, economy and matters of co-operation
2. the study, by both management and other employees, of the subjects mentioned under 1
3. the preparation, arrangement and development of curricula
4. the promotion of sound and proper rationalization as a means of raising productivity
5. the promotion of good co-operation within the individual company.

The new financial possibilities opened up by the fund have led to an increase in trade union training programmes. It has also resulted in the creation of educational committees within the different branches of industry, and in the training and engagement of training specialists. The type of training financed and carried out by means of money from the fund mostly consisted of advanced vocational training, supervisor training and general management training.

The revision of 1978 of the 'Basic Agreement' includes certain paragraphs which are beginning to have their effect on internal training programmes. The two main organizations intend to make this influence even greater in the future.

In the effort to give those working within the individual departments or working groups more opportunity to make decisions on their own during their daily work, it is, among other things, important to promote understanding of and insight into the financial position of the undertaking. Learning, development, information and consultation will increase the ability of the individual employee to take part in the decision procedure and create a basis for reducing alienation at work. The organizations therefore presume that the works council and working environment council of the individual enterprises will see it as an essential task to promote proposals about what can be done within the various fields of the enterprises to adapt conditions for such a development.

Experience shows that it is of little use to change jobs or positions in isolation, or to try to change the forms of organization and management within an individual group or department without any connection with the rest of the undertaking. Such changes need the support and active co-operation of the rest of the organization and may lead to larger or smaller changes also in other parts of the organization. Therefore, representatives of the various parts of the undertaking must be included in such development work.

The organizations emphasize that it is the duty of the top management and of the employees and their shop-stewards to take the initiative and actively support and take part in such development work. For their part, the organizations will, jointly and separately, support this work through various actions.

Effect of the Adult Education Act

The law on adult education is new and the effects in practice cannot yet be fully evaluated. The law itself clarifies the duties and responsibilities within the field of adult education. It introduces democratic principles in the organizational structure of institutions and organizations receiving financial support for adult education. It also introduces democratic principles in the learning process itself. The law also encourages the development of educational opportunities more relevant for adults with a practical background in working and community life. The law finally introduces financial arrangements which are intended to stimulate people in the direction of lifelong learning. As the law is regarded as a political instrument for democratization and equalization, it introduces the principle of positive discrimination, favouring educationally underprivileged groups.

The law has already had some effect on the school system. It makes it clear that the school or institution responsible for basic education within a certain field is also responsible for educational provision aimed at adjustment and renewal within the same field. Therefore the whole school system has to adjust its plans in order to make room for such adult educational programmes. The law also makes it clear that what is offered within regular basic education should be organized in such a way that it satisfies the need for alternating between education, work and other activities. This not only results in new educational programmes within the school system, it also makes it necessary to educate teachers with qualifications for adult education. As a result, adult education has become part of teacher training college programmes. Different organizations are also beginning to develop programmes for teachers in adult education.

Informal educational organizations are the main bodies carrying out adult education outside the schools. They undertake all kinds of adult education which do not lead to a formal qualification within the ordinary school system.

As these organizations include many of the educationally underprivileged groups, they are favoured by the law which gives them great scope for action and financial support. It is already evident that these organizations have increased their activity.

An organization must, in order to get financial support, be run on democratic principles: open and individual membership, a board elected by members, and recognition of adult education as a central task. As a consequence, many educational institutions are today trying to adjust their organization in accordance with these principles in order to get financial support.

The law opens up the possibility of financial support for internal training programmes within individual companies. Such programmes must be relevant to the activities of the company. The companies can engage or co-operate with the schools or the educational organizations in carrying out such programmes, or they may carry them out by means of their own internal resources. A condition for getting financial aid is that the programme is agreed upon by a body within the company with equal representation from the employer and the employees. This body is also to decide who should take part in the programme and who should carry it out. These conditions not only influence training programmes with financial support, but also introduce a general pattern of co-determination in training activities within companies, which will influence all training activities. The law also helps to further co-operation between the world of work and the school system as regards adult education in general, as most companies will depend on the school system for training personnel and facilities.

Another condition for financial support is that the students are to have a certain amount of co-determination as regards the aim, content, methods and progression in the learning process itself. This condition will undoubtedly have a general educational influence, but it is difficult to predict how strong this influence will be. At present there are experiments with unstructured learning programmes and with different forms and degrees of co-determination in many areas of adult education. But as the educational world submits to fashions almost as much as teenage girls, it is difficult to say which new fashion will have a lasting effect.

The law constitutes a great step towards recurrent education. As recurrent education implies alternation between work and education, periods of work become part of the educational process. This has led to a new recognition of the learning potential inherent in a work situation. Informal learning is emphasized more than before. This means that learning from work and the working environment is gaining in importance.

The result of adult education activities so far has not been what was intended. As in many other countries, the majority of those who have availed themselves of adult education opportunities have been those who already have a high degree of education, while the less educated and enlightened have largely ignored adult education opportunities. The gap has been widening, and to reverse this trend the law is based on the principle of positive discrimination. Groups with a low educational level, unemployed people, handicapped people, etc will be favoured with subsidies for adult education, while groups with high education and greater resources will be given lower priority. This will certainly lead to the development of new educational programmes for underprivileged groups.

When the law was passed in Parliament, it was made clear that it would have to be regarded as a preliminary effort to fill the vacuum of adult education, and that the law would have to be revised in the not too distant future. An adequate revision of the law necessitates an analysis of the effects of the law so far. This has given the newly established Norwegian Institute of Adult Education a great responsibility for carrying out research work. The Institute is today engaged in research in almost all fields of adult education, assessing who takes part, what methods are used, results, degree of co-determination, organization of educational institutes and organizations, the channelling of financial support, etc. One result of the law has thus been a great increase in the amount of research in adult education.

Present needs

The field of adult education has been strongly influenced by many different laws and agreements. New activities have been started, new organizations have taken up adult education, new demands made on the school system, new forms of financial support have been developed, new methods are being tested, etc. In this situation there is a great need for contact and co-operation and for co-ordination between the main bodies engaged in adult education. This is one of the most important tasks for the institutions and the organizations. The main responsibility for this, however, must be taken by the Adult Education Council.

We have at present different laws for the different parts of our educational system, and a special law for adult education. As all these laws deal with parts of the process of lifelong learning and as they all in varying degrees include alternation between school and work, there is a great need for coherence. At some time in the near future, this need will have to be met by the implementation of one comprehensive law uniting the whole educational system.

11. Strategic planning on a recurrent basis

Hans-Erik Östlund

Summary: The planning for recurrent education in Sweden has employed many ingredients in parallel. However, they can be fitted into a long-term strategy in the light of the conviction that recurrent education is not a reform to be implemented at one fell swoop.

The ingredients that comprise instruments of planning are the content and organization of the studies, admission policies, location and dissemination of education, financing and educational leave, information and outreach activities, and labour market policy.

The Swedish strategy may be said to have two lines of action. Measures which are chiefly of an organizational nature and less expensive have been undertaken on a big scale. This category of action principally includes such changes as in the organization of studies to make possible an increased alternation between education and work.

Measures which are more expensive are built up step by step as more economic leeway can be afforded. This category of action principally includes the financing of studies. Parallel with this build-up, measures are taken which can be regarded as favouring positive discrimination, eg outreach activities and opportunities to take educational leave.

Of vital importance for the Swedish strategy is the close interplay between educational policy and the labour market policy. Recurrent education is seen as an instrument to change working life as well.

The Swedish context

In 1975 the Swedish Parliament stated that 'the continued planning of the educational system shall proceed from recurrent education as an ordinary model for the individual's educational planning'. Actually, this statement did not signify the starting point for an innovation. If anything, it was the formal political confirmation of a development that has characterized at least a decade.

Recurrent education as a pattern in the individual student's behaviour is nothing new. But in the rapid development of education during the 1950s and 1960s, the trend had been moving increasingly towards a longer continuous period of education in youth. On the whole, too, youth education had become more general in its character. At the meeting of the European Ministers of Education held in Versailles in 1969, the then Swedish Minister of Education, Olof Palme, underscored the necessity of breaking away from this trend.

> It is evident that we cannot go on prolonging youth education by constantly adding new two- or three-year periods. Sooner or later the individual will have to take his part in the production process.

He outlined the idea of recurrent education and its implications. At that time there was a strongly-felt need to have educational planning develop patterns of alternation between periods of work and study and to support such interplay with different policy instruments.

At that time, too, the Swedish 1968 Educational Commission considered the overarching balance problems in the educational system, including the allocation of educational resources among different groups in society and the equilibrium between the needs of the labour market and the individual demand for education. Recurrent education was the answer to these balance problems. It should be noted that recurrent education was not seen as an addition to existing educational structures. On the contrary: the goal aimed at was a profound reorganization of the whole educational system after the period of compulsory schooling, and, as such, included the education of adults and young people. At the same time it was appreciated that the massive changes which were required could not be achieved overnight. Recurrent education was to be regarded as a long-term strategy, but it would influence every future decision within the educational domain. It was this that Parliament confirmed in 1975.

In the debate that went on between 1969 and 1975, not only the critics but also the proponents of recurrent education pointed to a question of great strategic importance. Will recurrent education confer even more chances on that section of the community which has reaped the greatest benefits from continuous education as a consequence of the free choice between future education and future work? Or will it mean broadened educational opportunities for new social groups? Will the educational opportunities be accumulated or be spread more evenly? There was widespread consensus that a great deal depended on the instruments used to implement the strategy.

Contents and organization of education

Compulsory education

A point emphasized at the outset is that the Swedish planning strategy mainly deals with the education which follows the period of compulsory schooling; however, this does not mean that the latter is left untouched. The foundation of attitudes to working life and continued studies is laid in the compulsory school. Since 1969 the compulsory school, whose equivalents abroad are the primary and lower secondary levels, has lacked all direct ties to vocational preparation. Such career training does not come until the next stage. On the other hand, the compulsory school gives a general orientation to working life through educational and vocational guidance in both theoretical and practical form. The latter encompasses first, study visits; and second, practical training in companies for two weeks during the ninth grade.

This arrangement has been the target of heavy criticism in recent years. It is argued that the picture which pupils form of the world of work is not particularly realistic. Some pupils leave school with a much too optimistic view of what working life can give. Other pupils are so unfamiliar with working life that they cannot make a realistic estimate on which to base their future career plans and studies.

Improving the contact with working life is one of the goals set in the decision which Parliament took in 1976 to change the internal working of the school. As part and parcel of this decision, practical vocational guidance is to be broadened in scope and be spread over several years. The goal is also widened. Contacts with working life are supposed to give experience of what kinds of problems are to be found at a workplace, what demands are put on the employee, how his relations are with workmates, supervisors and trade unions and what the working environment is like, physically and mentally.

In order to plan this and to improve contacts across the board between school and working life, local councils have been set up, on which school staff, employers, union officials and employment offices are represented.

Included with the strategy are changes in official syllabuses and in the training of teachers. A proposal for a new syllabus, which, among other things, is meant to introduce general technology as a compulsory subject, is being considered by Parliament in the spring of 1979. A commission on teacher training will put forward a proposal to the effect that anyone who applies for such training must have experience of gainful employment in another occupation of a specified duration. Incidentally, even now, teachers may obtain experience of other occupations for a couple of weeks with no deduction from their pay.

Upper secondary school

If a pattern of recurrent education is going to be viable, the design of the upper secondary school is of crucial importance. In any event, that is the opinion which prevails among school planners.

In order to understand this, it is important to recall two factors. One is the already-mentioned generalization of the compulsory school in 1969; it no longer affords any vocational preparation as that task is assigned to upper secondary school. In other words, the upper secondary school has a twofold bridging function, between studies and the labour market and between basic education and higher education. It is also scaled to receive virtually the whole cohort of 16-year-olds (at present 97 per cent).

The second factor is the question that many people have asked themselves, namely whether the upper secondary school is organized to meet that requirement. Since 1971, upper secondary education in Sweden has been of the comprehensive type. In that year, the former gymnasium, the two-year continuation school and the vocational school were merged to form a single integrated entity. Since this reform was chiefly organizational and did not change the content of the studies in any more drastic manner, it does not provide sufficient incentives to develop a pattern of recurrent education.

In the discussion that has been joined among educational planners and in the trade unions, one can discern two distinct demands for changes which seek to facilitate recurrent education. One is that all upper secondary education shall enable the students to make a choice between gainful employment and continued studies. 'Vocationalization' of upper secondary school has become the slogan. The second demand calls on society to shoulder its responsibility to ensure that those who do not go straight on to upper secondary school are regularly afforded job openings or study opportunities. This has been called the 'youth guarantee' in Swedish debate. Parliament endorsed the youth guarantee in 1978.

The first demand absorbed a large part of the public debate in the early 1970s and it would be wrong to say that it started out by enjoying strong support in the population at large. There may be many reasons why this was so. One was that the upper secondary school has been reformed recently and has struggled with quite a few difficulties. Another reason, surely, was simply the difficulty of the task. To bring vocational preparation into the traditional academic programmes of upper secondary school would be to violate centuries-old traditions, to make inroads on the domain of the 'learned' school. At the same time those who defended the traditional vocational training saw the risk of superficial vocational training.

Public opinion changed direction in the mid-1970s. An important reason for this was growing youth unemployment, which almost exclusively hit those who lacked some form of vocational training. Typically, it was mainly LO, the Swedish Confederation of Trade Unions, which pressed strongly for a transformation of upper secondary school in the direction mentioned.

On top of the labour market problems came the awareness that the hitherto existing structure entrenched the social selection for different kinds of education and training. Problems in the school, notably those which have caused a high drop-out rate, have led thoughts in the same direction.

The Parliament statement on recurrent education includes a statement saying that each and everyone who goes through upper secondary school should be given preparation both for gainful employment and for further studies. A consequence of this was the appointment of the 1976 Commission on Secondary Education, mandated to propose an organization which aims at recurrent education. Its terms of reference also look upon upper secondary institutions as a general educational resource, not exclusively for young people only. One of the assignments is to see how the school can be co-ordinated with the two dominant kinds of adult education: manpower training (vocational training courses for the unemployed) and municipal adult education.

Since the commission's first report is expected during 1979, no concrete proposals can yet be reported. However, it is relevant to mention one ingredient of the public debate which has suggested a new angle of approach to the classical notion that youth education ought to give maximal breadth and avoid premature specialization. This notion contends that, within the framework of recurrent education, the balance between breadth and specialization can be reached by another route. Breadth is to be reached through an interplay between practical experience and studies. An upper secondary course which prepares students both for jobs and for further studies is followed by several years of experience in the world of work. This is followed by a shorter or longer period of study, where subject matter does not necessarily have to relate to previous experience or education. Later study periods may also be less specialized than the earlier ones.

In a period of severe problems on the labour market, especially for young people, it will not do to sit back and simply wait for a commission to come up with proposals sooner or later. If recurrent education is an important strategy, it is already necessary to give all young people the chance to get off to a good start in the job world. The past few years have put the focus of attention on the so-called risk group, specifically those young people who leave the compulsory school so 'fed up' with studies that they cannot imagine any form of further education for themselves. As the structure is now built up they run the risk of not getting any form of basic vocational training.

Two principal measures have been taken to support the members of this group. One enjoins every municipality to follow the progress of those who have left school up to the age of 18 and to offer them different kinds of education or work. The other measure has set up a series of shorter courses which seek to motivate the disenchanted individuals and to intercept those who are unemployed or risk becoming so. These courses are so designed that they can be developed into a more comprehensive training programme either straight away or later, with periods of work sandwiched in between. Taken together, these measures comprise intruments of the so-called 'youth guarantee'. At the same time they constitute a sort of practical experiment which can be generally introduced in a reformed upper secondary school.

Higher education

The organization of studies which so far has been most consistently adapted to recurrent education is the one to be found in higher education. That might seem surprising at first glance, but two causal factors are involved: first, a spontaneous development; and second, the fact that the decision to reform the organizational structure, intake capacity and physical siting of tertiary-level facilities was taken just when recurrent education scored its breakthrough in the political debate (Ministry of Education, 1973a). On top of that, the terms and conditions governing entry into higher education have been changed step by step during the 1970s. (*See also* section headed 'Admission policy'.)

An element of recurrence has gradually emerged since the mid-1960s in that a growing number of older students have come to the universities and colleges for further education in some form, added to preceding periods in secondary school and in gainful employment. As a rule these older students have not aspired to a full degree programme but have been content to take single courses in line with their previous work experience. For this group, recurrent education has become largely synonymous with adult education and the so-called overbridging function has been dominant. For these older students recurrent education opens a door that had been closed to them when they were young. Economic factors and an altered admission policy have paved the way for this change.

In the reform of higher education, however, consistent efforts have been made to build up an organization of studies which can help to promote recurrent behaviour. Among the new features of this organization, three in particular are worth noting:

1. An increased output of single courses.
2. Division of curricula into stages.
3. Development of new, short-term curricula which explicitly require a specified term of work experience for admission.

The privilege of signing up for single courses was available even earlier to undergraduate students enrolled in the faculties of arts and social sciences. This privilege has now been extended to include the whole field covered by tertiary education. In principle, all those courses which enter into the post-secondary curricula can be offered as single courses. It is also expected that innovative activity at the universities, colleges and other tertiary schools will lead to new courses that tie in more directly to previous work experience; indeed, this lofty ambition has already been realized in part.

Work has begun on taking an inventory which seeks to reorganize longer-term curricula so as to enable undergraduates to interrupt their studies after a certain stage and go out into the world of work. So far, not many curricula have been divided up in this fashion. One example is the law curriculum, which since January 1978 has been divided into two stages. Another example is the curriculum in medicine; a separate curriculum was recently offered to nurses, who by reason of their previous education and experience are permitted to exclude certain courses and in that way receive a 'time rebate' on the road leading to a medical degree. Both the individual tertiary schools and the National Board of Universities and Colleges (UHÄ) are pursuing a development project aimed at bringing out even more stage-divided curricula.

By contrast, what may be regarded as a pure innovation and as a direct outflow of the debate on recurrent education are the short-cycle technical programmes which were introduced on a trial basis in 1975 and which will form a definite part of higher education in 1979 (Dahllöf, 1977).

These curricula have been developed in response to learning the lesson that the interest in further studies among persons with experience of practical work and with a vocational training background is closely tied to the practical work situation. It is also clear that new patterns for decision-making and new methods of work in manufacturing industry will make it necessary to arrange training of high calibre which focuses on practical work situations.

It is in agreement with such ideas that the experimental programmes have evolved in higher education. The programmes have concentrated on the needs of the manufacturing industry and the study period is normally two years. The following requirements are specifically set for admission: completion of vocational training within upper secondary school and at least three years of on-the-job experience in the particular industry or line of business.

The creation of these short-cycle programmes can be seen as embodying a quest to develop higher education so as to suit students with long vocational experience, at the same time as meeting an educational need of the labour market. Obviously, it must be an attempt to adapt university courses more generally to the needs of adults and with that to bring in their experience as an asset to instruction in the classroom.

That development is bound to take time, of course, but if we ask what effect such changes will have on future applicants for higher education, it is legitimate to pass the following judgement. For that generation which still finds itself in school, the new organization of studies together with the new admission policy will mean greater freedom of choice. It also means that there will be more chances to make up for less good results as measured by grades, with credit given for work experience upon application to a university or college. The dominant problem — seen with reference to the political goals that have been formulated for recurrent education — is this: what social groups will take advantage of these new opportunities? Will there really be new groups or will the new opportunities accumulate to those who are already well looked after? It is obvious that changes confined to the content and organization of studies are not enough to guarantee a more equitable distribution of educational opportunity. The instruments that are being tried out in Sweden to make progress in this direction will be discussed in the following sections.

Admission policy

If it is going to be a real possibility for each and every person to return to studies after a period of gainful employment, short or long, the terms governing admission to continued studies will have to be changed. In 1972, the Swedish Parliament adopted a policy resolution with the following purpose. Every student who has completed an upper secondary programme of at least two years' length, be it academic or vocational in character, will have the right to be accepted for higher education, provided that he or she has at least two years of Swedish and English at upper secondary level. For adults over 25 years of age, five years of occupational experience or work in the home are regarded as equivalent to the completion of upper secondary school. In most cases, moreover, knowledge of specific subjects is required for admission to specific curricula.

Some experimentation under these rules has been taking place since 1969. Beginning with intakes for the 1977/78 academic year, this was carried out for admission to all higher education as a general rule. The only change that was made was to lower the requirement for the gainfully employed period from five to four years. Additional support for undergraduates with occupational experience comes from the selection rules which were introduced at the same time. Anyone who has occupational experience is permitted to add credit points to his grade marks for up to five years of gainful employment.

This system obviously makes it easier in most cases for the person who has occupational experience to start or resume higher studies. Since the system has been applied for only two years, the student population involved is still too small to justify any definite conclusions. It is certainly clear that the intake rules have attracted new groups to try their hand at higher studies. Conversely this means that competition has become keener for those who made up their minds early to go directly to courses with a very limited intake.

When the proposal was first put forward, ideas were mooted in public debate to make gainful employment mandatory for admission to higher studies. However, that demand was rejected for both practical and ideological reasons. It would be difficult to produce a sufficient number of meaningful jobs. And according to another argument advanced from a background of similar experiences, it would have a negative effect on the social selection to higher studies.

Location and dissemination of education

If recurrent periods of education are going to be a real alternative for every citizen, the courses on offer must be made available in the municipality or its vicinity. Seen generally, Sweden enjoys a favourable starting point in this respect. Because the municipality is vested with planning responsibility for the compulsory school, upper secondary school and a substantial part of that adult education which corresponds to these school levels, there is ample provision for a geographically even distribution of educational opportunities. Those areas of adult education which are administered by voluntary educational associations and by trade unions have a tradition of widely spread spatial distribution. The same can be said about that form of adult education specific to Scandinavia called the folk high school. The missing link in this location pattern has been higher education, which, up to the reform of 1977, was concentrated in six cities or towns.

The tertiary school reform signifies a decision in principle to locate higher education in 19 towns. At the start in 1977, higher education was expanded to four new towns and facilities will be gradually expanded in these localities. Moreover, opportunities are already open to those who are geographically confined to take part in so-called decentralized university education at many towns. As a result of the strong commitment to decentralization, the idea of having an Open University along British lines has been rejected. Sweden has been divided into a number of tertiary school regions and every tertiary school is responsible within its region for the whole educational output, irrespective of whether this is offered at the school venue itself or through so-called long-distance tuition.

Over and above the foregoing, and by contrast with the very centralized organization of higher education so far, in the new organization, local authorities (including representatives of the community) wield a decisive influence over education both in content and organization. In that way, an important contact has also been forged at this stage between education and working life.

Generally speaking we can say that an even geographic distribution of the educational resources is the goal that has been easiest to reach for Swedish educational policy. It is also worth noting that the inflow of students into different kinds of education is very evenly spread across the country despite the very uneven demographic distribution. However, an exception must be made for the three metropolitan areas (Greater Stockholm, Göteborg and Malmö), where enrolments are higher than in the rest of Sweden.

Educational leave and financing

In the Swedish debate on recurrent education, the financing of study has been regarded as the most strategic question. To choose to study in preference to gainful employment is to abstain from earned income in whole or in part. Here, a major factor bearing upon the individual's choice is the trade-off he or she perceives between likely future benefits, as in the form of expected income from employment, and the costs of studying. The question the student must answer is whether the benefits of education in the form of increased wages and so on outweigh the drawbacks in the form of economic sacrifices which are bound up with full-time studies.

Weighing-up of this kind plays a much greater role for the person who is already gainfully employed and who plans to go back to the classroom than for the teenager on a continuous educational path who has to make up his mind about moving from one educational stage to the next. Moreover, the former often have responsibility for other persons and they are bound to ask whether a changeover to studies is acceptable, not least on economic grounds in view of the situation of those people who are dependent on them.

The study financing system that has been offered in Sweden up to recent years has been completely designed for continuous and uninterrupted youth education of the traditional type. It is actually divided into two systems, one for persons under 20 years of age, another for those who are above that age. The former system is on a very modest scale and builds on the notion that the young person is still a part of the family finances. The latter system affords much greater economic scope, but is designed for young students with relatively small financial obligations. In any event it does not offer a reasonable alternative for the adult who relinquishes income from employment in order to study on a full-time basis.

It is therefore only natural that those who have acted in favour of recurrent education, above all the trade unions, should intensely argue the case that adult students must be provided with special financial aid. Particularly vigorous action was taken after Sweden acceded to the ILO Convention and Parliament adopted a law on the right to take time off to pursue studies.

This law came into force on 1 January 1975. It gives every worker, manual and non-manual, the right to take educational leave from his or her employment. The law holds for all employees, both in public and private service, at workplaces large and small. To be eligible for leave the worker must normally have been employed either for the past six months or for a total of at least twelve months over the past two years. No limitation is made as regards the kind of education. It is left to the worker to decide personally on the direction that the education should take. However, exclusively pursued private studies are not covered by the law. The length of leave is not limited by law. On the other hand, the employer is allowed some discretion to postpone the requested leave, normally by up to six months. If he wants a longer postponement, he must obtain consent from the trade union concerned.

During the first year when the law was in force, the only forms of financial aid available were the traditional ones. However, a parliamentary decision in 1975 created a third, more favourable form for economic support, known as adult education grants. In principle these are intended to cover the income foregone by an industrial worker. In reality, the adult grants scheme consists of three different aid forms. One is for full-time studies lasting at least one month, one is for hourly compensation chiefly intended for participants in study circles, and the third gives daily compensation for shorter courses.

A scheme of financial aid on this scale is inevitably accompanied by restrictions. The number of persons who can qualify for such assistance is determined by annual decisions of Parliament. Financial aids to students are distributed among the applicants by adult education boards, one in each county. The wage-earner organizations are represented on these bodies. Since the amount of aid money is limited, and in order to satisfy the equality and recurrence aspects, top priority will be accorded to persons of low basic educational attainments and with difficult working conditions, eg shift-work. Similarly, basic education is given priority over higher education.

The adult education grants scheme is perhaps the ingredient of planning for recurrent education which has been most deliberately devised to stimulate a more egalitarian distribution of educational opportunities. According priority to persons of scant educational background serves as a clear-cut example of what is usually called positive discrimination.

Another part of the study assistance system which is strategically vital is that form of aid which is payable to pupils in upper secondary school. This has long been the evil conscience of Swedish educational policy. The present system assumes that the student is part of the family finances and the level is adapted accordingly. Since this form of aid was introduced it has lagged behind others. Inasmuch as other supportive measures of social welfare policy on behalf of young people and families terminate once the children are 16 years old, the net burden on the family finances increases as soon as a child starts attending upper secondary school. If one wants to ensure that everyone gets vocational training in upper secondary school, the achievement of that goal is stymied by the low level of financial aid. Hence it is necessary to increase economic and social security to a level such as to entice young people to enter upper secondary school and complete it. A special commission of inquiry has now been empowered to overhaul the level and organization of the various forms of study aid. However, no proposal has yet been defined.

Information and outreach activities

Apart from financial stimulus, another important part of the quest to distribute education more evenly is represented by efforts to reach the poorly educated with information and to encourage them to take advantage of educational opportunities (Ministry of Education, 1973b).

As a matter of course, society's combined resources for educational and vocational guidance include the conveyance of information which promotes recurrent education. In recent years these resources have been enlarged both at secondary and tertiary levels.

In the Government Bill of 1975 on higher education, the Swedish Minister of Education had this to say:

> In my opinion a cardinal mission for educational and vocational guidance activity, within and in association with the tertiary school, should be to provide information about recurrent education during the next few years. For this purpose collaboration should be established with the labour market parties.

But the operation of a linkage between information and active studying is going to necessitate much more active efforts, which in Sweden have been referred to as outreach activities. This denotes the taking of measures which aim straight at the individual and as such require not only information but also active stimulus. A pilot scheme of experiments with outreach activities has been in progress since the early 1970s. It has concentrated on the poorly educated and the experiments have been directly conducted at workplaces and in residential areas. The services of personnel employed with the voluntary educational associations have been used for outreach activities to the utmost extent. This means that the 'outreacher' has often been a workmate in whom confidence is felt out of sheer intuition.

Since 1975 the outreach activities have been cast in firmer moulds and received fixed appropriations in the annual budget. The activities are in charge of the voluntary educational associations, with active support forthcoming from the law on the status of shop stewards which Parliament enacted in 1974. This law also embraces the organizers of studies employed by the trade unions. These officials are legally entitled to perform union-related work, including outreach activity for studies, on paid work time.

As pointed out earlier, three of the ingredients in planning for recurrent education — namely, outreach activities, adult education grants and the law on the right to take time off for studies — must be regarded as the most vital components for reaching adults of low educational attainments and hence for realizing a part of the equality goal. It is also an indication that the planning for recurrent education must span a much wider field than educational policy if the intended effect is going to be achieved.

Recurrent education — a social policy

A typical feature of Swedish planning is that it has stressed social policy and labour market policy pre-requisites every bit as much as the educational policy pre-requisites. This is wholly in line with the educational reforms during the 1960s, which have been consistently regarded as social reforms. Where that view prevails, recurrent education also becomes a strategy for changing working life, since in the basic philosophy of recurrent education, work and education are means of equal worth for contributing to personal development.

In recurrent education one looks at education and working life as equivalent instruments for learning and development of the individual. In that case, of course, one also wants to see that these develop in the same direction according to certain commonly held value judgements. But we must be clear in our minds that we have to do with two different systems, with their own impacts and their own inner tensions. It should also be recognized that the value judgements which education and working life embody may be in tension, that they undergo never-ending change and that they do not necessarily develop in the same direction. The contact is as likely to lead to conflicts as to concerted action towards similar goals. A trend towards recurrent education will require sweeping changes in the *modus operandi* of the educational system, but, and this is perhaps most important to underline, a deepened education/working life partnership is hard to imagine unless profound changes are made in the world of work. In Sweden, such changes have generally been linked with the trend towards industrial democracy. (*See also Chapter 7.*)

If the interplay between education and working life is seen in a dynamic perspective of this kind, the main problem will be to develop each system so that it contributes to a positive development in the other.

References

Dahllöf, U (1977) *Reforming Higher Education and External Studies in Sweden and Australia* Acta Universitatis Uppsaliensis: Uppsala, Studies in Education 3

Ministry of Education (1973a) *Higher Education. Proposals by the Swedish 1968 Educational Commission* Stockholm

Ministry of Education (1973b) *Continued Outreaching Work for Circle Studies in Adult Education* Stockholm

12. West German experience of 'popular' higher education

Helmuth Dolff

Summary: For a long time, little consideration was given in West Germany to a cause for which the *Volkshochschulen* had been fighting for decades: the integration of adult education into the general system of education, on an equal basis with the so-called traditional sectors of school, university and vocational training.

In 1966, when the *Deutscher Bildungsrat* was instituted by the President of the Federal Republic, a new initiative was taken. A so-called Federal-Länder-Board (*Bund-Länder-Kommission*) on educational planning, created in parallel to the Educational Council, was to take up the suggestions of the Council, carry out concrete planning and implement it nationally, in the Länder and municipalities. The leading idea was the concept of 'lifelong learning' and the provision of equal educational opportunity for all. The plan for the structure was ready in 1970. It argues for the establishment of institutionalized continuing education as an educational domain complementary to compulsory schooling. Continuing education includes further vocational training, re-training and adult education.

Apart from the theoretical ideas, discussions on educational organization and structure were held in the field of continuing education itself, particularly at the level of the Länder which are competent authorities according to the constitution. The outcome is a network of legislation for continuing education, out-of-school youth education and professional training, representing a first step in the right direction and supported by increased resources and a greater planning capacity.

The chapter concentrates on the main sector of continuing education in the Federal Republic, the *Volkshochschulen*. It describes their position, functions, programmes and organizational requirements, and ends by considering future possibilities. Many traditions will have to be abolished. Continuing education will have to develop completely new forms independent of existing patterns. Controversies over responsibility, frequently of a political-ideological nature will have to be resolved. Educational provision will have to be re-distributed among the different sectors. Only then will the continuing education institutions take their rightful place beside school, university and vocational training.

Historical factors and planning

For a long time little consideration was given in the Federal Republic to a cause for which the *Volkshochschulen* ('folk high schools') had been fighting for decades: the integration of adult education into the general system of education on an equal basis with the so-called traditional sectors of school, university and vocational training.

Based on the conventional idea of an educational system which subdivides life into a period of learning and another period in which one then applies what has been learned, public opinion often gave to adult education the task of merely supplying later on in life what had been missed at school and of being a pleasant complement to general and more decorative cultural activities. This state of affairs was not changed by the fact that after the war the *Volkshochschulen* began to make the teaching of civics, education in democratic responsibility, or (as it has since come to be called) political education, one of their central and basic activities – thus gradually assuming cultural, educational, and social functions which did not fit easily with those misconceptions. At about the same time, the problem of overcoming the traditional opposition between education and training began to be discussed: the alleged incompatibility of vocational training and so-called liberal education. Nevertheless, people became aware of these difficulties to the extent that the *Deutscher Ausschuss für das Erziehungs- und Bildungswesen* in 1960 tabled a comprehensive study on the 'Task of Adult Education in the Federal Republic of Germany', thus clearly initiating a re-examination of the problem.

There is no doubt that one of the merits of the *Deutscher Ausschuss für das Erziehungs- und Bildungswesen* is to have started – in the mid-1950s – discussion on reform of education in the Federal Republic of Germany. Through a series of much-discussed reports, such as the reports on 'Adult Education' and on 'Political Education', the committee stimulated interesting trains of thought in the field of out-of-school education. Although the proposals and analyses of the committee initiated a process of self-examination within the adult education institutions, they remained without practical consequences as far as the State – the Federal authorities, the Länder (individual states) and the municipalities, – was concerned. The State, which was not represented in the committee, was apparently not much inclined to discuss seriously the thoughts of the independent authors of the reports and to urge the Executive to take action.

In 1966, when the *Deutscher Bildungsrat* was instituted by the President of the Federal Republic, a new initiative was taken. This time, the Federal authorities, the Länder and the municipalities participated in the Council in an advisory fashion right from the beginning. A so-called Federal-Länder-Board (*Bund-Länder-Kommission*) on educational planning, created in parallel to the Educational Council, was to take up the suggestions of the Council, carry out concrete planning and implement this planning nationally, in the Länder and in the municipalities. The purpose of the Council's activities was to propose, within a plan for the structure of education (*Strukturplan für das Bildungswesen*), the basic timetable for educational reform in the Federal Republic, and to explain the different educational areas through expert comments. The leading idea was the concept of 'lifelong learning' as a unity and the provision of equal educational opportunity for all. The Board was to take the necessary action on behalf of the Executive by establishing a comprehensive educational plan (*Bildungsgesamtplan*) and to help prepare the financial basis for the reform proposal by working out a long-term educational budget.

The plan concerning the structure was ready in 1970, the comprehensive educational plan in 1973. Although many of the political questions — especially as far as the interaction between the Federal Government and the governments of the Länder are concerned — remained unsolved, the objective of establishing guidelines for the future has been attained.

This is true in particular for out-of-school education, which has been defined for the first time as being a fully integrated fourth main section of public education, with equal status. The relevant paragraph of the plan concerning the structure reads:

> School and vocational training will provide only the first phase of education in future for more and more people. Today it is already obvious that the training received during this first educational phase cannot satisfy the requirements a person has to face later, even if this training were aimed at broad and profound knowledge and at the satisfaction of expected needs. More and more people have to be able to obtain new knowledge, skills and aptitudes to face growing and changing vocational and social requirements. Lifelong learning means extending education to later phases of one's life and changing radically the attitude towards education. The traditional concept of life being divided into two phases which — exclusively and separated from each other — are identified with the acquisition and application of training, will be replaced by the concept of organized learning not limited to a training phase at the beginning of life. It is necessary to establish institutionalized continuing education as an educational domain complementary to compulsory schooling. Further education as the continuation or resumption of former organized learning forms a whole, inter-connected with pre-school and classroom learning processes.

Continuing education includes further vocational training, re-training and adult education. It supplements the conventional closed educational cycle and continues it under post-school conditions. At the same time, it tries to relieve the educational system of social pressure resulting from unsatisfied educational needs and requirements.

If the curricula of the first educational phase are adapted to the phases of continuing education, re-distribution of educational efforts will have a relieving effect on university and upper secondary levels; if this distribution is done intelligently, the duration of training may in some cases be shortened. Continuing education cannot be limited and confined to a functional connection with technical progress. Its objective, in fact, is to enable people consciously to participate and co-operate in the development and transformation of all aspects of life and by this to form their personalities.

Legislation and present situation

Apart from the theoretical statements which are now no longer seriously questioned, the discussions on educational organization and structure were carried on in the field of continuing education itself, particularly at the level of the Länder, which are the competent authorities according to the constitution. The outcome is a network of laws for continuing education, out-of-school youth education and professional training which, taken individually, represent first steps in the right direction, with greater resources and an improved planning capacity; all in all they meet – albeit only partially – theoretical demands depicted above. The economic depression with its consequences for the public budget, coinciding with this eagerness for reform, helped to deepen federalist, ideological and historical differences between the individual legislatures of the Länder in terms of the material support they provide.

None of this should, however, conceal the fact that, with some exceptions, all acts fortify retrospective financing policies and offer only limited developmental possibilities for educational provision, and this only in some of the Länder. We are still far away from comprehensive legislation for continuing education as a public duty, derived from the needs of a structural overall education plan.

In addition, since the *Volkshochschulen* as the central institutions for adult education in the Federal Republic dominate the public field for continuing education, pedagogical and methodological schemes have to be developed for them and those involved in their work. These schemes have at present from the historical point of view no established patterns such as are used in the 'classical' field of the educational system, at least as a starting basis for reforms. On the other hand the rush to public continuing education has, despite – or because of – widespread economic, ideological and political uncertainty, never been as important as it is at this moment. The requirements in style, complexity, and variety of continuing education have never been so extensive as today.

The range of proposed measures and practical models which are being worked out now in many places comprises

1. The inclusion of specialized technical colleges (*Fachschulen*) and universities (*Fachhochschulen*) in a so-called comprehensive university (*Gesamthochschule*).
2. The transformation of vocational education and training.
3. The establishment of agencies for continuing scientific education.
4. The inclusion of continuing education in an educational guidance system.
5. The interrelation between upper secondary level and continuing education measures at comprehensive school level.
6. The systematizing of a part of the continuing education programme through a 'modular system' composed of various certificates for adults.
7. Statutory measures to ensure continuing education through the Federal State and the Länder, and therefore through the assumption of public responsibility.
8. The statutory guarantee of educational leave for all employees.

9. The establishment, by Federal law, of statistics on continuing education.
10. The setting up of measures to bring about continuing education provision covering all the regions of the Federal Republic.

The position of the Volkshochschule

The description of the *Volkshochschule* in the context of an overall system of continuing education reads as follows:

> Conditions of work are undergoing structural changes which call for a high degree of adaptability in the persons concerned. This adaptability presupposes an understanding not merely of individual functions but of human life as a whole. Our present-day society, being based on the provision of services, requires the ability to co-operate based on awareness and experience. With so many consumer goods and so much leisure time available, selective judgements and creative imagination are necessary. Both of these need guidance and encouragement. Mass media are providing more and more information, and means are required of enabling people to evaluate this critically. The growth of international contacts makes it necessary for people to be linguistically and mentally equipped for dealing with unfamiliar problems and people from other countries. Free and democratic ways of life can be maintained and developed only if the people representing them are well-informed, discriminating, and willing to take decisions.
>
> In helping people to meet these requirements of society, adult education should also, as far as possible, help each person to satisfy his own individual wish to discover what he can do and how to act responsibly.

Adult education is therefore an essential element of the educational system as a whole. With such a multiplicity of functions, the institutions providing adult education must be able to supply the organizational framework and the careful planning necessary for an extremely varied programme. The *Volkshochschule* is particularly suited to this task, being distinguished from other organizations which also provide adult education by the fact that this is its only purpose and that it is open to all.

The statement that adult education is the only purpose of the *Volkshochschule* means that it does not work on behalf of particular ideas and limited interests. The *Volkshochschule* regards the educating of adults as its *raison d'être*. Being open to all implies that the *Volkshochschule* serves the public as a whole, thereby helping to integrate society. Just as attendance at the *Volkshochschule* is independent of the economic, political, or denominational background of the participants, so is the selection of subjects and teachers essentially free of restrictive regulations. The *Volkshochschule* invites public criticism of its activities by the regular publication of reports about its finances, the number of people attending its courses, and the subjects dealt with.

The functions of the Volkshochschule

Fundamentally, the *Volkshochschule* has three functions to fulfil in its programme:

1. Helping people to learn.
2. Helping people to keep informed and develop their powers of judgement.
3. Helping people with their leisure activities.

These three functions are regarded by modern educational theory as complementary, and in the *Volkshochschule* they have equal rights. They meet the need for knowledge, communication, and recreation. Although they cannot be made to fit exactly into particular groups of subjects, each of them requires its own methods.

The programme of courses

There can be no central control of how programmes are drawn up. Local conditions with regard to cultural matters will always have to be considered. There are, however, certain general points, arising from present-day ways of life and what we can foresee of the future, which apply to all. Modern living conditions place an increasingly heavy burden on our creative mental powers, which are only able to develop properly if our emotional needs are satisfied. Adult education is therefore concerned both with factual matters and with personal contacts. Part of the *Volkshochschule's* programme should consist of systematic courses, graded according to their standard of difficulty and related by subject matter, while another part should offer assistance on matters of particular importance.

The programme should provide evidence of the wish for continuity and topicality; in other words, it should contain some activities dealing with concrete problems and situations, and others forming planned courses of study. A point which requires particular examination is the extent to which television — especially its educational programmes — can be incorporated into the work of the *Volkshochschule*.

These general principles mean that the *Volkshochschule's* programme should, as a rule, consist of the following types of activity:

1. Courses of instruction, lectures and lecture series providing information. These apply principally to the publication of new discoveries in all fields of learning and to the presentation of topical problems, especially when it is not yet possible to adapt the material to courses and study trips. They may also serve to draw on new reserves of participants.
2. Study and discussion groups dealing with social, intellectual, political, and religious problems. These also include the treatment of problems about life, and advanced language courses. Because of the

opportunities for discussion which are afforded, meetings extending over a weekend, a whole week, or the duration of a study trip are particularly favourable for this field of activity. Longer courses as part of university extension schemes are very useful.
3. Working groups for the promotion of leisure activities. These cover especially imitative and creative activities such as singing and painting, subjects such as hygiene and health education and domestic science, and also activities of a more technical nature, such as photography.
4. Performance of plays and films, concerts and exhibitions. These are included as a contribution to cultural life, especially when courses of preparation and discussion are arranged in connection with them, or when no other local organizations exist to provide such features.

It is not possible for every *Volkshochschule* to include every one of these activities in its programme. What should be done in every case, though, is to examine how far the *Volkshochschule* — if necessary in conjunction with other educational establishments — can contribute to the expansion of further education schemes, and how it can facilitate transfer within the educational system. The study and discussion groups, representing the traditional principle of the symposium, should evolve into long-term courses of study. Where a *Volkshochschule* is too small to obtain suitable supervisors of studies, lecture series can take the place of courses of study.

It is reasonable for the participants to wish for something in writing to show that they have attended the courses. To meet this wish, the *Volkshochschule* should issue attendance certificates; this is not the same as a record of achievement, which must be restricted to those courses where the degree of achievement can be judged by reference to accepted standards.

Organizational requirements

If the *Volkshochschulen* are to carry out their function of providing co-ordinated education they must be sponsored by bodies whose legal position is established. These may be local authorities, registered companies, or other kinds of legally recognized organization.

At regular intervals a *Volkshochschule* should publish a programme valid for a fixed term. Besides laying down its work for this period, this programme will also serve as very useful publicity. Good public relations should be sought after by being on friendly terms with the Press, maintaining close contacts with influential persons and authorities, and presenting useful statistics.

To meet these organizational requirements, the *Volkshochschule* needs an office with rules of procedure, a filing system, and regulations concerning registration for courses, fees payable, and the payment of teachers. It should have regular hours of business when it can be visited by members of the public, who should also be able to obtain advice on the choice of courses. Permanent accommodation for teaching with a stock of teaching aids is essential. If it is to carry out to the full the work required of it, and particularly if its work is not to be restricted to the evenings, the *Volkshochschule* must have premises of its own. In order to carry out the various tasks described above, the *Volkshochschule* requires a permanent staff. This applies just as much to the conduct of its business affairs as to the continuity of its teaching. Regular meetings and conferences of the staff must be held to discuss the significance of past experiences and to plan and improve the programme.

Two things which can do a great deal to place the work of the *Volkshochschule* on a firm basis are an advisory committee of teachers and some form of representation of the participants. In the town, it should be a matter of course for the *Volkshochschule* to have a full-time principal, and larger *Volkshochschulen* need a full-time staff of qualified heads of departments and teachers. Adult education in smaller parishes is best served by the organization of some form of co-operation between villages, such as the organization of district *Volkshochschulen*.

Outlook

Many traditions will have to be abolished. Continuing education will have to develop completely new forms independent of existing patterns. Controversies over responsibility, frequently of a political-ideological nature, will have to be overcome. The provision of education will have to be re-distributed among the different sectors. Only then will the continuing education institutions take their rightful place beside school, university and vocational training.

13. Lifelong education policies in western and eastern Europe: similarities and differences

Ettore Gelpi

> Summary: The author cautions against the arbitrariness of the distinction between eastern and western European countries. Educational policies and legislation, as well as educational experiences, are taken into consideration, noting that most of the countries are concerned with lifelong education at a global policy level and no longer at a sectoral level. The international, as well as the technical and social division of labour, is stressed in its relationship with education. Several indicators are proposed to evaluate the European educational systems (eg participation of workers' children at all levels of education and abolition of rank between the so-called manual disciplines and the so-called intellectual disciplines). Worker and union education is considered as well as the relationship between the system of education and the system of production. The configuration of new types of educators that exist, but are not recognized by the formal education system, is explored. The article ends with the hypothesis that the non-economic dimension of education is one of the most relevant features of European education trends.

The distinction between eastern and western European countries is very imprecise as far as the geography is concerned, because there is not only an eastern and a western Europe, but also differences between southern, central and northern Europe. Only for reasons of simplification do we use this distinction between eastern and western European countries; their main difference is economic organization, but State control of economic, collective property and private ownership are not always the same within the sub-region 'eastern countries' and the sub-region 'western countries'. The arbitrariness of this distinction does not prevent a useful comparative analysis of the common and specific trends of education in Europe.

Educational policies and legislation as well as educational experiences have to be taken into consideration in a comparative analysis of lifelong education in European countries. What is common, what are the differences, what is new, what are the perspectives? Today, this initial appraisal and comparative analysis is possible and necessary within each country.

Most of the countries are concerned with lifelong education on a global policy level, and no longer at a sectoral level. This means a progressive institutionalization of lifelong education and a national concern at the planning level; educational planners, and not only philosophers of education or adult educators, are involved in lifelong education. The pressure on the planners is two-fold: political and technocratic. Politicians are aware of the relevance of this educational approach and they ask for broader educational policies; technocrats apply pressure, because they feel the necessity of a more rational and productive use of investments in education, and lifelong education policies appear to be a possible answer.

Futurologists are becoming concerned with lifelong education. Education appears to be a possible answer to a variety of socio-economic problems that are on the rise in our societies. At the same time, education seems to provoke further problems because of an increase of better-qualified people, because of the irrelevance of some jobs for well-educated people and because of increasing social demands. If there is a predominant trend in future education, it is a greater concern for the global environment of man and not only for traditional institutional education; the environment, place of work, leisure and the like are becoming much more related and relevant to educational debate than in the past.

The debate on comparative education with its notes of optimism and pessimism (Debeauvais, 1978: 28) leaves us with some doubts on the validity of the comparative analysis of educational systems if we limit ourselves to educational institutions, content and methods. Our inquiry must take into consideration the relation between (a) social and political systems, (b) the systems of production and (c) education, and should try to avoid formal educational declarations or comparisons. The dialectic dimension of lifelong education is more and more accepted in pedagogical debates; social and counter-cultural forces are taken into consideration, even if the contradictory nature of these social forces is underlined (Suchodolski, 1978: 28-9).

The impact of international and regional economic organizations (more than just those of an educational nature) on educational trends has to be considered. There is no doubt that the Organization for Economic Co-operation and Development (OECD), the European Economic Community (EEC) and COMECON (the COMmunist ECONomic community) have an impact on the educational schemes of the different member states of European sub-regions. It seems that the educational schemes of western and eastern European sub-regions are approaching common ground: nine or ten years of basic education, better integration of initial and subsequent training, and integration of vocational education in the formal educational system are some examples of these common trends. The biggest difference between and within the sub-regions, is the evaluation procedures within the educational system; societies with some technocratic orientation tend to be tougher in evaluation procedures (eg Sweden, Federal Republic of Germany, Democratic Republic of Germany, Hungary); stronger class societies tend to be less rigid because selection is made at the social level, or because class struggle is pushing towards a more egalitarian society (eg France, Italy, Spain), or because of both.

The international division of labour is found both in eastern and western Europe and has a relevant impact on education, even if it is ignored by official regional bodies. It is quite clear that the division has heavy consequences corresponding to ideological and political differences. Vocational and higher education as well as research policy are strongly influenced by industrial investment in this or that part of Europe; the scarcity of formal education for migrant workers and their children is another consequence of the division of labour that most affects southern Europe (Italy, Yugoslavia, Spain, Portugal, Turkey).

The relevance of the migrant labour market is a factor increasingly acknowledged by educators, and from a quite different angle, than a few years ago when full employment was a common reality in most European countries. Division of labour, job rotation, cultural and social functions within the place of work — these are becoming a permanent concern for educators engaged in continuing as well as initial training.

In the 1970s several educational plans and new laws incorporating the lifelong education principle (eg in Poland, Yugoslavia, Federal Republic of Germany) were prepared; in the implementation of these plans, there was some regression because a few of the principles were considered too Utopian, but still some fundamental ideas were retained. Popular participation in educational management, integration between initial and further training, less rigid separation between the different streams of secondary education, institutionalization of adult education — these are some of the main aspects that we find in the new educational plans and legislation.

The problem of new educational ideas concerns educational planners of different countries: they are aware of the increasing irrelevance of school curricula, and of the meagre attention given to the cultural dimension in institutional education. There is a search for non-scholastic educational experience, but in general, educational institutions do not take the risk of directly involving the cultural and social groups that can provide new content in education.

The search for instruments of evaluation is acute in most countries both among the 'Malthusians' and the 'Keynesians' of education. Traditional evaluation seems to be irrelevant and tautological: to boast about or to denigrate education is no longer the most important game in the European education debate. There is an increasing interest in analysing and evaluating educational results, in assessing motivation and interest in education, and in monitoring educational systems through a permanent evaluation process. The quest for new indicators is common to several countries, because failures in new educational experiences are not unusual. Scarcity of educational means, as far as financial aspects are concerned, is now more and more the case in many European countries; therefore, people feel the need to evaluate educational progress and failure.

For example, in many countries a simple analysis of the population in adult classes shows the selective role of adult education. The relationship between the system of education and the system of production leads to selection in two ways: people attached to the system of production are usually seeking and achieving some kind of social mobility through education, adults only loosely attached to the system of production are staying on in school and further education systems related in only a marginal way to the labour market (Dubar, 1977).

In most countries, people with little initial training do not take advantage of further training for its own sake; further training laws and regulations benefit people with high levels of education or, above all in recent times, people who are marginal in the labour market and who get involved in training activities because of unemployment and under-employment, and not necessarily for the sake of the vocational education that is proposed. This may often be irrelevant to their potential needs in their place of work.

We can analyse the European educational systems through the following indicators:

1. Participation of workers' children at all levels of education.
2. Participation of workers themselves at all levels of education.
3. Use of educators who are not teachers in the educational systems.
4. Active participation of workers (in industry, farming) as educators.
5. Education as an instrument not only of individual advancement but also of community advancement.
6. De-streaming of upper secondary education.
7. Abolition of the different streams of secondary education.
8. Abolition of inequalities between schools in urban and rural areas.
9. Introduction of folk culture, oral and written, as an integral part of the school curriculum.
10. Abolition of status difference between the so-called manual disciplines and the so-called intellectual disciplines.
11. Integration of general and vocational education.
12. Increase in the consumption of cultural goods (books, newspapers, films).
13. Progress in participation in community life (political parties, trade unions, village associations, district associations).
14. Improvement in the cultural content and methods of the mass media.
15. Making work experiences more interesting from the educational point of view.
16. Significant development of experiments in self-instruction.
17. Participation of schoolchildren and students in the management of educational institutions.
18. Integration between initial and subsequent training.
19. Provision of facilities (eg paid leave, scholarships, instructional materials) to underprivileged groups to enable them to profit from the educational system.

Referring to the numbered indicators above, we find resistance, with very few exceptions, in eastern European countries as regarding points 4, 7, 9, 10, 15; we find more positive approaches in western countries to points 13 and 17; a more positive approach in eastern countries to points 11, 18, 19; and as far as the other indicators are concerned, there are positive trends in most European countries.

The development of the concept of lifelong education as far as educational practices are concerned allows us to make a comparative analysis of several aspects of educational systems — the reform of education, school systems, leisure-time activities, relationship between work and education, worker education, initial and subsequent training. The integration of western and eastern countries (OECD, EEC, COMECON) has some implications for educational activities, even if the formal educational systems are sometimes only partially affected by this integration.

Educational systems with a high degree of selectivity, especially where higher education is concerned, feature in both eastern and western European countries (Federal Republic of Germany, Hungary); others are less selective (Italy, Belgium, Yugoslavia). In both cases, problems are on the rise, whether because of strong selection or the lack of it.

A new tendency of all European educational systems to try and assure some kind of vocational or pre-vocational qualifications at the end of one's educational career (compulsory or higher secondary education) is a recent concern. This concern was present in the educational systems of most eastern countries but was absent in western countries with a few exceptions (mainly the Federal Republic of Germany): under-employment, unemployment, the tension between initial training and the educational needs for productive work are pushing all the educational systems towards a greater concern for future working activities. The gap between educational objectives and practices in the school system and the system of production is still a pressing problem in western countries; some experiments are trying to close this gap, but either vocational education comes too early, or educational experiences that are work-oriented are very poor. The Yugoslavian propositions contained in the educational reform project are appealing to most European countries:

> In preparing for work, special attention should be paid to linking theory and practice and training for creativity in work; young people have the opportunity to join the labour force as soon as possible, youth and adults have access to recurrent education in order to acquire new knowledge and raise their level of qualification — in accordance with the needs of new technology in production and in other spheres of human activity. Special efforts are being concentrated on this latter demand. (*Yugoslav Survey*, 1978)

But educational reforms have to face the problem that in western and eastern countries the technical division of labour still implies a social division and vice versa. In some cases, western societies are more class-divided societies than eastern ones (eg through the effect of inherited wealth and private property) but as far as the social implications of the technical division of labour are concerned, eastern and western societies tend to accept the same logic. Therefore they are very far from 'the model based on vertical polyvalence and the rotation of functions, and more specifically on the abolition of unskilled, repetitive and frustrating tasks as the lifelong work of certain categories of citizens' (Visalberghi, 1973). New educational reforms can contribute to a vertical job rotation and they can provoke very strong pressure in this direction.

The nature of trade unions, which is quite different in the various European countries, heavily influences the nature of the unions' education programmes; in Latin European countries and in Yugoslavia, the involvement of unions in economic planning or self-management or in some kind of control of production within the place of work means a very intensive permanent education in the various fields of social, economic and political life and not only in bargaining skills.

It appears that as far as workers' education is concerned, an increase of workers' control within the factory implies an increase in educational demand, eg the '150 hours' in Italy (De Sanctis, 1978), self-management in Yugoslavia, industrial democracy in Great Britain, co-operative systems in Hungary and so on. Further exploration of these implications, which are neglected by educational institutions that do not profit from the dynamics of worker participation in the productive system, would be interesting. These dynamics seem to be a significant trend:

> The demand for the participation of workers in management is one of the universal processes which is connected with the foremost trends of today. Workers' self-management represents a real challenge to the contemporary world. As an authentic socialist alternative of social development, self-management represents an 'opening towards the possible' and an escape from the 'myriad contradictions into which the bourgeois society and statist type of socialism were steeped'. (Mitrovic, 1978)

The integration of education with production and research can change the functions of the school system:

> Once the integration of education with production and research has been optimally achieved, school continues to represent the main formal socialization agency, yet it fundamentally changes its social function: the educational system becomes able to generate new social structures, a new division of labour, and to open up prospects and trends towards removing essential differences and interweaving manual and intellectual work. (Mahler, 1978)

The dual system of education (vocational versus grammar school) has largely been eliminated at the first level of secondary education but is still in existence in upper secondary education. Some reforms try to attack this dualism and concurrently another type of dualism — that which exists — between adults and young people. A case in point is the Yugoslavian reform:

> Proceeding from the concept of lifelong education, the reform actually accentuates education acquired during employment, education practised in relation to work and education received directly at work. This is a further important aspect of the process of elimination of the previous dualism in the system of education and training which separated adults from young people. (European Centre for Leisure and Education, 1978: 92-3)

As far as formal and non-formal education are concerned, we can say that there is a shift in an opposite direction in western and eastern countries. In the 1960s, socialist countries were mainly concerned with institutionalized education and they very often neglected the non-formal aspect of education. Western countries, faced with strong economic development, were eager to find new solutions in non-formal learning and in more flexible educational institutions. During the late 1970s, non-formal educational experiences were explored in some socialist countries because of the growing relevance of this approach to the young and adult population. At the same time in western countries, a more integrated educational approach to the working experience was becoming a new feature in education, because of the new structures of the labour market.

The real motivation and the social conditions of learners were analysed in many European countries where extended provision for education was not necessarily used by the section of the public for whom it was intended. It seems that adults are much more interested in non-formal educational and cultural experiences than was supposed. The concept of integration of initial and subsequent training is being explored both by European states and regional organizations (Council of Europe, 1978). This integration is related to an increasing institutionalization of adult education in Europe which is a new trend in western Europe.

Citizens' initiatives in the field of education are a parallel and sometimes opposite trend to the institutionalization of adult education in several eastern and western European countries: housing, leisure, environment, politics and folk customs are the main concerns of these initiatives. Popular movements and initiatives in the field of education appear to be very relevant in a period of change (Melo, 1978: 45). Popular participation in educational, cultural and intellectual life in Czechoslovakia in the 1960s (Richta, 1977) is another example of this wide participation in the shaping of a new society. Studies are needed to evaluate the contribution of popular movements in education.

Another trend in some countries is the decentralization of education (Italy, Yugoslavia) and a growing interest in rural areas that were neglected in the past (Hungary, Yugoslavia, Poland, Italy). The spread of pre-school education is also an emerging trend in many European countries. Both the educational and the social dimension are stressed in the new kindergartens and nursery schools.

Two other trends are the education of migrants and a more balanced relationship between rural and urban education; western European countries (plus Yugoslavia) are concerned with the first trend. Some eastern countries (Poland, Yugoslavia, Bulgaria) and, in a more limited way, a number of western European countries, are concerned with the second trend. These two trends are obliging educational systems to have a more open educational approach because of the universality of the educational demand made by parents, youth, children and the entire community. As far as non-European migrants' and workers' education is concerned, the eastern European countries are involved in a very limited way (some non-European young workers are present in some of these countries) but only for training purposes.

The geographical dimension is also being explored because decentralization can be another and parallel aspect (mass media, cultural centres in the capitals, etc). Further exploration can be envisaged to find some forms of integration between decentralization and centralized distance-teaching instruments (group discussions led by local teachers, local research, local educators serving as relays to national broadcasting and educational institutions).

New infra-structures in several countries reflect a lifelong education approach to education: polyvalent community facilities are emerging and are under study to allow full use of these infra-structures by all members of the population, children, teenagers and adults (UIA, 1976; Regione Toscana, 1978).

The recognition that libraries, museums, summer camps, factories, social life, mass media and the environment are all part of education implies the emergence of new types of educators who exist but who are not recognized by the formal educational system. In the field of vocational education, new openings are seen in some educational systems regarding the employment of educators other than teachers (Art. 47: 'The teaching staff for vocational education is provided by the care of the bodies running vocational schools and all the other forms of worker training mentioned in the present decree; they are selected among the best engineers, masters [foremen] and other experts from the industry, as well as among the educational staff' [Romania, 1977]).

New types of educators are emerging in many countries, even if there is a gap between legislation formally acknowledging their contribution and its actual impact. There is an awareness that formal educational systems are not providing necessary skills for vocational, social and political education (Pflüger, 1978).

A very interesting hypothesis is developed by Adamski in relation to the future of post-secondary education (Adamski, 1978): non-economic factors are becoming relevant to the motivation of students to enrol in education and this is combined with a worldwide trend of a decline in return on investments in post-compulsory education, especially where higher education is concerned. Education is demanded for better quality work and not only for a better salary.

This hypothesis has to be explored in order to have a better understanding of the motivation of young and adult learners who are aware of the discrepancy between educational planning and labour market planning. The non-economic dimension of education is one of the relevant features of European educational trends (Kallen, 1978).

References

Adamski, W (1978) *Continuing Education in Western and Eastern European Societies* European Cultural Foundation: Amsterdam

Council of Europe (1978) *Permanent Education: Final Report* Council of Europe: Strasbourg

Debeauvais, M (1978) Les rôles des organisations internationales dans l'évolution de l'éducation comparée *Recherche, Pédagogie et Culture* May-August 1978

De Sanctis, F M (1978) *L'Educazione Degli Adulti in Italia* Editori Riuniti, Paideia: Roma

Dubar, C (1977) Formation continue et différenciations sociales *Revue Française de Sociologie* 18: 543-75

European Centre for Leisure and Education (1978) *Adult Education in Europe* Studies and Documents No 4

Kallen, D (1978) L'éducation récurrente dans les pays d'Europe occidentale *Perspectives* 8 2

Mahler, F (1978) *The integrated system of school, work and research, its impact on the changes in the future occupational and social statuses* The Research Centre for Youth Problems: Bucharest

Melo, A (1978) Experiments in popular education in Portugal 1974-76 *Educational Studies and Documents No 29* UNESCO: Paris

Mitrovic, L R (1978) A contribution to the definition of the relationship between participation and self-management *Socioloski Pregled* Belgrade

Pflüger, A (1978) *Training and Retraining of Adult Educators* Council of Europe: Strasbourg

Regione Toscana (1978) *Educazione Permanente e Territorio* Commissione Nazionale Italiana per l'UNESCO: Firenze

Richta, R (1977) The scientific and technological revolution and the projects of social development *Scientific-Technological Revolution* SAGE: London

Romania: The Council of State of the Socialist Republic of Romania (1977) *Organization and Operation of Vocational Education in the Socialist Republic of Romania* Bucharest

Suchodolski, B (1978) L'éducation permanente à la croisée des chemins *Education Permanente – Une Confrontation Internationale d'Experiences* AFEC March: 28-9

UIA (1976) *Seminar on Integration of Educational and Community Facilities, Athens, 2-6 October 1976* The Technical Chamber of Greece: Athens

Visalberghi, A (1973) *Education and Division of Labour* Martinus Nijhoff: The Hague

Yugoslav Survey (1978) *The Educational Reform in Yugoslavia*

Note
The author would like to emphasize that the views expressed in this article are his own, and not necessarily those of UNESCO.

14. Lifelong basic education for the 'absolute poor' in Africa

Marjorie Mbilinyi

Summary: This chapter presents a detailed analysis of the form and content of Lifelong Basic Education Reform (LBER) presently being promoted specifically for the 'absolute poor' in Africa. A critique of LBER is developed which sets the reform in the context of African under-developed economies. By exploring the LBER critique of schooling systems, and its own programme, it is possible to identify the underlying problem which LBER cannot adequately confront or resolve. This is the growing impoverishment of peasants, which forces them to seek alternative means of subsistence in wage labour or in informal occupations. Since schooling remains the gateway to wage labour occupations, the tremendous expansion in schooling is thereby explainable.

It is argued that LBER has risen in response to schooling expansion and growing peasant impoverishment, in order to create a differentiated and dual education system which would contribute to the social control of the masses in the poorest countries of Africa and elsewhere. The development of an alternative education reform movement in Africa is identified, which provides the peasants and workers with the skills, knowledge and consciousness necessary to engage in the struggle for national liberation and socialist revolution.

Introduction

The aim of this chapter is to analyse and explain the increased demands for more education and the form these demands have taken, arising from two opposing social forces. On the one hand, peasants and workers in the independent African countries are demanding more education at all levels of the formal schooling pyramid, and they are demanding education of a particular content and 'payoff'. On the other hand, the different international agencies representing the interests of global capital, as well as the majority of African governments, are confronting these demands with programmes for universal lifelong basic education. The contention of this chapter is that the kinds of education being demanded by these two different social forces are not the same, and that this struggle (over what *kind* of lifelong education) is a fundamental aspect of the class struggles in Africa today against imperialism and for socialism.

Within the worldwide context, there are different concepts of lifelong education which correspond to different ideological and material conditions. In the *advanced capitalist countries*, lifelong education is often referred to as recurrent education, on-the-job training or adult education, and is differentiated according to the target population for which it has been designed. Workers participate in training and adult education programmes intended to increase their productivity and adaptability to the constant technological changes in the labour process. The new petty bourgeois or middle classes are caught in a fundamental transformation of their work, often referred to as the proletarianization of white-collar work, which is related to de-skilling and the growing obsolescence of certain skilled or supervisory functions and tasks and the development of new ones. This helps to explain the urgency with which 'recurrent education' programmes are being promoted specifically for the middle classes, related to 'mid-career' changes in occupation, the use of leisure time, the development of hobbies and study programmes to offset the alienation of the workplace. Greater adapatability to changes in the labour processes, as well as the development of new skills, is one goal of lifelong education oriented to the middle classes. Whether for the working class or the middle classes, lifelong education has developed to promote greater productivity through both skills training and ideological control, in order to enrich capitalists.

In *under-developed capitalist countries*, on the other hand, lifelong education reform sponsored by international agencies and the governments concerned is referred to as non-formal, basic, adult or workers' education, or as a work-oriented, functional literacy programme. The target population in the poorest under-developed countries is predominantly rural peasants, although on-the-job training and education programmes for workers are also important. The nature and goals of such programmes are analysed in detail in Section II. Lifelong education for peasants arises out of growing rural impoverishment and accompanying demands of peasants for a higher standard of living and the means to attain it, education being one means with wage labour the ultimate goal. The *lifelong basic education programmes* have arisen to counter such demands and to provide basic manual vocational skills and changes in attitude, ie ideological control.

Lifelong education programmes in the industrialized and under-developed capitalist countries are conceptualized as *lifelong education reform for capitalist exploitation*. Alternatively and contradictorily, *lifelong education for socialist revolution and reconstruction* has developed in the context of national liberation and class struggle in capitalist *and* socialist countries, its form and content depending on the specitic historical material conditions of each country. Basic skills and *scientific and technological knowledge* are an important aspect of these programmes, not only to increase productivity through the development of the productive forces, but also integrally related to transformation in the social relations of the education institution. Hence, the ideological aspect includes the destruction of capitalist, and the promotion of socialist, attitudes and expectations. The goal is therefore *not* adaptability to capitalist social relations but rather the struggle against them. Moreover, and most important, lifelong education for socialist revolution and reconstruction arises *as an integral part of* overall struggles of the producer classes led by the working class to seize and maintain control of the state in order to ensure dominance in production and in ideology. It should therefore be clear that these two forms of lifelong education — lifelong education reform for capitalist exploitation and lifelong education for socialist revolution and reconstruction — are diametrically opposed to each other.

Section II analyses the concept of lifelong education for capitalist exploitation which is being promoted for the 'absolute poor' in underdeveloped countries generally and in Africa in particular. Section III explains the origins of lifelong education in terms of contradictions inherent in the political economy of these countries as well as in their educational systems. Lifelong education for socialist revolution and reconstruction is briefly discussed in Section IV, drawing on the historical experience of the struggles for socialist education in Tanzania and elsewhere.

Lifelong basic education reform

A great deal of confusion arises in the literature about the nature of lifelong education, its aims, structure and content and whose interests it is serving. This confusion arises because of failure to distinguish between the two forms of lifelong education, and because of ignoring the different social contexts in which lifelong education policy has emerged.

There is a need to be more specific in our analysis of education, taking into account the nature of each society, its economic, political and ideological aspects and the struggles which develop within it. At the same time, it is important to set the analysis of education in its wider context, given the reality of the capitalist global economy. The processes of internationalized production and trade integrate the economies of underdeveloped African nations with those of the advanced capitalist world. The internationalization of educational reform accompanies the development of a global capitalist economy.

Hence, side by side with the need for more specific analysis, there is also the need to abstract out and generalize about the problem posed by lifelong education reform as designed for the absolute poor in African countries. Radical education reforms *in appearance* have been developed by international agencies. The World Bank has been closely identified with the policy of lifelong basic education reform for its target population of the 'absolute poor' (World Bank, 1974). The countries categorized as the poorest in Africa (including Tanzania) share certain characteristics:

1. The vast majority of the total adult population are rural peasants, and a small to miniscule proportion are engaged in industrial wage labour.
2. There is great disparity in overall economic development by region and between urban and rural areas.

3. The average *per capita* income is strikingly low; when the range of incomes is considered, a very wide gap is found between the incomes of the middle class and the producer classes.
4. The majority of poor peasants (as compared to rich or kulak peasants) are increasingly *unable* to subsist with the means of production (land and/or cattle, implements of production, finance) at their disposal, and have had to be fed through famine relief and other state-sponsored programmes, often financed by international agencies who have also provided food products directly to such programmes.

Schooling in Africa

The schooling structure in all of these countries is hierarchical and pyramid-shaped, in similar and different ways from that of advanced capitalist countries (Bowles and Gintis, 1976). First of all, in nearly all African countries (Tanzania being one exception where universal primary education has nearly been achieved) half or more of the school-age population never enter even the first standard of primary/elementary school. A relatively large proportion drop out during the primary grades, and after primary/elementary education, a very small proportion go on to secondary and higher education. Hence, the schooling system resembles Figure 1 more than an actual pyramid. In some West African countries like Nigeria and Ghana, the schooling system has expanded such that the first level includes the equivalent of junior secondary education, whereas in East Africa, the first level refers to seven years of primary education. In general those who drop out or are structurally rejected by the schooling system at the base level (primary/junior secondary) do not secure industrial wage labour, and must subsist either through agricultural production as smallholder peasants or seasonal farm labourers, or through work in the 'informal' sector as petty traders, prostitutes, apprentice craftsmen (such

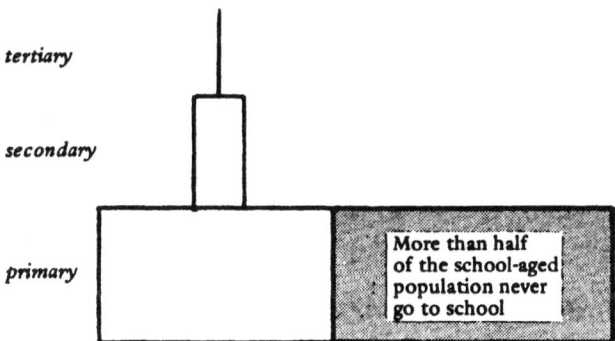

Figure 1 *The Schooling System in Africa*

as under-the-tree mechanics) and the like.

Access to primary and post-primary levels of schooling has been found to be determined by regional, class and urban/rural location. Children of poor peasants have the least access to schooling at all levels — partly because of their inability to pay school costs, partly because the opportunity involves 'freeing' the labour of children from agriculture production to go to school (Mbilinyi, in press; Court and Ghai, 1976).

Final examinations are the basis for promotion in the school system, acquisition of certificates and wage labour. The examinations tend to be paper-and-pencil, 'bookish' in nature, measuring rote memory more than problem-solving, discovery or critical thinking, and structured deliberately to compare and contrast individual performance in order to select a small number of 'top' performers. Given the reliance on examinations for selection purposes, they have a strong backwash effect on the content and social relations of schooling at lower levels.

The children of the bourgeois and petty bourgeois classes tend to perform better than those of the peasants and working class, both in meeting everyday demands of the classroom as well as in the final examinations. They are at a distinct advantage because of the material and human resources found at home, including access to the language used as the medium of instruction, which generally is not the home dialect. Moreover, schools tend to recruit children predominantly from one class partly through location and the operation of differential school costs. They have differential resources in terms of qualified teachers, textbooks and other teaching materials, and semi-permanent buildings. Permanent buildings are crucial during the lengthy rainy and cold seasons of the year — those who say otherwise have neither lived nor worked under a leaky grass roof with non-insulated, dripping wet and muddy walls. An important complex of ideological factors also contribute to explain differential performance. Bourgeois/petty bourgeois children are encouraged and expected to 'pass' by teachers and parents and thereby enter the class of origin or move upwards. 'Low-performer' children of such backgrounds are mobilized by teachers to succeed. The schooling structure and material constraints which teachers face within the classroom (eg 45 to 90 or more children per class, insufficient books and equipment, a rote-memory exam system based on a centrally determined syllabus) condition teachers to single out the most-likely-to-succeed students for special attention; they discourage the efforts of other students to win the attention of the teacher or to succeed in fulfilling school demands. A large proportion of working class and peasant students give up on school learning as a result of these factors, which helps to explain the growing phenomenon of school-leaver illiteracy in Africa.

The critique of schooling by the Lifelong Basic Education Reformers and a counter-critique

This is the schooling system now under attack by the Lifelong Basic Education Reformers (LBER) for being ill-suited to the needs of the rural areas where the majority of the poor reside. What are the arguments given against schooling (Coombs, 1969; Coombs *et al*, 1973; Coombs and Ahmed, 1974; and World Bank, 1974)? It is bookish and irrelevant to the needs of peasants, inegalitarian, and promotes expectations for upward mobility in the schooling system and class structure which are not fulfilled, leading to frustration and conflict. Students are no longer 'adaptive' at school and at the workplace (Coombs, 1969). The reformers also argue that universal primary education is impossible to achieve in the poor under-developed countries because of the resource demands (eg qualified teachers and other personnel, teaching materials and equipment, buildings). The most alarming issue, however, appears to be the rapid expansion in primary schooling due to popular demand, and the accompanying ever-growing demand for *more* and *better* education (Coombs, 1969).

At the same time, little or no attention is given in the LBER critique to the authoritarian relationship between teacher and student, symbolized by the prevalence of caning as the 'reinforcement device' most relied upon at primary and secondary school, and the basic cognitive and attitudinal outcomes of the school learning process. Cognitive outcomes include rote memory and non-critical, non-creative, non-problem-solving thought; attitudinal outcomes include individualism, competition based on self-orientation and invalidation through the constant experience of failure for all but a minority.

Lifelong Basic Education Reform (LBER) has three related dimensions:

1. An alternative education system for adults and children who did not go or are not going to school, or have dropped out prior to the acquisition of certain basic skills and personality traits.
2. An alternative, second-chance education programme for those who were structurally rejected by the schooling system and thereby blocked from receiving the necessary if not sufficient certification to acquire wage labour.
3. Reform of the schooling system itself at the level of mass education, which includes primary/elementary schooling and adult education.

These reforms are often an integral part of 'rural development packages' which combine social services and production inputs. The most commonly stated objective of LBER is to increase peasant productivity, which is *then* related to bettering the economic and social well-being of the individual producers and the development of the country as a whole. Likewise, the definition of rural development is the increased skill and productivity of farmers, craftsmen and small entrepreneurs (Coombs and Ahmed, 1974).

The generalization which follows about the form and content of LBER represents a simplification of the multitudinous programmes under way in

Africa and elsewhere in under-developed countries. (Sheffield, 1976, provides an exhaustive list; in particular, Coombs and Ahmed, 1974; Coombs *et al*, 1973; Grandstaff, 1978; Sheffield and Diejomaoh, 1972; World Bank, 1974.) It is necessary, however, to abstract from these programmes and the literature the general trends in order to make sense of them, to clarify the characteristics which are common, and to explain the LBER movement itself. In this endeavour, the critique of the reform from 'the right' — the so-called traditionalists in education — is often as instructive as the material produced by the reformers in bringing out the confusion and inherent contradictions integral to LBER (for example, Oxenham, 1976; Simkins, 1978; Williams, 1976). The ultimate conclusions differ, however, in that I am arguing the necessity and possibility of reform of schooling, but in an entirely different direction.

The most salient characteristic of LBER is that it leads to a differentiated curriculum set within the context of a dual structure of education. The present schooling *structure* is retained, such that a small minority receive post-elementary education, whereas, for the majority, elementary 'basic' education is terminal. Curriculum reform of a radical nature is aimed at the elementary and adult education levels, that is, *mass education*, whereas the topmost levels are left intact.

The curriculum basically includes the content of knowledge, how it is organized, and the instructional and evaluation strategies used to achieve and monitor it. (*See* Bernbaum, 1977; Sharp and Green, 1975; Levitas, 1974; Young, 1971 for analyses of curriculum change.) Of all these aspects of curriculum, however, change is primarily demanded of content, and to a limited extent, instructional strategies. The content is defined by the famous 'minimum essential learning needs' (Coombs *et al*, 1973: 14) as follows:

1. Positive attitudes toward co-operation, work, community and national development, further learning.
2. Functional literacy and numeracy.
3. Scientific outlook with reference to health, agriculture, etc . . .
4. Functional knowledge and skills for raising a family and household operation.
5. Functional knowledge and skills for earning a living.
6. Functional knowledge and skills for civic participation.

These objectives are to be achieved through instruction which includes practical out-of-the-classroom activity side-by-side with normal classroom routine. The content is primarily rural-oriented, related to the work of a smallholder peasant producer.

The concept of *minimal* is associated with the concept of *terminal* education — the minimal number of skills that everyone ought to have — a few will, of course, get something different, something more. It is also argued that the amount of resources necessary to achieve such objectives is less than that normally found in the school system. LBER questions the need for qualified teachers, permanent school buildings, well-stocked school equipment and teaching materials — including textbooks for teachers and students. A large number of recent research reports sponsored by the World Bank and others employ the 'production function' to investigate the factors most often associated with school performance. Their findings tend to reinforce the argument being put forward, that since any one of these factors *singly* does not contribute a significant amount of variance in school-based tests of performance, they are therefore non-essential (Alexander and Simmons, 1975).

For example, the report *Education, Poverty and Development* (Simmons, 1974) is one of the more thorough and critical analyses of education in under-developed countries using the production function. Nonetheless, Simmons develops a technicist conception of the problem of schooling and school performance which is conditioned by the need to 'fit' the analysis into a quantitative mathematical model. Lifetime earnings is the dependent variable and is used as the basis for the rate-of-return analysis. The so-called independent variables are quantified and used as if they *were* independent of each other and linear in nature. The use of a continuous linear scale for differentiated incomes hides the reality of the exploitation relations between capitalists and the workers and peasants.

The whole thrust of the analysis is the question of how to improve the *effectiveness* and *efficiency* of the investment in 'human capital'. Effectiveness refers to the minimal *amount* of education necessary to achieve functional skills. Efficiency explores the possibilities of *reducing costs* of education at the same time. The *kinds* of skills to be trained are to be determined by *manpower needs of employers*.

The critique of Jenck's *Inequality* and the quantified survey approach used to explore the complex question of school policy and student performance in the United States is applicable with respect to the under-developed world as well (*Harvard Education Review*, 1973; Bowles, 1977; Carnoy, 1975; Mbilinyi, 1977). Moreover, the basic assumptions upon which such procedures are based are even less appropriate in conditions of stark poverty co-existing with enormous wealth, where no common *lingua franca* exists, where there are gross discrepancies in resources available and used across region, urban-rural and school location, and between illiterate peasants and workers and the university-educated middle class. Assumptions such as full resource utilization which underlie such procedures therefore do not apply.

Given the policy orientation of such research, it directly legitimizes the measures being taken in the name of LBER to provide an even cheaper low-cost education programme for the peasants and workers than before. The impact of LBER is conditioned by the perpetuation of the examination-based selection system tied to the deformed pyramid structure. Second-rate cheap mass education programmes, which are explicitly terminal and geared for peasants and workers, are thereby promoted side by side with a well-endowed school system serving the petty bourgeoisie.

The analysis above encompasses the first and third dimensions of LBER, an alternative education system for the under- and un-schooled, including adults and children, and school reform at the elementary level. The programmes for primary school leavers, the second dimension, share a similar orientation towards the reproduction of manual vocational skills. The skills and knowledge taught are stratified and differentiated like the school pyramid. School costs, resources available, the kind of certification acquired, and the *value* of the knowledge acquired, all vary. On the one hand, there is a proliferation of cheap, practical, one to two year courses in rural areas in village artisan skills like carpentry and masonry for boys, domestic science for girls. These courses usually lack adequately trained teachers, materials, and certification, and are explicitly geared *not* towards further training or wage labour but rather towards smallholder peasant production. The skills acquired appear less important than the 'cooling out' of school leavers' expectations for further education and employability in wage labour. On the other hand, there is a much smaller number of urban courses in industrial skills, sometimes built into government-sponsored apprenticeship schemes, which lead to grade tests and immediate employment in wage labour.

The rural artisan programmes are beset by demands to provide similar industrial skills and grade testing. Hence, the reformers' concern about the people's insistence to have more education of a nature relevant to employment in wage labour. This is *not* the concept of relevance espoused by LBER, which is instead preparation to be a peasant producer within the context of *present* exploitative social relations.

The contradictory nature of LBER

LBER is riddled with contradictions which are partly due to the technicist theoretical framework underlying its analysis of schooling and work. Faced with the phenomena outlined earlier such as the school leaver problem *and* growing school expansion, technical solutions are sought. By orienting curriculum content towards rural manual vocational skills, and using examination devices to ensure the terminality of mass education, it is assumed that 'attitudes' will change and people will adapt to being poor peasant producers. Moreover, increased productivity in peasant production will be achieved by this vocationalization process. Experience has shown thus far, however, that such technical solutions fail to induce acceptance of a minimal terminal education and adaptation to the poverty of peasant production (Mbilinyi, 1979a). The growing phenomenon of school leaver functional illiteracy illustrates the failure even to attain minimal basic skills (UNDP, 1976). Hence the alarm over rising school costs and the 'inefficiency' of schooling accompanied by the 'social turmoil' aroused by the demands of school leavers for more education and wage labour employment (Dag Hammarskjold Foundation, 1974). As Coombs puts it, 'universal (mass) education is a "white elephant" which later will eat the *recipient* (sic) out of the house and home' (Coombs, 1969: 131).

School education has a dynamic of its own, such that the more it is expanded, the greater the demand for it at all levels. The phenomenon of inflation applies. That is, education expansion alone does *not* alter social relations of exploitation nor unequal opportunity in education (Karabel, 1972). Nevertheless, as universal mass education is achieved, there is increasing pressure on the bottleneck(s) in the school structure to open up. The differential payoffs of different kinds of certification become increasingly visible and difficult to legitimize. This necessitates the promotion of a differentiated curriculum at primary and secondary level, plus growing 'scientification' of the selection examinations.

Reformers to the contrary, peasants and workers have eagerly accepted innovations which appear to have visible material benefits. Indeed, LBER is *not* responsible for initiating the many different programmes being referred to. On the contrary, educational expansion *precedes* LBER and is the product of the efforts and demands of peasants and workers in the rural areas. LBER is a desperate effort after the fact to systematize and redirect the ongoing 'people's expansion' of schools.

Hence, the web of inconsistencies which ensnare LBER reformers. The conclusion of the 1974 Dag Hammarskjold 'Seminar on Education and Training and Alternatives in Education in African Countries' is illustrative. For example, schooling is correctly criticized for promoting passivity and dependence, and suppressing creativity and initiative. At the same time, the report deplores the people's insistence on building more schools, demanding more places in higher education and more wage labour employment. Such insistence and the efforts made to realize them in fact reveal the initiative, determination and independence of the people.

LBER on the one hand arises to equalize educational opportunity, and on the other hand, actually strengthens the dual structure of education. The large diversity of programmes is praised for providing greater flexibility, local relevance and local participation but the trend is actually towards greater centralization, rationalization and rigidity as 'non-formal' programmes become incorporated into the schooling network of control. The demand for more local participation is denied again by the increasingly hierarchical, specialized and technicized function related to LBER programmes, typified by the new expertise of non-formal/adult education. The aim of fostering certain basic minimal skills is contradicted by the *diminishing* resources allocated per student in mass education.

The increasing shift onto peasants and workers of the development and recurrent costs of education is indicated by the reliance on self-help labour to build and maintain schools and teacher housing, school fees, students' own provision of books and other materials, and even productive inputs like seeds and hoes, plus the opportunity costs of releasing children's labour from farm production to go to school.

This form of local self-reliance is offset, however, by growing dependence on international funding agencies to finance LBER. Indeed, the funding is often geared to the training and support of national LBER reports, and does not flow directly into the education programmes themselves. Instead, a proliferation of curriculum developers, evaluators, inspectors and managers are trained within a technicist framework to operate such programmes.

Finally, despite all the production function researches claiming that cutting school costs will not hamper school objectives, we find a growing number of illiterate school leavers, and adult education drop-outs. The enthusiasm with which educational expansion is supported by the people indicates that inadequate home interest in school is not the cause. Rather, *inadequate* and *unequal* school resources *and* home resources combined with the structure of schooling and the limited and unequal opportunities for higher education and wage labour employment condition poor student performance. The value of schooling as the means to escape the poverty and drudgery of peasant production persists.

Raised literacy rates have rarely kept up with increased rates of exploitation of peasants in Africa. The argument that exploitation is due to illiteracy, and its obverse, that *literacy* would liberate the poor is thereby stood on its head (Dag Hammarskjold Foundation, 1974). Indeed, LBER contributes to reproducing the conditions which foster exploitation. This is clearly revealed by the following conceptualization of the 'new deal' in LBER, which means 'removing any *sense* of inferiority or shame for what you are' (Dag Hammarskjold Foundation, 1974: 17, *emphasis added*). The underlying relations of exploitation are not challenged or destroyed but rather, the peasant or worker is supposed to adapt to them. As the LBER literature documents, peasants and workers continue to resist and reject the adaptive aspects of LBER. Nevertheless, LBER has permeated the national education policies of most African governments.

Impoverishment of peasants

What underlies the struggles in schooling and schooling reform outlined above? Educational expansion has developed in the context of a continuous primitive accumulation process in the countryside. Peasants are less and less able to maintain themselves with the land, cattle and other means of subsistence at their disposal.

The 'subsistence budget' of necessary maintenance needs has risen, partly due to the process of capitalist commoditization in agriculture production, whereby inputs are cash-based and more costly in terms of labour demand. Moreover, with uneven development between urban and rural areas, peasants have begun to expect and demand the kinds of social services such as medical dispensaries, water supply and schools as well as commodities like sugar and tea, *and* good clothes, radios, etc which were not formerly a part of the subsistence basket. Hence a household of elder, wives, grown and young children must work much harder merely to maintain themselves at a minimal subsistence level. In absolute and relative terms, peasants are often experiencing a lower subsistence level than before, due to the above factors plus soil erosion and other results of labour intensification.

Elements of pre-capitalist modes of production are continually being eroded at the same time. For example, women and young people in general resist the relations of subordination identified with 'traditional' lineage social relations and seek alternate means of subsistence. Traditionally, land, cattle and the rest, are controlled by male elders who allocate the labour of women and youth in household production and control the labour product as well. Such oppressive relations are even more difficult to sustain when bare subsistence is problematic (Bryceson and Mbilinyi, 1978; Mbilinyi, 1979b). The growing overall peasant impoverishment referred to above plus the search for an *independent* means of subsistence explain the 'insistence' of peasants on searching for wage labour employment or else informal work including prostitution, petty trade, and beer brewing.

The significance of schooling as a means of acquiring wage labour is also understandable in such a context. As schooling at all levels expands, contradictions increase, in that the productive forces are unable to absorb and utilize all the potential workers who have participated in schooling (Keith, 1975). On the one hand, the 'soil' rejects the peasants, especially youth and women who do not have independent access to the means of production. On the other hand, such under-developed economies are not sufficiently industrialized to absorb this surplus labour.

LBER has developed as one effort to resolve such contradictions, and must be related to rural development programmes geared to increase labour intensification and labour productivity of peasants. Right now in agriculture-based economies like Tanzania, it becomes vital for capital to keep the peasants on the land and increase their capacity to produce more efficiently, using less labour and making labour inputs more cost-effective. In this way, peasants will produce more of the raw materials like cotton demanded by productive capital, and more of the food necessary to maintain themselves at the same time. To achieve increased labour intensification and productivity, greater social control of peasants is required and schooling becomes a major instrument of mass social control. More than the specific skills to be acquired, schooling represents the indoctrination of submissiveness, obedience, punctuality, apathy and external orientation required to fit into bureaucratic social relations at the workplace of the village as of the factory. Curriculum reform becomes vital to ensure that such indoctrination occurs; and to correct the dangers of an over-educated and resistant labour force.

Post-primary schooling then becomes the gateway to wage labour employment, guarded by ever more 'scientific' testing apparatus. The demands for greater efficiency and effectiveness in education are a part of the rationalization and centralization process in mass education on an international scale.

On the one hand, LBER is a response to peasant demands for more schooling at all levels. On the other hand, as elementary and adult education expands under the LBER policy, the demand for post-elementary schooling *and* wage labour will grow, in spite of curriculum reform. As noted above, such demands are not caused by schooling curricula but rather by the primitive accumulation process in the countryside. Rural development programmes established to offset peasant impoverishment have thus far failed, in that they are based on a technical understanding of the problems and therefore present technical solutions. For example, peasants may adopt modern farm practices to grow cotton, but so long as the price received in the international capitalist market remains too low to subsist on, poverty remains or increases due to debt. Only the transformation of underlying imperialist social relations and the struggle for socialism can resolve such contradictions.

Lifelong Education for National Liberation and Socialist Revolution (LENLSR)

What therefore *appears* to be 'radical structural reform' is rather a reflection of the capitalist struggle to control the peasants and working class in the under-developed countries in the context of growing impoverishment and heightened class struggle. Struggles over lifelong education reform reveal that global capitalism and its agents are not omniscient. LBER has arisen out of class struggles in schooling *and* in production. The form it has taken partly reflects mass demands for a certain kind of schooling. Mass resistance to aspects of LBER which are not in their interests and the consequences of such resistance clarify the dialectical nature of education reform.

What kind of schooling reform is necessary to create Lifelong Education for National Liberation and Socialist Revolution (LENLSR)?

1. It is in the interests of peasants and workers to demand a 'universal' curriculum, *not* differentiated and *not* second-rate. This does not ignore the importance of practical and local relevance, but such relevance is a *part* of the universal curriculum and is *not* an end in itself.
2. Literacy *is* a necessary weapon for the liberation of the masses. Recent World Bank efforts to deflect energies from achieving mass literacy and *replacing* it with the use of mass communication systems like the radio must be rejected (Jamison and McAnany, 1978; Allen and Anzalone, 1978).
3. Universal schooling represents the most efficient and effective means of advancing the skills, knowledge and consciousness of the masses — de-schooling is no answer.
4. Literacy is only a first, though a necessary, step towards the development of the (human) productive forces *and* the class consciousness and understanding necessary to engage in the struggle against imperialism. Hence, adult education begins with universal literacy and then should go on to universal schooling, and finally, the universalization of the university.
5. Mass manual vocational skills are no basis for development, and

instead, emphasis must be placed on science and technology in mass education, in line with a policy of basic industrialization.
6. Social relations in the school must be developed which enhance co-operation, group effort and group solidarity, which are necessary attributes for the anti-imperialism struggles ahead. Likewise, teaching techniques which foster creativity, critical thinking, self-confidence and problem-solving must replace the neo-colonial authoritarian techniques of today.
7. Mental and manual work must be *united* through a process of combining production with training, scientific experimentation and problem-solving.
8. In order for such goals to be achieved, teachers require a supportive system of on-the-job training: formative evaluation which emphasizes such changes; teaching materials which have, built into them, the kinds of group process and problem-solving tasks desired, and the new knowledge to be learned and shared by both students and teachers. Schools in turn require an ever more qualified teaching force to achieve such school objectives.
9. Selection for post-elementary levels of education should be based on a combination of factors, to include the school's continuous assessment, some form of evaluation tests plus work performance and local recommendation, eg sponsorship by one's own village.
10. Selection for post-elementary education of different kinds can then include adult learners as well as youth; so-called non-formal or out-of-school programmes can thus become organically a part of the overall education system.
11. To be successful, schooling reform must be structurally integrated to total mass mobilization. For example, a literacy campaign becomes a massive *political* campaign in which many different cadres and mass organizations participate, as in the 1961 Cuban literacy campaign (Kozol, 1978; Lorenzetto and Neijs, 1968).
12. It must be recognized that although schooling is a *necessary* instrument for the liberation of the masses, political struggle to seize command of the national economy and the state is ultimately the *sole* means of liberation. Participation in this struggle is *the* education for liberation of the peasants and workers in Africa.

There is a growing number of programmes in Africa which combine education and production, research and action in a combined process, to be referred to here as *Lifelong Education for National Liberation and Socialist Revolution (LENLSR)*. Often categorized as *participatory research*, what distinguishes LENLSR is its political position in solidarity with the united struggles of peasants and workers to destroy imperialism in Africa and to build socialism. Working within a historical materialist perspective, LENLSR engages in concrete investigation and active struggle which combines the knowledge of intellectuals with that of peasants and workers. Immediate short-term material solutions to concrete problems are sought and implemented as a part of LENLSR. In the process, there is growing clarity about the long-term revolutionary goals and the struggles ahead (*Participatory Research Approach in Africa*, 1979; Christian Council of Tanzania, 1976 and 1977; Community Development Trust Fund, 1977; Swantz *et al*, 1977; Dag Hammaskjold Foundation, 1978).

Appropriate technology in grain storage

One such programme is the grain storage project which took place in an Ujamaa village situated near Morogoro in central Tanzania (CDTF, 1977). It will be useful in conclusion to describe the project briefly in order to raise the issues in this chapter in concrete form.

It must first be noted that Tanzania continues its struggle for national liberation and socialist revolution. Its economy remains an integral part of the international capitalist economy, and the majority of its people are suffering from the exploitation and peasant impoverishment noted above. One of the most common short term material problems is that of grain storage. Vital grains are attacked by rodents and insects, and the loss often equals half or more of an annual crop. A team of national and international experts and peasants of the target village identified grain storage as an important problem to investigate and resolve.

The team began by pursuing the historical background to the problem. They discovered that grain storage was a critical problem for *poor* peasants in the village, but not for the richer peasants. It became necessary to create two prototypes of grain storage, an effective type within the resources available to poor peasants and another more costly type. The prototypes were developed through investigation and experimentation with traditional and modern technology. Experiments were also conducted with insecticides at the village primary school, in order to determine the correct proportion and type of insecticide to use. Villagers shared the results of this work with the teachers and pupils, with both the pupils and adult villagers developing very high motivation to learn in the process.

Records were kept by some of the peasant participants of insecticide use. Village members were contacted regularly to contribute information about insecticide purchase, use, results, and evaluation. Insecticides were used successfully by many of the villagers, and the prototype grain storage units were also adopted and built. As a result of the project several of the village peasants lectured on grain storage systems at the Faculty of Agriculture of the University of Dar-es-Salaam at Morogoro. The significance of this is illustrated by the undergraduate response to their guest lecturers. The students refused to believe they had been taught by illiterate and semi-literate peasants, and challenged them as impostors. Indeed, it was a significant event to have university students take notes vigorously from peasant lecturers!

Several aspects of the project stand out. It was geared to a concrete, immediate and high priority problem from the point of view of poor peasants. The resolution of the problem was to be of immediate and material benefit. Local level obstacles such as lack of certain materials and bureaucratic red-tape were successfully overcome. Both traditional and modern knowledge of science and technology were found useful in a material way (not romanticism about the past). Understanding of basic principles of scientific investigation as well as the science and technology relevant to grain storage was learned in the process. More than that, participants also learned how to organize themselves to conquer specific problems with resources at hand. In doing so, they also were forced to recognize the limits to struggles confined at the local level.

Participation in every aspect of the programme became an educational process. Moreover, the primary school was incorporated as a *part* of the total village programme. Here we see the concept of education widened to include development projects which may never carry the labels 'education' or 'school'. At the same time, *false* antagonism between the school and the overall village project was avoided. At the village level, it was possible to solve the grain storage problem, but the exploitative relations which impoverish the peasant were *not* destroyed by this kind of limited action. Nevertheless, it is through participation in such forms of combined production and training, investigation and action, within the methodological approach of historical materialism, that peasants begin to clarify the nature of the underlying reality which must be transformed and their necessary role in that revolutionary process.

References

Alexander, L and Simmons, J (1975) The determinants of school achievement in developing countries: the educational production function IBRD Staff Working Paper No 201: Washington, DC

Allen, D W and Anzalone, S (1978) Learning by radio: the first step to literacy *Prospects* 8 2: 202-10

Bernbaum, G (1977) *Knowledge and Ideology in the Sociology of Education* Macmillan: London

Bowles, S (1977) Unequal education and the reproduction of the hierarchical division of labor Paper presented to the Bellagio Conference on Social Science Research and Education Effectiveness (25-29 July)

Bowles, S and Gintis, H (1976) *Schooling in Capitalist America* Basic Books: New York

Bryceson, D F and Mbilinyi, M J (1978) The changing role of women in production: from peasants to proletarians Paper presented to the Sussex Conference on Women and Development

Carnoy, M (1975) Can educational policy equalize income distribution in Latin America? ILO Working Paper: Geneva

Christian Council of Tanzania (1976) *Elimu ya Ufundi Vijijini Tanzania (Vocational Education in Rural Villages of Tanzania)* Kicheba Report: Dar es Salaam

Christian Council of Tanzania (1977) *Elimu ya Ufundi Vijijini Tanzania, Maoni, Mapendekezo na Utekelezaji* Tabora Report: Dar es Salaam

Community Development Trust Fund (CDTF) (1977) *Appropriate Technology in Grain Storage* Dar es Salaam

Coombs, P H (1969) *The World Education Crisis* Oxford University Press: New York

Coombs, P H et al (1973) *New Paths to Learning for Rural Children and Youth* International Council for Educational Development: New York

Coombs, P H and Ahmed, M (1974) *Attacking Rural Poverty: How Non-Formal Education Can Help* World Bank/Johns Hopkins Press: Baltimore, Md
Court, D and Ghai, Y (1976) *Education, Society and Development* Oxford University Press: London
Dag Hammarskjold Foundation (1974) Seminar on Education and Training and Alternatives in Education in African Countries: Conclusions *Development Dialogue*
Dag Hammarskjold Foundation (1978) Seminar on Educational Alternatives for Southern Africa *Development Dialogue* 2: 73-9
Grandstaff, M (1978) Non-formal education as a concept *Prospects* 8 2: 177-82
Harvard Education Review (1973) *Perspectives on Inequality* Reprint Series No 8
Jamison, D T and McAnany, E G (1978) *Radio for Education and Development* Sage Publications: Beverly Hills, Ca
Karabel, J (1972) Community colleges and social stratification *Harvard Education Review* 42 4: 521-62
Keith, S (1975) Education and dependent capitalist development: a case study of Jamaica *LACDES Quarterly* 4 2: 4-19
Kozol, J (1978) A new look at the literacy campaign in Cuba *Harvard Education Review* 48 3: 341-77
Levitas, M (1974) *Marxist Perspectives in the Sociology of Education* Routledge: London
Lorenzetto, A and Neijs, A (1968) The Cuban literacy campaign *Convergence* 1 3: 46-50
Mbilinyi, M J (1977) Inequality and underdevelopment Paper presented to the Bellagio Conference on Social Science Research and Education Effectiveness (25-29 July)
Mbilinyi, M J (1979a) Peasants' education in Tanzania *The African Review* 6 2
Mbilinyi, M J (1979b) The changing sexual division of labour and social transformation: the Shambaa case Paper presented to History Department Seminar series, University of Dar es Salaam (in press)
Mbilinyi, M J (in press) *Who Goes to School in East Africa?* East African Publications: Arusha
Mbilinyi, M J and Omari, C K (in press) *Peasant Production in Tanzania*
Oxenham, J (1976) Reflections on the 1974 education sector Working Paper *in* Williams (1976)
Participatory Research Approach (PRA) in Africa (1979) Papers to be submitted to the June Conference on PRA in Africa in Dar es Salaam and later published as proceedings
Sharp, R and Green, A (1975) *Education and Social Control: A Study in Progressive Primary Education* Routledge: London
Sheffield, J R (1976) The rediscovery of poverty: a review of aid policies in education *in* Williams (1976)
Sheffield, J and Diejomaoh, V P (1972) *Non-Formal Education in African Development* African-American Institute: New York
Simkins, T (1978) Planning non-formal education: strategies and constraints *Prospects* 8 2: 183-93
Simmons, J (1974) Education, poverty and development IBRD Bank Staff Working Paper No 188: Washington, DC
Swantz, M L et al (1977) *Jipemoyo 1* Ministry of National Culture and Youth: Dar es Salaam
UNDP (1976) *The Experimental World Literacy Programme* UNESCO: Paris
Williams, P (1976) *Prescription or Progress? A Commentary on the Education Policy of the World Bank* Institute of Education Studies in Education 3: University of London
World Bank (1974) *Education Sector Working Paper* Washington, DC
Young, M F D (1971) *Knowledge and Control* Collier-Macmillan: London

15. Education in China: a lifelong process
Peter Mauger

十 年 树 木　　10 years to grow a tree
百 年 树 人　　100 years to educate a person

Chinese proverb

Summary: This chapter describes the problems which faced China on the establishment of the People's Republic in 1949 and the necessity for education of the whole population. Governmental guidelines for education, based on the concept of education as universal, lifelong and completely politically-orientated, were developed in the liberated areas prior to 1949. During the period 1949-66, priorities were debated between mass education or selective education. Achievements in formal education were considerable; mass literacy campaigns were organized.

After the Cultural Revolution there was a clear victory for the mass line policy and the decentralization of education. School curricula were closely geared to local needs, and run on a part-work, part-study basis, achieving a combination of education with productive labour. There was selection for higher education but social and political criteria were deemed more important than educational level. The development of workers' colleges was a more technical form of higher education. The May 7 cadre schools and party schools were intended to prevent bureaucratic methods of leadership and to provide better political leadership.

The People's Liberation Army was transformed into an army of a new type, an educative as much as a military force; it had close ties with the civilian population. Spare-time education embraced workers' study groups, correspondence courses, and radio and television programmes. Changes since 1977 include more formalized education to raise standards, the reintroduction of university entrance examinations and a mass scientific movement to aid 'four modernizations'. China is still a poor country, but successes in dealing with starvation, homelessness, and drought are largely a result of mass and lifelong educational policy.

Aims and achievements, 1949-1966

When Mao Tsetung and the Communist Party established the People's Republic of China in October, 1949, they faced almost insuperable problems. Exhausted by over twenty years of bitter civil war and Japanese invasion, the country was bankrupt, its few industries in ruins, its people ragged, hungry and often homeless. The mass of the predominantly peasant population was illiterate, backward and superstitious. To establish a socialist society, to transform the economy, to give the people confidence in their power to make great changes, the whole population had to be educated — or rather re-educated, since their lives had been an education in passivity and resignation to lifelong exploitation and poverty. The education of the adult population was an even more immediate and urgent task than the education of children.

The temporary Constitution issued by the government in 1949 included broad guidelines for the development of education for the whole population:

> The culture and education of the People's Republic of China are new democratic, that is national, scientific and popular. The main tasks for raising the cultural level of the people are: training of personnel for national construction work; liquidating feudal, comprador,* Fascist ideology; and development of the ideology of serving the people . . .
> In order to meet the widespread needs of revolutionary work and national construction work, universal education shall be carried out. Middle and higher education shall be strengthened; technical education shall be stressed; the education of workers during their spare time and the education of cadres who are at their posts shall be strengthened; and revolutionary political education shall be accorded to young intellectuals and old-style intellectuals in a planned and systematic manner. (Fraser, 1965: 83)

This concept of education as universal, lifelong and completely politically-orientated reflected the experience of the Yenan period when, at the end of the Long March in 1935, the Red Army under Mao Tsetung had occupied North Shensi and had set up a Communist government. The prime necessity in those days had been to mobilize the people in the fight, first of all against Chiang Kaishek and the Kuomintang and then, from 1937, against the Japanese; Mao saw the Red Army, under the control of the Communist Party, as a political and educational as much as a military force. To defeat the enemy it was essential for them to earn the confidence and even the love of the peasants, who had learned through the ages to hate and fear the marauding, raping, looting soldiers of *any* side.

To this end they were given strict instructions; 'Do not take a single needle or piece of thread from the masses . . . return everything you borrow . . . pay for everything you damage . . . do not hit or swear at people . . . do not damage crops . . . do not take liberties with women.' The soldiers had regular discussions on the policy, strategy and tactics of the war. Western observers were astonished to see soldiers during rest periods sitting in a circle while one of their comrades taught them characters scratched in the dust. The soldiers in their turn conducted literacy campaigns among the peasants, who gradually came to accept the Red Army as a body of men they could trust.

The thirst of the peasants for education had been noted by Mao in 1927:

> The moment the power of the landlords was overthrown in the rural areas, the peasants' movement for education began. See how the peasants who hitherto detested the schools are today zealously setting up evening classes! . . . The peasants are very enthusiastic about these schools, and regard them, and only

---

* Chinese wholesalers who acted as go-betweens, between Imperialists and native merchants

them, as their own. The funds for the evening schools come from the 'public revenue from superstition', from ancestral temple funds, and from other idle public funds or property . . . The development of the peasant movement has resulted in a rapid rise in their cultural level . . . (Mao Tsetung, 1927: I, 53)

Jack Belden describes the beginnings of mass education in the areas liberated from the Kuomintang between 1946 and 1949:

The Communist solution was both simple and typical. They combined education with life. Instead of drilling the peasant in school (except in winter) the Communists began teaching him how to read by showing him characters connected with his daily life and occupation. Thus a shepherd would be taught the characters for sheep, dog, stick, grass and so on. A farmer would learn the characters for field, millet, wheat, mule and the like. The methods of teaching were also as ingenious as they were pleasant. A school child would go around at the noon recess to the homes of five or six housewives and paste on the front door, the living room table, and the kitchen stove the characters for each of these objects. While continuing to do her work, the housewife would memorize the characters. The next day, the school child would bring three new characters. Or, as I saw, a farmer ploughing in his field would put up one character on a big board at each end of the field. Thus, going back and forth all day, even his primitive mind could grasp the complex convolutions.

In village after village I have seen these clods of the soil, hitherto barred from any education, poring over lessons, trooping to the winter schools, watching rural dramatic teams perform on the threshing ground, listening to newscasts broadcast through hand megaphones, and studying the slogans painted on the walls, spelling them out in their tortured but patient way. (Belden, 1970: 116)

Thus, when the Communist government took over in 1949, the principle of mass education was already established. There were, however, fierce struggles within the Party about its implementation, indeed about the whole question of educational priorities at a time of shortage of buildings, materials and teachers. Liu Shao-chi, Party vice-chairman, took the view most often held by educationists in developing countries. Rapid industrialization and modernization of agriculture was urgent, necessitating the education of experts in every field, scientific, technological, managerial, educational. To these ends the scarce resources should be deployed in selected and selective secondary schools and universities. This view was in direct contradiction to Mao's policy of universal, mass, lifelong education.

In the event the achievements of the government in the first ten years of the People's Republic were remarkable. From 24 million children attending primary school (aged 7 to 12) in 1949, the number in 1960 had risen to 90 million — about 80 per cent of the child population in that age range. The number in middle schools of various kinds had risen from about one million to around 10 million — a significant advance, though still only some 13 per cent of youngsters between the ages of 13 and 18.

At the same time a number of mass literacy campaigns were organized. The labelling method described above by Jack Belden was introduced into many villages, and 'literacy check-points' were set up in country market places where passers-by were stopped and given a reading test. In 1956 the Party and the State Council issued a joint directive setting out the aim of wiping out illiteracy in five to seven years, and in the next year Mao edited *Socialist Upsurge in China's Countryside*, a collection of articles describing the changes taking place in agriculture and written to encourage the people 'to complete the transformation from semi-socialist to fully socialist co-operatives' and to speed up 'the socialist transformation of China's handicrafts and capitalist industry and commerce'. The vital part played by education is described in this widely-read book and, in the usual Chinese fashion, a particular place was picked out as an exemplar.

Yinta is a small town of 318 peasants, in Kansu province. Members of the agricultural co-operative were very worried because they could not read or write the accounts of the work-points on which their income was calculated. Li Mao-yuan, head of a production brigade, said: 'I myself cannot read. Who knows whether the tally-man keeps a correct record of work-points!' (Che Hung-chang, 1955: 433). The co-operative needed at least eight book-keepers and 32 tally-men, one radio monitor and four literacy school teachers — a minimum of 45 people with four to six years' schooling. But the whole township had only 32 literate people. In 1954 the 13 tally-men were still semi-literate and attending a 'quick method literacy class'. 'When registering the work-points, some wrote 15 as 105 and 8 as 18. Because of the wrong accounts disputes occurred with the members of the co-operative when work-points were counted' (Che Hung-chang, 1955: 434). Four experimental winter schools were set up in 1950, followed by crash literacy courses. The teachers were given work-points for each class hour and, as their educational level was low, the cultural and educational committee of the co-operative called them together for studies once every two weeks to exchange experiences and help to solve difficult teaching problems. In 1954 the four schools were amalgamated to form one literacy school, attended by 173 adult students.

The timetable of the literacy school classes was arranged to meet the different demands of farming in busy and slack seasons — two hours an evening before the spring sowing, then a month's vacation during the sowing period, followed by shorter lesson periods and more self (private) study. The school used nationally-produced textbooks — *Peasants' Vocabulary Textbook, Chinese Reader for Peasants* and *General Arithmetic for Workers and Peasants*. They held written tests and monthly examinations in language and arithmetic, and oral tests for political study. The *Socialist Upsurge* article goes into considerable detail about the difficulties encountered — lighting, heating, teachers' salaries, timetable clashes — and how they were overcome. For instance a different timetable was evolved for the co-operative functionaries, too busy with many meetings to join the normal classes. They were taught two characters a day and were tested twice a week. 'Wang Hsueh-lu, chairman of the first branch of the co-operative, could only read a few names before he began studying. Now he not only can read the *New Chiuchuan Daily* and the *Kansu Peasant*, but can also write simple letters. At meetings he can jot down brief notes. He was chosen model student' (Che Hung-chang, 1955: 438). At the end of a year 57 peasants could read 300 characters, 35 could read 500, and the senior class of 43, who were younger and had received some schooling previously, could read 800 characters. As a result more and more people wanted to read books and newspapers, and the practice began — still a common feature of life today — of co-operative members reading papers or listening to papers being read aloud in rest periods during field work or in their spare time in the evening.

These considerable achievements were publicized throughout China to encourage others to follow the example of Yinta township. The shortcomings were not glossed over.

> Many comrades still lack a comprehensive understanding of the political significance of the peasants' spare-time educational work in serving agricultural production and the mutual-aid and co-operative movement directly . . . Comrades working in rural areas, therefore, should know the far-reaching political significance of raising the cultural level of the peasants. (Che Hung-chang, 1955: 439)

As always in China, everything must be related to political aims: 'To teach students to read while neglecting their ideological education is an incorrect attitude.'

Literacy campaigns were also carried on in factories. A Ministry of Education decree of 1958 required factories to provide education for the workers. Large factories set up schools at all levels; smaller ones established literacy classes. Spare-time schools were set up for workers, and a western observer who visited about 38 industrial enterprises in 1966 wrote that most of them claimed to have reduced the illiteracy rate from well over 50 per cent to under 10 per cent (Richman, 1969).

There were also part-work, part-study schools; one such school is described by Rewi Alley, a New Zealander who has lived in China for many years. In 1966 he visited Wusih Diesel Engine Factory in Kiangsu province, a factory with over 3,000 workers. He found a school of 900 students, all having come as 16-year-olds from secondary school. The staff numbered 202, including teachers, cadres, technicians and workers. The curriculum included politics, mathematics, physics, Chinese language, mechanical drawing and the techniques required in the factory. Alternate weeks were spent in practical and classroom work. The factory paid for the practical work done by the students, the money being used to run the school (Alley, 1973: 551).

The great proletarian cultural revolution

Rewi Alley visited the Wusih and other part-work, part-study schools during the turmoil of the Cultural Revolution, and I must say something about this great upheaval which is so widely misunderstood in the West and is still the subject of controversy in China itself. Very briefly, the movement started with the revolt of students who considered that, although there had been an enormous increase in the scale of education at all levels, the content and methods had remained much the same as before

1949. Courses were too long, their content classically 'academic' and far-removed from the realities and the needs of the new China. Entrance examinations favoured the children of the bourgeoisie and party cadres, and there was a danger of creating a new élite who would become counter-revolutionary and in fact 'take the capitalist road'. By the middle 1960s China's socialist economy was fairly well established; the base was sound, but the cultural super-structure was still too widely influenced by capitalist ideology.

As we have seen, there had been controversy within the Communist Party itself over educational policy during the transition to socialism. Mao's policy of mass, universal education won the day in 1966, and in August the Central Committee issued the *Sixteen Articles*, urging the fullest, countrywide discussions of the implications of the Cultural Revolution; the following extracts show the guidelines which were indicated in this important document.

> Although the bourgeoisie has been overthrown, it is still trying to use the old ideas, culture, customs and habits of the exploiting classes to corrupt the masses, capture their minds and endeavour to stage a come-back. The proletariat must do just the opposite; it must meet head-on every challenge of the bourgeoisie in the ideological field and use the new ideas, culture, customs and habits of the proletariat *to change the mental outlook of the whole of society (emphasis added)* . . . It is normal for the masses to hold different views. Contention between different views is unavoidable, necessary and beneficial. In the course of normal and full debate, the masses will affirm what is right, correct what is wrong and gradually reach unanimity.
>
> The method to be used in debates is to present the facts, reason things out, and persuade through reasoning. Any method of forcing a minority holding different views to submit is impermissible. The minority should be protected, because sometimes truth is with the minority. Even if the minority is wrong, they should still be allowed to argue their case and reserve their views . . . The struggle of the proletariat against the old ideas, culture, customs and habits left over from all the old exploiting classes over thousands of years will necessarily take a very, very long time. Therefore, the cultural revolutionary groups, committees and congresses should not be temporary organizations but permanent, standing, mass organizations. They are suitable not only for colleges, schools and government and other organizations, but generally also for factories, mines, other enterprises, urban districts and villages.
>
> It is necessary to institute a system of general elections, like that of the Paris Commune, for electing members to the cultural revolutionary groups and committees and delegates to the cultural revolutionary congresses. The lists of candidates should be put forward by the revolutionary masses after full discussion, and the elections should be held after the masses have discussed the lists over and over again. (Chen, 1970: 117)

There followed a period of intense and heated discussion over every aspect of cultural life. Experiment was the order of the day; everywhere we went in 1972, for instance, we were told: 'We are in an experimental period; please give us your criticisms of what you have seen.'

An essential feature of the Cultural Revolution was decentralization. Mao's 'directives' and the Central Committee's resolutions were broadly-based; their implementation had to be worked out by the men and women in the organizations concerned, taking into account local conditions. This was necessary both because of the vast size of the country and the wide variations in climatic, geographical, economic and social conditions, and because the long drawn-out and often painful working-out was an essential part of the education of the whole population in socialist ideology.

The education of women

In old China women had no status except that of slaves or chattels, no rights over property, no rights of custody over their own children, no say in who married them. The whole structure of social relationships, including that between men and women, was underpinned by the deeply-rooted ideas of Confucianism. Women were governed by the 'Three Obediences' — obedience to the father and elder brother when young, obedience to the husband when married, and obedience to the sons when widowed.

The 1949 Constitution established the legal equality of women, and the Marriage Law of 1950 gave women the right of divorce and remarriage, and made female infanticide, concubinage, polygamy, prostitution, and buying and selling of women illegal. The Land Reform Act of 1950 gave women for the first time a legal entitlement to land. Other measures include equal pay for equal work, all jobs being formally open to women. Free contraception and abortion have liberated women from constant child-bearing.

But, as Mao said (in a conversation with André Malraux in 1958):

> Of course it was necessary to give them (women) legal equality to begin with. But from there everything remains to be done. The thought, culture and customs which brought China to where we found it must disappear and the thought, customs and culture of proletarian China must appear. The Chinese woman does not yet exist among the masses, but she is beginning to exist. And then to liberate women is not a matter of manufacturing washing machines.

In fact, of course, women have not attained full equality with men; the customs and culture of thousands of years are not so easily overthrown. But the social, economic and political position of women has advanced to an astonishing degree in a mere thirty years; women are *asserting* their right to equality, and the very considerable degree of liberation they have achieved has made it possible for them to play an increasingly important part, both as teachers and students, in the educational developments which we shall now discuss.

School management

Mao had emphasized that:

> To carry out the educational revolution, it is imperative to have the leadership of the working class and its participation, together with the revolutionary three-way alliance of the soldiers of the People's Liberation Army (PLA), students and teachers, and the activists among the workers who have resolved to carry the proletarian educational revolution through to the end. Workers' propaganda teams should remain at the schools for a long time to share the

task of 'struggle-criticism-transformation' and to perpetuate their leadership there. In the countryside, schools are to be run by the most reliable allies of the working class — the poor, lower and middle peasants. (Chen J, 1970: 155)

This call for participation by the whole working population in the educational revolution was taken up, notably by the revolutionary committee of a county in Kirin province, whose plans for education were published in the *People's Daily* in 1969 and adopted on a wide scale (*People's Daily*, 1969). The schools were to be managed by the 'poor and lower-middle peasants' (ie those who, before Liberation, had been exploited peasants rather than exploiting landlords), organized in revolutionary committees with teachers and students. These committees were responsible for appointing, dismissing and paying teachers, building and maintaining the schools and providing all equipment, and supervising and revising the curriculum.

School curriculum

The Kirin Report made definite proposals for curriculum reform. The primary courses were to be politics and language, arithmetic, revolutionary literature and art, military training and physical culture, and productive labour. The five courses in middle schools were to be politics (including modern and contemporary Chinese history), basic knowledge of agriculture (including mathematics, physics, chemistry and economic geography), revolutionary literature and art (including language), military training and physical culture, and productive labour.

Thus the curriculum was closely geared to the needs of agriculture. We must remember that China was just emerging from centuries of peasant food shortage and many periods of actual starvation for millions, and that with 20 per cent of the world's population China has under 8 per cent of the world's arable land. Mao had advised that 'teaching material should have local character. Some material on the locality and the villages should be included', and the Kirin Report echoed this: '... Aside from the teaching material compiled by the state, localities should organize workers, peasants and soldiers and revolutionary teachers and students to compile teaching material on the area as supplementary teaching material' — another instance of lay adults being drawn into the educational process.

Schools were to be run on a part-work, part-study basis, and in vacations, weekends and spare time generally 'they should participate in production' on the land, working with and being taught by the local peasants.

City schools followed a similar pattern, with students working regularly in factories or in workshops attached to the school, using obsolescent machinery from local factories and actually producing goods for sale, taught by factory workers seconded to the school for a period. Mao once said, 'Every capable person can teach', and this use of lay adults in schools is typical of modern Chinese life. Workers' propaganda teams were assigned to schools after the Cultural Revolution to prevent the re-appearance of the old 'ivory tower' or, as the Chinese call it, 'treasure pagoda' attitude to education and to maintain the correct political orientation. For the same reason old people come into the schools to tell the children about the 'bitter past'.

City and country schools alike were enjoined to 'encourage the students to investigate for themselves', and in place of the former concentration on book learning, 'open-door schooling' became the favoured method, with students spending a considerable portion of their time outside the classroom, visiting communes, factories, mines, questioning workers and peasants and reporting their findings back at school.

Nurseries and kindergartens

Political education starts even in nurseries.

> Near the end of his second year the toddler begins to see the large, colourful posters that introduce him to Mao's Thought; he first hears the stories of the heroes in simple form for a few minutes each day . . . He learns to play co-operatively and helpfully with other children, to control impulsive behaviour, to follow routines, and to participate in a rigorous outdoor life of games, races, exercises and use of playground equipment. Moral education is stimulated through songs and dances celebrating the five loves – Chairman Mao, workers-peasants-soldiers, the Communist Party, the Great Socialist Motherland, and physical labour. (Kessen, 1975: 57)

Political and moral education (and it is difficult to distinguish between the two) is continued in the kindergarten. Stories are told emphasizing the virtues of care for the community and putting the needs of others before one's own. Language lessons are used as a framework for more training; the teacher describes a situation in which children have a choice of actions, and the young pupils discuss which alternatives will best 'serve the people'.

Higher education

When universities reopened in about 1968 a new system for admission was introduced, to ensure that the students would be predominantly of working class or peasant origin. The main selection criteria were: completion of middle school education, a minimum of two years' work in a factory, on a commune or in the PLA, and a personal application endorsed by the applicants' fellow-workers after thorough discussion of their characters and their degree of social consciousness; were they applying in order to 'serve the people' better, or to 'seek fame or fortune for themselves'? This policy resulted in the proportion of worker and peasant students increasing greatly. Also, with the new emphasis on open-door schooling there was, for the first time, fairly frequent contact between working adults and university students. And, as in schools, workers and peasants occasionally taught in appropriate university and college departments.

'July 21' workers' colleges

Only a small proportion of China's youth can go to university — the present number is only around 600,000 — and the Chinese have developed other forms of further and higher education. Perhaps the most noteworthy of these is the development of 'July 21' colleges — so-called from a directive of Mao's of that date in 1968:

> It is still necessary to have universities; here I refer mainly to colleges of science and engineering. However, it is essential to shorten the length of schooling, revolutionize education, put proletarian politics in command and take the road of the Shanghai Machine Tools Plant in training technicians from among the workers. Students should be selected from among workers and peasants with practical experience, and they should return to production after a few years' study. (Mao Tsetung, 1968)

By 1976 there were 15,000 workers' colleges with a total enrolment of nearly 800,000 students. They are operated by enterprises of all sizes — factories, steel mills, mines, oilfields, railway worksites, ships on the high seas. Most courses are in engineering and allied disciplines, but some are in medicine and liberal arts. Some are full-time, some part-time, some run on a part-work, part-study basis. Those I visited in 1976 were running courses of two years' duration, with half the day spent in theoretical study and half in the various factory departments. Subjects studied included advanced mathematics, mechanics, electricity, mechanical engineering and political economy. Students are selected in the main by and from the factory workers, and the selection is by no means confined to young workers.

'Workers' colleges have shown themselves to be not only a way to meet the need for technical personnel, but to build a contingent of working class intellectuals' (*China Reconstructs*, 1975). Colleges with similar aims are being developed in the countryside, the subjects studied including agronomy, water conservation, hydrology, stock breeding and veterinary science.

Teachers at Futan University, Shanghai, told us in 1976 that the university was co-operating with July 21 colleges in several ways. For instance:

> Our micro-wave department runs education jointly with the Shanghai No 26 Wireless Radio Factory. They have formed a unified Party Branch Committee, and a leading group of three-in-one combination of teachers, workers and students. This leads both the discipline and the factory in education, scientific research and production. We mixed students of the discipline and students of the factory July 21 workers' college to accomplish the typical tasks of discipline and factory, for instance, the study of micro-wave networks. Our students go to that factory and the July 21 factory students come to the university.

The teachers told us that the university had helped some 20 factories to run July 21 workers' colleges, with an enrolment of over 1,500 students, and that there was interchange of teaching staff between the university and workers' colleges. These developments are probably not typical of China as a whole, since Shanghai is the most advanced industrial city; but, as often in China, they are being publicized as exemplars. The Futan teachers told us

> In mapping out their three-year and eight-year programmes, industrial departments under the State Council and some provinces, municipalities and autonomous regions have assigned the job of training more than half the urgently-needed new technicians to factory-run schools, especially the July 21 workers' colleges.

There is in fact an enormous variety of full-time, part-time and spare-time schools and classes springing up all over China, to speed the 'four modernizations' — agriculture, industry, national defence and science and technology. Part-work and part-study is the general practice, whether the courses last for two or three years or, for short-time specialized courses, for only a few months. As well as full-time teachers, technicians and veteran workers and peasants from factories, communes, scientific research institutes and universities are invited to give lectures. These schools are financed in different ways: factory-run schools are self-financed, peasants' colleges are state-subsidized.

May 7 cadre schools

These schools stem from another of Mao's 'directives' (7 May 1966). He warned that some people within the Party might use their positions to gain privileges for themselves and in time form a new bourgeois element endangering the development of socialism. All cadres, Party or non-Party, were subject to the temptation not only of using their positions for corrupt ends, but also of becoming complacent, bureaucratic and intolerant. Therefore all cadres should receive re-education; and re-education, in Chinese terms, always means taking part in basic production, collective labour side-by-side with the 'broad masses', and at the same time studying Marxism/Leninism/Mao Tsetung Thought.

May 7 cadre schools have sprung up all over the country since late 1968. They are generally set up in the more unproductive parts of the countryside so that the students, while re-educating themselves, take part in land reclamation. A cadre is anyone who holds a responsible position in Party, government or local organizations, and as such makes decisions affecting others. The Chinese define responsibility widely; shorthand typists and switchboard operators, for instance are included, as their work tends to isolate them from rank and file workers and peasants.

Courses vary in length from three months to as long as two years, and are all organized on a part-work, part-study basis. The task of the schools is:

> to train a corps of cadres armed with Marxism/Leninism/Mao Tsetung Thought who are willing to work at any level, whether or not in a leading position, who have close ties with the masses and serve the people wholeheartedly. To realize this, the cadre schools are set up in the countryside. The students study Marxism and take part in collective labour in production. They also spend a period of time in the surrounding villages learning about life there. All this

> helps them remould their world outlook and better take the stand of the labouring people. It is an important measure for consolidating the dictatorship of the proletariat and preventing revisionism. (Lin Yu-sheng, 1974)

It is intended that every male cadre under age 60 and every woman cadre under age 55 should attend, and that they should return periodically for political and physical refreshment. Cadres have to apply for a place, but are clearly expected to apply. However, there is no indication that the schools are intended in any way as corrective labour camps. Students at a school I visited near Peking in 1972 were obviously enthusiastic about the benefits they were receiving; they were fitter, they enjoyed the sense of adventure and the satisfaction of sheer hard manual work in creating a fertile farm from arid wasteland, and they were gaining an understanding of China's pressing needs in the most practical way possible. Their political studies, half of each day in the slack season and two and a half hours a day during sowing and harvest times, were more concentrated and thorough than in their normal working lives.

Party schools

There have been schools for Communist Party members since 1936. They have a different aim and role and different points of emphasis from May 7 cadre schools. To a great extent they have been allowed to lapse in recent years, but are now being revived at provincial, municipal and autonomous regional level.

> The Central Committee holds that the most important subject for Party schools at various levels is the systematic reading of works by Marx, Engels, Lenin and Stalin and by Chairman Mao, the comprehensive and accurate grasp of Marxism/Leninism/Mao Tsetung Thought as a system, the diligent study of Chairman Mao's great theory on continuing the revolution under the dictatorship of the proletariat. The reading of the original works and self-study should be the main form of study. The style of study characterized by closely integrating theory with practice should be encouraged. (Central Committee, 1977)

The People's Liberation Army

It seems odd to think of an army as a cultural and educational force, and the very idea would have been ludicrous in the old China. But, as we have seen, Mao regarded the education of the Red Army as essential for the defeat of the enemy, whether it was the Kuomintang or the Japanese. 'An army without culture is a dull-witted army' he said 'and a dull-witted army cannot defeat the enemy' (Mao Tsetung, 1944: 235).

Edgar Snow, during a visit to a Red Army unit in 1936, wrote that a Red soldier's daily duties included, when not in the front line, two hours of political lectures and discussion and two hours of character-study.

> There were three character-study groups; those who knew less than 100 characters; those who knew from 100 to 300; and those who could read and write more than 300 characters. The Reds had provided their own textbooks

(using political propaganda as materials of study) for each of these groups... Only about 20 per cent of the 1st Army Corps, I was told, was still in the *hsia-tzu* class, or 'blind men', as the Chinese call total illiterates. (Snow, 1937: 293)

We have referred earlier to the literacy campaigns among the peasants organized by the Red Army. The tradition of keeping close ties with the civilian population has persisted. An officer of the 179th Division of the PLA, which we visited while in Nanking in 1976, commented:

In war or peace we try to keep the closest ties with the people and serve them in every way possible. We help them sow and harvest, dig wells, build roads and bridges. We do household chores like collecting firewood and carrying water. Our relationship with the people is like that of fish in water; fish cannot live without water, we cannot win battles without the people. With their trust and support we can conquer the biggest difficulties and the strongest enemies.

Army doctors tour the villages to give treatment and help to train 'barefoot doctors'. Every company has linked itself with a commune production team nearby and helps the peasants with sowing, harvesting, making compost... The Division has set up five small farms which supply all the vegetables and much of the meat they consume; apart from the financial benefit to the state, 'Experience has convinced all of us that work practice is essential for the army's ideological education as a whole and in revolutionizing the thinking of each individual.'

Officers and army men spend two days a week in political study and current affairs. There are lessons on the Party's basic line, class struggle and related subjects. Private study is combined with group discussion and individual tutorials. The educational role of the PLA is illustrated by their work in the Tibet autonomous region, where illiteracy was widespread before Liberation. For instance, when a people's commune was set up in 1969 in an isolated mountain village, there was not a single literate person. A PLA company stationed nearby made desks and benches to help the village establish a school, and the army men took turns in teaching. Army units run evening classes to teach peasants and herdsmen scientific and technical knowledge, and production and construction corps have shown the backward Tibetan peasants how to convert wasteland into fertile cropland and have introduced good strains of cereals, vegetables and tree saplings from other parts of the country (*Hsinhua*, 1973). 'The People's Liberation Army should be a great school,' said Mao in 1966, and during their two years in the PLA the political and educational level of the conscripts undoubtedly rises considerably. When they return to their villages it is reasonable to suppose that they, in their turn, play a significant part in raising the educational, cultural and technical level of the peasants.

Spare-time education

There are many opportunities for spare-time education; and there is considerable public encouragement, even pressure, for everyone to improve their cultural and technical level. As well as July 21 workers' colleges, most factories have formed workers' spare-time study groups, concentrating on subjects as diverse as philosophy, political economy, scientific socialism, history, international affairs, literature and art. In the countryside subjects studied include book-keeping, mathematics, languages, agricultural science, politics and first aid. *Hsinhua* News Agency reported in 1974 that over a million peasants were attending night school, two hours every evening, in Fulkien province alone (*Hsinhua*, 1974).

Correspondence courses have formed part of many universities' and colleges' work since 1952 and are widely used by the eleven million young city people who have gone to live and work on communes since 1969. For instance, a dozen Shanghai colleges and universities offer courses in politics, Chinese language, mathematics, electrical engineering, agriculture, medicine and public health, all designed to meet the needs of the rural areas. Courses are six months or a year in length; the students are organized into groups according to the subjects they study and their localities. They combine home study with group discussion, obtaining learning materials from Shanghai. I have met young teachers in commune primary schools who were improving their knowledge of maths teaching in this way.

A Marxist-Leninist college set up in 1975 in Tientsin initially enrolled 4,300 workers, peasants, teachers and educated young men and women who had settled in the countryside, in Chihsien county. Most were activists in theoretical study or teachers of politics at evening schools, and the period of study was three years. Private and group study alternated with broadcast lessons from the local radio station and periodic visits by the teachers — leading county cadres and political theory teachers and students from Nankai University (*Hsinhua*, 1975).

Radio courses in many subjects, especially in foreign languages, are widespread, and with the growing availability of television sets, television courses are now being offered. *Hsinhua* News Agency reports the opening of a television college in Shanghai in October 1978, offering correspondence courses in Chinese language, mathematics, chemistry, physics and medical work. The college publishes text books, notes and reference books, and has set up 55 stations to give supplementary lectures. Students on the medical course can attend tutorials in their localities to see films, read X-ray negatives and do dissections. University laboratories and workshops are open to television college students during their free time. The college plans to set up laboratories for the study of physics and chemistry in districts and counties and to establish experimental centres with modern equipment in the city. In this development Shanghai, as the largest city in China, has led the way; doubtless this television college is the first of many (*Hsinhua*, 1978a).

Shanghai also leads in the provision of cultural activities, with eleven 'palaces of culture'. Ten thousand workers come to the largest of these every evening. With the current interest in science and technology new items have been added recently. Last year, 25,000 workers saw an exhibition of science and technology in other lands; films and books on these subjects are provided, television centres give courses in foreign languages and mathematics, and skilled workers give demonstrations of advanced engineering techniques. The palace of culture also organizes music festivals, dance dramas and *chuyi* (ballad singing, story-telling and comic cross-talks) (*Hsinhua*, 1978b). These last features are very much a part of Chinese life today; from nursery to cadre school very well-produced songs, dances and sketches portray their problems, solutions and aspirations with lively humour.

Conclusion

Since 1977 changes have been made in various aspects of education, all designed to speed the four modernizations. Entrance examinations for higher education have been re-introduced, and play a larger part in selection now than during the last ten years. There is more emphasis on formal education. Foreign textbooks have been studied and from these studies new Chinese texts are being issued by the Ministry of Education, to some extent taking the place of the material produced in the localities. It would be a great pity if this general tightening up in order to raise standards in any way dampened the local initiative that has characterized Chinese education since the Cultural Revolution. Recent developments show this to be unlikely. To give one example, at the 9th National Trade Union Congress in October 1978 a leading member of the central committee of the Communist Party urged trade unions to:

> encourage the workers to study Marxist theory, politics, economics, management, science, technology and culture. Trade unions should run workers' spare-time middle schools, university and other courses. (*Hsinhua*, 1978c)

The whole population, in fact, is being encouraged to study science, following a national science conference in 1978 which formulated an eight-year development programme. Tens of millions have been drawn into a mass scientific movement — scientists, engineers, technicians, teachers and students, workers and peasants. In different parts of the country study courses and lectures are being organized on scientific subjects including the use of electronic computers, uses of atomic energy, genetic engineering and plant tissue culture. This movement has wide ramifications: to give just one example, over half the production teams, brigades, communes and counties in China have set up agricultural science organizations, popularizing new techniques and training large numbers of technical personnel.

Indeed, very few Chinese remain untouched by the range of educational facilities that have sprung up all over the country. In addition to those outlined above, group political discussion forms a part of the daily life of workers and peasants. It is a common sight to see a group of workers in a factory, or peasants in the fields, studying an editorial in the *People's Daily*, or one of the classic Marxist works, or discussing the local implications of the current national campaign and the part that they are playing in it. This involvement of the whole population is a central part of Party and governmental policy. There can be little doubt that it is this policy of lifelong and continuous education and re-education that is largely responsible for the astonishing — indeed unparalleled — rise in the living standards of the Chinese people in the short space of thirty years.

References

Books

Alley, R (1973) *Travels in China* New World Press: Peking
Belden, J (1970) *China Shakes the World* Monthly Review Press: New York and London
Che Hung-chang (1955) How Yinta Township started spare-time education for peasants *in Socialist Upsurge in China's Countryside* (1957) Foreign Languages Press: Peking
Chen, J (ed) (1970) *Mao Papers, Anthology and Bibliography* Oxford University Press: London
Fraser, J (1965) *Chinese Communist Education* Vanderbilt University Press: New York
Kessen, W (ed) (1975) *Childhood in China* Yale University Press: New Haven
Mao Tsetung (1927) Report on an investigation of the peasant movement in Hunan *in Selected Works of Mao Tsetung* (1967) Foreign Languages Press: Peking
Mao Tsetung (1944) The united front in cultural work *in Selected Works of Mao Tsetung* (1965) Foreign Languages Press: Peking
Mao Tsetung (1968) *in Strive to Build a Socialist University of Science and Engineering* (1972) Foreign Languages Press: Peking
Mauger, P et al (1974) *Education in China* Anglo-Chinese Educational Institute: London
People's Daily (1969) Programme for primary and middle schools in the rural areas (draft) *in* Mauger, P et al (1974)
Richman, B (1969) *Industrial Society in Communist China* Random House: New York
Selected Works of Mao Tsetung I (1967) Foreign Languages Press: Peking
Selected Works of Mao Tsetung III (1965) Foreign Languages Press: Peking
Snow, E (1937) *Red Star over China* Gollancz: London
Socialist Upsurge in China's Countryside (1957) Foreign Languages Press: Peking
Strive to Build a Socialist University of Science and Engineering (1972) Foreign Languages Press: Peking

Periodicals

Communist Party of China Central Committee Decision (1977) *Peking Review* 20 43: 7
Hsinhua News Agency (1973) Weekly Issue 235: London
Hsinhua News Agency (1974) Weekly Issue 261: London
Hsinhua News Agency (1975) July 20: London
Hsinhua News Agency (1978a) Weekly Issue 504: London
Hsinhua News Agency (1978b) May 16: London
Hsinhua News Agency (1978c) October 13: London
Liu Yu-sheng (1974) The Nanniwan May 7 Cadre School *China Reconstructs* 23 7: 6-7
Staff Reporter (1975) Factories run their own colleges *China Reconstructs* 24 11: 4

16. Asia and the South Pacific: the exchange of ideas with Australia

Chris Duke

Summary: The rationale for including a chapter referring to Asian non-formal education is considered, along with the diversity within the Third World. The state of educational provision and of thought about this provision in the region is briefly described, including the increasing acceptance of non-formal education as a possible road for the future. Aspects of Australian tradition and outlook are summarized, especially its stance towards Asia and the status of recurrent education in Australia. This suggests a basis for exchange of ideas between Australia and countries of the region, including some existing means and modes for such exchange. Issues of importance to Asian non-formal education and Australian recurrent education alike are identified.

Introduction

This chapter may appear out of place in a collection of readings most of which are from and about recurrent education in the West — the wealthy, largely industrialized countries which comprise the membership of the Organization for Economic Co-operation and Development (OECD), to which organization, more than to any other source, we owe the concept and strategy of recurrent education. OECD has a 'Pacific circle' group of members: the United States and Canada, Australia, New Zealand and Japan. All are however urbanized, industrialized and affluent relative to the rest of the world, and especially compared with the countries of the South in what is often called the North-South dialogue.

On reflection, the inclusion of this chapter may not appear so strange. The relationship between the 'North' and the 'South', the developed and the developing, the industrialized and the Third World, is among the most important and problematic issues facing mankind.* Australia chances to have some special opportunities as well as problems in this respect, as a

---

* No terms are fully satisfactory, ie descriptively accurate without unacceptable connotations. The preference here is for 'western world' and 'Third World', partly because of what seems most commonly acceptable in the region. 'Developing/ developed' has a connotation of convergent linear development and of western superiority which is misleading as well as unacceptable. 'Industrialized/ non-industrialized' and 'traditional/modern' are similarly inaccurate and misleading.

result of its history and its geographical location (Blainey, 1966). Omission of all reference to the Third World would be a limitation. Also, despite the obvious and often stark contrasts between the western and the Third World (contrasts which are dramatized and simplified by the uni-dimensional economic perspective commonly employed) there are interesting and illuminating parallels and analogies between thought and policy options in education in these two groupings of countries. These comparisons are the basis of this chapter; without them there could be little prospect for exchange of ideas between Australia and the other countries of this region (New Zealand excepted). We have, however, to clarify the similarities and differences between the recurrent education (RE) of the western world and non-formal education (NFE), an emergent concept and strategy for the Third World.

This chapter does not provide a full profile of either recurrent or non-formal education. The *World Yearbook of Education* as a whole gives a quite comprehensive understanding of the meaning of recurrent education and of different approaches to it from country to country. The intention here is to sketch some characteristics of Asian countries, and to point out the problems facing educational planners. In this context, the attractiveness of community-based and other alternatives to trying to extend the western model of compulsory school-based education for the whole population should become evident. Secondly, I sketch some distinguishing characteristics of Australian society, including the education system which reflects them, before indicating both theoretically and in practical ways what exchanges of ideas between Australia and Asia and the South Pacific might appeal to Australians. This includes a brief account of some recently developed channels and mechanisms. Finally, I mention important unanswered questions which apply with similar force to RE in the western world and to NFE in the countries of the region, and which might attract comparative study of mutual benefit. While no systematic account is provided of the different approaches to alternative and non-formal educational structures considered in the region, the references provide starting-points for those who wish to pursue this further.

A dichotomy between the industrialized western world and the Third World (or between North and South) has been implied. This should be qualified before we proceed to consider in turn NFE in Asia and the South Pacific, RE in Australia, and exchanges (actual and conceivable) between them. Eastern Europe and the USSR, which is also a major Asian power, are excluded since neither RE nor NFE is a common concept in these countries; otherwise I might have opted for the term North-South in this discussion. Japan, as well as being Asian, is one of the three industrial super-powers within the OECD club. Australia, on the other hand, is knocking at the door seeking admission to the Organization's 'second division' within the more sophisticated break-down of the two broad categories of nations. Within the Asian region, one hears more these days of the 'Korean miracle' than of the Japanese: its industrialization is if anything more dramatic than the earlier Japanese transformation. Other countries of East and South-East Asia are not far behind, and ASEAN (the Association of South-East Asian Nations) is becoming a significant economic force in the region. On the other hand India, for all its successful industrialization and exporting capabilities in Asia and Africa, yet contains half the world's illiterates, and it is common to speak of the Fourth World, or the 'least developed countries' (LDCs) as a distinct category. Asia has its share of these: not only Bangladesh but also countries smaller in size or population like Afghanistan and Nepal. Indonesia has a large population which suffers severe overcrowding and under-nourishment, notably in parts of Java, and India itself is sometimes included in the category of countries which one school of economists has maintained should be abandoned, development aid being concentrated instead on the economic 'take-off' countries of the Third World. Those who belong to or work in Bangladesh vary in their outlook: a few adopt similar counsels of despair. More remain extraordinarily optimistic about the prospects of a resilient and resourceful people in the face of daunting population and resource problems.

Non-formal education — Asia and the South Pacific

Asia and Oceania is, then, a very diverse area. And the economic diversity is matched by cultural diversity. English is becoming the universal *lingua franca* for international meetings and increasingly common as a business language, but there is no common language that reaches as far into the general population as the Spanish of Latin America, much less the unifying language of the Arab world. Despite the diversity of cultures, history, languages and religious traditions as well as contemporary socio-economic circumstances and social-political systems, there is a sense of commonality, at least in regional, political, professional and administrative exchanges, which is expressed in terms such as 'the Asian way'. The same may be said, but as a distinct region, of the broad reaches and tiny dispersed populations of the South Pacific or Oceania. This region still includes colonial territories. It is superficially dominated by British, French and American influences, but there is an underlying and unifying Oceanic culture or 'Melanesian way'. The characteristics sketched here are well displayed by UNESCO's organization in the region: the UNESCO Regional Office for Education in Asia, located in Bangkok, is the earliest and strongest of that Organization's regional offices. Recently it has acquired all regional co-ordinating functions, not just educational ones, and has added Oceania to its title (ROEAO). This acknowledges the feeling in the South Pacific that Oceania is a distinct region and should not be treated as merely an appendage of the huge and heavily populated Asian region. As we shall see, the non-governmental regional organization relevant to RE/NFE, the Asian and South Pacific Bureau of Adult Education, has followed the same path but gone rather further than UNESCO in this direction (ASPBAE, 1974-, 1978).

Most countries throughout the region have been strongly influenced by the West. Whether by direct colonization or indirectly, they have set themselves in the direction of creating a formal education system essentially similar to that which emerged during the later years of industrialization in western countries: universal, compulsory primary education; the gradual introduction of secondary education for all and the progressive raising of the school-leaving age; a small but increasing proportion of the population going on to higher education and even to graduate studies. For many countries, higher education has to be taken abroad in a number of subject areas, since local resources are lacking for specialized study. Many countries are but a short way along this path but on the whole all have looked in the same direction.

The model of educational provision familiar in Europe and North America, and thus introduced to Asia, grew out of the needs and circumstances of urban industrial societies in the nineteenth century. Socio-economic changes transformed traditional institutions and structures, including the extended family and many of the roles and relationships in local rural society. The school came to acquire educational, custodial and socializing functions formerly carried by other institutions, and to be quite significantly segregated from other institutions and social activities, with specialized resources and increasingly professionalized personnel. The dysfunctions which this has generated in western societies have been much documented and debated. Conclusions range between the more extreme variants of de-schooling to the more conservative variants of recurrent education. In Asia and the South Pacific this cost-intensive approach to schooling and an education system has been introduced to countries which are still predominantly rural, and which have no possibility of affording the teachers, buildings and other facilities implied by such a model. The model is thus doubly irrelevant: it seeks to transfer functions to the school which can better be left with the family and other institutions of traditional society; and it demands an expenditure for these partly unnecessary specialized services which the budget of most Third World countries precludes.

This is the context for understanding the present salience of NFE in the Asian and South Pacific region. The 'world crisis in education' belongs as much to the Third World as to the West, and the gulf between present provision and perceived need yawns wider. 'Recurrent education' is not a Third World concept; the term is scarcely known and almost never used. Likewise, 'continuing education', the term increasingly preferred in western societies (including Australia and New Zealand) to encompass all forms of non-credit education for adults, has not been widely introduced in Asia. 'Adult education' has a narrow connotation in many places. Although some use it broadly to encompass many objectives, strategies and programmes — Thailand and India for example — it still tends to be equated mainly with basic literacy for adults.* The term 'non-formal

---

*The analogous problem in Australia and similar countries is the identification of adult education with non-vocational, liberal, and often recreational courses at the

education' has made a recent but rather dramatic appearance in the region, encompassing school-age and post-school-age youth and adult education. It has tended to displace the earlier term 'out-of-school' education, meanwhile extending its scope more firmly to include alternatives throughout the age range, and not mainly for youth and adults.

'Non-formal', like 'out-of-school', education is a negative definition, especially if understood as merely ancillary to what is provided in school. What is remarkable is the extent to which the term has very recently come to be defined positively and purposefully. It seems that a new paradigm is already developing. Quite suddenly, policy-makers and senior administrators are turning to NFE to by-pass the insoluble resource problems of the formal system. 'NFE and alternative structures' is the subject of seminars and workshops, and prominent in major regional meetings (UNESCO, 1976, 1977, 1978a, 1978b). Two years ago, a UNESCO regional seminar stressed the importance of treating NFE as a continuing and attractive alternative for all ages, levels and groups, and not merely a stop-gap until more schools were built and more teachers trained (UNESCO, 1976). Now the point seems to have been won among many in the international community of Asian educationists. The attention is more on questions of linkage, bridging, the relationship between the formal system and non-formal alternatives, even on possible means whereby the latter might influence and 'deformalize' the former. NFE has thus become a positive factor and a possible force for system-wide change, early though it is to predict that such will occur. The attention given to NFE at regional level, and in the plans and programmes of several countries, suggests that a general alternative approach, even possibly a 'rival system', already all but exists. The Philippines, for example, appointed an Under-Minister, now Deputy-Minister, for NFE; she holds a key political and administrative position in the Department of Education and Culture and probably in government itself. Indonesia has recently launched a massive World Bank programme exceeding 30 million dollars, and Thailand is part-way through a somewhat similar World Bank programme. Despite the diversity of terms employed, including social and community as well as adult and non-formal education, a common pattern appears to be emerging. In some countries the shift towards NFE is feared as a threat to 'essential' mainstream school education — a concern expressed by the Nepalese delegation to the UNESCO/APEID† consultation meeting in March 1978. More countries are turning to NFE, however, even clutching at it as the only alternative to the obviously unbridgeable gulf between the resources required to extend the cost-intensive western model to the whole population and the resources conceivably available for education (UNESCO, 1978a).

Some analogies with the purposes and difficulties of recurrent education

expense of other aspects; there has been a practice in Australia of protecting this tradition by referring to other non-formal and adult provision as 'the education of adults'.

†APEID — Asian Programme of Educational Innovation for Development

will readily be discerned. Like RE, NFE is potentially a strategy for educational reform in the direction of lifelong learning. It also displays a mix of socio-educational values including democratization, mobilization and participation, with pragmatism. The quantity of ingredients in the mix is not always clear, and this makes judgement as well as evaluation difficult. It is generally agreed that RE is a strategy for educational reform, although the main thrust tends, for practical reasons, to be at the upper secondary levels and perhaps increasingly into the higher and adult education sectors. Application of RE to basic school levels is mainly speculative at present. NFE by contrast appears to offer a means of bringing education to children denied access to schooling at all, at a cost which society can contemplate. For example, Project IMPACT of the South East Asian Ministers of Education Organization Centre Innotech makes it possible for one teacher to manage up to 200 pupils, using the community and its resources as aids to learning. The In-School Off-School (ISOS) programme in the Philippines has children spend alternate weeks on individual and group learning projects in the community, which relate to the classroom weeks while allowing schools to double their intake.

The combination of principle (democratization) and necessity (scarce resources) is revealed in a preoccupation with defining a basic educational cycle or core curriculum. This is much more advanced in Asia than in OECD member countries. It holds out the possibility of removing a year from the compulsory basic cycle period of education. Studies are being attempted of how children may be able to acquire concepts through work experience and community projects, especially scientific concepts; the difficulty is that the natural rhythm of productive village life may not lend itself to the sequential learning whereby subjects are pursued to more difficult and abstract levels in the school curriculum (UNESCO, 1977). There is concern, on the one hand, that NFE might be second-rate stop-gap education, or disguised productive employment and domestication of the rural (and maybe the urban) poor rather than education at all. There is also, on the other hand, a concern that bureaucratic dynamics will turn it instead into a rival system competing for funds and in the process becoming scarcely less formal than the system whose deficiencies fostered its creation. The emphasis has thus shifted not only from talking of an NFE system, which has been rare, or non-formal and alternative structures, which is still perhaps imprudent, to speaking of non-formal provision and modes, and to looking for means of diversifying and 'deformalizing' the 'system' of provision. Again, there are parallels with recurrent education.

Some characteristics of Australia

Australia enjoys one of the highest standards of living, at any rate in economic terms, and has one of the highest levels of consumption of any country in the world. It is highly urbanized, largely industrialized and, by most criteria, a western nation. Its political and cultural orientation is still largely towards Britain, for all the real and simulated hostility to the former motherland. It also looks a great deal to the United States, culturally as well as politically and for security. While New Zealand is said to recall Victorian England, or at least the England of the earlier years of this century, Australia, and especially Sydney, is said to resemble America, and to follow the main American fashions a few years later.

Australia is still in the main a primary producer, its chief trading partner being highly industrialized Japan. Most of the capital to develop Australia comes from abroad — from Britain, from America, and increasingly of late, from Japan and elsewhere. Traditional Australian culture, that is Aboriginal culture, has been harassed to near extinction. Although there is now more than a little renaissance, there is not the recognition, respect and mutual penetration which reportedly characterizes white and Maori societies in New Zealand. There are some distinctively Australian works of art — painting and literature — and the beginnings of a distinctive cinema and television film industry, but the mass media are largely dominated by American and British productions.

Australia is thus of mixed identity: partly western and developed, but economically developing and culturally uncertain. A characteristic obeisance to overseas authority and expertise has been called the 'Australian cultural cringe'. Australia is in fact an increasingly rich and diverse society, containing vigorous cultures from all parts of Europe and many parts of Asia, as a result of its very youth (as a European society) and the scale and variety of immigration throughout its modern period of history, and especially from World War II until the time of the present recession. Even today, the unplanned and uneasily accepted immigration of Vietnamese, and possibly also of East Timorese, is adding to the cultural diversity.

There remains a strain of ethnocentrism in Australia which expresses itself periodically as fear or hostility towards Asia and Asians. Documents recently available suggest that Australia may have played a key part in persuading the United States into full military engagement in Vietnam. The domino theory (or fear of the 'Asian hordes' or the red or yellow peril) still has powerful support from the political right.

Australia has an unusually easy-going and open society and this manifests itself in its education reform. Higher education, for all that there is room for reform, has always been much more open than the British and various European systems. The popular expression of this is the egalitarianism and acceptance known as mateship. But as a former British colony, although the majority of the population is not of British extraction, there is still an orientation toward Britain and America accentuated by the monopoly of positions of influence and leadership occuped by Anglo-Saxons. Add to this an easy-going style characterized as 'she'll be right, mate', a centrifugal federal system and tradition such that many state politicians consider themselves Western Australians or Queenslanders first and Australians second, a degree of isolation which has provided insulation from most direct threats and encouraged a parochial outlook, and one has the main ingredients of what was described some years ago in a popular analysis as the lucky country (Horne, 1964). After 23 years of Liberal (conservative) administration, Whitlam's Labour administration (1972-75) already seems something of an aberration in an essentially conservative country, even though a number of its domestic and foreign initiatives have survived. These included recognition of China and Vietnam, as well as a higher profile abroad generally, the creation of a Technical and Further Education Commission to stimulate this much-neglected sector of education, abolition of tertiary fees and greatly enhanced federal expenditure on education and other social services.

This outline may pose the question of what, if anything, and by what means, Australia can hope to give or gain in exchange of ideas with Asia and the South Pacific. To this question I now turn more directly. Let it first be said that not all the characteristics identified above stand in the way of exchange of ideas, for all that learning from Asia is, on the face of it, implausible. On the other side we might note openness and willingness on the part of many Asian countries for exchange with Australia. Despite the recent emphasis on regional and endogenous forms of development, on finding an 'Asian way' and terminating dependence on the North, many countries of the region still seek the know-how of technologically advanced countries, for instance through research and development and training. Australia, despite its mainly western and sometimes frankly racist stance, is seen as a non-threatening, though not non-aligned, country, almost as part of the region. When Australia transferred from the European to the Asian region of UNESCO for programme purposes at the 18th General Conference of UNESCO, the change was warmly welcomed within the region; that welcome has been sustained, for all that membership has been little more than token. The official and professional relationship, other than in conventional aid terms, has been less than the Asia-philes and development-oriented in Australia would like, but there has also been considerable contact with parts of the region through tourism (both students and package tours for middle-aged suburbanites) and also through trade. The Liberal Government in 1978 established a Committee on Third World Relations which, if perhaps cynical in part, also no doubt reflected a real concern with this increasingly pressing aspect of foreign relations.

So far new ideas about education have come mainly from Britain and America, and increasingly also from the relevant inter-governmental organizations, especially UNESCO and OECD. Because of the latter, recurrent education has been prominent. It is still normal in the mainstream of Australian education to look for wisdom and inspiration to Britain or America, and the majority of academic and professional visitors, keynote speakers and advisers hail from these countries, even when such subjects as community education, external studies and adult education are under consideration. The report of the Faure Commission, *Learning to Be* (UNESCO, 1972), made a considerable impact in Australia, as in New Zealand. National Commissions for UNESCO in both countries took advantage of it to organize national seminars, and in the case of Australia also a regional seminar, on the report. This brought to Australia first Dr Champion Ward from the United States, but on the second occasion Dr Majid Rahnema, the Asian member of the Commission, and a number of Pacific and Asian educationists interested in the theme. While the term 'lifelong education' has made little headway in administrative parlance in either Australia or Asia, and is indeed treated with some impatience in Asian countries which find it, like NFE, a source of semantic distraction, the underlying philosophy and concept have had more success.

Recurrent education has made more substantial ground especially among planners and administrators in Australia, probably because of its apparent moderation and practicality (Duke, 1976). Although the first major national seminar on recurrent education was not until 1977 (Duke, 1978a) there were regional and local seminars on the subject earlier, and advisory groups or working parties appointed by various bodies. The interim council preceding the Technical and Further Education (TAFE) Commission took recurrent education as its philosophical underpinning, and it appeared prominently in policies of the Universities Commission, as well as indirectly through recommendations for more open access to universities (ACOTAFE, 1974; AUC, 1975). The Schools Commission appointed a working party and gave cautious support to the concept (Schools Commission, 1975). The Education Research and Development Committee, a federal funding body for research and development in education, has made RE one of its priority areas, and it is among the terms of reference of a major Committee of Inquiry into Education and Training. Australia has enhanced the flow of ideas and materials from OECD in Paris by means of a national OECD Education Advisory Committee which was responsible for the national 1977 seminar as well as for other less conspicuous exercises in dissemination. The Labour administration also appointed an Education Counsellor to the Organization in Paris, a position which has fallen victim to economies in recent times. In these and other ways, recurrent education has been actively promoted in Australia, and has secured the verbal blessing of many official and professional authorities and gatherings.

This is not to say that there is a policy of recurrent education in Australia. There is still considerable confusion over both ideological and practical aspects. For instance, does RE represent democratization and a second chance, or rather a second creaming? Is it economically defensible? By what economic criteria? Even if it is, how are resources to be generated or transferred and mechanisms devised, to make it possible? Does it require greater direction and control, including possibly compulsory re-accreditation? If so, how is this to be reconciled with a quest for decentralization and diversification, and with the desirable principle of choosing to study rather than being compelled? Does the Australian practice of long-service leave mean it will be easier or harder to introduce paid educational leave? Is it the immoral sacrifice of a generation to encourage under-achievers to leave school early when there is as yet no integrated RE system? Is the target, the 'client', of an RE system the individual, his community or group, or the whole society? Does it represent enhancement of learning or enslavement to schooling? Is it a means whereby educators betray their mission and education becomes the handmaiden of employers and the economy?

These and similar doubts are probably shared in most countries where RE is discussed. For all its openness, however, Australia tends to be somewhat dismissive of new people and ideas — a style known popularly as knocking or rubbishing. Australia has a somewhat *laissez-faire* western socio-political system, in contrast to the planning approaches attempted by many of its Asian neighbours of both the left and the right. It is also a federal system, like Canada and Germany, in which education is mainly a state responsibility. Federal policy-making and advisory bodies have to contend with eight (other) education systems. This makes it still less likely that we will soon be able to speak of *a* recurrent education system in Australia, even though piecemeal changes, economically rather than educationally motivated, are moving Australia in this direction.

Exchange of ideas

Overseas influences on Australian education seem to have increased in recent years, and especially to have diversified from the UK/USA domination of earlier times, even though these remain overweening. UNESCO and OECD have been the means for a wider spectrum of influences and experiences to infiltrate themselves, including, from UNESCO, indirect Third World influences. RE and NFE are rather distinct concepts, sets of literature and programmes generated in response to different circumstances and perceived needs. Yet this cursory sketch has indicated points of similarity; and we have noted some tendency for Australia to feel and conduct itself as part of the region within which it is physically located. Exchanges and mutual learning, then, are less implausible than might at first appear. There is the Australian programme membership of the Asian region of UNESCO, and the educationally strong Regional Office in Bangkok. This has created the important mechanism of the Asian Programme of Educational Innovation for Development (APEID) a network approaching a hundred associated centres identified as being involved in educational innovation throughout the member countries of the region. Australia joined this network by means of three associated centres at the end of 1977. Heads of centres took part in the March 1978 Regional Consultation Meeting to complete planning of the second four-year cycle of APEID (UNESCO, 1978a). In 1978 there was also the first APEID programme (on distance teacher education) to take place in Australia, one of a number of educational and other programmes arranged in Australia by the UNESCO National Commission which has involved significant Asian participation. Two additional associated centres (one State Technical and Further Education system and one Schools Authority) are likely soon to bring Australian membership of the network to five, widening and diversifying the person-to-person and agency-to-agency web of connections through which ideas can be exchanged.

The philosophy of APEID makes clear that Australian participation (like that of any country, from the two financial donor members Japan and Iran to impoverished states like Nepal) is on a basis of equality and partnership. Learning is mutual. The political, administrative and intrinsically educative processes whereby Australia moved cautiously into this form of association are instructive. Many involved or consulted initially could not conceive that any exchange could benefit Australia. They saw it paternalistically as just another form of aid from a sophisticated to a backward country. The extent to which the APEID philosophy could be accepted, or even grasped, provided a measure of the extent to which exchange of ideas might indeed be expected to occur.

This is the more important since APEID represents a coming of age in Asia, a confidence that Asian ways can be devised which are more relevant and by many criteria and values 'better' than the imported ways — which do not rely on ever-enhanced state-of-the-art technological sophistication, nor automatically define traditional attitudes, institutions and modes as obstacles to development. We have described NFE as a new paradigm of education. The same phrase has been used about 'development' (Schramm and Lerner, 1976). Nowhere is the 'new paradigm of development' more evident than in education. This paradigm replaces the linear, convergent assumptions of economic and technological development in trailing pursuit of the receding — and now tarnishing — western growth model with emphasis on choice of levels, means and technologies. Questioning both of the western model and indeed of any single model or solution seems quite general, together with a revived interest in the educative potential of traditional institutions and forms which it would be short-sighted to stigmatize as either romantic or Luddite (UNESCO, 1978b). APEID provides a practical and convenient, decentralized network approach to exchange of ideas between countries of the region, including Australia. Its philosophy is inimical to that inequality which in most aid relations inhibits mutuality.

Another means for exchange is the non-governmental Bureau, ASPBAE, mentioned earlier. ASPBAE was established at a UNESCO Regional Seminar in Australia in 1964, with an Indian Chairman and a New Zealand Secretary resident in Australia. After early activity, a series of misfortunes curtailed programmes for several years. Recently it has proved increasingly successful as a non-governmental means of exchanging ideas and personnel, and co-operating in programme development. The size of the region has encouraged a measure of decentralization. There is now a separate South Asia office located in Tehran. The German Adult Education Association secured from its Government in 1977 a substantial programme development fund for the Bureau region spanning East and South-East Asia, the headquarters of which (and the nerve centre for the network) is in Australia. This is the first substantial German adult education development grant not conditional on engaging a German national as administrator on the spot, itself a significant step towards recognition of regional maturity and autonomy. The South Pacific region was designated a distinct Bureau region, with an Oceania-wide executive and headquarters in Suva, in 1978 (ASPBAE, 1978). Despite continuing colonialism in the South Pacific there is within the region, and manifested especially in the outlook of recently independent Papua New Guinea, a stance of regional autonomy, an emphasis on national self-reliance, an aspiration to win some measure of disassociation from the world fiscal and economic system and to regulate kinds and levels of production and consumption, which matches the new spirit in Asia. The philosophy and approach of the Bureau resembles that of UNESCO and APEID, with which there is practical co-operation. Australia's role in fostering the Bureau network, like its recent membership of APEID, thus provides a means for exchange of ideas in the field of RE, NFE and educational innovation, insofar as there is a will and an interest to engage in such exchange.

At a policy level, it must be admitted, participation in the educational affairs of the region seems grudging and largely token. This may reflect a political view of Australian self-interest which is refuted, albeit unsuccessfully, by increasing numbers of educationists and education administrators. At non-governmental and personal levels a shift seems to be occurring, a quickening of Australian interest in the activities of nearby countries, a dawning recognition that such involvement may be professionally challenging and rewarding as well as making good sense. Apart from Australia's traditional long-sightedness (long in distance rather than time) which has kept the British and American scene in clearer focus than the Asian, differences of terminology, culture, social structure, economy, language and resource base have made it hard for most Australians to see and understand what is happening in Asia, much less to see it as relevant to the local situation. Greater familiarity with these concepts and their relationships (for all the dismissiveness with which they tend to be greeted at first) and some capacity to think comparatively and across dissimilarities, are reducing the barriers. The increase in tourism and trade with the region, and the gradual further diversification and cultural enrichment of the Australian population itself from non-European quarters (as well as perhaps from the diversity of the European population in Australia) has also played a part. So, no doubt, has the apparent non-aggressiveness of Maoist and post-Maoist China, and the evident fallacy of the domino theory in Indochina. The exercise of political will in most countries of Asia, for all that this may be manifested in ways repugnant to one or another section of Australian society, makes it probable that the Asian variant of RE, the much wider NFE strategy, may be introduced more widely and rapidly than RE in Australia. Once the analogy between western-style RE and Asian-style NFE is acknowledged it becomes possible also to see other comparative dimensions and common concerns beneath the variety, and to gain from the exchange rather than dispute its possibility.

Some issues which could be illuminated by exchange have been mentioned. To these might be added the question of to what extent non-formal or recurrent education can be conceived, facilitated and orchestrated as a single planned system. How far can it be provided with and through resources specifically defined and identified as educational, as part of a deliberate 'education system'? For NFE the answer is in the negative; the more far-reaching NFE and adult education schemes reach down deep in efforts to tap other community resources, as well as to engage with other ministries and departments. The moderate adherents of recurrent education, especially those who espouse it selectively from a policy and administration perspective, tend to treat it as a matter of schools and colleges. The nexus of RE with industrial democracy has, however, frequently been shown. This quickly takes it beyond the confines of formal education. In this and other ways RE, like NFE, is not to be treated in a vacuum but rather as part of an integrated approach to planning along with manpower, social welfare and other considerations.

We have mentioned already another important common concern. Will close association of NFE with the formal system help to free the latter, or will it lead, rather to bureaucratization of the former? How can association and beneficial interaction be fostered without loss of distinctive value and virtue? What administrative arrangements will best permit interaction while protecting NFE from over-formalization? Beneath these clusters another set of questions about staffing, including the deployment of teachers from the formal system in recurrent and non-formal programmes, and training of NFE facilitators which avoids excessive and perhaps disabling over-professionalization. Strategies for RE, especially refresher, continuing and work experience elements, soon lead into similar questions.

The most sensitive and perhaps the most important question for NFE in Asia is also of considerable importance in the RE debate, for all that it tends to be somewhat muted in the softer and less clear-cut circumstances of western societies. This is the question: education for what? In Paulo Freire's terms, is education for conscientization, liberation, mobilization, or rather for domestication? This is a difficult question for any country, especially for any country young in independence, scarce of resources, and uncertain about its internal security and its national unity. The diminution of parliamentary democracy and of the classic political freedoms in many countries of the region causes a crisis of purpose and conscience for some in Australia who are committed to Asian involvement and partnership. Recent clashes within UNESCO over the control and use of mass media illustrate the point; a western tendency to rush to judgement can be myopic and even ethnocentric. The question is pertinent because NFE implies mobilization of local community resources, active participation of the people in defining and meeting their own learning needs. This is not easily reconciled with close central direction and control, such as some Asian governments may consider essential to their own, and possibly their country's, survival. Once again, the analogies with recurrent education are obvious. In western countries, though, the issue is less directly political, more a question of fashioning or domesticating individuals to the changing requirements of the workplace versus active engagement with the society and economy which might thereby itself be refashioned.

Conclusion

The scope of this chapter is wide. Space precludes elaboration and illustration of the issues raised. It should be clear, for all that, that exchange between Australia and Asia holds promise of being fruitful, more perhaps for Australia than for Asia, and that recently created or activated channels and mechanisms are already making this possible in some measure in areas especially relevant to the theme of this book. It should also be clear that although recurrent education is little discussed in Asia (even OECD member country Japan may find it slightly bemusing, given the differences between RE's Scandinavian industrial democracy test-bed and the Japanese socio-industrial system) there are parallels between questions central to this concept and the NFE approach more typical of Asia. Both are strategies for educational reform, and each is in danger of being forestalled or side-tracked, especially by the dynamics of bureaucracies. Finally, to make explicit what has been implied, exchange of ideas between Australia and its Asian-South Pacific region are increasingly likely because Australia and Australians have no choice but to live in the region. They need to know and come to terms with their neighbours. Luckily, for many in the lucky country, this is coming to be seen less as a threat or hardship.

References

Ahmed, M and Coombs, P H (1975) *Education for Rural Development: Case Studies for Planners* Praeger: New York
Asian and South Pacific Bureau of Adult Education (ASPBAE (1974-) *Courier Service* Canberra
ASPBAE (with South Pacific Commission) (1978) *Regional Planning Conference on Adult Education in National Development* Report: Noumea
Australian Council on Technical and Further Education (ACOTAFE) (1974) *First Report on Needs in Technical and Further Education* Canberra
Australian Department of Education (1978) *Recurrent Education: Trends, Tensions and Trade-Offs* Canberra
Australian Universities Commission (AUC) (1975) *Sixth Report* Canberra
Bhasin, K (1977) *Participatory Training* FAO: Rome
Blainey, G (1966) *The Tyranny of Distance* Sun Books: Melbourne
Duke, C (1974) *Recurrent Education — Policy and Development in OECD Member Countries: Australia* OECD: Paris
Duke, C (1976) Recurrent education — refurbish or reform? *in* Browne, R K and Margin, D J (eds) *Sociology of Education* Macmillan: London
Duke, C (1978) Australia in Asia — comparison as learning *in* Charters, A N (ed) *Handbook of Adult Education* Jossey-Bass: San Francisco
Duke, C (ed) (1978a) *Recurrent Education: Trends, Tensions and Trade-Offs* Australian Department of Education: Canberra
Horn, D (1964) *The Lucky Country* Pelican: Harmondsworth
Schools Commission (1975) *Report for the Triennium 1976-78* Canberra

Schramm, W and Lerner, D (1976) (eds) *Communication and Change: the Last Ten Years — and the Next* University Press of Hawaii (especially Rogers, E M 'The passing of the dominant paradigm — reflections on diffusion research')

Srinivasan, L (1977) *Perspectives on Non-Formal Adult Learning* World Education: New York

UNESCO (1972) *Learning to Be* (The Faure Report) UNESCO: Paris

UNESCO (1976) *Lifelong Education, the Curriculum and Basic Learning Needs* (Final report of the regional seminar at Chiangmai) UNESCO: Bangkok

UNESCO (1977) *Alternative Approaches to School Education at Primary Level* (Final report of the regional seminar at Manila) UNESCO: Bangkok

UNESCO *Prospects* (quarterly) UNESCO: Paris 1971-

UNESCO (1978a) *Towards Implementation of the Second-Cycle Plan, Final Report of the 5th Consultation Meeting of APEID* UNESCO: Bangkok

UNESCO (1978b) *Draft Final Report of 4th Regional Conference of Ministers of Education and Those Responsible for Economic Planning in Asia and Oceania* UNESCO: Colombo

Part 4: Trends in Britain

17. Recurrent education: perceptions, problems and priorities

Frank Molyneux

Summary: This chapter considers recent developments in Britain in relation to different concepts of recurrent education. It is believed that most recent British developments relate to pragmatically derived extensions to existing structures best described as continuing education. These are outcomes of the British traditions of highly devolved and decentralized approaches to educational provision. A greatly increased awareness of the wider international thinking about recurrent education is traced over the last five years. It is argued that this, together with powerful social and economic trends, will produce shifts towards future systems of education in Britain based on the recurrent principle. Certain urgent priorities are considered and the question asked, 'To what extent can Britain's fragmented approach to educational provision provide the evolutionary impetus needed to produce the alternative strategy of recurrent education urgently demanded by changed national circumstances?'

Introduction

The main purpose of this contribution is to attempt to identify and evaluate recent developments in Britain which relate to the concept of recurrent education as an alternative to the present structures and processes of provision. In doing so, it will be argued that much contemporary British usage of the term relates more to adjustments and additions to existing structures than to any wider view of an alternative strategy. However, as other contributors clearly demonstrate, the rather grander version of recurrent education has much international significance in the late 1970s. It will thus be justified to consider, however briefly, the major views of recurrence as a basis for alternative future strategies before examining the peculiar complexities which constitute British educational provision. The nature of this context helps to explain the apparent reluctance of government and administrators to think in terms of general strategies for educational development in Britain despite events elsewhere. However, a greatly increased awareness can be demonstrated in recent years and it is argued that certain general social and economic trends form a framework within which specifically educational problems will become so acute that major changes in attitude by both the providers and recipients will occur. These circumstances are likely to produce the traditionally pragmatic responses which typify educational change in Britain.

Nonetheless, it is my view that the ultimate outcome will be substantially different patterns of provision in Britain which will effectively constitute an overall system of recurrent education. As in the case of the move to comprehensive secondary education, the main political impetus is likely to come from the left, but a wide consensus with regard to purposes and basic principles seems probable in face of changed conditions in society. The progress towards recurrence in Britain is unlikely to be a function of the systematic research and development characterizing educational reform in some countries, notably Sweden, where the tradition of fervent national debate on educational policies is strong and there is arguably a more receptive climate for the political and educational visionary.

Perceptions and terminology

As Open University students were advised some five years ago, the first major problem in coming to grips with the principle of recurrent education is that of terminology (Open University, 1974). (*See also Chapter 3.*) So far as recent British usage is concerned, the term 'continuing education' has become prominent since the mid 1970s, notably in the Open University's 'Report of the Committee on Continuing Education' (*see Chapter 19*) and in the title of the long-awaited Advisory Council for Adult and Continuing Education in 1977. However, in addition to the Open University's consideration of recurrent education in its educational studies course, 1974 also saw the compendium *Recurrent Education — A Plea for Lifelong Learning* appear as the first semi-popular work advocating the principles of recurrence (Houghton and Richardson, 1974). Subsequently, one can trace a marked increase in public discussion notably via the reporting of events under the term 'recurrent education' by the *Times* Newspaper Group. Thus from a complete absence of the term in 1974 one finds 26 entries in 1977, and no less than 21 in the first six months of 1978.

Of major significance to this coming-of-age of the term in Britain was the international seminar on recurrent education organized in Glasgow by the Department of Education and Science and the Scottish Education Department in November 1977. The documentation for the seminar is useful to the purposes of this paper in spotlighting two aspects of the term in Britain. These lead to a distinction between the Organization for Economic and Cultural Development (OECD) view of recurrence as an *alternative* strategy to existing provision and *elaboration* of the traditional model so as to increase learning opportunities at the post-compulsory level. Leonard Cantor, in updating his 1974 review of British developments related to recurrent education, summarizes this other less far-reaching view of recurrent education thus:

Another and broader concept of recurrent education does not tie it fundamentally to the principle of alternation between periods of organized educational activity and periods of work or leisure. These activities need not necessarily alternate but may often be concurrent and sometimes synonymous. This view of recurrent education requires that educational provision be so planned that after leaving full-time education and starting work, individuals can make use of it throughout their life in response to the intermittent demands of personal development, status, ability and ambition. (Cantor, 1974)

It seems to the writer that this 'supplementation' version is essentially the sort of thinking implied currently in Britain by the use of the term 'continuing education'. There is little or no stress upon notions of related social change or of fundamentally different relationships between providers and receivers in learning systems. This contrasts markedly with the OECD/Council of Europe views where the stress is on the evolution of a new strategy for educational provision as part of a wider spectrum of social and economic change. There is a firm belief in the capacity of a recurrent strategy to achieve widely accepted educational objectives more effectively than has been the case thus far via the traditional model. In addition there is the expectation that education thus provided will prove more effective in relation to the achievement of social and economic improvement. This is well summarized by the seminal OECD paper of 1973:

The basic assumption underlying this report is that the strategy being proposed under the label 'recurrent education' has the potential to facilitate such a shift in each of the goal areas discussed above, ie, to provide better opportunities for individual development, greater educational and social equality, and better interplay between the educational and other social sectors, including a better contribution to the potential for necessary economic growth. (OECD/CERI, 1973)

One must, however, appreciate that the existing provision of education in the United Kingdom (UK) is such as to render any sudden shift towards a recurrent strategy, let alone its imposition from the centre, virtually impossible. A detailed analysis of the complex and highly permissive approach to the provision of education and training in the UK is far beyond the scope of this paper. However, it is necessary to indicate some of the major characteristics of powers and structures in England and Wales, Scotland and Northern Ireland relevant to the sort of changes which would be necessary to bring about a major strategical shift.

First, educational responsibilities reflect the general political devolution within the United Kingdom of Great Britain and Northern Ireland. Thus the Secretary of State for Education and Science has responsibility for all aspects of education in England, for further education in Wales and for universities throughout Great Britain. The Secretary of State for Wales is answerable to Parliament for nursery provision and schools at all levels in Wales. The Secretaries of State for Northern Ireland and Scotland have full responsibilities for educational provision at all levels in their countries with the exception of universities in Scotland. Second, administration of publicly provided schools and post-school provision (excluding universities) is on a decentralized basis. Central authority rests with three government departments; the Department of Education and Science (DES), the Scottish Education Department (SED) and the Northern Ireland Department of Education. Local authority, in terms of day-to-day running of schools and colleges, is vested in local education authorities (known as LEAs in England and Wales and as EAs in Scotland). These are derived from the local government structure of counties, regions and metropolitan districts established in 1974-75. In Northern Ireland the counterparts to LEAs are known as Education and Library Boards.

Despite this devolved and decentralized approach, the organization of education in each country follows recognizably similar lines and can be viewed in three common stages: primary, secondary and further/higher. Schooling is compulsory throughout the United Kingdom from the age of five to 16 years with the primary stage from age five to 11 or 12 and secondary following to age 16 or age 18 or 19 on a voluntary basis. Post-compulsory education may, therefore, begin in the upper secondary schools or in institutions of 'further' or 'higher' education. This latter and increasingly difficult distinction reflects the old and deep dichotomy between vocational and non-vocational education in Britain. Traditionally, the universities and institutions of teacher training are classified as 'higher education', though included in this is a rapidly growing range of courses regarded as 'advanced further education' associated particularly with the development of polytechnics in England and Wales. 'Further education' (FE) is thus a general description of most of the post-school provision outside universities and teacher training institutions.

The complexity of educational provision increases as one moves through the stages. This may be ascribed to two main factors: first, the reorganization of secondary education on comprehensive lines; second, the considerable increase in the numbers seeking education after the age of 16. Thus today over 75 per cent of pupils in secondary schools in England and Wales attend comprehensive schools, compared with about one-third ten years ago. About one in three of young adults received some form of post-school education in 1978, compared with some 20 per cent in 1965.

Comprehensive reorganization followed the Labour Government's bid to end selection at the age of 11 in the mid 1960s via the DES Circular 10/65, which urged LEAs to plan comprehensive schools and approved six patterns of reorganization. The result in 1978 is a veritable patchwork quilt of secondary systems varying from middle schools (age nine to 13 years) at one end to sixth form or junior colleges (age 16 to 19 years) at the other. One must add to this the remaining, passionately defended outposts of selective schooling in the maintained sector, including the politically contentious direct-grant schools, funded directly by the DES, and note the continuing, robust good health of Britain's well-established independent (fee-paying) school sector. In 1975, over a million parents (many of them articulate and politically influential) had children in fee-paying schools. These children represented only one in 20 of the total school population but 10 per cent of those over age 15 (CSO, 1978). Their subsequent presence in higher education is disproportionately greater again.

There is thus little doubt as to the complexity of the initial education base which would need to be accommodated within any total strategy of recurrent education in Britain. One must also stress that while the British school system traditionally abhors the notion of centralized curricula and there is no national system of school-leaving certification, schools are, in many ways, dominated by a well-established system of public examinations. In England and Wales, the critical interface between initial and further/higher education is represented by the two main groups of examinations. The older and more critical group, in terms of access to post-school provision, consists of eight independent boards awarding the General Certificate of Education (GCE) at two levels. These boards to a large extent reflect the interest of the universities in monitoring and influencing the academic standards of the secondary schools. It would be difficult to overestimate their influence on the curricula and methodology of secondary schools in England and Wales. This is a matter of obvious concern to the advocates of the recurrent strategy for whom initial education's prime role is the fostering of the means and will for subsequent learning in the *total* school population rather than to act as a selection mechanism for further study by relatively *few* at age 16 or 18. A newer sector in the public examination structure is that associated with the Certificate of Secondary Education (CSE) dating from the mid-1960s and administered by 14 Regional Examining Bodies whose target population is that larger portion of the 16-year-old group not judged capable of reaching the standards of the GCE ordinary-level examination. The advent in the mid-1960s of CSE and the current moves towards reformed examination structures at ages 16 and 18 are indicative of the difficulties encountered as the traditional 'front-end' model tries to cope with mass secondary education. A common system of examining at 16+ is almost certain to be a reality by the mid-1980s in England and Wales. Public examinations in Scotland and Northern Ireland, while administered somewhat differently, have much the same characteristics, functions and significance for post-school provision.

One might suggest that the establishment of the Council for National Academic Awards (CNAA), which has the power to award degrees and other qualifications comparable with those of universities, to students who successfully complete approved courses in institutions without their own degrees, reflects the same basic problem. By 1977 the Council had some 118 institutions under its aegis, offering over 1,200 approved degree and Diploma in Higher Education (DipHE) courses to an enrolment of over 100,000 students — about a quarter of the total higher educational enrolment in the UK. Further developments by CNAA could well include degree courses designed entirely for mature students without conventional entry qualifications (Kerr, 1977).

At the post-compulsory level there is a considerable diversity of provision on a full-time, part-time or 'sandwich course' basis, but deep and much criticized organizational divisions can be identified. These are notably between the upper secondary schools and further education colleges at the

16 to 19 age level, and between the universities and the so-called 'public sector' institutions (particularly polytechnics and regional colleges), at the post-18 stage. The principal institutions from which any system of recurrent education would be formed beyond the base of compulsory education are the 45 universities and 30 polytechnics in England and Wales, the 14 Scottish central institutions with concentrations of advanced courses, Ulster Polytechnic (formerly the Ulster College) and over 700 other colleges. The latter include several large and recently-created institutions of higher education in England and Wales within which many former colleges of education have been absorbed since the sharp reduction in teacher training places after 1975. The great majority, however, were derived from former local technical colleges and are now termed colleges of further education. These represent the most widely spread institutions capable of generating a closely spaced network of centres for any formally institutionalized system of recurrent education in Britain. Their potential is well demonstrated by the pioneering efforts at the Nelson & Colne College of Further Education in Lancashire (Moore, 1977).

Thus, though total participation at post-compulsory level is not quantitatively outstanding by international standards, the diversity of provision as reflected by the following table is obviously a potential advantage in any move to develop a recurrent system in Britain.

The table does not include significant numbers of older people involved in those organized educational activities outside the main areas of higher professional and technical education typically described as 'adult education'. In 1974/5 about 2.7 million persons over 18 years of age attended courses classified thus and provided by LEAs, adult education departments of universities and various voluntary bodies. Of these the Workers' Educational Association (WEA) is the largest, usually working closely with the extra-mural departments of universities. This is an amorphous area of educational activity in Britain, the boundaries of which have become increasingly blurred. Financially, it traditionally accounts for a very small proportion of national educational investment but in Britain, as elsewhere, its practitioners are understandably prominent among those advocating educational reform on recurrent lines. Awareness of its growing significance as well as its problems of identity and purpose led to a major review via a government committee in 1973 (DES, 1973). The outcome of this, known popularly as the Russell Report, will be considered presently.

Finally, in concluding this brief and necessarily selective review of the British educational context in the late 1970s, one should draw attention to the large and expanding body of industrial training schemes existing alongside, or intermingled with, the public educational systems. Significantly, these activities are largely regulated by the Employment and Training Act of 1973, the outcome of a period of growing concern about the performance of the British economy in the post-war period and serious doubts as to the adequacy of the industrial training available. This concern led to the Industrial Training Act of 1964 and the establishment of 27 statutory Industrial Training Boards (ITBs). Thus by 1978 one has another

Table 1 Persons Continuing Education in Great Britain Aged 16 and over 1974/75
(All figures in thousands)

— Age on 31 December 1974 —

	Total 16 and over	Total 16-17			Total 18-20			Total 21-24			Total 25 and over	
		No.	C(%)	R(%)	No.	C(%)	R(%)	No.	C(%)	R(%)	No.	R(%)
Total Population *		1,670.0			2,360.0			3,120.0				
Full-time & Sandwich Students												
a. Schools	648.5	595.0	35.6	91.8	53.1	2.2	8.2	—	—	—	—	—
b. Further Education	373.0	131.9	7.9	35.4	122.4	5.2	32.8	70.6	2.3	18.9	47.9	12.8
c. Colleges of Education	119.8	—	—	—	63.8	2.7	53.3	32.9	1.1	27.5	23.0	19.2
d. Universities	257.7	2.2	0.1	0.9	131.6	5.6	51.1	85.2	2.7	33.1	38.6	15.0
e. Total Full-time & Sandwich Students (e = a + b + c + d)	1,399.0	729.1	43.7	52.1	370.9	15.7	26.5	188.7	6.1	13.5	109.5	7.8
f. Part-time Students † in Further Education	3,326.5	451.6	27.0	13.6	453.2	19.2	13.6	Total 21 and over 2,421.7			72.8	

C — percentage of age-group (column percentage)
R — percentage in that category of education (row percentage)
* — Registrar General's Estimate for 1 January 1975
† — of which 2,541.1 or 76.4% were *evening* students

Sources: DES : SED : Department of Education (Northern Ireland) as in *Annual Abstract of Statistics*, HMSO, 1978.

area of post-school provision but also further division and complexity in terms of the providing bodies. These are essentially the Department of Employment and the Manpower Services Commission (MSC). The latter is the means by which Britain seeks to achieve a satisfactory manpower policy and operates largely through the Employment Service Agency (ESA) and the Training Service Agency (TSA). When one recalls the OECD's belief in the recurrent strategy's greater potential for the achievement of 'necessary economic growth' it is evident that the advent of this other area in the overall complexity of post-school educational activity is of major significance to any consideration of recurrent developments in contemporary Britain.

Towards recurrent education?

It was suggested earlier in this chapter that most of the developments in Britain in recent years relevant to concepts of recurrent education were more directly related to a broader notion of increasing the opportunities for adults to participate in a wider range of education and training than with total alternative strategies linked with social and economic change. The term 'continuing education' seems more appropriate to this approach where the emphasis is on *addition to*, rather than *replacement of*, the familiar front-end model. The preceding sketch of Britain's complex and essentially decentralized systems of educational provision makes it clear that the circumstances are not such as to favour educational reforms in the manner which has occurred in more centralized systems since 1945. However, a serious debate has started, and mounted over the last five years, concerning the wisdom of continuing to invest the great majority of educational expenditure in a system designed primarily for the under-25 age group with the bulk of post-school provision going to those successful in competitive attainment tests at age 18.

One might, therefore, single out some of the more notable concerns in this intensifying debate, asking to what extent they represent the suggested distinction between (a) a pragmatic supplementation approach with a stance of relative practical neutrality (continuing education) and (b) the wider more ideologically-based approach perhaps more properly associated with recurrent education in the international sense which assumes 'that there exists a dialectical relationship between the overall social system and the education system' (Rodriguez, 1972).

In institutional terms, undoubtedly the best known example of British innovation with regard to continuing education is the Open University (OU). Its organization and methods as a non-residential university providing part-time degree and other courses via the electronic media and summer schools since 1971 are well documented (Open University, 1977). By 1978, with a student body of over 55,000 and an output of nearly 6,000 graduates per year representing one in 14 of the British total, the Open University would seem to have confirmed the belief in a substantial measure of educational under-achievement derived from traditional practices, particularly from early selection in compulsory education. About one in four of the 1976 graduates had less than the normal university entry qualifications. That is, significant numbers of older people, effectively debarred from full-time further study by the constraints of Britain's version of the front-end model, clearly possess the abilities to benefit from higher education. Analyses of the OU student body, however, make it quite clear that, thus far, it does not represent fully the obvious casualties of the decades of rigidly selective secondary education, particularly children from the lower socio-economic groups who failed to secure entry to the grammar school (Table 2). Though graduates from manual and routine non-manual occupations have increased in number they still represent little over one in ten of the total. Thus the OU's critics ask to what extent it would succeed with a socially wider student body and some doubt its continued success once the generation of grammar school under-achievers has passed through. Obviously, with less than a decade of operation and evaluation available, there is insufficient evidence in these directions. However, as with the Adult Literacy Scheme the outcomes are richer in terms of our understanding of success and failure in human learning than could have been foreseen (Jones and Charnley, 1978). Certainly, the debate on alternative educational strategies is much enhanced by the presence and experience of the OU. Its creation was a political act of faith as much as a radical experiment in the extension of existing opportunities, a belief in the potential of continuing education at university level. The lessons from it may well run deeper so far as alternative educational futures in Britain are concerned.

Indeed, by 1976, the OU's corporate strength was such that it was able to produce a major study on the wider possibilities for continuing education and the application of the principles of recurrence. The Venables Report (*see Chapter 19*) added further weight to the views of Russell's 1973 committee on non-vocational adult education concerning the need for a national development council devoted to the future of adult and continuing education.

One should note at this point that the general concern about adult learning in Britain led to a Scottish counterpart to Russell, the Alexander Report, a few years later (SED, 1975). Certainly, in 1974 government consideration was being given to the establishment of a national council but as the then Minister for Higher Education reminds us, 'Russell had reported at the moment when economic gloom was turning to long-running crises, a development council — not least because of the implications of the word 'development' — was seen as a new pressure group, demanding the commitment of resources which were not available in the foreseeable future' (Fowler, 1977). However, it was to be the autumn of 1977 before the long-awaited Advisory Council for Adult and Continuing Education (ACACE) came into being under the chairmanship of Dr Richard Hoggart. (*See also Chapter 17.*) Predictably, the Council falls short of the hopes of many in terms of its powers and brief. Gerald Fowler's successor at the

Occupational Group	1972 No.	%	1974 No.	%	1976* No.	%	1978* No.	%
At Home	3,763	11.0	4,858	14.6	6,958	13.8	6,461	14.4
Armed Forces	577	1.7	851	2.6	1,419	2.8	1,209	2.7
Admin & Managers	1,572	4.6	1,221	3.7	2,334	4.6	2,025	4.5
Education	10,327	30.2	9,620	29.0	11,653	23.1	9,519	21.2
Professions & Arts	4,283	12.6	3,894	11.7	5,811	11.5	5,479	12.2
Scientists & Engineers	1,486	4.3	1,009	3.0	1,615	3.2	1,227	2.7
Technical Personnel	4,084	11.9	3,251	9.8	5,148	10.2	4,425	9.9
Skilled Trades	1,017	3.0	1,004	3.0	2,055	4.1	1,580	3.5
Other Manual	772	2.3	818	2.5	1,641	3.3	1,333	3.0
Communications & Transport	476	1.4	493	1.5	1,085	2.2	967	2.2
Clerical & Office	3,224	9.4	3,355	10.1	5,686	11.3	5,287	11.8
Shop & Personal Sales Staff	1,514	4.4	1,408	4.2	2,691	5.3	2,230	5.0
Not Working	1,066	3.1	1,380	4.2	2,183	4.3	3,056	6.8
In Institutions	61	0.2	58	0.2	61	0.1	41	0.1
Totals	34,222	100.1	33,220	100.1	50,340	99.8	44,839	100.0

* applications

Source: Analysis of Applications for Places with the Open University, 1978. Open University, November 1977

Table 2 *Open University — occupational analysis of applicants*

DES clearly faced the same problem from the Treasury concerning the financial implications of any statutory development role for the Council so that Minister Gordon Oakes resisted pressure for a body with anything beyond the advisory role. Nonetheless, the Council's brief is explicit concerning its duty to 'promote the development of future policies and priorities, *with full regard to the concept of education as a process continuing through life*' (DES, 1977, *emphasis added*). Its response to the DES discussion document on the future of higher education in Britain (see below) reflects the advocates of recurrent education among its members:

> We think the fundamental issue facing the educational system as a whole, and higher education in particular, is the urgent need for a transition from a 'front-end' model based upon full-time initial higher education for a relative few to an 'open-ended' model based upon the continuing or recurrent provision of full-time and part-time further and higher education for all who, by virtue of ability, experience and motivation are able to benefit from it regardless of age. (ACACE, 1978)

Indeed, notable among the organizations pressing for, and consulted about, the Advisory Council was the Association for Recurrent Education (ARE), established in 1975. Much of the impetus behind ARE came predictably from OU staff and adult educationists in other universities. However, its executive represented all levels of the educational system from its inception and with the then Minister of State for Higher Education as its President, the Association offered further evidence of growing awareness and acceptance with regard to the recurrent concept in Britain from the mid-1970s onwards. Its constitution (*see* Appendix) was used among the starter definitions by the DES/SED Conference on Recurrent Education and its views were sought by the government prior to the establishment of the feasibility study into educational credit transfer in the United Kingdom in 1977.

This study, now proceeding under the direction of Dr Toyne at Exeter University, represents a further significant shift with regard to British thinking and attitudes on continuing and recurrent education. Some reactions to it, notably from the university sector via the Association of University Teachers (AUT), are predictably defensive, stressing the autonomy of academic institutions and professional bodies (ARE, 1977), but the implications of the inquiry are obvious in terms of the growing awareness of the inadequacy of the existing procedures with regard to the extension of educational opportunity through the age range.

A final event in this catalogue of growing awareness of the possibilities of recurrent education in Britain was the appearance of the DES discussion document 'Higher Education in the 1990s' in February, 1978. The concerns of government reflected in the document remind us of those changing social and economic circumstances of Britain in the late 1970s which seem likely to force the serious consideration of recurrent strategy by those hitherto unresponsive to the international debate on its principles and ideology. Whereas the Canadians and the Dutch (Alberta, 1972; Ontario, 1972; Kemenade, 1975) were moved in the late 1960s and early

1970s to debate publicly at the highest level the problems of further extending the front-end model *before* the full impact of internationally experienced inflation and major changes in demographic trends, Britain's response is firmly linked to these more immediate socio-economic trends. Though Britain's higher education system has almost tripled in size since 1960, as the document lucidly demonstrates, it will soon be faced with the consequences of the sharply falling birth rate which has already affected the teacher training component. The immediate problem underlying the discussion document is that the total number of full-time and sandwich course students is expected to continue to rise until the mid-1980s, then to stabilize for five or six years before a serious contraction sets in during the 1990s. A more fundamental problem is that all the document's projections must, of necessity, rest on the continuation or otherwise of known conditions. Thus, if the so-called 'Robbins Principle' is maintained whereby 'higher education courses should be available for all who are qualified by ability and adjustment to pursue and who wish to do so', (Cmnd No 2154, 1963) and the overall strategy remains that of the front-end model, with higher education concerned predominantly with the 18 to 25 age group, then certain highly unpalatable political consequences seem inevitable. The present higher education system, the major recipient of British educational investment since the 1950s, requires even more expenditure to meet front-end demand in the next decade, but thereafter will be disproportionately over-size, over-manned and arguably uneconomic. In the face of such disturbing circumstances, the document offers five models for the future development of higher education and invites comments on what it deems to be the 14 principal questions involved. (*See also Chapter 17.*) To many these suggest that DES thinking in 1978 is still unable adequately to conceptualize recurrent education as a serious alternative strategy for *all* provision in Britain, one which would ultimately affect compulsory initial education as much as universities, polytechnics and colleges (ARE, 1978). Nonetheless, it must be admitted that the following extract (Paragraph 7) is far removed from the stance of a former DES Deputy Secretary who at the OECD Conference on Future Structures of Post-Secondary Education in Paris in 1973 found recurrent education 'more confusing than clarifying' (Cantor, 1974):

> Another possibility is that the demand, which is already beginning to make itself felt, to devote more educational resources to those already in employment might result in more systematic opportunities for recurrent education for mature students. Priority might be given at first to those who had missed higher education opportunities at normal entry age. *But this might not preclude more radical developments*, such as a systematic scheme for continuing education at an advanced level, or indeed at a non-advanced level. This kind of possibility would be of direct concern not only to the education service, but also more widely, and particularly to the TUC and CBI, in so far as it might have implications for employment levels and for the terms and conditions of employment of individuals. Any more detailed examination of the possibility of increasing participation by those in employment would need to take this aspect fully into account. (DES, 1978, *emphasis added*)

Conclusions

The above extract helps to draw together the underlying arguments in this review of the recent developments related to recurrent education as a serious alternative strategy in Britain. Terminological imprecision and ambiguity remain a serious problem. The difficulty is, however, appreciated and ARE offers a forum for ongoing debate at a serious academic level (Lawson, 1977; Griffin, 1978). A growing awareness at a variety of levels, particularly governmental, is indisputable. The nature of the British context is such that the majority of thinking and action to date seems to relate more to that looser view of the principles of recurrence which the term continuing education represents, than to the strategical concept of recurrent education typified by OECD and the Council of Europe. However, Britain's continuing obsession with what successive governments see as their most acute problem, the failure to harness a sufficient proportion of its resources for productive industry and thus to secure adequate economic growth, has brought the nation's total educational enterprise under intense political scrutiny. This externally-derived accountability was given focus by Prime Minister Callaghan's initiation of the so-called 'Great Debate' on Education in 1976 in his speech at Ruskin College. To many, his preoccupation with attainment in compulsory education seemed misguided and the immediate response of the DES again was indicative of a failure to think in adequate strategic terms (DES, 1976):

> Ironically, the 'Great Debate' is concerned almost exclusively with schools and their role in servicing society ... Therefore, instead of asking whether there is a fundamental design flaw in our traditional educational model, we subject its working to an almost morbid scrutiny to see if tinkering with the engine will make it perform more effectively. (Fowler, 1977)

By 1978 Britain's economic problems appear to some to have generated what may be regarded as serious long-term structural unemployment, particularly acute in certain geographical areas and among those of the 16 to 19 age group who have fared worst in the examination-oriented secondary schools. New ages and stages of retirement begin to be considered at the other end of working life, in face of growing demand for workers with more skills dependent on higher educational achievement but in relatively smaller numbers, as automation bites more deeply into the structure of industry. Yet the workers in question will, for at least another 20 to 30 years, be the children of the 'bulge', products of the tripartite age of secondary schooling with its well-documented underachievement correlated with social class. Comprehensive reorganization has thus far failed to produce any dramatic improvement in the eyes of many employers and mass upper secondary education becomes more of a reality each year as individual expectations and youth unemployment rise. Yet, without an unprecedented increase in the participation of comprehensive school leavers in higher and advanced further education, the demography of the late 1980s will bring acute pressures on government from the providers of this expensively assembled sector of British provision. All these external and internal pressures on the various levels of educational provision make for a major crisis of educational identity and purpose as the 1970s draw to a close. Such an atmosphere may well be that which forces political consensus about alternative educational strategies and ends the era of British in-fighting about access within the front-end model. It is thus possible that the radical British editorials of today concerning the potential of recurrent education in its wider sense will be the political orthodoxy of tomorrow:

> The third need is the most important of all. It is for education for participation. The old authoritarian structures, at work, in the community and in the home are crumbling . . . Perhaps it is not an exaggeration to suggest that the role of recurrent education in the birth of social and industrial democracy may be as important as that of compulsory elementary education in the creation of the political democracy of the last century. (THES, 1977)

Be that as it may, certain hard, practical questions will need to be faced and answered during the evolution of any system of recurrent education in Britain. The more obvious concern is the urgent need to question some of the major assumptions underpinning post-compulsory provision; at each turn one can confidently anticipate protest from well-established sectional interests and governmental pleas of chronic national poverty.

The question of paid educational leave will need to be resolved before there can be any serious prospect of continuing education on a recurrent basis for that great majority of adults who did not succeed sufficiently at school to attract mandatory awards for further study. The system of such awards will need reconsideration.

The future of higher education will require review in much wider terms than those at present apparent. That is, it will be necessary to 'think laterally' about purposes, processes and appropriate structures in the universities and polytechnics of the 1990s and not only about the means whereby adequate numbers of students may be found to ensure that present structures and procedures are maintained. The question of credit transfer is urgent, even within the present front-end model in Britain. In any future system seeking to accommodate mixed modes of study and mature entrants with a variety of previous learning experiences, a national system of validation and accreditation would seem a necessity. There is already substantial experience in Sweden of admission to university on a basis of work experience rather than formal attainment. (*See also Chapter 11.*) Serious comparative research and larger pilot experiments will need to be funded in Britain if the fundamental question of mature entry is to be faced. Work like that of the Sheffield Group on Mature Entry to Education is indicative of the growing awareness of the problem.

In the related area of guidance and counselling for adults, Britain can claim internationally acclaimed expertise in the shape of the Educational Guidance Service for Adults in Belfast — ironically facing closure in 1978 (ARE, 1978) — and point to other pioneering ventures, eg at Hatfield

Polytechnic. Again a national service would seem a necessity to a recurrent system and this brings us to the basic national question. Can Britain's decentralized approach to educational provision provide the necessary evolutionary impetus? Paradoxically, the separation of responsibility at the centre appears to be increasing with DES and Department of Employment acting as the contemporary representatives of the uneasy relationship, as yet unresolved in Britain, between education and training. The question of effective power at the centre thus becomes vital. There are those who argue that the fragmentation of educational decision-making in Britain inevitably buttresses educational conservatism and that any major strategical shift must have the legislative backing of Parliament. It seems safe to presume that any effective system of recurrent education in Britain will be slow to evolve without a clearer commitment to its principles by one or both of the major political parties.

The need for legislation is perhaps most apparent when one faces the massive problems related to the least-mentioned aspect of change associated with recurrent education — that demanded of compulsory education. Clearly, the foundation of any successful recurrent strategy will be found in the nature of the learning experiences of the pupils in its schools. Five years ago, I argued that:

> ... while *education* is a social process systematically organized and institutionalized, *learning* is a personal experience. It begins and ends with the individual student and the time has come to invest him with considerable choice in deciding where, when and how he will seek to learn. (Molyneux, 1974)

Such a principle applies no less to the school child than the adult but its effective application has, so far, eluded every major school system, particularly at secondary level. Compulsory education within a recurrent system cannot afford significant numbers of school leavers lacking the skills and confidence to profit from continuing education. It will still need to foster academic excellence and maintain a critical interface with the frontiers of knowledge in higher education, but its priorities and purposes will be significantly different from those found in Britain today. Their achievement will require attitudinal changes among its practitioners arguably more daunting than those required at the post-compulsory level in the British system.

Appendix: Extract from the Constitution of the Association for Recurrent Education

The Association exists to promote discussion of and the establishment of activities within a wide variety of settings which come under the heading of recurrent education. Recurrent education constitutes a comprehensive educational strategy including all levels of educational provision. Its essential characteristic is the distribution of educational opportunity throughout the life span of the individual. It allows the alternation of periods of structured educational experience with work, leisure and retirement. It is to be regarded as an alternative to the traditional pattern of educational provision in which the great majority of formal education is experienced in the first 25 years of life. Its acceptance will require a reconsideration of every facet of existing educational provision in that it seeks not only to review the interaction between schooling, work and leisure, but also to make more meaningful the relationship between the acquisition and the application of human knowledge. It, therefore, represents a new contribution to human rights in which learning is acknowledged as a personal matter and each person's claim on educational provision represents more clearly his or her preference for a particular pattern of learning, work and leisure. Its goal is the learner with greater autonomy, better equipped to participate in the continuous shaping and re-shaping of his or her environment and society.

References

Advisory Council for Adult and Continuing Education (ACACE) (1978) Draft response to DES discussion document *Higher Education in the 1990s*

Alberta (1972) *Choice of Futures* Report of the Commission on Educational Planning in Alberta (The Worth Report): Edmonton

Association for Recurrent Education (ARE) (1977) The national credit transfer feasibility study *Association for Recurrent Education Newsletter 5*: Nottingham University

Association for Recurrent Education (ARE) (1978) Guidance and counselling for adults — Higher Education in the 1990s *Association for Recurrent Education Newsletter 6*: Nottingham University

Cantor, L (1974) *Recurrent Education Policy and Development in OECD Member Countries United Kingdom* OECD: Paris

CSO (1978) *Annual Abstract of Statistics 1978*: 118 Table 5.1 Central Statistical Office HMSO: London

Department of Education and Science (1963) *Report of the Commission on Higher Education* (The Robbins Report) Cmnd 2154 HMSO: London

Department of Education and Science (1973) *Adult Education: A Plan for Development (The Russell Report)* HMSO: London

Department of Education and Science (1976) *Schools in England and Wales Current Issues: An Annotated Agenda for Discussion* Welsh Office: Cardiff

Department of Education and Science (1977) Members appointed to new Advisory Council for Adult and Continuing Education: Press Release 18 October 1977

Department of Education and Science (1978) *Higher Education in the 1990s* (discussion document) DES: London and SED: Edinburgh

Fowler, G (1977) Agenda for better days *Times Higher Educational Supplement* 15 April

Griffin, C (1978) Curriculum models of recurrent and continuing education *Association for Recurrent Education Discussion Paper 3*: Nottingham University

Houghton, V P and Richardson, K (eds) (1974) *Recurrent Education: A Plea for Lifelong Learning* Ward Lock: London

Jones, H A and Charnley, A (1978) *Adult Literacy: A Study of Its Impact* NIAE: Leicester

Kemenade, J A Van (1975) *Contours of a Future Educational System in the Netherlands* (English version summary of a discussion memorandum) Ministry of Education and Science: The Hague

Kerr, E (1977) CNAA and recurrent education. Report of 1977 Annual Conference *Association for Recurrent Education Newsletter 5*: Nottingham University

Lawson, K H (1977) A critique of recurrent education *Association for Recurrent Education Discussion Paper 1*: Nottingham University

Molyneux, F H (1974) International perspectives *in* Houghton and Richardson (1974)

Moore, D (1977) Nelson and Colne College community-based approach to RE Report of 1977 Annual Conference *Association for Recurrent Education Newsletter 5*: Nottingham University

OECD/CERI (1973) *Recurrent Education: A Strategy for Lifelong Learning* OECD: Paris

Ontario (1972) *The Learning Society* Report of the Commission on Post-Secondary Education in Ontario (The Wright Report): Toronto

Open University (1974) *Recurrent Education – An Alternative Future?* Educational Studies E221, Unit 16. Open University Press: Milton Keynes

Open University (1976) *Report of the Committee on Continuing Education* (The Venables Report) Open University Press: Milton Keynes

Open University (1977) *An Introduction to the Open University* The Open University Information Services: Milton Keynes

Rodriguez, C (1972) Lifelong education *Bulletin of the International Bureau of Education* Year 46 No 185 The Fourth Quarter UNESCO: Paris

SED (1975) *Adult Education: The Challenge of Change* (The Alexander Report) HMSO: Edinburgh

18. A comprehensive system of education for adults

Naomi E McIntosh

Summary: General agreement about the inevitability of continuing education as the new educational form has not yet led to clarity about what this will imply in reality. Impetus has been given to the task of working it out through the mandate given to the Advisory Council for Adult and Continuing Education (ACACE) by the government to promote the development of the concept of education as 'a process continuing throughout life'. Discussions have also been stimulated by the five possible models for Higher Education in the 1990s proposed by the Department of Education and Science.

ACACE argues that these proposals do not go far enough and that it is necessary to move to an 'open-ended' model based upon the continuing or recurrent provision of full-time and part-time further and higher education for all who by virtue of ability, experience and motivation are able to benefit by it regardless of age.

To achieve this, it is argued, it is necessary to adopt a student-centred approach and begin by determining the educational needs and wants, both overt and covert, of *all* adults, not just those who have hitherto been participants in adult education. The key shift of emphasis is to the provision of 'education for adults'.

Four main barriers to the access of adults to educational provision are discussed: geography, finance, educational qualifications and structural barriers, and some requirements of an effective system of continuing education are outlined.

In conclusion, one possible strategy, that of giving all adults educational entitlements (or credits) as a right is suggested.

Background

While there is growing understanding among educationists and politicians that some form of recurrent or continuing education will become an increasingly important part of the overall education system over the next twenty years or so, there is as yet little clarity as to what form such developments should take, and how the necessary changes are to be achieved. In one sense, the spate of words being written on the subject, and the lip-service being paid to it may be self-defeating, as they give an illusory sense of general agreement which makes the way ahead seem clearer than it is.

The setting up of the Advisory Council for Adult and Continuing

Education (ACACE) by the Secretary of State for Education in October 1977 provided, in England and Wales, the first tangible sign of government commitment to this new concept. Adult education has been for too long the Cinderella of the education system. It has had little collective consciousness, no professional armies pressing for it, scanty funds, scarcely any buildings of its own — and no glamour. Adults themselves have not yet started to demand their rights in the field of education as they expect to do as citizens in other areas of their lives. The Russell Report (DES, 1973) must be the government report which received most praise for its recommendations, but which resulted in least official or governmental action. Van Straubenzee (1976), in explanation, suggested that the report had not been timely: the Committee had taken too long in its work, and by the time of its publication the economy of the country was on the down-turn and such funds as were available had already been committed to the setting up of the Open University.

There has been little political protest about this lack of implementation. Several years have passed between that time and the awakening interest shown, for example, by the Trade Union Congress in their recent statement on *Priorities in Continuing Education* (TUC, 1978). This lack of political interest has been paralleled by the lack of academic interest in the intellectual development of the discipline of adult learning. The dominance of initial education has carried with it, in virtually every country, a concentration on pedagogy at the expense of the subject the Dutch and Yugoslavs teach as 'androgogy'. The assumption that what has been discovered about child learning can be straightforwardly applied to adult learning across the whole life-span is not well founded. (*See also Chapter 4.*) At the same time adult educators have been content until now to acquire their skills and expertise on the job rather than through formal training, in the pursuit of theoretical knowledge. As Purvis (1976) points out, there is no general consensus concerning the definition of the territory of activity of adult education, there is a paucity of systematic knowledge and research in the field, the structure of decision-making covering the area within the Department of Education and Science is fragmented, and so is the structure and method of financing in the country as a whole. All of these factors, she argues, contribute to the current low status of adult education.

Education for adults

Although any move forward requires more than just re-labelling, a change of name may well prove to be an essential prerequisite to a change of attitude and thence to changes in educational, political and financial commitment. More important than whether or not the model adopted is labelled 'continuing', 'recurrent' or 'lifelong', however, is the determination embodied in the terms of reference given to the Advisory Council to look at 'education for adults'. The shift of emphasis involved in looking at 'education for adults' rather than adult education immediately makes it clear that the task is vast and challenging, requiring a new perspective.

The Council's terms of reference are:

> To advise generally on matters relevant to the provision of education for adults in England and Wales, and in particular
> (a) to promote co-operation between the various bodies engaged in adult education and review current practice, organization and priorities, with a view to the most effective deployment of the available resources; and
> (b) to promote the development of future policies and priorities, with full regard to the concept of education as a process continuing throughout life (DES, 1977).

In a letter to Dr Richard Hoggart, the Council's Chairman, giving 'Notes of amplification' for its first meeting, the DES made it clear that the use of the phrase 'education for adults' was intentionally broader than 'adult education' (Lloyd Jones, 1977). Since these notes provide important guidance for the Council, it is worth quoting the key paragraph:

> The second strand of the terms of reference brings us to the concept of continuing or recurrent education. Increasingly we have come to realize that education and training cannot adequately be provided by school and immediately post-school (front-end) provision; for a variety of personal, social and vocational reasons, adults need to be able to return to education and training throughout life, to explore new avenues or pursue existing interests further — adult education probably never was, and certainly cannot now be regarded as, a discrete area. Post-school education and training is increasingly seen as a continuum permitting many different combinations of modes of attendance, subject areas and levels of study intended to meet the almost infinite variety of students' needs and motivation. Adult education and all the other administratively convenient bundles of provision do not therefore have rigid boundaries. Continuing education requires us to think in a student-centred rather than an institution-centred way. (Lloyd Jones, 1977)

The relevance of Higher Education into the 1990s

It is obviously too early for the Council to have developed such an overall framework, and the Committee charged with the task has only recently started work. Its initial thinking, however, has been spurred on, as has the thinking of many others involved in post-school education, by the publication of the discussion document *Higher Education into the 1990s* (DES, 1978). Prompted by the dramatic decline in the birth-rate which has already affected primary schools and teacher training, the document asks a number of questions about various policy options open to the country both in the short-term, to meet the demand for higher education generated by the last peak in the birth-rate from the early 1960s, and in the longer term, when demand from the conventional age-group is likely to decline dramatically. The government could decide not to expand higher education provision over the next few years to meet the natural demand generated by the last peak. This is the policy recommended by the Government's Central Policy Review Staff Unit and described as 'tunnelling through'. Such a policy, not surprisingly, does not find much support among existing institutions, nor does it seem equitable to that particular 'accidental' generation of teenagers who will suffer in the short term. Whether or not the government chooses to expand fully over this time period, there will be an inevitable contraction of demand from the conventional age-group in the late 1980s and 1990s.

The document suggests five possible scenarios as outcomes. The first of these, Model A, postulates expansion to meet the full demand, followed by sharp contraction with all the difficulties that implies. Model B involves reducing the scale of expansion after 1981 and therefore the need for so much contraction after 1990. This option would involve a break with the Robbins principle on which higher education has been based for many years and a reduction of opportunities for qualified applicants during the peak time period. The third model involves catering fully for student numbers, but causing universities to do it more cost-effectively, eg, by using higher student-staff ratios, or by applying the principles of educational technology. Model D is more radical in its approach and considers shorter courses (two rather than three years), more part-time study, more sandwich courses and the possibility of deferment of entry.

The relevance of this discussion for the future of continuing education is the fifth scenario, Model E, described by Gordon Oakes (the Minister of State for Education) on the day of the paper's publication as having a great deal of appeal for him personally (Oakes, 1978). It envisages that there should be no contraction, but that the places released by demography in the late 1980s and 1990s would instead be used to expand opportunities for the children of manual workers and for adult students. The discussion document states explicitly:

> Another possibility is that the demand, which is already beginning to make itself felt, to devote more educational resources to those already in employment might result in more systematic opportunities for recurrent education for mature students. Priority might be given at first to those who had missed higher education opportunities at normal entry age. But this might not preclude more radical developments, such as a systematic scheme for continuing education at an advanced level, or indeed at a non-advanced level. (Paragraph 33)

ACACE, in its response to the discussion document (ACACE, 1978) welcomed the recognition that:

> It is quite possible to envisage a pattern of higher education in the 1990s which differs in significant respects from that which obtains today. . . . and the higher education system itself might reach out to embrace different types of students and meet fresh needs such as that of recurrent and continuing education.

Faced with the stark reality of demography, it is not surprising that many responses to the Minister have welcomed Model E as a possible way ahead, though there is as yet little clarity about what the Model might involve, and many institutions appear to consider that it will mean no more than opening up existing opportunities to a wider age-range.

ACACE argues strongly that the discussion document, in confining itself to the implication of demographic trends for higher education, is too limited and that a similar study is required for further education. It considers that:

> the fundamental issue facing the education system as a whole, and higher education in particular, is the urgent need for a transition from a front-end model based upon full-time initial higher education for a relative few to an 'open-ended' model based upon the continuing or recurrent provision of full-time and part-time further and higher education for all who by virtue of ability, experience and motivation are able to benefit by it regardless of age. ... The ultimate aim must be a flexible student-centred pattern of higher education catering for the emerging needs of students irrespective of age. (ACACE, 1978)

The rationale for continuing education has been spelled out in detail elsewhere and does not need repeating here. The problem that remains is to translate the principle of this country's agreement, at the European Ministers of Education Conference at Stockholm in 1975, into a workable plan appropriate for the situation in this country. Obviously no plan can be implemented 'at a stroke', but equally it is important that in the transitional period, any changes that are made are consistent with the general direction of an overall plan. The time-scale involved is likely to stretch to the end of this century.

Of course this does not imply that all education will change. Much already exists which qualifies as continuing education in every sense of the word, and which will provide a firm foundation for future developments. Any plan will also need to ensure that the good aspects of current provision are not lost in the interest of more ambitious, but not yet realized, goals. At the same time it will have to be recognized that a diversion of resources towards continuing education will undoubtedly mean fewer resources being available for some other claimants.

A student-centred approach

The key to an understanding of ACACE's position at this stage is the acceptance of a student-centred approach to the provision of education. Although some 'continuing education' already exists, and although strategies for its extension are likely to be implemented to a large extent through institutions as we now know them, to get a clear view of the change in concept it is necessary to approach it, not in terms of existing structures, existing institutions and existing power-groupings, but through an analysis of the educational needs of all adults. It is useful to start, as ACACE's discussion paper does, from generalizations about education, in terms of:

1. The needs and motivation of adults, at differing stages of their lives.
2. The purposes of the educational provision.
3. How access to this educational provision can be secured for all adults.
4. What are the likely social and economic consequences of this provision.

The educational needs of adults

The provision of education has until now, in all countries, been determined more by what providing institutions wish to provide or think people need, or what they think society needs, than by any systematic attempt to discover what individuals themselves actually want or need. And existing provision is made through a variety of different structures attempting to meet different educational needs, without any overall policy. While educationists and politicians may understand the rationale for these different overlapping and often competing structures, adults who simply want more education may be excused for feeling bewildered. The lack of integration of education and vocational training causes particular difficulties and inequities, for example the payments made to unemployed teenagers to study while sixth formers continuing normally at school are unsupported.

To discover what people would wish for, provided the more obvious barriers to access, such as geography or finance, were removed is not an easy task. It is important, however, to make a start. The first stage of a 'needs assessment' — actually asking people about their experience and needs — is a step in the right direction, and ACACE is commencing a study along these lines. It is however argued, particularly by the TUC, that those whose needs have always been neglected are also those who fail to perceive the relevance of education in their lives. These people will not even know that they want education. Some commentators will suggest that it does not matter if a majority of the population remains uninterested in education for most of their lives, and that it is arrogant of educationists to assume they should. Others, of whom Hoggart is one, argue strongly that this state of affairs should not be allowed to continue and that 'it is not good enough simply to take for granted what Lessing called "the *wantlessness* of the poor"' (Hoggart, 1978). It is part of the TUC's case that there should be a radical shift in the allocation of resources for continuing education from the 'haves' to the 'have-nots':

> Post-school education has tended to reinforce inequality by allocating the greater share of resources to those who gained the highest attainments at school, and least to those with the greater educational and social needs. (TUC, 1978)

The identification of the needs and demands of adults for education must be a priority task. The identification of overt needs and demands is the easier part of this, but unless the covert needs of the educationally under-privileged are also brought into the open, the major task will not be done. This may well necessitate a total change in people's attitude to education so that they do not just screen it off as irrelevant, but look on it as a right, a pleasure and a benefit to themselves and their families.

The purposes of education: general and vocational

Distinctions continue to be made between vocational and non-vocational education or between vocational and general education. The mandate of ACACE is clearly in the area of general education. It is part of my thesis, however, that this distinction, although it may be necessary for funding, organizational and administrative purposes, is not helpful as far as the consumer of education is concerned. While some courses are clearly vocational in nature, many other general courses may well have significance for occupational purposes, for example the simple possession of a degree. What is general for one person may well be vocational for another. Similarly the same course, taken at one point might be vocational, or taken at another point in relation to one's career might be general. A critical feature of any future plan will be to ensure that any organizational boundaries drawn for administrative or financial purposes between general and vocational education and training do not prevent adults from having access to the type of education or training they need.

Access to educational provision

Four major barriers impede the access of adults to existing educational provision: geography, finance, educational qualifications and the structure of existing provision. For many, the right course is not geographically accessible and study would mean leaving home temporarily, or moving house. For others, financial pressures and family responsibilities mean that the financial sacrifice involved in studying full-time, even if a mature student grant is available, is too great. And of course many are debarred by lack of appropriate qualifications. Discussions on recurrent education tend to concentrate on the notion of *alternating* periods of work with periods of education. The experience of the Open University has shown that many adults wanting a degree appear to prefer to study *while they continue to work* (McIntosh and Woodley, 1978). While for some this is a negative choice, due to lack of money, for others it is a positive choice related to their desire to continue in their careers. The assumption that the majority of adults, if given the choice together with adequate financial support, would prefer to study — even for a degree — full-time for three to four years, often in another place, is not well-founded. It often means giving up an existing job, usually with no guarantee that it or another one will be available. For the great majority of courses below the level of degrees, part-time study has, of course, always been seen as an acceptable and appropriate mode for adult students.

Geographical barriers

Geographical barriers are of particular significance to some categories of potential students. While the young can be expected and often prefer to move to distant universities and polytechnics, older students are tied by families and jobs and limited to opportunities which are physically accessible to them. Longer journeys may be justified for full-time study, but the physical location of part-time study has to be near the student if it is to be of any use. To be compelled to attend one physical location two, three or maybe four times a week for several years outside working hours, or on top of looking after a family, is a major barrier to access. Decreasing availability of public transport locally does not help in this respect.

Structural barriers

For all those who do not wish or are not able to study full-time, access is also prevented by the lack of part-time courses, or at least part-time courses available on terms which take account of the other proper demands on adults' lives. While a number of students, having tested out the loneliness of the OU's distance-learning system, will prefer to study through conventional institutions, many others will simply not be able to meet the physical attendance requirements of some courses. Educationists, traditionally, have viewed part-time study as an inferior method compared to full-time study, and this has been reinforced by ways in which the funding for these areas has been calculated.

If part-time education is indeed the preferred mode for the majority of adults, this in itself has major implications for its status and for decisions about its future funding and provision. While full-time study can be provided through a limited number of regionally spread centres, part-time provision has to be within reasonable travelling distance of part-time students to be effective. This argues for a wider spread of smaller centres rather than a limited spread of larger centres. The implications of this for some areas of study, particularly if there is to be a reasonable choice of curriculum, may well be the widespread use of co-operatively produced common core materials which can be provided locally through the *mediation* of a local tutor.

Financial barriers

Adequate financial support has to take account not only of the cost of tuition, but of the additional costs of study, or of travel to enable study, and also of the cost to the household of the student studying.

Traditionally in Great Britain the individual consumer has not paid directly for his or her education. At school level, education is free to the individual and paid for through a combination of rates and taxes. The comprehensive mandatory grant system has similarly ensured that much of post-school education has been effectively free to the individual. To demarcate some areas of post-school education as not free, or to provide them with inadequate financial support, will undoubtedly limit their accessibility, and particularly their accessibility to educationally disadvantaged groups.

Looking back nostalgically to the late 1940s at a time when, after the war, adult students were the norm rather than the exception in universities, and were also highly successful, one significant difference appears to be in the adequacy of financial support provided to them and their families. Students could at that time study without great sacrifice by their families. It is also true that fewer of them were doing it at the expense of their jobs and careers, since most of their careers would have been dislocated by the war.

The barrier of educational qualifications

The barrier of educational qualifications is still a formidable one, although faint hearts should now be able to take courage from the evidence provided by the Open University of the ability of 'unqualified' students to study successfully. Suffice it here to say that motivation and experience are likely to prove as significant, if not more so, as formal educational qualifications. Greater flexibility in entrance requirements and in arrangements about credit recognition and transferability are an essential prerequisite to the removal of this barrier.

Some requirements of an effective system of continuing education

In its response to the discussion document on the 1990s, ACACE identified at least five different requirements of an effective system of continuing education (ACACE, 1978):

1. *The establishment of an effective system of information and publicity.* Interest in the country in developing mechanisms for the provision of educational advice and guidance is increasing, and a committee of ACACE under the chairmanship of Peter Clyne is currently making recommendations about systems which are educationally and financially appropriate. The matching of adults' needs to existing opportunities is obviously critical and is unlikely to be achieved through existing institutional structures. The provision of an adequate information service should, it is argued, assist in identifying unmet need and demand, and help to shape future provision.
2. *A comprehensive system of student awards and financial support.* There is no question that financial problems form an important barrier to access, and existing grant schemes are of more assistance to some categories of people than others. Provision for support for full-time study is at the moment less of a problem than it is for part-time study. If, therefore, more part-time study is to develop, or mixed modes of full and part-time, then the discretionary area of awards will need rethinking. Similarly if transferability is to be encouraged, then rules which debar people who have previously followed or

started a course from being awarded a second grant will need to be reviewed.

The idea of 'paid educational leave' is gaining ground and obviously has some merit. (*See also Chapter 9.*) It does not, however, provide an adequate framework for all categories of people, and if pursued headlong may well only provide patchwork provision. As currently discussed, it does not cover those who are not employed: this includes women temporarily out of the labour market, the unemployed, people who have been made redundant or who have retired prematurely. Another important group likely to be less well provided for are employees of small firms.

The employer's role with regard to vocational education is clear, and the majority of employers are likely to accept it, providing the financial implications are dealt with. But what many adults want is general and not vocational education and existing information, for example about employers' attitudes to Open University study, indicates that the majority do not feel that general education is their responsibility. Paid educational leave is therefore likely to make only a partial contribution to the problem, and should not be thought of as the unique solution replacing all other provision.

It will be important for any new scheme not to be pursued at the expense of existing ones: current grants and sponsorship schemes in the country provide substantial possibilities for mature students with few strings attached.

3. *Developments in educational technology, distance learning and independent learning systems.*

An increasing number of adults are going to want education to be more available to them. The role of the media and of educational technology in making education directly available more cost-effectively is obviously important. What is equally important is its ability to provide education in more flexible ways both in terms of time and geography. Technology enables education to be provided to some people who simply would not be able to have access to it in its traditional form. New developments such as Prestel, VCRs and telephone teaching are all important and need to be utilized to extend the range of educational opportunities open to all. However there are institutional barriers to be overcome if the use of new technologies is to spread, for example the fact that funding currently is related to teaching hours. It is also important that older distance methods such as correspondence teaching should not be too easily discarded in the scramble for glamour.

4. *The training and re-training of staff in post-school education.*

Discussions concerning the training of staff in further and adult education are continuing at a national level at the moment, with major proposals for an increase in training. A shift to continuing education will increase this need, particularly in methods appropriate to mature and post-experience students for whom the traditional patterns developed for 16 to 21 year-olds are unlikely to be suitable. Given the security of tenure enjoyed by the teaching profession at all levels, re-training is likely to be more important than initial training.

5. *The provision and adaptation of buildings.*

Whether one likes it or not, society's investment in the bricks and mortar of existing buildings is also a powerful determining factor in future provision. The impact of declining enrolment has already released several former college of education buildings and numbers of primary schools, either for demolition or for change of use. One problem is that the location and structure of these buildings is not necessarily appropriate for new uses. A very fashionable option, particularly in areas where it is financially not possible to justify another building, is to have dual use of buildings, opening up to the community the existing primary or secondary school. This appears on the face of it to be a very desirable development, integrating as it does the community with the school. However, to some adults who have been screened out of education by just such a school, to have to re-enter it through the same doors and even under the same teacher's eyes may well be a serious barrier. A change of location and image for some people may be a necessity as a passport to entry.

If schools are to be used as dual-purpose buildings then this must be planned for, and the buildings adapted where necessary. It is simply not good enough to expect adults to sit at child-sized desks without even facilities for coffee and social interchange.

These are only some requirements of an effective system of continuing education, and need to be added to. The significant point is that entry into the problem does not come from the point of view of existing institutions or from existing provision, but from the point of view of the student or potential student.

To endeavour to provide a comprehensive range of provision assumes a world of perfect knowledge and infinite resource. The strategy is, therefore:

1. To make the most of existing resources by making them more accessible.
2. At the same time to get adults to articulate their needs and make their demands felt.
3. These demands then have to be matched against and married with society's demands.
4. The resultant gaps in provision will then become clearer and society can move towards filling them.

The assumption behind this is that existing provision will be forced to respond to the more overt expression of needs and demand.

A possible strategy

It will be clear that changes in educational provision will not happen overnight, and that the key to change is seen to come through a change on the part of adults in their expectations and demands. Society accepts without question the right of a child to have access to education. Society now needs to move to a similar acceptance of that principle for adults. The simple giving of that right to adults will, it is argued, change qualitatively people's attitude to it. It is unlikely that the right will be abused, since education for most adults is not an easy option, to be lightly undertaken. The question of financing such a scheme has been deliberately left out of this discussion. Of course it will have a cost, but it will also have benefits.

It will not be easy to work out an effective way of giving adults a right to education. One possible way into the problem is outlined here, as a personal contribution to the debate and to start realistic discussion going. The suggestion is that all adults be given educational credit units (or entitlements) as a right. Such credit units would be taken to cover the right to study, the right to leave from work if that were necessary and the right to adequate financial support. They could be used for any type of study whether general or vocational, certificated or not. They could be of two sorts: the first sort would be several large units covering the five years of education normally taken as full-time immediately post-school from 16 to 21. If individuals preferred not to continue with post-school education end-on, they would simply bank these large credit units and cash them in later on, if and when they wished to embark on major full-time study over long time periods. At the same time individuals would accumulate smaller credit units at the rate of, say, one week for every year of their adult life, irrespective of whether or not they were in paid employment. These could be cashed in as and when the individual chose, either being used for small periods of study such as evening classes, or being accumulated for longer periods to enable chunks of full-time study or prolonged part-time study. They could be used at whatever level individuals preferred. Many might well not use their entitlement, but many others would be encouraged to take advantage of the opportunity. Such a scheme would recognize and build on the additional benefit accruing when adults have themselves chosen to participate in more education.

Of course, the financing of such a scheme has major implications for the country, but a lot of this would be redistributive in effect rather than involving new expenditure. The implications for the relationship between education and training, and the provision of opportunities made available through employment rather than through educational institutions needs further study. Additional vocational training for example is still likely to be needed.

Maybe such a scheme is wildly unrealistic. However, the emphasis is clear, and it is that in order to co-ordinate a comprehensive system of education for adults, it is necessary to start from the point of view of the needs of adults and match provision to their needs. We are not expecting vast changes on a grand scale in the short term. The richness and profusion of existing structures both in adult education and further education provide a foundation on which to build in order to ensure that the comprehensive educational opportunities now available to children are also made available to adults.

References

Advisory Council for Adult and Continuing Education (ACACE) (1978) Council's response to the DES discussion document *Higher Education into the 1990s*: Leicester

Department of Education and Science (1973) *Adult Education: A Plan for Development* (The Russell Report) HMSO: London

Department of Education and Science (1977) *Memorandum of Arrangements for the Advisory Council for Adult and Continuing Education* HMSO: London

Department of Education and Science and the Scottish Education Department (1978) *Higher Education into the 1990s (discussion document)* DES: London and SED Edinburgh

Hoggart, R (1978) *After Expansion: A Time for Diversity* ACACE: Leicester

Lloyd Jones, D E (1977) Letter to Richard Hoggart: London 14 October 1977

McIntosh, N E and Woodley, A (1978) *Combining Education with Working Life or The Working Student* Paper presented at the 4th International Conference on Higher Education University of Lancaster, September 1978

Oakes, G (1978) Minister of State for Education and Science *The Universities and Britain's Future* Address to the AUT/THES Conference 23 February 1978

Purvis, J (1976) The low status of adult education — some sociological reflections *Educational Research* 19 1: 13-24

Taylor, J (1978) The Advisory Council for Adult and Continuing Education *Adult Education* 51 4: 209-15

Trade Union Congress (1978) *Priorities in Continuing Education* London

Van Straubenzee, W R (1976) *Whither the Open University?* Lecture to Open University Students Association Bristol University 9 April 1976

19. Co-ordinating vocational education for adults

Ron Johnson

Summary: From the manpower angle, adult education is closely linked with vocational training in meeting people's employment learning needs. Helping adults learn requires more than providing courses in colleges. It involves managing a variety of situations in which adults are consciously helped to develop their own potential, whether this is initiated by their employers or whether it arises from the individual's desire to improve his or her employment prospects through study.

Account must be taken of employment prospects and the nature of labour markets. Such studies may indicate new opportunities for apt educational provision. Current learning opportunities are provided through a diversity of education and training institutions and by employers.

Effective co-ordination must be directed towards well-defined ends, to ensuring that the realistic requirements of people, employers and society are met. Problems arise from the plurality of responsibilities for education and training, from the difficulty many people have in gaining access to the tuition they require and from the cost of developing appropriate curricula.

The way forward is to build on the evident strengths of present institutions — the richness of variety, the adaptability of their staffs, and their many contacts with other sectors of society. At the same time there is a need to remedy certain weaknesses in the system by improving communications, especially at the local level, by helping individuals and institutions to adapt and change and to focus upon the needs of people.

Introduction

In the United Kingdom the term *adult education* has been used to indicate the extension of general education into adult life and as such it has excluded the main areas of higher, professional and technical education. In recent years increasing collaboration between the education and vocational training bodies, coupled with the developing notion of continuing education, embracing vocational and non-vocational studies, has blurred this definition.

The manpower angle on adult education is naturally concerned with people and employment and, in particular, ways in which education can help individuals to prepare themselves for employment, find it, perform well in their jobs, enjoy their working experience and become equipped to continue their personal growth and development within realistic limits.

Studies of the employment scene indicate the need for people who can adapt to changes in their jobs and who will probably move to other kinds of jobs during their working lives.

This suggests that the initial education, training and work experience of young people should be deliberately geared to helping them to acquire learning skills along with the knowledge and skills related to their jobs. For those who have left full-time education, whether they are employed or unemployed, there is a need to provide a comprehensive array of learning opportunities to help them to cope with changes as they occur.

Helping adults learn

In the minds of many people education and training is something that happens over a specific time in a special place called a school or a training centre. Worse still, some people think of education as something that is done to young people on a once-and-for-all basis. Happily such notions are being challenged by ideas of continuous education and training where the need for adults in all kinds of jobs — and those without jobs — to re-enter education and training programmes is recognized. This need arises in part from the external pressures of changing technology, job structures, legislation and the like. But these pressures also arise because more people today want to develop their own abilities and explore their potential for growth in relation to work and in other spheres.

It is probably natural that in the work context these ideas are highly developed in the management field where it is increasingly recognized that good managers are developed over a period of time and the learning that takes place on the job (for good or ill) is often more important than the learning that takes place in an education or training establishment. We now speak of management development in terms of 'any attempt to improve managerial performance through a planned and deliberate learning process' (Manpower Services Commission, 1978a). A lot of management learning happens by accident, but management development is concerned with trying to make this learning a positive, conscious, purposeful activity. This concept can be applied to individual managers, to management teams, and to whole organizations. They can be used to improve present performance, to encourage organizational cohesion or to help provide well-prepared managers for the future. If we consider the individual manager, he needs to be encouraged to learn by being enabled to see the relationship of learning to performance and rewards. In many cases this will result in managers taking more responsibility for what they learn in peer-learning groups or in resource-based programmes rather than content-based programmes. In this scenario, education and training programmes become a component of self-development/management development programmes. Although these ideas have often been developed for managers they will have other parallels and applications. Recent work on the training of training officers (Manpower Services Commission, 1978b) points to similar problems — and perhaps some parallel solutions. There has also been some work done where people with employment problems have been helped by programmes combining group work with individually pursued studies.

The traditional forms of education and training have a vital role where relevant areas of knowledge, skill and understanding are to be acquired quickly by a number of people with shared needs. When, as is so often the case with adults, the tutor is confronted with a group of people whose learning styles and prior knowledge vary widely, programmes with a considerable measure of self-paced work and sub-group activity will be required. Where the group contains people whose learning needs vary widely, a large measure of self-directed learning assisted by tutors and other appropriate resources will be more appropriate. There are also arrangements whereby individuals can be attached to educational centres to pursue self-directed studies.

This concept of human development as a continuous process assisted by periods of education/training will give rise to new demands and challenges in adult education, but it may in fact be one of the keys to effective co-ordination by helping us to focus on the learning needs of people. Co-ordination will arise naturally if we put the learner first and if we make effective working links between the providers of education and training in seeking to meet these needs together. Talk-shops between educators of various kinds and trainers will produce hot air. Workshops where these same people meet to tackle real problems will produce imaginative solutions, understanding and collaboration.

It may be worthwhile to illustrate this by a few examples. If we consider the training of craftsmen — be they engineering, construction or bakery workers — there is clearly a need for the acquisition of theoretical and practical skills coupled with experience of a variety of tasks which must be accomplished at commercially viable speeds. In other words the learning is a combination of education, training and (one hopes, planned) experience. Education alone cannot produce a craftsman; nor can training. Some skills can only be developed on the job. Quite apart from the technical aspects of the job, an effective craftsman is generally working with a number of other people — the supervisor, other craftsmen, machine operators, perhaps clerical workers. He or she must cope with these relationships as well as with the piece of metal or the loaf of bread being fashioned.

The individual may aspire to become an instructor, a supervisor or a technician. Further personal growth is indicated and more knowledge and skills will be required. Many effective schemes have been devised by local co-operation between company trainers and college lecturers to meet the learning needs of such people. Much of the general theory and practice can be covered by the colleges, while the company-specific procedures (eg industrial relations procedures and management information systems) will be dealt with by company training.

These schemes work best when people get together to examine specific problems and to provide specific solutions. The problems of adults moving into technician-type work are likely to increase. We should not think in terms of putting adults through the normal education courses. Special courses must take account of their existing knowledge and experience, and also the different approach they may have to learning in the classroom.

Adult vocational learning needs

The initiative for education and training for adults in employment may come from the employer or from the individual. The unemployed adult may seek education and training as a way of improving his or her job prospects. If vocational education is to be of real value it must be related to jobs which are, or will become, available to the individuals concerned. What then, will be the size and shape of the labour market in future?

Employment prospects

Forecasting the economy and employment prospects is a fascinating but highly imprecise art where judgement plays as big a part as historical quantitative data. (In a fast-moving world data collected at the national level is normally out-dated by the time it is assembled.) Nevertheless it is necessary to look for some trends on which to base employment, education and training plans and policies. It is fortunate that towards the training end of the spectrum it is often possible to arrange programmes at short notice, provided suitable accommodation and equipment can be mobilized. On present evidence (Manpower Services Commission, 1978c) unemployment in the UK is unlikely to diminish appreciably over the next five years. During this period more people will be entering the labour market, especially young people, graduates and mature women.

Employment opportunities are expected to increase gradually in the social, professional and other services. Growth in employment in manufacturing and construction will probably be slender. The net effect will be to increase the numbers of people employed in occupations demanding education and training at the expense of those demanding little learning. Graduate employment opportunities will improve in health, in education and in certain parts of the public sector, but probably not enough to satisfy the number of graduates produced so that some graduates will be doing lower level work and the domino effect will push its way down the market. Those with least education or training will find it most difficult to get jobs. It is likely that growth in certain occupations will occur in unexpected places, eg more technicians and draughtsmen in the public sector and in services.

These global trends will not apply uniformly to each region. Indeed variations in the pattern of employment within regions is likely to continue to be marked. Particularly acute problems will be presented by the long-term unemployed and inner-city areas.

Labour markets

An account of the co-ordination of education in relation to employment would be incomplete without an understanding of labour market concepts. The term internal labour market is sometimes used to describe the movement of people between jobs, or the change in the nature of the jobs which people continue to do, but where they are retained by the same employer. This notion covers transfers, promotion, job enlargement, organizational changes and the like. There is an enormous variety of educational and training needs associated with internal labour market problems. For example, large numbers of people are appointed to management posts for which they need, but do not receive, education and training. Technological change often requires skilled workers or craftsmen to take on technician-type work where problem-solving skills are required and must be acquired.

There are also a smaller number of individuals who move from comparatively narrow functional management positions to demanding general management jobs where they need to broaden their perspectives and to have an appreciation of organizational functions where their knowledge is often scant. The increase in participation by workers in the broader aspects of the affairs of their organizations can so easily lead to unnecessary friction, delays in decisions and other phenomena. These impede the effectiveness of the organization and impose stress on people. There will always be differences of view but often improvements can be made by effective education and training programmes that increase understanding in relevant areas.

The term 'labour market' is generally used to describe movements of people in and out of employment or between one employer and another. It has been estimated that there are about nine million job changes each year in Great Britain. It is convenient to consider labour markets in three dimensions, ie occupational, geographical, and sectoral. If a carpenter, a bricklayer, an accountant or a biochemist is dissatisfied with his or her employer, the individual will most likely look for another job as a carpenter, bricklayer, accountant or biochemist respectively. This is the occupational dimension. Most carpenters and bricklayers will be reluctant to move house in order to change employer and they will probably look for jobs within the 'travel to work' area based on their existing homes. On the other hand the accountant may be quite prepared to move to another part of the country and the biochemist ready to move to another country altogether. This is the geographical dimension. The accountant will be able to move into any sector of employment (eg, distribution, engineering, insurance) whereas the biochemist will be limited (as a biochemist) to sectors of employment where there is an interest in biochemical matters, eg, pharmaceuticals, food, health. This is the sector dimension. Of course people can change their occupations. They can build on their existing expertise. For example, the carpenter or bricklayer can be trained to become instructors, the accountant and biochemist can become college lecturers. People can also break free from the notional constraints of their past experience and training to take up completely new occupations.

Education and training programmes can be provided to assist in this process of helping people to develop and to cope with the changes in the labour market caused by technological, economic, social, political and market forces. Indeed all the available evidence suggests that very large numbers of people will experience quite profound changes in their jobs during their working lives. Our education and training system must be geared up to meet the learning needs that will arise.

Much of the discussion at present tends to emphasize the occupational and industrial sector dimensions of labour market problems, because our society is largely organized along these lines, with occupation-based trade unions and professional bodies, sector-based employers' organizations and subject-based educational schemes. From the point of view of setting educational and training standards there has been great merit in this approach. It means that people who are experts in the sectors of employment and in occupational knowledge and skills have had a major hand in prescribing curricula and terminal standards.

In the future employment scene, however, these pre-occupations will need to be balanced by two very serious considerations, ie, the need for flexibility and the importance of the regional dimension. While we are grappling with high unemployment there are jobs around waiting to be done. In construction for example, a builder who employs a dozen people cannot afford to do a minor job on your house. His overheads would make the cost prohibitive. Yet a man working alone or in a very small firm could do it — if he could manage the money side and the form-filling. Perhaps we should, therefore, consider educating and training some craftsmen to cope with simple financial and administrative procedures, geared to his especial needs.

Current provision

Training tends to focus on learning how to perform, whereas education tends to focus on personal development (Johnson, 1977). Some people grossly over-emphasize the difference between the two approaches whereas in practice much training contributes materially to personal development and most education helps people to perform — eg to read, to write, to do sums, to solve problems. In the UK context a discussion of adult education must perforce include coverage of the adult training efforts. The interface between vocational education and training for adults is such that no single government department can be said to have overall responsibility. Although the bulk of education is provided by the education services, many of the programmes of the national training agencies and of employers' training centres are educational in intent and in practice.

Education services

Adult education is carried on by universities and university colleges, local education authorities and by a wide variety of voluntary organizations. The University Council for Adult Education provides a forum for the interchange of ideas on extra-mural education. The National Institute of Adult Education and the Scottish Institute of Adult Education provide a means of collaboration between the various forces and agencies involved in adult education and the Advisory Council for Adult and Continuing Education brings together many interests to formulate advice to the Government. Universities in the UK are under the general supervision of the University Grants Committee which advises the Government on the support grants awarded to augment the modest funds already available from charitable bequests, industrial support and income from fees.

Apart from the university sector, the education services operate on the basis of the distribution of responsibility among central government, the local education authorities and the teaching profession. The day-to-day running of the education service is left largely to the local education authorities although there are some far-reaching proposals in the pipeline about the future management of higher education (Oakes, 1978).

The local authorities have a duty to provide and run the schools and colleges in their areas. Education services are under the general supervision of the Department of Education and Science (England and Wales), the Scottish Education Department and the Northern Ireland Department of Education.

Training services

Responsibility for the training services in Great Britain lies with the Manpower Services Commission (MSC) and in particular with its Training Services Division. In Northern Ireland the Department of Manpower Services discharges similar responsibilities. The MSC works closely with some 40 sector training bodies which bring together representatives of employers, employees and educationists who consider the training requirements for sectors of employment. Twenty-three of these sector bodies are statutory industry training boards which receive considerable financial support through the MSC. In considering the training requirements for their industries these sector bodies also take into account further education programmes which may be coupled with training programmes.

Over the past few years a programme jointly sponsored by the MSC and the DES has been concerned with the experimental provision of unified vocational preparation programmes where elements of education, training and work experience are combined to form a coherent scheme of learning for young people starting work in occupations which have, in the past, involved little training.

The MSC also organizes a nationwide scheme of training opportunities for adults through its Training Services Division (Manpower Services

Commission, 1978d). This 'TOPS' scheme provides travel and subsistence allowances and tuition fees to enable adults to attend vocational courses from four to 52 weeks in length. More than half of these individuals attend courses in higher or further education establishments. Although the rules and guidelines are established centrally the scheme is administered through regional and district offices which seek to relate the provision of vocational training awards to the jobs available. Advice is also sought through a network of over one hundred District Manpower Committees.

Employers and trade unions

The third major group providing education and training is employers. Training by employers can certainly be traced back to the twelfth century and 1563 saw the introduction of the Statute of Artificers which sought to regulate apprentice training (Perry, 1976). Currently the vast bulk of apprentice training in Great Britain is undertaken by employers and this is often accompanied by a further education course on a day-release basis. The Confederation of British Industry and the Trade Union Congress would prefer to see this principle extended by agreements between employers and trade unions in particular sectors and do not favour Government action to extend this pattern of training arbitrarily.

Employers now train their staff in a wide range of skills. For example, training for salesmen is particularly well developed in some industries and management training and development has grown enormously in importance over the last two decades. Many in-company courses, especially those offered for managers and supervisors, are blends of education and training.

The trade unions take a keen interest in continuing education (Trade Union Congress, 1978) and are particularly involved in training their members in their representational roles in association with the Workers' Educational Association, certain educational institutions and the British Broadcasting Corporation Further Education Department.

Co-ordination needs

In the United Kingdom, as in so many western countries, education and training for people who have left school has arisen in what appears to be a haphazard manner, in response to needs. The natural inclination of a bureaucrat would be to try to bring order out of chaos by imposing a central system recording, classifying, and closely controlling what happens in this field.

There are two good reasons why this would be a disaster. In the first place people's needs for learning vary from person to person, from place to place and from time to time in a way that defies planning on the grand scale. The very nature of the problem demands flexibility, and the encouragement of entrepreneurial educational initiatives. In the second place, centralized control does not really work very well for the British, and from what we can see it does not seem to work all that well for other Europeans or for the North Americans. People will apply their ingenuity to beating the system if it impedes our educators and trainers from meeting what they see to be the real needs of the hour. This conflict within the system exists to some extent even now, and detracts from the optimum use of scarce resources in the educational sphere. There is a need for each part of the system to be accountable at appropriate levels (ie local authorities and the central government must control public expenditure). This can be achieved in a way that encourages the imaginative, effective and efficient use of resources — or it can be attempted in a way that suppresses initiative and emphasizes detailed accounting at the expense of efficiency and effectiveness.

How can we achieve co-ordination without rigid controls? To answer that question we must first ask why: why co-ordinate? Co-ordination is surely not an end in itself. We can learn to live with untidiness and in the education sphere this is not a crime. The real problems are twofold. Are we sure that the legitimate claims on educational and training resources — by individuals, employers and society — are being met? We shall return to that question later. Second, are the existing resources being used efficiently, or are scarce resources wastefully duplicated and under-used? These are serious issues and there is evidence around that improved co-ordination could materially improve the answers to these questions. (There is also a clear need for action to rationalize the plethora of regulations governing the payment of educational course fees and related grants for maintenance, travel, books etc, but that problem is outside the scope of this chapter.) Effective co-ordination, therefore, should be directed to well-defined ends, towards ensuring that the realistic requirements of people, employers and society are met, and that high quality is achieved and maintained.

This involves a co-ordinated approach to identifying needs where, for example, information on learning needs gathered by manpower and training bodies is passed on to educational bodies. Co-ordination will certainly require improved communications so that people become more aware of the resources available and of the knowledge and methods developed through research and experimental programmes. Such knowledge is particularly needed at the regional and college level where most of the really important decisions regarding the provision of education are taken. The individual and the company training officers also need to know what educational resources exist, especially at the local level.

Responsibilities

One of the problems of co-ordination is the division of responsibilities among the government, the local authority and the college. But the solution lies not in simplifying these relationships, but in making them work by recognizing that our way of life is based on these balances of power. We need to recognize the legitimate claims of various interested parties: the individual, the educational institution and its staff, the local community and the local authority, and society at large — the taxpayer and central government. Success lies in recognizing and managing constructively the many conflicts inherent in the system, eg, the desire for more educational resources *versus* the need to contain public expenditure, the needs of the individual for particular courses *versus* the need for economically-sized learning groups.

The division of responsibility can sometimes lead to two unfortunate effects: duplication of effort or inadequate provision. Duplication of effort can occur when nearby colleges offer similar courses in excess of local demand. This may occur when, for example, they are on opposite sides of local authority borders. Improvements in liaison can usually reduce this to a minimum. This problem can also arise when a polytechnic and a neighbouring university offer essentially similar courses. Since these two institutions are funded and controlled by separate systems, co-ordination in this sphere is more difficult. The growth of the training services has also given rise to the possibility of duplication of effort or competition for scarce resources.

The aim should be to ensure the delivery to those who need it of an effective help in learning, and not to be over-concerned with whether the offering is education, training or, that other vehicle of learning which is increasingly being recognized, a planned experience — or more likely a mixture of all three. There should not be over-concern about who gives the tuition, but rather with ensuring that the various resources are mobilized in the most fruitful way to meet real learning needs. Those who are employed in education and training will be rightly interested in making a full contribution to these developments and ensuring that their own status and employment are safeguarded. But the enormous needs for learning that will emerge in the coming years will surely require the full mobilization of all those who are competent in the education and training field.

Curriculum development

Duplication of effort may not be a disadvantage in the development of new courses. Indeed in some ways the staff development involved in devising new curricula and methods may be ample reward for the effort expended. At present an enormous amount of time is being spent in colleges and universities in developing new learning experiences — from programmes for the educationally disadvantaged to programmes for senior managers. One might wish to see a centrally designated college or two where this development work is focused and which dispenses recipes to all who need them. I believe this would be a mistake.

By decentralizing and allowing simultaneous developments to take place all over the country we are achieving three valuable results. In the first place, academic staff are being developed as they consider afresh the needs of the would-be learners, what they need to know and how best to present their material and manage the learning. Second, this process helps tutors to own the material and the programmes, making them more effective and more sensitive to the student's reactions to the material and to the learning problems posed. Third, from this rich exploration, fresh nuggets of insight are discovered.

Although central control of curriculum development would not be helpful, appropriate means of communicating insights to those who could benefit from them would be. The recent activities of, for example, the Further Education Curriculum Review and Development Unit (in the education of young people), and the Foundation for Management Education (in education for managers) have been valuable. But as Nancy Foy mentioned in her recent report (Foy, 1978) the major need here is for work-based links between key people.

Access to education

No government can afford to set up colleges within easy reach of everybody which will cater for all their reasonable needs. Colleges inevitably specialize in a range of subjects which (they hope) meet the needs of the majority of the people in their locality. People with needs outside this range generally have to travel to get the tuition they require unless some special arrangements are made.

In many subjects correspondence courses seem at first sight to be the answer. But anyone who has tried to learn alone by correspondence, even in these days of the cheap tape-recorder, will tell you that it is a hard grind. Most people need more stimulus and support if they are to succeed. One of the most successful ventures in this field has been the Open University. By adding to the correspondence material well-designed and produced television programmes, home experimental kits, support through local tutors (normally in colleges) and short residential periods the OU has tapped a new reservoir of human potential.

The Open University has taken a special interest in continuing education (Venables, 1976; *see also Chapter 20*) and is likely to play an increasing role in helping those who find it difficult to attend a normal university or college course. There have been suggestions that this concept should be extended more widely into the further education sphere with the formation of an 'open technical college'. Although this will work up to a point it is important to recognize the strengths and weaknesses of the OU system. The success is dependent in part on the very high quality of the learning aids produced coupled with careful course design. This process is expensive and time-consuming, but becomes viable and cost-effective if the number of people who will take the course is sufficiently large. People may find it difficult to attend a further education course because it is not offered locally or for personal reasons like family responsibilities or because they work shifts. When there is a large number of people who want to take a further education course which is not available to them, the OU system is a sensible option. However, more often than not the people who want to take a particular course in the further education area are too few in number to make an OU-type course economic. If the course is very important, the design of the curriculum and the production of the learning aids may be subsidized. There are a large number of courses, however, where this approach is not worthwhile.

One answer to this problem of access to courses is to encourage the concept of regional specialization where a particular department in a particular college is encouraged to develop distance learning material in the subjects where it has competence. Then links would be built up with local colleges who would provide tutors who would specialize in helping people to cope with learning, but who would not themselves be expert in the subject matter. Subject specialists would be available by telephone (perhaps eventually also on closed circuit television) at pre-set times so that the tutor and student at the local college could resolve questions relating to content.

A network of such departments/local tutors, where the specialist departments would not be grouped into one college, would probably have the degree of flexibility required to meet with the myriad needs of adults for learning. Moreover this system would encourage variations which would make the curricula more relevant to the regional labour markets. The Council for Educational Technology is working with other bodies to try out open learning systems of this kind. *(See also Chapter 5.)* Many people who require further education courses with a vocational bias would need the encouragement of a large measure of relevance to their own situations and this has been one of the great strengths of the further education system. A centrally prepared set of detailed curricula could easily diminish this flexible, apt response to people's learning needs.

In addition to the colleges, the traditional universities will play a very valuable role within this network. Indeed the university departments of adult education are already highly active in this field, providing a wide diversity of vocational as well as non-vocational programmes.

The way forward

A major reorganization of education for adults will merely throw the whole system into disarray for a decade. The sensible way forward is to recognize the strengths of the present system and to build on them, and to identify its weaknesses and to seek to overcome them.

The strengths of the present system are the richness of its variety, the adaptability of its teachers, the co-ordination in the field of curricula and standards through the examination bodies and other 'linking' organizations, the relevance fostered by the dialogue between teachers and companies, professional bodies, trade bodies and training bodies.

One weakness in the system — from the manpower angle — is that there is not enough attention paid to analysing the needs of the client groups served. The clients of today demand even more immediate practical value from their off-site learning experience. Analysis will help. The system has grown rapidly, but now it is generally in a steady state. This means that its teachers — many of whom had real industrial and commercial experience when they entered the colleges as tutors — have been in post a long time. They need the opportunity to spend time in a commercial environment and to help companies with their problems to ensure that they have the feel for the up-to-date situation. Some lack teaching skills but sensible steps are being taken to overcome this.

Another weakness of the system is that in a period of low growth (Department of Education and Science, 1978) the knowledge of some established teachers declines in importance relative to other subjects. Such teachers must be helped to recognize this fact and be re-trained to take on new challenges. The subject basis of further education, which has been a strength in the past, can so easily become a hindrance.

The reward system in education which encourages tutors to upgrade courses academically, even when this is not helpful to the client is yet another weakness. The reward system also favours long courses leading to academic qualifications as against shorter courses which may meet real needs. The more enterprising college staff find ways to meet people's needs in spite of these problems. There is certainly a need for reward structures and for colleges to be accountable for the economic use of public funds. At the same time there is a danger of under-using scarce resources if new ways of managing accountability and rewards are not evolved.

There is every prospect of building on the strengths of the system by encouraging healthy variety (but rationalizing in some areas), encouraging the adaptability of teachers by supportive programmes of secondment, re-training and, most important of all, by assisting self-development and coaching on the job. There is room for further co-ordination in curricula, particularly between universities, further education colleges and training bodies.

Inevitably this chapter has generalized and in many areas co-ordination is already very good. There is a rich variety of services provided by many kinds of institutions for a range of people differing widely in age, ability, aspirations and needs. In the UK there is an organic system adapting to different situations as they arise. The challenge is to develop that system, to mobilize its resources economically to meet real needs in imaginative ways and to foster improved communications in relevant areas.

References

Department of Education and Science and the Scottish Education Department (1978) *Higher Education into the 1990s (discussion document)* DES: London and SED: Edinburgh

Foy, N (1978) *The Missing Links — British Management Education in the Eighties* Foundation for Management Education: London

Johnson, R M (1977) *Meeting Needs — Training in Context* Association of Colleges of Further and Higher Education: London

Manpower Services Commission (1978a) *Management Development: Policy and Activities of the MSC* MSC: London

Manpower Services Commission (1978b) *Training of Trainers: First Report of the Training of Trainers Committee* MSC: London

Manpower Services Commission (1978c) *MSC Review and Plan* MSC: London

Manpower Services Commission (1978d) *TOPS Review 1978* MSC: London

Oakes, G (1978) *Report of the Working Group on the Management of Higher Education in the Maintained Sector* HMSO: London

Open University (1976) *Report of the Committee on Continuing Education* (The Venables Report) Open University Press: Milton Keynes

Perry, P J C (1976) *The Evolution of British Manpower Policy* British Association for Commercial and Industrial Education: London

Trade Union Congress (1978) *General Council Report 1978* (paragraphs 249-56) TUC: London

The opinions expressed in this chapter are the author's and do not necessarily represent the views of the organizations with which he is associated.

The author would like to record his appreciation of the help he has received from Mr David James, Director of the Department of Adult Education, University of Surrey.

20. The Open University and the future of continuing education

Peter Venables

This chapter was completed by Sir Peter Venables just before his death in June 1979.

Summary: Far-reaching post-war changes in industry and commerce and employment generally under the impact of science and technology, together with changes favouring a more egalitarian society, have engendered changes in education and training, and sharpened demands for increasing educational opportunities. A proposal for a 'University of the Air' in 1966 led the government to establish in 1967 a Planning Committee 'to work out a comprehensive plan for an Open University'. A Royal Charter was granted in 1969 which laid down several objectives. The first was 'to provide education of university standard through the advancement and dissemination of learning and knowledge by teaching and research by a diversity of means...', and this was successfully under way by 1974. The remaining objectives included 'the provision of education to professional standards, and the promotion of the educational well-being of the community generally: and these too by a diversity of means including broadcasting, correspondence tuition, residential courses and seminars'. Initial difficulties with establishing professional post-experience courses pointed strongly to the consideration of new developments in a much wider context and, in 1974, the Open University established a Committee on Continuing Education, which published its report in December 1976. In the national context new developments included the government-financed Adult Literacy Resource Agency (ALRA), and the BBC's programmes 'On the Move'. The OU report emphasized the necessity of a greatly increased scale of co-operation between established institutions and agencies. This article discusses the report and its main recommendations, records steps forward taken since the report and considers some aspects of future developments.

Introduction

In Britain the three post-war decades were characterized by increasing educational opportunity, including the large growth in the universities following the publication of the Robbins Committee Report (HMSO, 1963), and the substantial growth in further and higher education in the polytechnics and colleges, all largely on traditional lines. However, developments include the use of modern mass media, as in the Open University (established in 1969) and the BBC's literacy programme 'On the Move', alongside the work of the government-financed Adult Literacy Resource Agency (ALRA), which was supporting the Local Education Authorities (LEAs) and voluntary bodies in tackling the nationwide problem of adult illiteracy (ALRA, 1978). After four years' delay following the publication of the Russell Report on Adult Education (DES, 1973), the Department of Education and Science established, late in 1977, a national Advisory Council for Adult and Continuing Education (ACACE).

From the foregoing it might appear that the future of continuing education is assured, but this would be to ignore the very inadequate level from which the developments began, the evident and latent needs to be met, and the adverse determining factors which still persist. The assessment of the situation made by the Open University Planning Committee in its report (DES, 1969) has not been invalidated in the last decade:

> In the past limited opportunities for education, determined by social, economic and political factors, have resulted in a low educational attainment on the part of a vast number of individuals. This low level of attainment has been taken as firm evidence of limited innate ability, which in turn was held to justify an absence of any increase in educational provision. It is both unjust and unwise to ascribe the adventitious hazards of nurture to alleged inherited defects — unjust to the individual, and unwise for society thus to deny the greatest educational opportunity to the greatest number of its citizens. For long regarded as a privilege of the few, the opportunity to engage in higher education is at last becoming widely accepted as a basic individual right. In these changes in recent years, science and technology have proved to be the most powerful catalysts of educational demand and development. Moreover, education generally, and higher education in particular is, at one and the same time, a necessary condition of a modern technological society and a defence against its abuses. (DES, 1969)

Industrial processes, manufacturing generally, and the structure of traditional industry have been profoundly affected not only by the nature of the scientific and technological developments, but also by the increasing rate of change at which they have come about. Industries have been transformed in the post-war decades, others made obsolete, and new scientifically-based ones increasingly established. Such fundamental changes have been accompanied by economic and social changes no less profound, as in conditions and practices inimical to the well-being of the family, and in the formerly unthinkable sustained scale of unemployment now almost passively accepted on the threshold of the 'silicon chip revolution'. Many of these changes, largely irreversible, demand large scale innovations which have hardly begun.

Education in future must be much wider in scope, and can never be provided as a one-off self-sufficient piece of educational capital to last the whole of adult life. It must be recurrent and lifelong. As a matter of natural justice it must be more widely and more equally available to all citizens. In addition, those who in the past have been denied educational opportunities must, by a determined policy of retrospective egalitarianism, be accorded them during their adult life.

The tasks are immense, and would be daunting were we to continue to think on traditional lines, but with the advent of distance teaching and with computer programming to deal with large enrolments and fixed deadlines, science and technology are coming to our aid once more.

It was such considerations as the foregoing which animated those who developed the concept of the 'University of the Air'. This was initiated by the then Leader of the Opposition, Mr Harold Wilson MP, in his speech in Glasgow on 8 September 1963, and was committed by him to the dynamic concern of Miss Jennie Lee MP in March 1965. The main outcome was the appointment by the Secretary of State for the DES of the Open University Planning Committee in September 1967, and the subsequent publication of its report (DES, 1969). The Charter incorporating the Open University was given Royal Assent on 23 April 1969, and the first courses began in January 1971 (Perry, 1976). The Planning Committee gave much thought to defining the objects of the university and these were explicitly set out in the Charter:

> The objects of the University shall be the advancement and dissemination of learning and knowledge by teaching and research *by a diversity of means such as broadcasting and technological devices appropriate to higher education, by correspondence tuition, residential courses and seminars and in other relevant ways, and shall be to provide education of university and professional standards for its students and to promote the educational well-being of the community generally.* (Emphasis added.)

The statement begins in the manner of traditional university charters up to the mention of research, but the remainder is markedly unorthodox, and it is this latter part which was to become the preoccupation of the Committee on Continuing Education (OU, 1976).

It was inherently impossible to try to attain all the objects from the outset, and the Planning Committee decided that work of university standard would more readily and surely establish the academic credibility of the institution, most of all by attracting staff of the requisite quality and originality to initiate the enterprise. The progress made is summarily conveyed in Table 1.

The Open University Committee on Continuing Education

Despite intense preoccupation with the initial task of establishing undergraduate courses, there was a persistent concern to develop post-experience courses at an early date, as strongly recommended by the Planning Committee. However, the attempt brought many difficulties and cumulative frustration, and the university felt compelled to reassess its whole policy on these courses in 1974. As a result the post-experience programme was limited and regarded as experimental for the next few years. The problems required consideration in a wider context; consequently the Senate of the University in December 1974 and in Council in January 1975 approved the terms of reference and mode of operation of a Committee on Continuing Education as follows:

1. To make recommendations on the nature and scale of the Open University's future contribution to the national development of

Year of entry	Number of inquiries*	Number of applicants†	Provisionally registered new undergraduates (September) 1 January	Finally registered new undergraduates (April)	Finally registered students as percentage of provisionally registered	Annual total undergraduate numbers	Cumulative total of graduates
1971	123,556	42,992	24,220	19,581	80.8	19,581	
1972	77,722	35,182	20,501	15,716	76.7	31,902	898
1973	71,757	32,046	16,895	12,680	75.1	38,424	4,538
1974	81,392	35,011	14,976	11,336	75.1	42,636	9,718
1975	109,858	52,537	19,823	14,830	74.8	49,358	15,187
1976	86,433	52,916	16,311	12,230	75.0	51,035	21,214
1977	75,541	49,956	19,886	14,971	75.3	55,127	29,204
1978	81,335	45,293	20,882	15,669	75.0	58,788	32,526

*This column represents the number of formal written inquiries received in the Admissions Office and does not include contacts made with other University Offices nor with Open University students or staff. The figures contain an unknown but not very large number of those who inquire more than once.

†The figures from 1972 onwards reflect the fact that a sizeable proportion of the applicants who fail to get a place in any one year reapply for admission in the following year.

Table 1 *Open University inquiries, applications, admissions to undergraduate courses, and graduations 1971-1978 (updated from Appendix V of the Report)*

continuing education, including professional education and training and to the educational well-being of the community generally.
2. To establish plans for the phased development of a long-term programme of continuing education, to estimate the resources needed for its implementation and to propose a structure for its organization.

The Committee, which included external non-OU members, met first in May 1975 and held its twentieth and last meeting in October 1976. Its unanimous report was published in December 1976 (OU, 1976).

The report was to be an internal one for the university, but consideration of the external and national scene could not be excluded. There was also a growing conviction that all post-secondary education will in future be seen as an entity. Evidence from public bodies, voluntary organizations and individuals was invited by public advertisement at the outset; and was taken into consideration in preparing an interim report. This was distributed widely, and there was a very interesting and useful response to it, which heightened the Committee's awareness of the complexity and diversity of the needs for continuing education. Furthermore the great range of bodies and organizations, both statutory and voluntary, working in this sphere of education made it crystal clear that no single institution could conceivably provide a comprehensive service on its own.

The evidence provided:

> overwhelming support for the idea that the Open University, in enlarging its efforts in the field of continuing education should do so largely, though not exclusively, through co-operation with existing agencies. Such collaboration could be not only with existing further, higher and adult educational institutions, but also with the professions, the training boards, the technician and business education councils, the correspondence colleges, and a wide variety of voluntary bodies. There will also be occasions when the Open University would be an inappropriate partner in a collaborative scheme, when other bodies will want to co-operate with each other, and when the size and scale of the Open University will be unsuited to particular needs. A realistic assessment by the university of its own special identifiable skills is a necessary prelude to any wider transfer of such expertise to assist the development of continuing education, particularly through collaborative schemes (OU, 1976: 44, para 55).

Such considerations apply in differing measure to the growing international contribution of the university, especially in under-developed countries.

The Committee took 'continuing education' to include 'all learning opportunities which are taken after full-time schooling has ceased. They can be full- or part-time and include both vocational and non-vocational study.' The education of 16- and 17-year-olds was excluded from consideration, and this was largely true of the undergraduate programme of the university.

The Committee's recommendations

Two sets of recommendations were made to the university's Council: (A) concerning the national scene, and (B) concerning the Open University's own contribution to continuing education. They are of course amplified by arguments in the main text of the report (of some 28,000 words, plus 12 Appendices). Only the recommendations can be given here (and unfortunately the report is now out of print):

A. The national scene
The Council should lend its support to the following efforts to increase and sustain continuing education. First of all to preserving access for the largest number of students, recognizing that fees charged to students are a major adverse factor, and also that the government has yet to fulfil its undertaking to the International Labour Organization convention on paid educational leave. Fees should be kept as low as possible and be reduced for those who have been given less by the educational system so far. Positive discrimination should be exercised in favour of those who have not had paid leave, and also for those who have not benefited previously from a mandatory award. Action should be taken in concert with other appropriate bodies to secure an adequate provision of educational facilities and allowances for the disabled student. At the postgraduate level increased opportunities for part-time study should be provided generally at universities in the United Kingdom.

A national Educational Advisory Service for Adults should be established to help all the intending students, not as a recruiting agency exercising selection for one particular institution but as an integrated service embracing the whole of adult education. Integrated development and use of library services, both public and in educational institutions such as universities, polytechnics and colleges are indispensable to the general improvement of this national resource in continuing education. Sustained analysis of difficult inherent problems should not be deferred, but set in train from the outset — regarding copyright, contracts, compatibility of technical equipment, editorial responsibility and other operational and legal problems.

Two recommendations to the OU Council were quickly overtaken by events. First, as already noted, the DES established ACACE, but without the funding powers recommended by the OU report, which would have given it the resources to become a truly enabling body for future developments. The second recommendation was that the Council should support pressures to increase considerably the time available for educational broadcasting, particularly for continuing education. This was overtaken by the publication in March 1977 of the Annan Report on the Future of Broadcasting (Home Office, 1977), which recommended the establishment of a Fourth Television Channel under an Open Broadcasting Authority, which 'should encourage productions which say something new in new ways: it should include educational programmes, including those for the Open University; programmes made by individual Independent Television companies, including ITN; and programmes from a variety of independent producers, some of them commissioned by the Authority.'

B. Recommendations concerning the Open University
In relation to the Open University contribution to continuing education, the Committee's recommendations were as follows:

Educational advice and counselling
1. The Council should encourage the university, especially through its regional services, to stimulate and support the development of an educational advisory service for adults.
2a. Preferably in collaboration with other relevant bodies, the Open University should undertake research into the educational needs of adults in order to determine appropriate provisions.
2b. The Open University's own developing contribution with others should be continuously evaluated.

Learning skills and preparatory courses
3. The Council should give support to the Post-Experience Unit for the early development and provision of a course available to all teachers to increase their understanding of mathematical ideas.

Adult concern courses and materials
4. The university should commit itself to the development of adult concern courses both on its own initiative and in conjunction with others.
5. The Open University should, after discussion with interested parties, produce experimental packages of learning materials covering topics of adult concern, which may be offered for use by other institutions.

Accreditation of adult concern courses
6. When the Open University presents a course to its own registered students, that course should offer optional assessment and certification.
7. The Open University should pursue exploratory schemes of collaboration with a number of existing examination boards and should lend strong support to any moves made nationally to provide accreditation of adult concern courses at standards equivalent to GCE 'O' and 'A' levels and CSE 'O' and 'H' grades.

Tutor training
8. The university in developing its commitment to professional and vocational education should do so particularly in relation to the training of adult education tutors and through collaboration with other appropriate institutions.

Professional and vocational courses and materials
9. The Council should encourage collaboration with appropriate interested bodies in the production of further post-experience courses in the professional and vocational fields and should investigate the development of initial 'core' training materials in particular areas.

Development of current non-undergraduate activities
10. The university should increase the provision of updating and refresher courses at the postgraduate level, open both to graduates and appropriately prepared non-graduates.

Special concerns
11. The Open University should not become directly involved in home-based distance teaching designed specifically for 16- and 17-year-olds.
12. The positive statement of interest made by the University Council, to meet the needs of disabled students on existing courses, should apply equally to those who enrol on new courses in a continuation programme.
13. The university, in all its regions, should investigate the possibility of developing local collaborative schemes which take due account of the differences in regional needs and the resources available to meet them within the region.
14. In its continuing education programme, the university should develop still further its relationship with the other branches of Scottish higher, adult and community education, in order to have regard to the distinctiveness of Scottish circumstances and the Scottish dimension.

15. The university should develop still further its collaborative links with appropriate educational bodies in Northern Ireland for the benefit of continuing education in the province.
16. The university should investigate the possibility of developing local collaborative schemes, in relation to the provision of courses and materials which will take due account of the special needs in Wales.

Use of facilities
17. The university should seek to initiate pilot experiments with polytechnics and colleges of further and higher education whereby part-time students using independent learning methods might spend one day a week or equivalent in local laboratories or other work space provided by such institutions.

Broadcasting resources
18. The university should investigate the desirability and feasibility of establishing regional and local pilot developments involving the appropriate broadcasting agencies.
19. There should be greater reciprocity of use between educational programmes prepared by the BBC and the Open University, as suggested by the Further Education Advisory Council of the BBC, and action to enable this to be achieved should be taken as soon as possible.
20. In the initial stages of planning of all continuing education projects, the university should give adequate study to the choice of the most appropriate means of production and distribution of any audio-visual components whether by broadcasting or by cassette, disc or other methods.
21. The university should proceed quickly to investigate the setting up of teleconference links between study centres through means of appropriate telephone services.

Learning resources centres
22. The university should maintain close links with appropriate national bodies concerned with open learning systems and educational resources, and in particular the Council for Educational Technology and the Scottish Council for Educational Technology, to encourage the development of a national network of resource centres.
23. The Council should take immediate steps to introduce the phased development of an Open University Learning Resources Centre, for information, materials, advice, training, design and production.

The Continuing Education Division
24. The Council should draw up a constitution for a Continuing Education Division (along lines set out in Appendix 11 of the Report), with a Delegacy to which Senate would delegate certain agreed powers to administer the development of all those aspects of continuing education in the university's own work, and of such joint schemes as may be agreed with the respective co-operating bodies. The former do not include those relating to first and higher degree programmes, but do cover the provision of courses and their accreditation, liaison with collaborating institutions, and the development of a Learning Resources Centre.

Finance
25. Council, in developing the work of the university in pursuance of all the objects in the Charter, should ensure that its contribution through degree courses and research is properly safeguarded and that the proposed expansion of the continuing education programme should be financed from additional funds.
26a. The university should make submissions to the government for additions to the present block grant, earmarked for the development of a programme of continuing education, and that such grant be not wholly recoverable from

student fees;
26b. the university should continue to seek sponsors for specific projects in the programme of continuing education; and
26c. the university should recommend that the proposed national Advisory Council for Adult and Continuing Education should have funds made available to it to facilitate the collaborative creation of a national programme of continuing education, using existing facilities wherever possible.

Phased development
27a. The level of underwriting for the post-experience programme already agreed to for 1977-79 should be maintained; and
27b. the following organizations and other proposals should be implemented as evidence of a firm commitment to the progressive development of continuing education:
(i) the establishment of the Delegacy for Continuing Education and the planning of the Division with the Post-Experience Unit as a nucleus;
(ii) an investigation of the Open University as a Learning Resources Centre;
(iii) the planning of continuing education course provision and materials, production for the years after 1979;
(iv) the drafting of a resource submission for 1980-82, for incorporating in the university's general submission to the Department of Education and Science for that triennium.

Course arrangements and design

From the outset the Open University has been designed as an institution of continuing education, and the report discusses the creation, production, distribution/transmission, and accreditation of courses designed for distance teaching and learning in the university against which expansion in continuing education is to be considered.

Implementing the foregoing recommendations will increase the range and number of courses very substantially, and the total number of students enrolled with the university directly and through other agencies collaboratively may even increase ten-fold over present undergraduate numbers (see Table 1). The university will remain 'open' in that *no* academic qualifications will be required (ie, *no* examination certificate) for undergraduate courses, and it is improbable that they would be required for non-degree courses. The flexible arrangements of two-stage registrations of students (ie provisional in September and final in April), followed by the successful completion of two Foundation Courses, opens the way to degree courses and so to graduation. These arrangements will hardly apply to future non-degree courses, which will generally be of much shorter duration. However, the practice of designing courses by particular course teams, gathered specially for the purpose and having external specialists and representatives of co-operating bodies, will continue to prevail.

Neglect over long periods or emotional blocks due to a variety of causes all too often prevent people from joining courses which manifestly would be of benefit to them: the damaging deprivation persists, as the individual personal testimonies given in the BBC literacy programmes showed so movingly. Besides literacy, numeracy also contributes to the basic skills which must be acquired before adults can help themselves to resolve their own difficulties. The Committee wished strongly to encourage courses of 'adult concern', that is courses related directly to their adult experience and expectations. Such courses can be designed at various levels of intellectual challenge specifically for adults, and assessed by appropriate methods. The scope of this development is indicated in Recommendations B. 4-7 above, and as listed in Appendix VII of the Report on Adult Concern Courses and Materials, as follows:

1. *Day to day problems of dealing with different authorities* — housing, taxation, education, social security, employment
   - individual rights and responsibilities
   - financial management and taxation
   - the choice of your child's school
   - improving your home
2. *Understanding the rules, procedures and policies of particular authorities* and the methods by which they are made accountable
   - learning to live with local government
   - how central government affects the individual
   - local transport problems
3. *Participating in change*, where a major issue arises or where a group is conscious of conflicting priorities with an authority
   - how tenants' associations work
   - running a local pressure group
   - planning your neighbourhood
   - parents, managers, governors and schools (and perhaps one may add, colleges, polytechnics and universities?)
4. *Understanding how society affects the individual*
   - young people and unemployment
   - industrial relations, work and its rewards
   - problems of a multi-racial society
   - social implications of science and technology (or how technological change affects decision-making)
   - resources and the environment
5. *Understanding the individual in society*
   - family relationships in middle life
   - child development in single parent families
   - health: your rights and responsibilities
   - the handicapped person in the community
6. *Basic educational skills*
   - numeracy: as a supplement to a course for teachers
   - literacy: supporting the initiatives begun by the Adult Literacy Campaign, and extending to communication skills in general.

Developments since the publication of the report

In the OU report, the Committee expresses its debt to those who contributed written evidence and helped in other ways in response to the interim report. Subsequent general reactions to the report itself have been very encouraging, indeed quite heartwarming. Other publications indicate the growing importance of continuing education, for example, the discussion document 'Higher Education into the 1990s' (DES/SED, 1978) and the Trade Union Congress published statement 'Priorities in Continuing

Education' (TUC, 1978). *(See also Chapter 17.)*

Within the Open University most of the boards and committees had discussed and commented on the report by March 1977. Arising therefrom the Vice-Chancellor identified a strategy for the closer consideration of specific proposals, and resolutions – mainly in principle – were taken at the September meeting of Senate. The first definitive result was the approval in December 1977 of the full-time appointment of a Pro-Vice Chancellor (Continuing Education), to which Professor Ralph Smith (Professor of Mathematics of the University) was appointed with effect from February 1978. The second step forward was the approval given in April 1978 to establishing an Interim Delegacy for Continuing Education, which held its first meeting in November 1978. Third, certain proposals for phased development (Recommendation B. 27 p.279) are in process of implementation or active consideration by the university.

Two important conferences to discuss the role of the OU were held in May 1978, one with the Trade Union Congress (TUC) and the other with the Confederation of British Industry (CBI). In each case a conference report was to be published, and there should be other valuable outcomes. Examples are individual seminars with the CBI on a regional basis, and conferences with representatives of Industry Training Boards (ITBs) and of industry on a regional basis. There may well be a greater emphasis on ways in which the OU could meet the education and training needs of particular industrial groups, with its new Continuing Education Division involved.

From the TUC conference, for example, three of the discussion groups have since been in contact in order to facilitate practical developments, and these are: the Counselling Advice and Information Group, the Opportunities for Women Group and the Race Group.

More generally some brief examples may be given of the sponsorship and types of co-operation already achieved, which are capable of repetition on an increasing scale:

1. *Funding of staff to work on course development*

    In 1977-78 the Department of Health and Social Security (DHSS) contributed the salary costs and expenses of a medical consultant, a nurse and a social worker to join the team producing course P252 – *An Ageing Population.* In professional areas such as this, staff costs are a crucial element in the course. The social worker post was funded via the Central Council for the Education and Training of Social Workers (CCETSW), and such relevant professional involvement is vital. A second example is the provision of consultants for the Community Education short course P912 – *The Pre-School Child*, where staff of the Pre-School Playgroups Association were released to contribute to the development of the course free of charge to the university.

2. *Fee sponsorship*

    For some courses, particularly for the *Diploma in Reading Development*, LEAs have arranged bookings on courses, the fees then being refunded en bloc by them. Eleven hundred 'free' places were sponsored on the Community Education short course P911 — *First Years of Life* by the Scottish Health Education Unit and the Health Education Council, the latter having also contributed towards the design and graphic costs of developing course material. Well designed and illustrated materials and publicity are manifestly important in attracting students to non-degree courses. The attractive leaflet which advertises courses P922 and P912 includes two others, which these days are clearly of 'adult concern' — *Energy in the Home* and *Consumer Decisions*.

3. *Voluntary work on the piloting of materials*

Materials within existing OU courses are being scrutinized with a view to extracting particular units on various themes eg *Government and Industry, Industrial Archaeology, Doing History* and *Water Conservation*, and turning them into short (40 hour) courses. To ensure that these units and materials could be used effectively in this way, help was specially sought from particular groups of people. For example, the Norfolk Federation of Women's Institutes volunteered to advise in this way, free of charge, in collaboration with the Wensman Lodge Adult Education Centre, with the help of the OU Regional Office in East Anglia.

Future development

The OU report defined a wide range of potential developments in continuing education for the university and nationally, and the conferences with the TUC and the CBI made it very evident that needs are not articulated and are not readily translatable into quantifiable demands. Certain long-term problems are already evident, for example, the provision of advisory services which must be inexpensive on a per capita basis. The choice of priorities to be adopted, and the nature and methodology of the provision to be offered is also apt to be very difficult, with a high risk element, especially with conflicting pressures from different professional groups. Another persistent problem, which will occasion no surprise to anyone familiar with the social background of students, is the continuing tendency for students to be drawn largely from groups already advantaged by education and occupation. 'To him that hath shall be given . . .' and there is no sign as yet of a substantial democratic breakthrough for the less fortunate groups in our society. Without the full implementation of many of the recommendations urged in the OU report, this social determinism will prove to be the most formidable barrier to promoting 'the educational well-being of the community generally'.

The recommendations entail necessary finance, and the Committee felt strongly, despite the unpropitious inflationary times of the 1970s, that the scale of national expenditure on continuing education should be increased annually by £0.1m in 1978-79 to £20m in 1984-85 (at mid-1976 price levels). In addition, extra capital expenditure would be required of not less than £6m up to 1983-84. However, scale of development is one thing, rate is quite another. We may note the Annan Committee's reservation that 'the Fourth Channel should not be allocated until the nation's economy will permit the kind of service we have outlined' (Home Office, 1977). With the massive need to develop continuing education in mind — 'how long, O Lord, how long?'! Rather should the pragmatic Churchillian aphorism determine development: 'It is an inconvenient rule that nothing can be done until everything can be done.' The government followed the Annan Report with a belated White Paper on *Broadcasting* (Cmnd 7294, HMSO) on 26 July 1978 which was debated the same day. The last year of a minority government was hardly likely to produce effective action, and legislation by the new government is awaited.

Establishing the Open University to meet its first main objective was a great educational and practical challenge, in meeting which the partnership with the BBC was a vital factor. Dramatic attainments resulted well within ten years, thoroughly justifying the Tenth Anniversary celebrations in 1979. To fulfil the rest of its objects by participating in a nationwide development of continuing education may appear less of a challenge in its second decade, but it will be very different in kind and scope. Less dramatic, less prestigious perhaps, but it will affect the lives of a far greater number of citizens in the community at large. However this cannot possibly be achieved by treating them merely as passive recipients. The report is emphatic that the challenge must be met by:

> promoting people's ability to respond to and participate in meeting the changing needs of the whole community to understand them *and to be able to influence them* and to develop the wisdom, through educational as well as practical experiences, which will enable them to recognize what their rights and responsibilities are as members of society.

Moreover continuing education may be undertaken to achieve personal objectives: the acquisition of new skills, the achievement of intellectual and aesthetic satisfaction, the furtherance of a career or the expansion of job opportunities. Many such individual and personal benefits may have a social effect and enhance the contribution individuals may make to the community.

In the furtherance of these objectives perhaps the most stimulating educational challenge to the Open University will be in the nature and range of the co-operation which will have to be achieved with many other established institutions and agencies in the field of adult education.

References

Adult Literacy Resource Agency (ALRA) (1978) *Adult Literacy in 1977-78: A Remarkable Educational Advance* HMSO: London

Department of Education and Science (1969) *The Open University* Report of the Planning Committee (Chairman, Sir Peter Venables) HMSO: London

Department of Education and Science (1973) *Adult Education: A Plan for Development* (The Russell Report) HMSO: London

Department of Education and Science (1977) *Members appointed to new Advisory Council for Adult and Continuing Education (with terms of reference)*: Press Release 18 October 1977

Department of Education and Science and the Scottish Education Department (1978) *Higher Education into the 1990s* (discussion document) DES: London and SED: Edinburgh

Home Office (1977) *Report of the Committee on the Future of Broadcasting* (The Annan Report) Cmnd 6753 HMSO: London

Open University (1976) *Report of the Committee on Continuing Education* (The Venables Report) Open University Press: Milton Keynes

Perry, Sir Walter (1976) *The Open University: A Personal Account by the First Vice-Chancellor* Open University Press: Milton Keynes

Robbins, Lord (1963) *Report of the Commission on Higher Education* (The Robbins Report) Cmnd 2154 HMSO: London

Trade Union Congress (1978) *Priorities in Continuing Education* TUC: London

Part 5

Signposts

Gerry Fowler

Signposts are hard to find in *terra incognita*. When you cannot see beyond the next hill, and you are not sure of the direction in which you are going, they are also difficult to erect. It is clear from the essays in this book that that is the major problem in writing about recurrent or lifelong education.

As several of the chapters reveal, the terminology itself conceals basic differences of philosophy. Are we discussing the cultural development, throughout life, of ever wider sections of the population? Are we aiming to prepare people for the fruitful use of increased leisure stemming from technological advance? Let us leave aside the question of what is 'fruitful' and what is not; most answers to it entail the imposition of intellectual and middle-class values on groups with very different inherited or socially determined preferences. The standard example of a bad or pointless use of leisure is 'sitting in front of the television screen'; yet part of the argument that lifelong learning for all is becoming practicable, as well as desirable, is precisely that more and more information can be made available to everyone through the medium of television. In any event, such an approach to lifelong or permanent education means that it becomes primarily an extension of traditional adult education, which in Britain has hitherto described the liberal education of those of mature years (the word 'liberal' is itself worthy of note), but excluded exclusively vocational studies.

Alternatively, the argument for a new educational philosophy may be based more directly upon the effects of technological and industrial change. The days are past, it is argued, when a man or woman could learn a skill or trade in youth, the exercise of which would then sustain him or her until retirement. That was a concept apposite only to the period before the first industrial revolution. In the West, the pace of change has grown ever faster since the late eighteenth century. In the developing world the revolution in techniques and the pattern of employment has been compressed into a few decades, resulting not in a new stability, but in entrapment on the steeply mounting escalator of industrial 'progress'.

The rapid pace of technological change means that few entering employment today can expect to be doing the same job in the same way throughout a working life. The amanuensis has been replaced by the shorthand typist, but career opportunities in secretarial work will disappear as it becomes practicable to transfer much (and doubtless ultimately all) of the work to electronically controlled machines. The medical doctor will always be necessary, but even a seven-year apprenticeship in universities and medical schools will in future avail him little, for his skills will be largely antiquated by the time he has reached middle age. The aesthetic judgement of the architect and the civil engineer are indispensable, but the laborious calculation of stresses and of ergonomics that we once expected of them are perhaps already better performed by machine. Many of the technicians upon whose aid they relied will become redundant. As for the unskilled labourer, his work will increasingly be done mechanically.

This scenario may or may not be exactly accurate; the history of technological forecasting inspires little confidence, and what is technically possible is not always financially or socially desirable. But there is no doubt that we live in a Heraclidan world: everything is in a state of flux. In many countries there is increasing concern with the updating or revamping of skills, as a means of counteracting rising unemployment and to ensure that critical skills (such as those of the doctor) remain up to date. The vocational argument for lifelong education is therefore simply that the retraining of most members of the workforce, whatever their level of qualification or skill, will in the future be essential. This has little connection with 'culture' or with the use of leisure. It is partly a question of remaining competitive internationally: if one country successfully adapts its workforce to changing technology and its commercial rivals do not, it has a great advantage over them in world markets. It is also partly a matter of fear: a steady and inexorable rise in unemployment, or in the size of the *Lumpenproletariat*, whether or not one objects to such developments on more liberal political grounds, is likely to produce political instability. The 'work ethic' still dominates the thinking of most people and to depend for one's livelihood on subsidies and handouts is to lose one's self-respect.

But there is a less cynical argument. Only successful adaptation to technological change can ensure a more pleasant and more leisured life for the mass of people. Terminological disputes between the proponents of lifelong, permanent or recurrent education should not therefore be allowed to cloud the central issue, for all the arguments point in the same direction. Vocationalism is not antithetical to a cultural or traditional 'adult education' approach; the two march hand in hand. In the long run, the more who learn new vocational skills, the greater is the number enjoying increased leisure. How each person does this is a matter of choice, but he or she should have the chance to acquire the knowledge or competence to make this choice possible.

However, it remains true that in most countries the political will to extend educational provision for adults is likely to be generated chiefly by the vocational or economic argument. The 1960s admittedly saw in Britain the establishment of the Open University, and in the United States that of such institutions as the University Without Walls and the Empire State University, which are not narrowly vocational in orientation. But the harsher economic climate of the 1970s has brought in most European countries a renewed emphasis on skill training and retraining. Thus, in France, paid educational leave from work seems so far to have been used for the development of skills related to work. In Britain, the annual budget for adult education has sometimes remained static, and sometimes even been reduced in real terms, while increasing sums have been spent on the training services provided by the Manpower Services Commission since its inception in 1973. This is one clear signpost to the likely future pattern of development.

In any event there can never be a rigid distinction between the vocational and the non-vocational, or between education and training. The vocational utility of learning lies, like beauty, in the eye of the beholder. What one man learns in order to improve his performance at his workplace, another studies because he wishes to take up a new hobby or leisure interest. This is true of many light craft skills, as the boom in do-it-yourself home improvement testifies. Equally, few who study literature do so with the intention of becoming professional critics or teachers, but some do. The acquisition of the most basic skills, literacy and numeracy, may be vital to the hitherto disadvantaged worker, but they are also essential to improving the quality of the life of the housewife who has no intention of seeking paid work.

For those who wish to see a broad approach to the development of lifelong learning opportunities for all, to take account both of changing vocational requirements and of the need to facilitate a richer use of increased leisure, earlier retirement and longer life expectancy, and to spread more widely than hitherto social and (in the most general sense of the word) political competencies essential to playing an active role in one's community or trade union, the danger lies less in the distinction between the vocational and non-vocational than in its institutionalization. If additional resources go only to agencies (such as the Manpower Services Commission) with a narrowly defined remit of matching the skills of the workforce to the nation's changing economic needs, we shall not see the creation of a genuine system of lifelong education. If funds for 'political' education are channelled only to those already elected or selected as trade union officials, worker representatives on company boards, community councillors or school managers, we may create a new élite rather than extend the control exercised by every citizen over his own and his family's life. A limited 'vocational' approach to lifelong education would particularly disadvantage women, for in every western country they form a lower proportion of the workforce and of those elected or appointed to community office than men.

At present, therefore, not all of the signposts point in the right direction. It is natural for all men, but especially for bureaucrats dispensing and accounting for public funds, to categorize and compartmentalize activities; but if we do this too rigidly in the development of lifelong education, we shall succeed only in depriving many people of the opportunities available to their fellows.

Dangers arise from fanatical adherence to any one narrow strategy for the development of lifelong education. Recurrent education is, as the title of one OECD publication makes clear, just such a strategy for lifelong learning. The concept has never been intended to exclude other possible approaches, but as other writers in this volume have said, some OECD work has emphasized the importance of paid educational leave for all workers. That emphasis seems to me to be right, but universal paid educational leave does nothing to help those who are not employed. Moreover, full-time learning is not necessarily superior to part-time or leisure-time activities, nor is learning undertaken away from the workplace superior to that undertaken at the workplace.

Those not in work include both the unemployed and the non-employed. I use the former term in its usual sense, to mean those who are seeking paid employment. By 'non-employed' I mean those who are neither in nor seeking paid employment — housewives, the retired, the infirm, etc. If they too are to be encouraged to acquire new skills and knowledge, we must supplement the European concept of paid educational leave with the American notion of 'financial entitlements'. As others have made clear, an entitlement would build up over an individual's lifetime and could be drawn on at any time to finance an approved course of study. It would also be possible to devise a scheme wherein an entitlement could be drawn in advance. As yet, there seems little European interest in this concept. In Britain, for example, there has been some discussion of educational vouchers for young people, which might be cashed at their parents' discretion to buy schooling in either the public or the private sector. The whole of this discussion has, however, taken place within the context of the traditional view of education as preceding adult life. It has served only to arouse the hostility of liberals to any such approach to education, on the grounds that the sole intention is to benefit private schools and more affluent families, able to supplement the voucher with money from their own pockets. Here, too, the signpost points in the wrong direction.

The value of part-time study is clear from the British experience of the Open University at one extreme, and of adult literacy programmes at the other. Most such students receive no personal financial support from public sources. Many full-time adult students, whether in higher education or receiving training in industrial or commercial skills, do get such support. There is no sign of a holistic approach to the development of lifelong learning. As for education at the workplace (which is not the same as narrow on-the-job training), it is reasonable to suppose that many adults will resume study more willingly if they are in a familiar environment and can see the relevance of what they are learning to their everyday concerns. Interest in the performance of their own firm and in its management and social structure is more likely than interest in the abstract disciplines of economics, sociology, and politics. But while some countries have experimented with this approach, in most the full-time educator rarely enters the workplaces of most of his fellow-citizens. On-the-job training is often given by those who are themselves untrained in teaching techniques, while the trained instructor does his job in premises perceived by some as just another school or college remote from their own work and its problems.

Implicit in these questions is the central problem of gaining acceptance for the concept of lifelong or recurrent education. Many now accept that education and training can no longer be confined to youth. But is learning in adulthood to be regarded as merely a supplement to what was done in the formal education which preceded adult life and work? Or is education throughout life to replace education for life? Those who adopt the former viewpoint are still wedded to the front-end model of education. Those who take the latter have adopted a new educational philosophy. It is not wholly new in as much as few have ever seriously believed that learning ceased with the end of formal schooling. (Socrates believed that no one was ever too old to learn, even if he was accused of corrupting the young specifically.) But we have in the past assumed that for the vast majority of people formal learning came to an end with entry into work, and that, while 'experience' was valuable, it was not normally necessary either to accredit it or to seek to build new formal learning upon it. Nor is the dichotomy between the two philosophies quite as sharp as I have made it appear. Few would argue that it is not important in early life to acquire the essential skills of literacy, numeracy and oral communication (perhaps in more than one language), some knowledge of the arts and the sciences, and a grasp of the principles of both deductive and inductive reasoning. But it is a question of whether one sees this process as producing a fully finished product, which may then be modified and updated from time to time, or whether one believes that the educational process (formal and informal) must for everyone be genuinely continuous throughout life.

Much practical political debate on education confuses the two philosophies. Thus, the mid-1970s in Britain saw some moves towards the recognition of the importance of adult learning. But in the autumn of 1976 James Callaghan, then Prime Minister, inaugurated what he called a 'Great Debate' on education with a speech which seemed to imply that schools should aim to turn out pupils at 16 with the knowledge and skills necessary for successful employment in industry and commerce. There was no suggestion that for everyone the educational process must thereafter continue, for vocational reasons and to enrich leisure, ensure fuller citizenship, and make possible a retirement meaning more than simply the cessation of paid work. Similarly, the leader of the British delegation to an OECD inter-governmental conference in 1973 had asserted (to an astonished audience) that in the United Kingdom we already had recurrent education; it was merely that we called it 'adult education'. This is an extreme version of the doctrine that the essence of education is what takes place in youth and that any learning thereafter, especially in a formal setting, is merely supplementary.

As an illustration of these fundamental difficulties in the development of a *system* of lifelong education we may assess changes in educational provision for adults in Britain between the elections of February 1974 and

May 1979, many of which have been mentioned in earlier chapters of this book. From 1975-78 the Government made available £1 million each year for a new adult literacy programme, initially through an *ad hoc* Adult Literacy Resources Agency. The British Broadcasting Corporation also mounted programmes designed to take adults through the first steps in learning to read. For three years the same notional sum was allocated to the task, but thereafter more than two-thirds of it was added to the general system of central government support for education and paid to local education authorities. The latter have many other functions and can allocate the grants they receive as they wish, provided that they perform their statutory duties. It might thus be argued that the burst of enthusiasm for aiding the most disadvantaged group of adults was short-lived. There was some discussion of a similar numeracy programme, but by 1979 no action had been taken.

At the other end of the academic spectrum, the budget of the Open University was protected by the then Labour Government and extra resources found to permit an increase in the number of degree students. The University's own report on continuing education, which if implemented would result in a wider range of provision at more than one academic level, was welcomed, though no extra money was forthcoming. The Education Act of 1975 gave a statutory right to financial aid to all students admitted to degree courses, irrespective of their previous educational attainments. This was designed to be of help primarily to mature students entering higher education. A new system of automatic financial support was introduced for students admitted to the six long-term residential adult colleges, all but one of which offered courses of two years' duration. In 1978 a Government discussion document on higher education suggested that as the number of 18-year-olds in the population declined in the second half of the 1980s, some of the surplus places in higher education might be filled by adult students. The suggestion bore however the *caveat* that there would have to be discussions with employers' and trade union organizations about the introduction of paid educational leave; by May 1979, no such discussions had taken place.

Paid educational leave was the subject of a publicly financed study inaugurated in 1977 under the aegis of the Society of Industrial Tutors and the National Institute of Adult Education. No concrete policy on the subject has emerged, however, and the in-service education and training of teachers, which in 1972 the previous Government had suggested should in part be undertaken on the basis of one term's leave in each seven years, has not developed as anticipated. Some local education authorities were generous with paid leave, but others much less so. Nevertheless, the Department of Education and Science has established a working party drawn from its professional advisers (Her Majesty's Inspectorate) to consider the practicability of establishing a system of recurrent education.

One British polytechnic established a degree by independent study, designed primarily for mature students. A few modular degree courses were mounted; in theory they ought to permit broken study and credit transfer between institutions more readily than the traditional British single-subject course. New technician-level courses under the aegis of the Technician and Business Education Councils were to be on a similar modular pattern, although the range of choice in each locality would be limited to what each further education college was able to offer. The Open University and the Council for National Academic Awards, which validates most degrees in Britain outside the universities, made an agreement on credit transfer, but the universities, which pride themselves on their independence *vis à vis* both the State (which provides most of their funds) and each other, did not become parties to this agreement.

The Workers' Educational Association, one of the voluntary bodies providing education for adults of all classes (despite its name) accepted from the Government new priorities – to concentrate on the socially and educationally disadvantaged, on those living in urban areas, and on political education. As ever, the word was easier than the deed; little extra funding was provided and it is always easier to add new activities to old than to substitute the former for the latter. The Government gave support to the Trade Union Congress to facilitate courses in trade union education for local and plant officials. Finally, a new Advisory Council on Adult and Continuing Education was established. The inclusion of the word 'continuing' in its title was deliberate, and from the outset it took a lively interest in the problems of moving towards a system of lifelong or recurrent education.

This list seems an impressive record of change in educational provision in Britain in the mid-1970s in the direction of recurrent education. But it is clear that these were piecemeal changes, and that the most important potentially, such as the research programme into paid educational leave, were an earnest of intent but not application. Nor were they manifestations of the will and philosophy of a single minister; in the five years there were nine incumbents of the three key ministerial posts in the Department of Education and Science. As for expenditure, by far the largest increase was in the vocational training and retraining of adults through the Manpower Services Commission. Although attempts were made to improve the liaison between the Department of Education and Science and this body, few thought them wholly successful. Most educational argument continued to be concerned with the schools, or youth education. In short, what was happening was a slow and bitty response to changing educational need, with increments to the existing front-end system of public education, rather than a fundamental review of educational philosophy.

Yet most of the issues central to a change towards recurrent education are now apparent. One of the keys is finance. Some countries have already legislated for paid educational leave (eg Sweden and France). Other countries cannot do so, by law (eg Switzerland, with its confederal system). In some countries the trade unions attach a high priority to the introduction or extension of such a system, while in others they attach little importance to it (Sweden here contrasts with the United Kingdom). But every country has the same interest in minimizing the displacement of existing private expenditure by new public expenditure, as paid educational leave (or entitlements) are introduced. Financial support, whatever its source, may have to be geared to the maximum benefit of those most in need, without commensurate advantage to those already enjoying private financing of their recurrent education, as many occupying professional or managerial posts do. With entitlement schemes, there is an added complexity, since it is not clear whether a financial entitlement dependent upon income should be settled by reference to the income of the individual or that of his or her family; this is especially important when we are considering provision for housewives.

Whatever the balance of funding paid educational leave or entitlements between the State (through taxation), the employer and the recipient (whether through a direct contribution or some form of educational insurance), care will be necessary to ensure that employing agencies are not relieved by public subsidy of financial responsibilities which at present they bear or undertake. The further education and training of his workers will always be of benefit to the employer as well as to the workers themselves. This suggests that we need detailed studies of the relative benefit to individuals, the enterprises in which they work, industries and nations to be derived from paid educational leave and recurrent education. The distribution of the burden of financing recurrent education is a matter for political as well as economic judgement: the Left will wish to place a greater responsibility on the employer and the taxpayer, the Right on the individual. But political judgements are best made upon the basis of sound economic appraisal.

Youth education offers the same basic diet to the great majority of pupils, although they also take optional extras. By contrast, recurrent education must focus on the developing needs and potential of each individual throughout his life, while taking account of the demands of the national and local economies. This too has implications for the system of financing recurrent education. It might suggest that it is the individual who should be directly financed, and educational institutions provided for only indirectly, through their clients (by fee income). On the other hand, any extreme version of such a system may produce unacceptable uncertainty in institutional budgeting, as German experience with the *Volkshochschulen* has already shown. Further, it would militate against provision to meet minority demands, whatever their importance, since such a system benefits institutions providing courses which attract large numbers of students.

Speaking to Parliament in 1861, Robert Lowe promised of the system of 'payment by results': 'If it is not cheap, it shall be efficient; if it is not efficient, it shall be cheap.' Recurrent education, if it is to be practicable at all, must be both cheap and efficient. That means that every opportunity must be taken to use centrally produced learning materials of high quality on standard topics, and the maximum use must be made of technological developments permitting the display of information and structured learning material on a television screen in the home, the local educational institution or the workplace. If changing technology has been a factor in making the front-end model of education no longer apposite, it can also provide some of the solutions to the new problems of recurrent education. We should, however, note that this calls into doubt some deep-seated doctrines or prejudices about education. The academic autonomy of the institution, dear to educators in Anglo-Saxon countries at least, is no longer so clear-cut when many of the learning materials it uses have been produced elsewhere. The freedom of the teacher to teach what he will as he will in his own classroom (however inefficiently and at whatever avoidable expense) is also called into question. One of the first tasks in recurrent education is to re-educate many of our educators.

Counselling is an essential key to the development of recurrent or lifelong education, and entails new training programmes for those who will attract adults back into education. It is at present offered by professional educators, by public and private employment agencies, by works training officers, by management and by trade unions. All of them have to some degree a sectional viewpoint, which makes it difficult for them to advise every individual in his or her best interests.

Here the Swedish experience of using shop stewards or works trade union officials as 'first-line' counsellors may be a signpost for other countries. The initial task is to communicate to the worker the range of opportunities available to him, the ways in which he may be advantaged by taking them up, and where he can go for specialist advice. The trusted workmate is a much better initial adviser than the unknown professional. Similarly, in the community, the postman, barman or social club organizer may be able to talk more easily to those who know and trust him than any teacher or government official. This does, however, require a considerable and continuing programme of part-time training for those who will perform this essential link role.

The second line of advice can, of course, come largely from public agencies, but here British experience suggests that there is not always adequate co-ordination between those concerned primarily with education (and hence with what the public education service can most readily offer), and those whose responsibilities lie in the fields of employment and training. It seems, therefore, that there will always be a need for independent advisory bodies, which may be partly or even largely publicly funded, but are not subject to the direction of central or local government. Such bodies can, moreover, offer specialist advice to the person whose needs do not fit any standard pattern, sometimes (perhaps) on the basis of psychological as well as educational expertise, in a way that lack of resources will deny to many smaller local government bodies. The best signpost here is the experience of the Educational Guidance Service for Adults in Northern Ireland. Although operating for 11 years in a climate of sectarian conflict and distrust, it has retained the respect of and remained accessible to members of both communities in the province, whereas agencies of government are viewed with fear and suspicion, particularly by the Catholic minority.

Counsellors will have to remember (as some Japanese experience indicates) that training without reference to subsequent job-function, or to management policies for career development, can lead to dissatisfaction among trainees. Further, training must take account of national and sectoral labour market changes. The development of skills which can never be used (except in leisure activities) can lead to an individual's dissatisfaction without improvement in economic performance.

They must remember, too, that there is a danger in removing the individual from his work-group for a period of education and returning him to it subsequently. This can lead to mutual alienation, without benefit to worker, group, employer, or the economy. At present there is little experience of group motivation and group learning schemes in recurrent education; it is urgently needed. Here (as in the introduction of paid educational leave) there are acute problems with small firms, simply because not many workers can be released for education or training at any one time. No country has yet fully solved these problems, although the solution undoubtedly lies in industry-based or locality-based schemes, designed to keep together members of the same interest-group even where it is impossible to operate with a unified work-group.

Despite all this, the individual must remain the final arbiter of his studies in recurrent or lifelong education. Adult learners, choosing studies on the basis of their own work and life experience, cannot be *directed* to courses which others consider good for them. Furthermore, because such education begins with the needs and the demands of the learner, it must be learner-centred rather than subject- or discipline- oriented. Educators will thus have to accommodate themselves to interdisciplinary methods. Here the experience of schools in 'project-based' studies and of higher education in 'independent study' are both relevant. The problem lies in diffusing the lessons of that experience more widely throughout the education and training system.

This demands that we develop new means of accrediting or validating learning achievement. We must also find ways of evaluating informal learning at the workplace and on the job, as the basis for future counselling and study. For most people, the ability to do or perform is more important than the accurate formal reproduction of facts and theory. We should therefore look less to the ability to reproduce knowledge in a set examination than to less formal means of assessing the learner's competence and potential — the practical project, the 'open-book' thesis, dissertation or essay, and skills manifested on the job. Some system of accreditation is demanded by the labour market, and for many students it provides positive motivation to maintain their studies. But accreditation should not be designed to mark a terminal point in learning, as most existing forms of certification do, but should provide the basis of counselling on future employment and further study. In short, what is needed is a 'transcript' of the individual's achievement and performance hitherto and an assessment of his or her potential, to guide both him and those who will counsel or teach him in the future.

However, if any system of accreditation is to be acceptable, there must be some guarantee of uniform standards. Its development thus poses in acute form one of the central problems in a system of lifelong or recurrent education — the distribution of power and control within it. There is no doubt that organs of government, both central and local, and teachers, employers and trade unions must all have a place in the structure of control, although the relative weight attached to each of these partners may vary according to political preference. On the other hand, at local community and plant level the individual learner must have a powerful voice in the planning process, if recurrent education is to be geared to his or her needs and to derive from them. The demands of providers, consumers, teachers and employers will in part be mediated and reconciled through the systems of financing recurrent education and of counselling adult learners which each country adopts. But there must still be devised a structure of policy-making which allows the needs of each individual to be determined and, so far as is practicable, to be met, while at the same time giving due weight to the demands of national and local economies and to changing social and political priorities. On the evidence of the essays in this book no country has yet devised a structure which does this wholly satisfactorily, if indeed it is an attainable objective.

Lifelong or recurrent education thus remains (to a large extent) *terra incognita*, and such signposts as exist do not take us much further on the journey, even when they point in the right direction. But this book does demonstrate that we are now in the process of building a bank of international experience which, if shared, can help ease the agonizing over policy choices which occurs in every country, developed or developing. The economic conditions of the 1970s have substantially altered the case for recurrent education. Already many and soon most countries in the world will have to examine the relative costs of social security support for increasing numbers of people, especially at the lower and upper ends of the age scale, and of progress towards recurrent education and training opportunities for all, integrated with a strategy both for the creation of new employment and for the use of leisure. Lifelong and recurrent education are no longer just theoretical concepts; their embodiment in practice is integral to the evolution of acceptable national economic and social policies.

Part 6:
Bibliography and Biographical Notes

Bibliography

The bibliography is divided into three sections. The first covers published books and pamphlets by individual authors; the second, publications (books and documents) issued by official bodies; and the third, articles and other papers.

It includes the majority of the references from individual chapters, omitting those which were relevant only to the specific context in which they were cited, rather than to recurrent education in general.

Other references of direct interest to the central theme have been added.

Section I: Books and Pamphlets

Abrahamsson, B and Broström, A (1978) Participation and the mandator role: some comments and an outline of a research project *in* Social Science Research Council (1978)

Abrahamsson, K, Nilsson, O and Rubenson, K (1978) *Recurrent Education – Ideals and Realities in the Swedish System of Higher Education* Stockholm Institute of Education: Stockholm

Adamski, W (1978) *Continuing Education in Western and Eastern European Societies* European Cultural Foundation: Amsterdam

Ahmed, M and Coombs, P H (1975) *Education for Rural Development: Case Studies for Planners* Praeger: New York

Alford, J (1968) *Continuing Education in Action* John Wiley & Sons: New York

Alley, R (1973) *Travels in China* New World Press: Peking

Anderson, D and Niemi, J A (1969) *Adult Education and the Disadvantaged Adult* ERIC Clearinghouse on Adult Education: Syracuse, NY

Argyris, C and Schön, D A (1976) *Theory in Practice: Increasing Professional Effectiveness* Jossey-Bass: San Francisco

Baltes, P B and Schaie, K W (eds) (1973) *Life-Span Developmental Psychology: Personality and Socialization* Academic Press: New York

Batstone, E (1978) Management and industrial democracy *in* Social Science Research Council (1978)

Batstone, E and Davies, P L (1976) *Industrial Democracy: European Experience* HMSO: London

Belasco, J A and Trice, H M (1969) *The Assessment of Change in Training and Therapy* McGraw-Hill: New York

Belden, J (1970) *China Shakes the World* Monthly Review Press: New York and London

Bernbaum, G (1977) *Knowledge and Ideology in the Sociology of Education* Macmillan: London
Best, F and Stern, B (1976) *Lifetime Distribution of Education, Work, Leisure: Research, Speculations and Policy Implications of Changing Life Patterns* Institute for Educational Leadership: Washington, DC
Bhasin, K (1977) *Participatory Training* FAO: Rome
Birren, J E and Schaie, K W (eds) (1977) *Handbook of the Psychology of Aging* Van Nostrand Reinhold: New York
Blainey, G (1966) *The Tyranny of Distance* Sun Books: Melbourne
Boaz, R L (1978) *Participation in Adult Education: Final Report 1975* DHEW, National Center for Education Statistics, US Government Printing Office: Washington, DC
Botwinick, J (1967) *Cognitive Processes in Maturity and Old Age* Springer: New York
Bowles, S and Gintis, H (1976) *Schooling in Capitalist America* Basic Books: New York
Broschart, J R (1977) *Lifelong Learning in the Nation's Third Century* United States Office of Education, DHEW (publication no OE 76-09102) US Government Printing Office: Washington: DC
Brunner, E DeS et al (1959) *An Overview of Adult Education Research* Adult Education Association of the USA: Chicago

Campbell, D D (1977) *Adult Education as a Field of Study and Practice* University of British Columbia, the Centre for Continuing Education: Vancouver
Cantor, L (1974) *Recurrent Education Policy and Development in OECD Member Countries United Kingdom* OECD: Paris
Che Hung-chang (1955) How Yinta Township started spare-time education for peasants *in Socialist Upsurge in China's Countryside* (1957) Foreign Language Press: Peking
Chen, J (ed) (1970) *Mao Papers, Anthology and Bibliography* Oxford University Press: London
Clark, B R (1956) *Adult Education in Transition* University of California Press: Berkeley, Ca
Coates, K (1978) *The Right to Useful Work* Spokesman Books: Nottingham
Coombs, P H (1969) *The World Education Crisis* Oxford University Press: New York
Coombs, P H and Ahmed, M (1974) *Attacking Rural Poverty: How Non-Formal Education Can Help* World Bank/Johns Hopkins Press: Baltimore, Md
Court, D and Ghai, Y (1976) *Education, Society and Development* Oxford University Press: London

De Sanctis, F M (1978) *L'Educazione Degli Adulti in Italia* Editori Riuniti, Paideia: Roma
Dolff, H (1973) *Die Deutschen Volkshochschulen* (2nd ed) Droste Verlag: Hamburg
Drucker, P F (1966) *The Effective Executive* Harper and Row: New York
Duke, C (1974) *Recurrent Education – Policy and Development in OECD Member Countries: Australia* OECD: Paris
Duke, C (1976) Recurrent education – refurbish or reform? *in* Browne, R K and Margin, D J (eds) *Sociology of Education* Macmillan: London
Duke, C (ed) (1978a) *Recurrent Education: Trends, Tensions and Trade-Offs* (report of a national seminar) Australian Department of Education: Canberra
Duke, C (1978b) Australia in Asia – comparison as learning *in* Charters, A N (ed) *Handbook of Adult Education* Jossey-Bass: San Francisco

Eisdorfer, C and Lawton, M P (1973) *The Psychology of Adult Development and Aging* American Psychological Association: Washington, DC
Elliott, J (1978) *Conflict or Cooperation? The Growth of Industrial Democracy* Kogan Page: London
Espinosa, J and Zimbalist, A (1978) *Economic Democracy: Workers' Participation in Chilean Industry 1970-73* Academic Press: New York

Farmer, M L (1971) *Counseling Services for Adults in Higher Education* Scarecrow Press: Metuchen, NJ
Feldman, K A and Newcomb, T M (1969) *The Impact of College on Students* Jossey-Bass: San Francisco
Ferguson, J (1975) *The Open University from Within* University of London Press: London
Finch, C B and Hayflick, L (eds) (1977) *Handbook of the Biology of Aging* Van Nostrand Reinhold: New York
Flippo, E B (1976) *Principles of Personnel Management* (4th edition) McGraw-Hill: New York
Ford, W (1977) Educational implications of industrial democracy *in* Pritchard (1977)
Fox, A (1974) *Beyond Contract: Work, Power and Trust Relations* Faber and Faber: London
Foy, N (1978) *The Missing Links — British Management Education in the Eighties* Foundation for Management Education: London
Fraser, J (1965) *Chinese Communist Education* Vanderbilt University Press: New York

Gagné, R M (1972) *The Conditions of Learning* (revised edition) Holt, Rinehart, and Winston: New York
Gershuny, J (1978) *After Industrial Society: The Emerging Self-Service Economy* Macmillan: London
Gladieux, L E and Wolanin, T R (1976) *Congress and the Colleges: The National Politics of Higher Education* D C Heath: Lexington, Mass
Gould, R (1978) *Transformations* Simon and Schuster: New York
Goyder, C (1977) *Sabbaticals for All* NCLC: London
Grattan, C H (1971) *In Quest of Knowledge: A Historical Perspective on Adult Education* (reprint) Arno Press and the *New York Times*
Gross, R (1976) *Higher/Wider/Education: A Report on Open Learning* Ford Foundation: New York

Hamilton, I B (1976) *The Third Century: Post-Secondary Planning for the Non-Traditional Learner* Education Testing Service: Princeton, NJ
Havighurst, R J and Orr, B (1956) *Adult Education and Adult Needs* Center for the Study of Liberal Education for Adults: Chicago. (Available from Syracuse University, Publications in Continuing Education: Syracuse, NY)
Hentschke, G C (1975) *Management Operations in Education* McCutchan Publishing Corporation: Berkeley, Ca
Herburgh, T M, Miller, P A and Wharton, Jr, C R (1973) *Patterns for Lifelong Learning* Jossey-Bass: San Francisco
Hoggart, R (1978) *After Expansion: A Time for Diversity* ACACE: Leicester
Hooper, R (1977) *The National Development Programme in Computer Assisted Learning: Final Report of the Director* Council for Educational Technology: London
Houghton, V P and Richardson, K (eds) (1974) *Recurrent Education: A Plea for Lifelong Learning* Ward Lock: London
Houle, C O (1961) *The Inquiring Mind* University of Wisconsin Press: Madison
Houle, C O (1972) *The Design of Education* Jossey-Bass: San Francisco
Houle, C O (1973) *The External Degree* Jossey-Bass: San Francisco
Husen, T (1970) *Lifelong Education in the Educative Society* School of Education: Stockholm

Illich, I (1978) *The Right to Useful Unemployment* Marion Boyars: London

Jacobs, E et al (1977) *The Approach to Industrial Change* Anglo-German Foundation for the Study of Industrial Society: London
Johnson, R M (1977) *Meeting Needs — Training in Context* Association of Colleges of Further and Higher Education: London
Johnstone, J W C and Rivera, R J (1965) *Volunteers for Learning* Aldine: Chicago

Jones, H A and Charnley, A (1978) *Adult Literacy: A Study of Its Impact* NIAE: Leicester
Joyce, B and Weil, M (1972) *Models of Teaching* Prentice-Hall: Englewood Cliffs, NJ
Katz, D and Kahn, R L (1966) *The Social Psychology of Organizations* John Wiley and Sons: New York
Kessen, W (ed) (1975) *Childhood in China* Yale University Press: New Haven
Kidd, J R (1962) *Financing Continuing Education* Scarecrow Press: New York
Kotler, P (1974) *Marketing for Non-Profit Organizations* Prentice-Hall: Englewood Cliffs, NJ
Knowles, M S (1970) *The Modern Practice of Adult Education* Association Press: New York
Knowles, M S (1975) *Self Directed Learning* Association Press: New York
Knowles, M S (1977) *A History of the Adult Education Movement in the United States* (revised edition) Krieger: Huntington, NY
Knox, A B (1974) Life-long self-directed education Chapter 2 in Blakely, R J (ed) *Fostering the Growing Need to Learn* Division of Regional Medical Programs, Bureau of Health Resources Development: Rockville, Md
Knox, A B (1977) *Adult Development and Learning* Jossey-Bass: San Francisco
Knox, A B (ed) (in press) *Adult Education Program Development and Administration* Jossey-Bass: San Francisco
Kurland, N D (ed) (1977) *Entitlement Studies* National Institute of Education: Washington, DC

Lauffer, A (1977) *The Practice of Continuing Education in the Human Services* McGraw-Hill: New York
Levinson, D J et al (1978) *The Seasons of a Man's Life* Knopf: New York
Levitas, M (1974) *Marxist Perspectives in the Sociology of Education* Routledge: London
Lindquist, J (1978) *Strategies for Change* Pacific Soundings Press: Berkeley, Ca
Lowe, J (1975) *The Education of Adults: A World Perspective* UNESCO: Paris
Luttringer, J M (1975) *Le droit des travailleurs à la formation* Armand Colin: Paris
Luttringer, J M (1975) *Les institutions de la formation permanente* Armand Colin: Paris

Maas, H S and Kuypers, J A (1974) *From Thirty to Seventy* Jossey-Bass: San Francisco
McHale, J (1976) *The Changing Information Environment* Westview Press: Boulder, Col
Mahler, F (1978) *The Integrated System of School, Work and Research, Its Impact on the Changes in the Future Occupational and Social Statuses* The Research Centre for Youth Problems: Bucharest
Mao Tsetung (1927) Report on an investigation of the peasant movement in Hunan in *Selected Works of Mao Tsetung* (1967) Foreign Language Press: Peking
Mao Tsetung (1944) The united front in cultural work in *Selected Works of Mao Tsetung* (1965) Foreign Language Press: Peking
Mao Tsetung (1968) in *Strive to Build a Socialist University of Science and Engineering* (1972) Foreign Language Press: Peking
Mauger, P et al (1974) *Education in China* Anglo-Chinese Educational Institute: London
Maurice, M (1975) *Shiftwork* ILO: Geneva
Moltke, K von and Schneevoight, J (1977) *Educational Leaves for Employees* McGraw-Hill: New York

Nakamoto, J and Verner, C (1973) *Continuing Education in the Health Professions: A Review of the Literature 1960-1970* ERIC Clearinghouse on Adult Education: Syracuse, NY
Niemi, J A and Jessen, D C (1976) *Directory of Resources in Adult Education* Adult Education Association (and ERIC Clearinghouse in Career Education at Northern Illinois University): Washington, DC

Pateman, C (1970) *Participation and Democratic Theory* Cambridge University Press: Cambridge
Perry, P J C (1976) *The Evolution of British Manpower Policy* British Association for Commercial and Industrial Education: London
Perry, W (1976) *The Open University* Open University Press: Milton Keynes
Peterson, R E et al (1978) *Toward Lifelong Learning in America: A Sourcebook for Planners* Educational Testing Service: Berkeley, Ca
Pflüger, A (1978) *Training and Retraining of Adult Educators* Council of Europe: Strasbourg
Pierce, R, Spencer, D and Weiss, L (1975) *Four Stages of Life: A Comparative Study of Women and Men Facing Transitions* Jossey-Bass: San Francisco
Pritchard, R L (1977) *Industrial Democracy in Australia* CCH Australia Limited: North Ryde 2113

Richman, B (1969) *Industrial Society in Communist China* Random House: New York
Richta, R (1968) *Civilisation au carrefour* Paris
Rogers, E M and Shoemaker, F F (1971) *Communication of Innovations* Free Press: New York

Schein, E H (1978) *Career Dynamics: Matching Individual and Organizational Needs* Addison-Wesley: Reading, Mass
Schramm, W and Lerner, D (eds) (1976) *Communication and Change: The Last Ten Years — and the Next* University Press of Hawaii
Schuller, T (1978) *Education through life* Young Fabian Pamphlet 47: London
Shaw, N C (ed) (1969) *Administration of Continuing Education* National Association for Public School Adult Education: Washington, DC
Shulman, C H (1975) *Premises and Programs for a Learning Society* American Association for Higher Education: Washington, DC
Skard, Ø (1977) *Learning and Democratization* Norwegian Employers' Confederation: Oslo
Smith, R M, Aker, G F and Kidd, J R (eds) (1970) *Handbook of Adult Education* Macmillan: New York
Snow, E (1937) *Red Star over China* Gollancz: London
Social Science Research Council (1978) *Industrial Democracy: International Views* Warwick University: Coventry
Srinivasan, L (1977) *Perspectives on Non-Formal Adult Learning* World Education: New York
Steele, S M (1973) *Contemporary Approaches to Program Evaluation and Their Implications for Evaluating Programs for Disadvantaged Adults* ERIC Clearinghouse on Adult Education: Syracuse, NY
Stonier, T (1976) The natural history of humanity: past, present and future, Inaugural Lecture, University of Bradford: Bradford

Timiras, P S (1972) *Developmental Physiology and Aging* Macmillan: New York
Trent, J W and Medsker, L B (1968) *Beyond High School* Jossey-Bass: San Francisco
Tunstall, J (ed) (1974) *The Open University Opens* Routledge: London

Vaillant, G (1977) *Adaptation to Life* Little, Brown: Boston
Visalberghi, A (1973) *Education and Division of Labour* Martinus Nijhoff: The Hague

Waniewicz, I (1976) *Demand for Part-time Learning in Ontario* The Ontario Educational Communications Authority: Toronto
White, R W (1961) *Lives in Progress* Holt, Rinehart, and Winston: New York
Williams, R H and Wirths, C G (1965) *Lives Through the Years* Atherton Press: New York
Willmott, P and Young, M (1973) *The Symmetrical Family* Pelican: London

Young, M F D (1971) *Knowledge and Control* Collier-Macmillan: London

Section II: Official Publications

Adult Literacy Resource Agency (ALRA) (1978) *Adult Literacy in 1977-78: A Remarkable Educational Advance* HMSO: London

Advisory Council for Applied Research and Development (ACARD) (1978) *The Applications of Semiconductor Technology* Cabinet Office, HMSO: London

Alberta (1972) *Choice of Futures* Report of the Commission on Educational Planning in Alberta (The Worth Report): Edmonton

Alexander, Kenneth (1975) *see* Scottish Education Department

Annan, Lord (1977) *see* Home Office

Asian and South Pacific Bureau of Adult Education (ASPBAE) (with South Pacific Commission (1978) *Regional Planning Conference on Adult Education in National Development* Report: Noumea

Association of Recurrent Education (ARE) (1977) *The National Credit Transfer Feasibility Study* Newsletter 5 Nottingham University

Association for Recurrent Education (ARE) (1978) *Guidance and Counselling for Adults; Higher Education in the 1990s* Newsletter 6 Nottingham University

Australian Council on Technical and Further Education (ACOTAFE) (1974) *First Report on Needs in Technical and Further Education* Canberra

Australian Universities Commission (1975) *Sixth Report* Canberra

Bullock, Lord (1977) *see* Department of Trade

Bund-Lander-Kommission für Bildungsplanung (1973) *Overall Plan for Education by the Joint Federal and Lander Committee for Educational Planning* Bonn

Christian Council of Tanzania (1976) *Elimu ya Ufundi Vijijini Tanzania (Vocational Education in Rural Villages of Tanzania)* Kicheba Report: Dar es Salaam

Commission on Non-Traditional Study (1973) *Diversity by Design* Jossey-Bass: San Francisco

Congressional Budget Office (1977) *Post-Secondary Education: The Current Federal Role and Alternative Approaches* Government Printing Office: Washington, DC

Council of Europe (1970) *Permanent Education: A Compendium of Studies* Council of Europe: Strasbourg

Council of Europe (1978) *Permanent Education: Final Report* Council of Europe: Strasbourg

Department of Education and Science (1963) *Report of the Commission on Higher Education* (The Robbins Report) Cmnd 2154 HMSO: London

Department of Education and Science (1969) *The Open University* Report of the Planning Committee (Chairman, Sir Peter Venables) HMSO: London

Department of Education and Science (1973) *Adult Education: A Plan for Development* (The Russell Report) HMSO: London

Department of Education and Science (1976) *Schools in England and Wales Current Issues: An Annotated Agenda for Discussion* DES: London and Welsh Office: Cardiff

Department of Education and Science (1977) *Memorandum of Arrangements for the Advisory Council for Adult and Continuing Education* HMSO: London

Department of Education and Science and the Scottish Education Department (1978) *Higher Education into the 1990s* (discussion document) DES: London and SED: Edinburgh

Department of Trade (1977) *Report of the Committee of Inquiry on Industrial Democracy* (The Bullock Report) Cmnd 6706 HMSO: London

Deutscher Bildungsrat (1970) *Strukturplan für das Bildungswesen (Structural Plan for the Educational System)* German Council for Education: Bonn

European Centre for Leisure and Education (1975) *Adult Education in Europe* Studies and Documents No 4

Faure, Edgar (1972) *see* UNESCO

Home Office (1977) *Report of the Committee on the Future of Broadcasting* (The Annan Report) Cmnd 6753 HMSO: London

Kemenade, J A Van (1975) *Contours of a Future Educational System in the Netherlands* (English version summary of a discussion memorandum) Ministry of Education and Science: The Hague

Manpower Services Commission (1978a) *Management Development: Policy and Activities of the MSC* MSC: London
Manpower Services Commission (1978b) *Training of Trainers: First Report of the Training of Trainers Committee* MSC: London
Manpower Services Commission (1978c) *MSC Review and Plan* MSC: London
Manpower Services Commission (1978d) *TOPS Review 1978* MSC: London
Ministry of Education (1973) *Higher Education. Proposals by the Swedish 1968 Educational Commission* Stockholm
Ministry of Education (1973) *Continued Outreaching Work for Circle Studies in Adult Education* Stockholm

National Advisory Council on Extension and Continuing Education (1977) *Proceedings of the Invitational Conference on Continuing Education, Manpower Policy and Lifelong Learning* NACECE: Washington, DC

Oakes, G (1978) *Report of the Working Group on the Management of Higher Education in the Maintained Sector* HMSO: London
OECD (1971) *Equal Educational Opportunity: A Statement of the Problem with Special Reference to Recurrent Education* OECD: Paris
OECD (1975) *The Role of Women in the Economy* OECD: Paris
OECD (1977) *Education Policies and Trends* OECD: Paris
OECD (1978) *Demographic Trends: Their Labour Market and Social Implications* OECD: Paris
OECD (1978) *Youth Unemployment Vols I-II* OECD: Paris
OECD/CERI (1973) *Recurrent Education: A Strategy for Lifelong Learning* OECD: Paris
OECD/CERI (1975) *Education and Working Life in Modern Society* OECD: Paris
OECD/CERI (1975) *Recurrent Education: Trends and Issues* OECD: Paris
OECD/CERI (1976) *Developments in Educational Leave of Absence* OECD: Paris
OECD/CERI (1978) *Alternation between Work and Education* OECD: Paris
Ontario (1972) *The Learning Society* Report of the Commission on Post-Secondary Education in Ontario (The Wright Report): Toronto
Open University (1974) *Recurrent Education — An Alternative Future?* Educational Studies E221, Unit 16 Open University Press: Milton Keynes
Open University (1976) *Report of the Committee on Continuing Education* (The Venables Report) Open University Press: Milton Keynes

Post-Secondary Education Convening Authority (1976) *A National Strategy for Lifelong Learning* Institute for Educational Leadership: Washington, DC

Regione Toscana (1978) *Educazione Permanente e Territorio* Commissione Nazionale Italiana per l'UNESCO: Firenze
Robbins, Lord (1963) *see* Department of Education and Science
Russell, Sir Lionel (1973) *see* Department of Education and Science

Schools Commission (1975) *Report for the Triennium 1976-78* Canberra
Scottish Education Department (1975) *Adult Education: The Challenge of Change* (The Alexander Report) HMSO: Edinburgh

The Carnegie Commission on Higher Education (1973) *Toward a Learning Society: Alternative Channels to Life, Work and Service* McGraw-Hill: New York

The Council of State of the Socialist Republic of Romania (1977) *Organization and Operation of Vocational Education in the Socialist Republic of Romania* Budapest

The National Commission on the Financing of Post-Secondary Education (1973) *Financing Post-Secondary Education in the United States* Government Printing Office: Washington, DC

Trade Union Congress (1978) *Priorities in Continuing Education* London

UIA (1976) *Seminar on Integration of Educational and Community Facilities* The Technical Chamber of Greece: Athens

UNESCO (1972) *Learning to Be* (The Faure Report) UNESCO: Paris

UNESCO (1976) *Colloque sur la Contribution des Non-Enseignants aux Activités Educatives dans la Perspective de l'Education Permanente* (ED-76/CONF.811/COL.2) UNESCO: Paris

UNESCO (1976) *Lifelong Education, the Curriculum and Basic Learning Needs* (Final report of the regional seminar at Chiangmai) UNESCO: Bangkok

UNESCO (1977) *Alternative Approaches to School Education at Primary Level* (Final report of the regional seminar at Manila) UNESCO: Bangkok

UNESCO (1978) *Final Report of 4th Regional Conference of Ministers of Education and Those Responsible for Economic Planning in Asia and Oceania* UNESCO: Colombo

Venables, Sir Peter (1976) *see* Open University

World Bank (1974) *Education Sector Working Paper* Washington, DC
Worth, W (1972) *see* Alberta

Section III: Articles and Working Papers

Allen, D W and Anzalone, S (1978) Learning by radio: the first step to literacy *Prospects* 8 2: 202-10

Baller, W R, Charles, D C, and Miller, E L (1967) Mid-life attainment of the mentally retarded: a longitudinal study *Genetic Psychology Monographs* 75: 235-329

Berrol, S C (1976) From compensatory education to adult education: the New York evening schools, 1825-1935 *Adult Education* 26: 4

Best, F and Stern, B (1977) Education, work and leisure: must they come in that order? *Monthly Labour Review* 100 7: 3

Blaug, M and Mace, J (1977) Recurrent education: the new Jerusalem *Higher Education* 6: 3

Booth, A and Knox, A (1967) Participation in adult education agencies and personal influence *Sociology of Education* 40 3: 275-7

Boshier, R (1976) Factor analysis at large: a critical review of the motivational orientation literature *Adult Education* 27 1: 25-47

Brown, W and Lawson, M (1973) The training of trade union officers *British Journal of Industrial Relations* 11: 431-48

Burdge, R J (1969) Levels of occupational prestige and leisure activity *Journal of Leisure Research* 1 3

Burgess, P (1971) Reasons for adult participation in group education activities *Adult Education* 22 1: 3-29

Carnoy, M (1975) Can educational policy equalize income distribution in Latin America? ILO Working Paper: Geneva

Centre INFFO (1978) *Actualité de la Formation Permanente* 35 July/August 1978

Christoffel, P H (1978) Future federal funding of lifelong learning *Lifelong Learning: The Adult Years* 1 10: 17-24

Coffey, J (1978) *Development of an Open Learning System for Further Education* Council for Educational Technology Working Paper 15 CET: London

Communist Party of China Central Committee Decision (1977) *Peking Review* 20 43: 7

Corbett, A (1978) Recurrent education *Scottish Journal of Adult Education* 3 3

Dahllöf, U (1977) *Reforming Higher Education and External Studies in Sweden and Australia* Acta Universitatis Uppsaliensis: Uppsala, Studies in Education 3

Darkenwald, G G (1977) Innovation in adult education: an organizational analysis *Adult Education* 27 3: 156-72

Davies, T C (1977) *Open Learning Systems for Mature Students* CET Working Paper 14 CET: London

Debeauvais, M (1978) Les rôles des organisations internationales dans l'évolution de l'éducation comparée *Recherche, Pedagogie et Culture* May-August 1978

Deleon, A (1978) Adult education as a corrective to the failure of formal education *Prospects* 8 2: 169-76

Dubar, C (1977) Formation continue et différenciations sociales *Revue Française de Sociologie* 18: 543-75

Fogarty, M (1976) The place of managers in industrial democracy *British Journal of Industrial Relations* 14

Fowler, G (1977) Agenda for better days *Times Higher Educational Supplement* 15 April

Freedman, D H (1978) *The Contemporary Work Ethic in Industrialised Market Economy Countries* Working Employment Programme Research Working Papers, ILO: Geneva

Freire, P (1970) The adult literacy process and cultural action for freedom *Harvard Educational Review* 40 2: 205-25

Fullerton, H N Jnr and Byrne, J J (1976) Length of working life for men and women 1970 *Monthly Labour Review* 99 2: 31

Gardell, B (1976) Reactions at work and their influence on non-work activities: an analysis of a socio-political problem in affluent societies *Human Relations* 29 9

Gosling, W (1978) *Microcircuits, Society and Education* Council for Educational Technology for the United Kingdom, Occasional Paper No 8: London

Griffin, C (1978) Curriculum models of recurrent and continuing education *Association for Recurrent Education Discussion Paper* 3: Nottingham University

Grugeon, D (ed) *Teaching at a Distance*: journal published by the Open University: Milton Keynes

Hackman, J R, Oldham, G R, Janson, R and Purdy, K (1975) A new strategy for job enrichment *California Management Review* 17 4: 57-71

Hsinhua News Agency (1973) Weekly Issue 235: London
Hsinhua News Agency (1974) Weekly Issue 261: London
Hsinhua News Agency (1975) 20 July: London
Hsinhua News Agency (1978a) Weekly Issue 504: London
Hsinhua News Agency (1978b) 16 May: London
Hsinhua News Agency (1978c) 13 October: London

Irish, G H (1975) Reflection on means and ends in adult basic education *Adult Education* 25 2: 125-30

Johnston, D F (1972) The future of work: three possible alternatives *Monthly Labour Review* 95 5: 3

Kallen, D B P (1978) L'éducation récurrente dans les pays d'Europe occidentale *Perspectives* 8 2

Keith, S (1975) Education and dependent capitalist development: a case study of Jamaica *LACDES Quarterly* 4 2: 4-19

Kerr, E (1977) CNAA and recurrent education Report of 1977 Annual Conference *Association for Recurrent Education Newsletter* 5: Nottingham University

Knox, A B (1975) New realities in the administration of continuing higher education *The NUEA Spectator* 39 22: 6-9

Knox, A B and Farmer, H S (1977) Overview of counselling and information services for adult learners *International Review of Education* 23 4: 387-414

Knox, A B and Sjogren, D D (1964) Achievement and withdrawal in university adult education classes *Adult Education* 15 2: 74-88

Kozol, J (1978) A new look at the literacy campaign in Cuba *Harvard Education Review* 48 3: 341-77

Lawson, K H (1977) A critique of recurrent education *Association for Recurrent Education Discussion Paper 1*: Nottingham University

Liu Yu-sheng (1974) The Nanniwan May 7 Cadre School *China Reconstructs* 23 7: 6-7

Lloyd, A S (1972) Freire, conscientization and adult education *Adult Education* 23 1: 3-20

Lorenzetto, A (1968) The experimental projects sponsored by UNESCO and the revolutionary element in literacy *Convergence* 1 3: 31-6

Lorenzetto, A and Neijs, K (1968) The Cuban literacy campaign *Convergence* 1 3: 46-50

McIntosh, N E and Woodley, A (1978) *Combining Education with Working Life or The Working Student* Paper presented at the 4th International Conference on Higher Education University of Lancaster, September 1978

Mbilinyi, M J (1979) Peasants' education in Tanzania *The African Review* 6 2

Melo, A (1978) Experiments in popular education in Portugal 1974-76 *Educational Studies and Documents No 29* UNESCO: Paris

Merriam, S (1977) Philosophical perspectives on adult education: a critical review of the literature *Adult Education* 27 4: 195-208

Mitrovic, L R (1978) A contribution to the definition of the relationship between participation and self-management *Socioloski Pregled* Belgrade

Monette, M L (1977) The concept of educational need *Adult Education* 27 2: 116-27

Moore, D (1977) Nelson and Colne College Community – based approach to RE Report of 1977 Annual Conference *Association for Recurrent Education Newsletter 5*: Nottingham University

Mulder, M (1971) Power equalization through participation *Administrative Science Quarterly* 16: 31-8

Penfield, K R (1975) Public service vs redeeming values: university extension in conflict *Adult Education* 25 2: 107-24

Pennington, F and Green, J (1976) Comparative analysis of program development processes in six professions *Adult Education* 27 1: 13-23

Purvis, J (1976) The low status of adult education – some sociological reflections *Educational Research* 19 1: 13-24

Richta, R (1977) The scientific and technological revolution and the projects of social development *Scientific Technological Revolution* Sage: London

Rodriguez, C (1972) Lifelong education *Bulletin of the International Bureau of Education* Year 46 No 185 The Fourth Quarter UNESCO: Paris

Rubenson, K (1977) *Participation in Recurrent Education: A Research Review* CERI/OECD: Paris

Simmons, J (1974) Education, poverty and development IBRD Bank Staff Working Paper No 188: Washington, DC

Sjogren, D D, Knox, A B and Grotelueschen, A D (1968) Adult learning in relation to prior adult education participation *Adult Education* 19 1: 3-10

Sorje, A (1976) The evolution of industrial democracy in Europe *British Journal of Industrial Relations* 14: 3

Stubblefield, H W (1974) Adult civic education in the post World War II period *Adult Education* 24 3: 227-37

Suchodolski, B (1978) L'éducation permanente à la croisée des chemins *Education Permanente – Une Confrontation Internationale d'Experiences* AFEC March: 28-9

Taylor, J (1978) The Advisory Council for Adult and Continuing Education *Adult Education* 51 4: 209-15

Tough, A (1971) *The Adult's Learning Projects* (Research in Education Series No 1) Ontario Institute for Studies in Education: Toronto

Tough, A (1978) Major learning efforts: recent research and future directions *Adult Education* 28 4: 250-63

Trade Union Research Unit (1977) *The Acquisition and Use of Company Information by Trade Unions* Ruskin College: Oxford

Truesdell, L R (1975) Persisters and dropouts in the Canada Manpower Training Program *Adult Education* 25 3: 149-60

UNESCO (1971) *Prospects* (quarterly): Paris

Viklund, B (1977) Education for industrial democracy *Current Sweden* 152 March

Williams, P (1976) *Prescription or Progress? A Commentary on the Education Policy of the World Bank* Institute of Education Studies in Education 3: University of London

Biographical notes on contributors and editors

J Myron Atkin (UK Consulting Editor) has been Dean of the College of Education at the University of Illinois since 1970. After teaching science for seven years at the elementary and secondary school levels, he became involved in curriculum development activities and teacher education. During the last 15 years his research and teaching activities have moved from science education to education evaluation to education politics. Recent writings focus on the effects on teachers and children of the shift of power from professional educationists to politicians and civil servants. He serves or has served on such bodies as the Advisory Committee for Science Education of the National Science Foundation, the Illinois Teacher Certification Board, the Committee on Governmental and Professional Liaison of the American Educational Research Association, the Executive Board of the American Education Research Association, and the Board of Directors of the National Association for Research in Science Teaching. He is a frequent consultant to universities and to governmental bodies.

Jarl Bengtsson (Chapter 1) is at present a counsellor and head of a research section at CERI, OECD, looking into the relationships between education and society.

Before joining OECD in 1972 he worked as an expert to the Swedish Ministry of Education and did research and teaching at the Social Science Faculty at the University of Göteborg, where he is also a Docent (Assistant Professor). His particular research and policy work over the last years has been directed towards major economic, social and labour market changes and the way they affect education.

Pierre Caspar (Chapter 9) was at first a mining engineer. He studied operational research in Berkeley (California) where he took his master's degree. He has been interested in adult education since 1963, when he began to work with B Schwartz in the 'Centre Universitaire de Co-operation Economique et Social' (ACUCES).

Engaged simultaneously in professional activities and university teaching and research, he became a doctor of sociology in 1969 for work on the relationship between education and change.

In 1970, he created, with F Viallet, a private institute specializing in educational engineering and development: Quaternaire Education. He is the chairman of this organization, which employs 30 full-time staff plus freelance people. It works with:

1. French firms: training plans, training of trainers, multi-media training problems of management and development.
2. Public administration: training of civil servants, development of adult education, interface between public services and population.
3. Cities: conception, planning of community facilities.
4. Foreign governments: implementation, on a large scale, of educational schemes.

Pierre Caspar, who also graduated from Stanford-Insead Business School, has written four books (Editions d'Organisation — Paris):

Formation ou transformation des structures (1969)
Créez votre entreprise (1972)
Pratique de la formation continue (1975)
Problèmes — methodes et strategies (1978)

He teaches at the French Ecole Nationale d'Administration.

Helmuth Dolff (Chapter 12) has worked in adult education since 1953. After school and vocational training he was appointed as Secretary of the State Association for *Volkshochschule* in Lower Saxony. He changed his position in 1956 to become Secretary General and later Director and Acting Member of the Governing Board of the *Deutscher Volkshochschul-Verband* (DVV, German Adult Education Association) in Bonn.

He serves on many national and international committees, associations and institutions in the field of adult education. In 1975 he was elected President of the European Bureau for Adult Education and as one of the Vice-Presidents of the International Council of Adult Education.

He has published a variety of books and articles about adult education, international cultural exchange, educational help for developing countries, and education and television in Germany and abroad.

Chris Duke (Chapter 16) was formerly a lecturer with experience of Third World students and immigrant communities in Woolwich and Leeds, and became the first Director of Continuing Education at the Australian National University in 1969. His interest in the sociology of education and in organizational and administrative questions, wedded to an interest in inter-cultural relations, led him to involvements with recurrent education as a strategy for educational reform in Australia and with educational developments in the Asian region. He has been closely involved in Aboriginal issues in Australia, and wrote the Australian OECD country paper on recurrent education in 1974. In that year he became Secretary, and later President, of the Asian and South Pacific Bureau of Adult Education, a regional adult education network. He is currently Chairman of the Bureau's East and South-East Asian sub-region, and of the Education Committee of the National Commission for UNESCO. His position in Canberra provides close contact with policies and developments in Australian education, especially at the federal level.

Gerald Fowler (UK Consulting Editor and author of Part 5) was a Member of Parliament in the UK until 1979, and is Professor Associate of Government at Brunel University. He has been in the past Professor of Educational Studies at the Open University, Assistant Director of Huddersfield Polytechnic, and Visiting Professor at Strathclyde University. In politics he has held high office as Parliamentary Secretary at the Ministry of Technology, as Minister of State at the Privy Council Office, and three times as Minister of State at the Department of Education and Science. From 1976 to 1978 he was President of the Association for Recurrent Education.

Ettore Gelpi (Chapter 13) has been responsible for lifelong education in UNESCO since 1972; he was active in the educational field in Italy between 1955 and 1972 (secondary, higher and adult education; teacher training; trade union education; migrants' education; cultural animation). His publications include:

Storia dell'educazione (History of education, 1967)
Scuola senza cattedra (School without chairs, 1969)
La formazione per l'educazione degli adulti (Training for adult education, 1969)
La formazione per l'insegnanento delle scienze (Training for science education, 1971)
European Renaissance and Reformation' (Education, history of; *Encyclopedia Britannica*, 1974)

He chairs seminars at the University of Paris and at the *Collège cooperatif de l'Ecole des Hautes Etudes en Sciences Sociales* on the subject of workers' culture and education and of comparative education. In 1979 his book in two volumes on lifelong education policies will appear in the Manchester Monographs series (Department of Adult and Higher Education, University of Manchester).

Geoffrey Hubbard (Chapter 5) was born in London in 1923. On leaving school he joined the Research Laboratories of the General Electric Company, working on the production and development of gas filled thyratrons and during this time he obtained a BSc in Physics and Mathematics from the University of London.

He joined the Civil Service in 1948 and held a variety of administrative posts mostly concerned with the management of science and technology in such varied fields as machine tools, aircraft development, atomic energy and high energy physics. While with the former Ministry of Technology he was concerned with the developing use of audio-visual and communication equipment in education, and became strongly convinced of the significance of new developments in educational method.

In 1969 he was appointed Director of the National Council for Educational Technology. He has been responsible for the development and execution of the Council's programme in the fields of information systems, training, innovation and resource development and management. On 1 October, 1973 the National Council was superseded by the Council for Educational Technology for the United Kingdom.

He has also written scripts for television programmes for small children, for both British and West German television, and a number of sound radio plays for the British Broadcasting Corporation and a number of Commonwealth broadcasting organizations. In 1965 he published *Cooke and Wheatstone and the Invention of the Electric Telegraph*, and his Pelican Original *Quaker by Convincement* was published in January 1974.

Ron Johnson (Chapter 19) has been with the Training Services Division of the Manpower Services Commission as its Director of Training since May 1974. He is responsible for an operational programme concerned with helping to improve the effectiveness and efficiency of the country's training effort through development work, research, information and advisory services to sector training bodies, professional institutions, and educational bodies.

Dr Johnson began his career with seven years as a food scientist in industry. He then moved into education where his posts included a lectureship at Chelsea College, University of London, and Head of Department of Food Science at the Polytechnic of the South Bank. He then became Chief Training Adviser to the Food, Drink and Tobacco Industry Training Board before taking up his present post. Dr Johnson is currently a member of the management board of the European Centre for the Development of Vocational Training (Berlin), the EEC Advisory Committee for Vocational Training (Brussels) and the management board of the DES Further Education Curriculum Review and Development Unit.

Denis Kallen (Chapter 3) studied social psychology and developmental psychology in the universities of Nijmegen (Netherlands) and Vienna (Austria). After work in sociology in the Federal Republic he participated in the UNESCO International Study of University Admissions. From 1962 until 1973 he was a staff member of the OECD in Paris. He was involved in – and responsible for – the organization's work on differentiation in lower secondary education, policies for educational research, the development of secondary education, curriculum development and, finally, recurrent education. He wrote, together with Jarl Bengtsson, the OECD policy report on recurrent education, *Recurrent Education: A Strategy for Lifelong Learning*.

He became a full professor of general and comparative education at the University of Amsterdam in 1973. He is closely associated with the Council of Europe's work on the contents and methods of adult education. Over the years he has published many articles on recurrent education and its affiliated concepts in Dutch, English and

German journals.

At present he is on leave of absence from the University of Amsterdam and is associated with the Institute of Education of the European Cultural Foundation in Paris. He teaches in the University of Vincennes in Paris, is a consultant on the OECD programme on compulsory education and is President of the Comparative Education Society in Europe.

James Roby Kidd (Chapter 8) was the organizing Chairman and has continued as a Professor in the Department of Adult Education, Ontario Institute for Studies in Education (OISE). He also served as Secretary-General of the International Council for Adult Education from the time of its inception in 1973.

His research interests have included learning theory and practice, the mature student, education in institutions: he was Chairman of the UNESCO UNDP Evaluation of the Experimental World Library Programme in 1974-75.

Before taking up his post at OISE, Dr Kidd served for 14 years as Director of the Canadian Association for Adult Education, and for six as Secretary-Treasurer for the Humanities Research Council of Canada and the Social Science Research Council of Canada. He has served as president or board member of many Canadian education and cultural organizations.

His international experience has included Presidency of the 1960 World Conference on Adult Education, Chairmanship of UNESCO's Advisory Committee on Adult Education, teaching at universities in India, the West Indies, Venezuela, and Alaska, Chairmanship of Adult Education for the World Confederation of the Organizations of the Teaching Profession, consulting with UNESCO and ILO.

He has published 16 books, the most widely known being *How Adults Learn*, now translated into seven languages. He was the Organizing Editor of *Convergence*, the international journal of adult education, has contributed to three encyclopedias and chapters to books on education published in a dozen countries.

Alan B Knox (Chapter 4) has served as an adult and continuing education administrator and professor of continuing education during the past 25 years at Syracuse University, University of Nebraska, Columbia University, and currently at the University of Illinois at Urbana-Champaign. He is Director of the Office for the Study of Continuing Professional Education, a research institute in the College of Education there. He was the 1978 recipient of the Okes award for outstanding research, by the Adult Education Association of the USA. An active researcher, he is the author of more than 60 articles, chapters, and books, including recently, *Adult Development and Learning* and *Enhancing Proficiencies of Continuing Educators*. Recently he served as Director of Continuing Education at the University of Illinois and as Chairman of the Commission of Professors of Adult Education in the USA. In addition to hundreds of talks and workshops in North America, Professor Knox has served as a consultant or speaker in other countries including France, Ireland, Mexico, Venezuela, and Norway.

Naomi E McIntosh (Chapter 18) is Professor of Applied Social Research at the Open University. After graduating in sociology from Bedford College, London, she spent 12 years as a market and social researcher at the Gallup Poll before joining Enfield College of Technology as Senior Lecturer in Market Research in 1967. She was an early recruit to the Open University in 1969, becoming Head of its Survey Research Department in 1972, and in 1977 Head of the Institutional Research Division, Institute of Educational Technology. She served as Pro Vice-Chancellor in charge of Student Affairs from 1974-78. Her expertise in research and evaluation has taken her to Europe and America to advise on evaluation of multi-media systems, for example the 1975 Satellite Technology Demonstration in the Rocky Mountain states. Appointed to the Advisory Council for Adult and Continuing Education (ACACE) in 1977, she chairs its sub-committee charged with developing an overall plan for continuing education. Her educational appointments include membership of the

CNAA Academic Policy Committee and the Steering Committee of the Educational Credit Transfer Feasibility Study. She is currently Project Director of the DES-funded scheme to assess the suitability of the Open University for younger students. She has written widely both on the subject of evaluation and on adult and higher education generally; notably *A Degree of Difference* (with Calder and Swift), published by SRHE/Praeger in 1976 and 'Access to Higher Education in England and Wales' (with Woodley and Griffiths) in *Innovation in Access to Higher Education*, International Council for Educational Development, 1978.

Peter Mauger (Chapter 15) graduated in modern history at Cambridge University in 1935 and was in commerce until the outbreak of war. During the war he was a flying instructor and lecturer in the RAF. In 1946 he started teaching in secondary schools. From 1957 to 1966 he was Head of a London secondary school and then was appointed Head of the Department of Education at Coventry College of Education; he retired early, in 1977, and is now a freelance writer and lecturer. He has written many articles on education, mainly on non-streaming and the liberalizing of the secondary curriculum. He is part-author of a history textbook for secondary pupils, *The British People, 1902 to the Present Day*. He has visited China twice, in 1972 and 1976, and is making a study of Chinese education. He is particularly interested in the Chinese view that education should be continuous from cradle to grave, that politics and education are inseparable, and that, as Mao Tsetung has said, 'Every capable person can teach'.

Marjorie Mbilinyi (Chapter 14) has been lecturing at the University of Dar es Salaam, Department of Education, since 1968. Her research has focused on issues of access to schooling among peasants, the historical development of colonial and post-colonial education systems, and women and the sexual division of labour in production. Teaching responsibilities have reflected these research interests. She has developed new courses in social psychology of teaching/learning and research methodology at the undergraduate level, and the postgraduate foundation course on education and society.

Interest in the problem of 'lifelong education' arose in the context of the historical analysis of Tanzania's education system. This has been crystallized through involvement in the Christian Council of Tanzania project on Rural Vocational Education, where intellectuals engage in joint study and investigation with peasants and church leaders at the village level. She is now associated with the West Bagamoyo (Jipemoyo) Project under the Ministry of National Culture and Youth. This is an ongoing participatory research programme among cultivators and pastoralists. She will be engaged in the concrete investigation of women and the sexual division of labour in peasant production among both groups.

Jacquetta Megarry (Series Editor) is a lecturer at Jordanhill College of Education, Glasgow. Her current work involves the education of teachers on pre-service and in-service courses, including the CNAA Diploma in Educational Technology which involves distance learning by teachers who are in post. Her interests include simulation/games and computer-assisted learning, methods and media for distance learning, curriculum innovation and evaluation. She is currently carrying out research into gender typing in Scottish education.

After teaching science and mathematics in secondary schools, she was a researcher at Glasgow University (1971-73), developing and evaluating multi-media materials for science teachers in the Highlands and Islands of Scotland. She was researcher on a secondary school computer-based games and simulations project at IBM's Scientific Centre in Peterlee in 1974-75 and has run summer schools in simulation/games at Loughborough University (1974 and 1975) and Concordia University, Montreal (annually since 1975).

She is closely associated with SAGSET (the Society for Academic Gaming and Simulation in Education and Training), she was its Chairman 1973-76, and has edited its Journal (*Simulation/Games for Learning*) since 1975. Her other publications include articles, chapters and research reports, mostly in the general area of educational technology, learner-based techniques and evaluation. She has also published a number of modules for the Jordanhill Dip Ed Tech course, especially on innovative techniques (eg, programmed learning, resource-based learning, computer-based learning).

Frank Molyneux (Chapter 17) is on the staff of the School of Education at the University of Nottingham where he completed doctoral work on school provision and planning begun at the University of Pittsburgh as a Fellow of the American Council of Learned Societies. From 1975 to 1978 he was general secretary of the Association for Recurrent Education and remains a member of its executive committee. He has continuing teaching and research interests in the comparative study of changes in systems of educational provision and since 1975 he has co-directed a large scale DES-funded investigation into spatial aspects of higher education in the East Midlands.

Hans-Erik Östlund (Chapter 11) is head of the Budget and Planning Secretariat within the Swedish Ministry of Education. Earlier he was head of the department of upper secondary education in the National Board of Education and before that lecturer at the Malmö School of Education.

As expert or member, he has taken part in most of the Swedish commissions on educational policy during the last 20 years, eg the 1957 Commission on Compulsory Education, the 1960 Upper Secondary Commission, the 1960 Teacher Training Commission, the Commission on Admission Policy, the 1968 Educational Commission and the 1974 Employment Commission.

Recurrent education has been one of his main areas of concern since the late 1960s. He has contributed to the debate on recurrent education both in the socialist press and in educational periodicals for more than ten years.

He has been involved, too, in the OECD/CERI project on recurrent education since 1970 and in corresponding projects in the secretariat of the Nordic Council of Ministers.

Maurice Peston (Chapter 6) is Professor of Economics at Queen Mary College, University of London. He was educated at the London School of Economics and at Princeton University. He has taught at the London School of Economics, and the University of California at Berkeley, before being the first Head of Department at Queen Mary College. He has been a member of the Council for National Academic Awards, and is currently a member of the Social Science Research Council. He has been Special Adviser to the Secretary of State for Education and Science and to the Secretary of State for Prices and Consumer Protection.

Tom Schuller (Chapter 7 and Subject Editor) is Research Director of the Centre for Research in Industrial Democracy and Participation at Glasgow University. He worked for four years on recurrent education at the Centre for Educational Research and Innovation at OECD, and has been a Research Associate at the Trade Union Research Unit, Ruskin College, and a Visiting Fellow with the Higher Education Research Group at Yale University. He is the author of a Fabian pamphlet, *Education Through Life*, and (with Jarl Bengtsson) a chapter on recurrent education and industrial democracy in *Power, Ideology and Education* (edited by Jerome Karabel and A H Halsey, Oxford University Press, 1977).

Øyvind Skard (Chapter 10) was first trained as a teacher and worked for ten years in the compulsory school system. While teaching, he studied psychology and took his MA degree in Minneapolis in 1947 and his Doctor's Degree in Oslo in 1951. After teaching psychology at the University of Oslo for six years, he went into research and consulting work on personnel problems and education in industry. After having worked as personnel director in Norwegian shipyards for some years, his interest in

318   BIOGRAPHICAL NOTES

management development and adult education in general made him Director of the Institute of Education and Management Development of the Norwegian Employers' Confederation. He has been a member of the government board preparing the new system of secondary education, member of the government board for adult education 1966-78, and he is at present Chairman of the Board of the Norwegian Institute for Adult Education. He represents the employers and adult education on several committees and councils, both in Norway and in international organizations, and has published several books on psychology, industrial democracy, management and adult education. He is especially interested in the relationship between learning and democratization.

Tom Stonier (Chapter 2) has held the founding Chair in Science and Society at the University of Bradford (UK), since 1975. He came to Bradford as Visiting Professor of Peace Studies in 1973. Prior to that he had been Director of Peace Studies at Manhattan College (New York) from 1971 to 1975, where he also held an appointment as Professor of Biology. Prior to joining the faculty of biology at Manhattan College in 1962, Professor Stonier held posts at Rockefeller University (New York) and Brookhaven National Laboratory (USA). He holds an AB degree from Drew University and an MS and PhD from Yale University. Professor Stonier is Chairman of Global Education Systems, a UK-registered limited company, providing education consultancy services.

Sir Peter Venables (Chapter 20) has been principal of several technical colleges, and of the College of Advanced Technology which became the University of Aston in Birmingham, and of which he was the first Vice-Chancellor, retiring in 1969. Throughout his career he has worked to improve educational opportunities for students, for instance in developing sandwich courses for technologists and technicians. More generally he was concerned with broadening the scope of courses and studies. He has served on many related national bodies and was President of the National Institute of Adult Education 1971-77. He was Chairman of the planning committee appointed by the government in 1967 to establish the Open University, and was the University's first Pro-Chancellor and Chairman of Council 1969-74. He was Chairman of the Open University Committee on Continuing Education, whose report he discusses in his chapter. He has published many papers in educational journals, and is author of a number of books, the latest of which is *Higher Education Developments: The Technological Universities* (Faber, London, 1978).

It is with great regret that we record Sir Peter Venables' death in June 1979, just after the typesetting of this book was completed — Editor.

Index

ACACE (Advisory Council for Adult and Continuing Education), 228, 235-6, 244-5, 263, 272, 276, 279, 293
  needs assessment, 249
  response to *Higher Education in the 1990s*, 247-8, 252
  terms of reference, 245-6
ACOTAFE, 217
ALRA (Adult Literacy Resource Agency), 242, 271-2
APEID (Asian Programme of Educational Innovation for Development), 213, 218, 219, 220
ARE (Association for Recurrent Education), 237, 239, 240
  constitution, 241-2
ASEAN (Association of South-East Asian Nations), 211
ASPBAE (Asian and South Pacific Bureau of Adult Education), 211, 219, 220
AUC (Australian Universities Commission), 217
AUT (Association of University Teachers), 237
Aboriginal culture, 215
Abrahamsson, B, 108
Access, to education, 250-2
Accounting, 101, 106
Accreditation:
  adult concern courses, 277
  learning achievement, 296
Active life, shortening, 22, 25
  see also Working life
Activities, adult learning, 65-6
Adamski, W, 174
Adaptability:
  LBER, 177
  personal, 87
Administration, adult learning, 67-72
  participation, 69-70
  personal qualities, 68-9
Admission:
  see also Selection
  flexibility, 252
  Swedish policy, 152-3
Adult concern courses, 277

Adult education, 86
  see also Further education; Higher education; Vocational education
  access, 250-2
  codification, 51
  education of teachers, 143
  financial barriers, 250-2
  France, 129
  geographical barriers, 250-1
  institutionalization, 169
  manpower aspects, 257
  needs, 248-50
  Norway, 137-45
  qualifications barrier, 252
  rise, 40
  selective role, 169
  staff selection and training, 70, 253-4
  structural barriers, 251
  student-centred approach, 248
  Sweden, grants, 155
  West Germany, 159, 161
Adult Education Act (Norway), 143-5
Adult Education Act 1970 (USA), 118
Adult Education Council, 145
Adult Education, report, 160
Adult learning, 59-63
  ability, 61-2
  administration, 67-72: leadership, 71; participation, 69-70; personal qualifications, 68-9; research, 71-2; resources, 70-1; staffing, 70
  characteristics, 83
  collaboration, 74
  development, 59-61
  historical studies, 72-3
  impact of societal contexts, 62-3
  objectives, 74
  programme development, 63-6
  research insights, 57-79
  speed, 62
  structure, 72
'Adult Learning Interests and Experiences', 122
Adult Literacy Campaign, 280
Adult Literacy Resource Agency *see* ALRA
Adult Literacy Scheme, 235

INDEX

Advice, 277
Advisory committees, *Volkshochschulen*, 166
Advisory Council for Adult and Continuing Education *see* ACACE
Afghanistan, 211
Africa, LBER, 176-92
  critique of schooling, 181-4
  schooling, 179-80
Aged *see* Elderly people
Agricultural extension, 113
Ahmed, M, 181, 182
Alexander, L, 183
Alexander Report, 235
Alford, J, 71
Allen, D W, 188
Alley, Rewi, 197
Androgogy, 245
Annan Committee, 283
Annan Report, 276
Anzalone, S, 188
Apathy, 187
Apprenti auprès du maître, 129
Apprentices, training, 264
Argyris, C, 69
Arithmetic, computer games, 38
Artistic skills, 35
Arts, support for, 121
Asia:
  exchange of ideas with Australia, 209-23
  non-formal education, 211-14
Asian and South Pacific Bureau of Adult Education *see* ASPBAE
Asian Programme of Educational Innovation for Development *see* APEID
Association for Recurrent Education *see* ARE
Association of South-East Asian Nations *see* ASEAN
Association of University Teachers *see* AUT
Atkin, J Myron, 312
Attendance certificates, 165
Attitudes:
  to education, 249
  to lifelong learning, 81-2, 121-2
Audio-visual:
  assisted materials, 42
  methods, effects on teaching process, 94-5
  reports, 42
Australia:
  characteristics, 214-18
  exchange of ideas with Asia and the South Pacific, 209-23
  leave, 217
Australian Universities Commission *see* AUC
Austria, demand trends, 18
Automation, 239
  displacement of workers, 21-2
  effects on employment, 26
  impact, 80
Autonomy, at work, 28
Availability, student wishes, 84

BBC (British Broadcasting Corporation), 36
  Further Education Advisory Committee, 278
  Further Education Department, 264
  literacy programmes, 271, 279, 292
  On the Move, 271
Baller, W R, 62
Baltes, P B, 61
Bangladesh, 211
Barker, R G, 63
Barratt Brown, M, 101
Bath College of Technology, 84
Batstone, E, 97, 105
Belasco, J A, 66
Belden, Jack, 195
Belgium, selectivity, 171
Bellamy, Edward, 120
Bengtsson, Jarl, 17-30, 312
Bennis, W G, 70, 73
Bernbaum, G, 182
Berrol, S C, 72
Bessent, W, 70
Best, F, 20
Bildungsgesamtplan, 161
Binstock, R H, 59
Birren, J E, 59
Black market work, 25
Blainey, G, 210
Blakely, R J, 73
Blaney, P, 65
Blaug, M, 46
Boaz, R L, 57, 69
Booth, A, 69
Boshier, R, 69
Botwinick, J, 62
Bowles, S, 179, 183
Bradford, L P, 65
Bradford College of Higher Education, 84
Bradford University, Science and Society Course, 41-3
British Broadcasting Corporation *see* BBC
Broadcasting:
  see also Radio; Television
  Open University, 278
Broschart, J R, 73
Broström, A, 108
Brown, W, 108
Bryceson, D F, 187
Buildings *see* Premises
Bulgaria, rural *v* urban education, 173
Bullock Committee Report on Industrial Democracy, 99
Bund-Länder-Kommission, 159, 160
Burdge, R J, 27
Burgess, P, 69
Byrne, J J, 25

INDEX

CBI (Confederation of British Industry):
  Conference on Continuing Education, 1978, 281-2
  vocational training, 264
CCETSW (Central Council for Education and Training of Social Workers, 281
CERI (Centre for Educational Research and Innovation), 17-18, 47-8, 50, 98, 229
CNAA (Council for National Academic Awards), 231, 293
COMECON (Communist Economic Community), 168, 171
CSE (Certificate of Secondary Education), 231
Callaghan, James, 239, 291
Campbell, D D, 71, 72
Canada, recurrent education, 237
Cantor, Leonard, 228-9, 238
Capital, conflict of interest with labour, 99
Capitalism, LBER, 177, 178
Careers:
  see also Jobs; Occupational:
  choice of, 35
  structures, changes, 50
Carlsson, Ingvar, 47
Carnoy, M, 183
Carp, Abraham, 122
Caspar, Pierre, 128-36, 312-13
Ceefax, 36
Central Council for Education and Training of Social Workers see CCETSW
Central institutions (Scotland), 232
Centralization, LBER, 184
Central Policy Review Staff Unit, 246
Centre for Educational Research and Innovation see CERI
Centre Inffo, 131, 132
Certificate of Secondary Education see CSE
Certification, 165, 231
  LBER, 184, 185
  re-, 125-6
Character-study, China, 204-5
Charnley, A, 235
Che Hung-chang, 196
Chen, J, 198, 200
Chiang Kaishek, 194
Children's Television Workshop, 36
China:
  cultural revolution, 197-207
  higher education, 201
  'July 21' workers' colleges, 202-3
  May 7 cadre schools, 203-4
  1946-66, 193-7
  Party schools, 204
  People's Liberation Army, 193, 199, 201, 204-5
  school curriculum, 200-1
  school management, 199-200
  spare-time, 205-7
  women, 199

China Reconstructs, 202
Chinese Reader for Peasants, 196
Christian Council of Tanzania, 190
Christoffel, P H, 72
Citizens' initiatives, 173
Civic education, 65
Clark, B R, 68
Class struggles, 177
  see also Middle class; Social: class
Clyne, Peter, 252
Coalition of Adult Education Organizations, 119
Co-determination:
  see also Industrial democracy
  Norway, 140-1
Coffey, J, 84
Collaboration, adult learning, 74
Collective rights, employees, 130
College experience, student personality, 61
Colleges of further education, 232
Commissions paritaires, 132
Committee of Inquiry into Education and Training (Australia), 217
Committee on Third World Relations (Australia), 216
Committee skills, 105
Communication:
  mass, 188
  rank and file, 108
  Volkshochschulen, 164
Communist Party, China, 204
Community:
  -based education, 40
  impact on adult learning, 62-3
  life, quality, 63
  service, teenagers, 39-40
Community Development Trust Fund, 190
Compagnonnage, 129
Compensatory education, 48
Comprehensive education:
  adults, 244-56
  reorganization, 230, 239
Compulsory education/schooling, 26
  Norway, 138-9
  role, 48
  Sweden, 147-8
Computer-assisted:
  learning, 37
  materials, 42
Computers:
  development, 32
  educational administration, 272
  electronic education, 36-7
  impact on education, 31
Concerts, 165
Condition of Education, 124
Confederation of British Industry see CBI
Conferences of European Ministers of Education, 47, 146, 248
Confucianism, 199
Congé-formation see Leave: educational

INDEX

Conscientization, education for, 221
Consumer interests, 107
Continuing education:
  compulsory, 125
  definition, 57-8, 123
  national expenditure, 282
  requirements (ACACE), 252-4
  USA, 114, 123
  West Germany, 159-66
Coombs, P H, 181, 182, 184
Co-operative systems, Hungary, 172
Correspondence courses, 253
  China, 206
  vocational education, 267
Co-sponsorship, 69
Council for Educational Technology, 268, 278
Council of Europe, 173
  éducation permanente, 51-4, 113, 115
  recurrent education, 229, 239
  role, 46
Council for National Academic Awards see CNAA
Counselling, 277, 295-6
  adult learning administration, 69
  lifelong learning, 122-3
Court, D, 180
Craftsmen, training, 259
Craig, R L, 64
Creativity, imagination, 35
Credit:
  -based economy, 33
  recognition, 252
  systems, 40, 58; USA, 113, 121, 126, 290
  transfers, 240, 293; educational, 237
  units, 255
Critical faculties, education for, 35
Cuban literacy campaign, 189
Culture/cultural:
  democracy, 54
  diversity, acceptance, 34
  functions, place of work, 169
  integration, European, 51
  policy, 51
  Shanghai, 206-7
  Volkshochschulen, 165
Curriculum:
  China, 200-1
  LBER, 182, 187
  universal, 188
  vocational education, 266-7
Czechoslovakia, popular participation, 173

Dag Hammarskjold Foundation, 184-6, 190
Dahllöf, U, 151
Dar-es-Salaam, Faculty of Agriculture, 190
Darkenwald, G G, 71
Davies, T C, 84
Debates, class, 42

Debeauvais, M, 168
Decentralization, 154, 173
Decision-making, participation, 50
Demand:
  satiation, 87
  trends, 18
Democracy, industrial *see* Industrial democracy
Democratization:
  adult education, 138, 143
  non-formal education, 214
Demography, 18, 247
Department of Education and Science, 230, 263
  ACACE *see* ACACE
  adult education, 245
  Circular 10/65, 230
  Higher Education in the 1990s, 237, 244, 246-8, 280 *see also* ACACE
  liaison with MSC, 293
  recurrent education, 237, 238, 292
  relationship with Department of Employment, 241
  seminar on recurrent education, Glasgow 1977, 228
  teacher re-training, 269
Department of Education of the State of New York, 121
Department of Employment, 234, 241
Department of Health and Social Security, 281
Department of Health Education and Welfare, 120
Department of Manpower Services, 263
De Sanctis, F M, 172
Deutscher Ausschuss für das Erziehungs- und Bildungswesen, 159, 160
Development, 219, 235
  see also Management: development; Personal: development
  adult education staff, 70
Developmental tasks, 60-1
Diejomaoh, V P, 182
Diploma in Higher Education (DipHE), 231
Direct-grant schools, 230
Disabled students, 144, 277
Discipline, 39
Discretion, at work, 28
Discussion groups, 164, 165
Dissemination, Swedish recurrent education, 153-4
Distance:
  learning, 251, 253, 268
  teacher education, 218
  teaching, 272, 277
District Manpower Committees, 264
Diversity, 80-5
Division of labour:
  international, 168-9
  technical and social, 167
Dolff, Helmuth, 159-66, 313
Domestication, education for, 221
Dorland, J R, 70

INDEX

Drop out periods, 25
Drucker, P F, 71
Dubar, C, 170
Duke, Chris, 209-23, 217, 313

EEC (European Economic Community), 168, 171
EIC (Educational Information Center), 123
ESA (Employment Service Agency), 234
Economies et Statistiques, 25
Economy:
    cyclicality, 93-4
    self-service, 20
Education:
    access, 250-2
    as a consumption good, 21
    as an investment, 32, 91
    compared with training, 91-2, 289
    co-ordination with employment and training, 295-6
    definition, 241
    equal availability, 272
    for employment, 34
    for life, 34
    for pleasure, 35-6
    for self-development, 35
    for the world, 34-5
    integration with production and research, 172
    integration with vocational training, 249
    interconnection with work, 53
    labour-intensity, 33
    life cycles, 17-30
    plurality of responsibility, 257, 265-6
    purposes, 221, 250
    relationship with training, 255
    reward system, 269
    services, UK, 263
Education Act 1975, 292
Education and Library Boards, 230
Education Authorities, 230
Education Permanente, 51-4, 113, 115
Education, Poverty and Development, 183
Education Research and Development Committee (Australia), 217
Educational:
    brokering, 122-3
    development, 49
    guidance, Sweden, 156
    institutions, location, 94
    leave *see* Leave: educational
    management, popular participation, 169
    means, scarcity, 169
    opportunity, equality, 49, 138-40, 143, 160
    policy: comprehensiveness, 51; interplay between labour market policy, 146, 157-8
    technology, continuing education, 253

Educational Commission, Sweden, 1968, 147
Educational Guidance Service for Adults in Belfast, 240
Educational Guidance Service for Adults in Northern Ireland, 295-6
Educational Information Centers *see* EIC
Educators, resistance to new technology, 37
Educredit, 113, 121, 126
Efficiency, 49
Egalitarian society, 168
Ego development, 61
Eisdorfer, C, 59, 61
Elderly people, 28, 38
The Electric Company, 36
Electronic education, 36-7
Electronic technology revolution, 31
Elementary and Secondary Education Act (USA), 118
Elliott, J, 98
Empire State University, 288
Employers, vocational education, 264
Employment:
    see also Unemployment
    co-ordination with education and training, 295-6
    education for, 34
    full, alternative, 21
    policy, 106
    shifts, 82
    trends, 18-19
    prospects, vocational education, 257, 260
Employment Service Agency *see* ESA
Employment and Training Act 1973, 232
Energy, constraints, 82
Enjoyment, cost-effectiveness of learning, 36
Entitlements *see* Credit
Environmental responsibility, 34
Environment, work, 106, 141, 142
Equality:
    opportunity, 49; LBER, 184
    pilot schemes, 53
    post-school education, 249
Espinosa, J, 104
Ethnocentrism, 34, 215
European Centre for Leisure and Education, 172
European Economic Community *see* EEC
European Ministers of Education Conference, Stockholm 1975, 248
European Ministers of Education Conference, Versailles; 1968, 47; 1969, 146
Evaluation, 169
    adult learning, 66
    self-, 81
Examinations, 231
Exhibitions, 165
Experience, adult education, 252

Expertise, 100-4
External orientation, 187
Extramural students, 40
Exxon Foundation, 120

Fachhochschulen, 162
Fachschulen, 162
Families:
  adult life cycles, 59
  effects of leisure, 95
  impact on adult learning, 62-3
  size, 28
Farmer, H S, 68, 69, 71
Fatigue, jobs, 28
Faure Commission, 216
Faure Report (*Learning to Be*), 51-4
Feedback information, 21
Fees, Open University, 276
Feldman, K A, 61, 63
Films, 38, 165
Finance, 106
  access to education, 250-2
  adult education, 255
  adult learning, 70
  continuing education, 252
  recurrent education, 86-96; Sweden, 154-6
Financial:
  information, shop stewards, 103
  policies, lifelong learning in USA, 113
  support, mature students, 292 *see also* Grants
Finch, C B, 62
Fitts, W H, 61
Flexibility:
  distribution over life cycle, 19
  human, 87
  open learning, 84
Flippo, E B, 70
Foggarty, M, 101
Folk high schools, 153 *see also Volkshochschulen*
Fonds d'Assurance Formation, 132
Ford, Bill, 101
Forecasting:
  see also Technological forecasting
  economic, 260
  techniques, 43
Foundation for Management Education, 267
Fourastie, 23, 24
Fowler, Gerald, 235, 239, 287-97, 313
Fox, Alan, 103
Foy, Nancy, 267
France:
  adult education, 129
  paid educational leave, 128-36, 289, 293
Fraser, J, 194
Freedman, D H, 20
Freire, Paulo, 64, 221
Full employment alternative, 21
Fullerton, H N Jnr, 25

Fund for the Improvement of Postsecondary Education, 117
Further education:
  see also Adult education; Higher education; Vocational education
  rise in, 40
Further Education Curriculum Review and Development Unit, 267
Futan University, 202-3
Future Directions for a Learning Society Project, 120
Future orientation, 43
Futurologists, 168

GCE (General Certificate of Education), 231
GI Bill 1944 (USA), 118
Gagné, R M, 61
Gardell, B, 28
Gelpi, Ettore, 167-75, 313-14
General Arithmetic for Workers and Peasants, 196
General Certificate of Education *see* GCE
Generalists, 41, 42
Geographical barriers, adult education, 250-1
Geography, computer games, 38
German Adult Education Association, 219
Germany (West), Federal Republic, 169
  demand trends, 18
  'popular' higher education, 159-60
  qualifications, 171
  selectivity, 171
Gershuny, J, 20, 22, 23
Gesamthochschule, 162
Ghai, Y, 180
Ghana, schooling system, 179
Gintis, H, 179
Globalization, pilot schemes, 53
Goals, oscillation, 126
Gould, R, 61
Government employees, educational support, 113
Grain storage, Tanzania, 190
Gramsci, 98
Grandstaff, M, 182
Grants, 251, 253
  continuing education, 252
Grattan, C F, 73
Great Britain *see* United Kingdom
'Great Debate', 239, 291
Green, A, 182
Green, J, 63, 64
Griffin, C, 239
Grotelueschen, A D, 66
Group:
  integration, 39
  learning schemes, 296
  motivation, 296
Growth, limits, 82
Guidance, Sweden, 156
Gymnasium, 139, 148

INDEX

Hackman, J R, 64
Hair, 114
Handicapped people, adult education, 144, 277
Harris, B M, 70
Hartle, 115
Harvard Education Review, 183
Hatfield Polytechnic, 241
Havelock, R G, 63
Havighurst, R J, 60
Hayflick, L, 62
Health Education Council, 282
Hentschke, G C, 70
Higher education, 150-2
  China, 201
Higher Education Act (USA), 115, 118, 123
Higher Education in the 1990s see Department of Education and Science
Hill, R, 59
Hill, R J, 65
History:
  avoidance of reconstructing, 46
  computer games, 38
  testing social theories, 43
Hoggart, R, 235, 246, 249
Holidays, 89
  see also Vacations
  entitlement and take-up, 24
  increases, 20
  longer, 22
  twelve weeks, 23
Holland, recurrent education, 237
Home-based education, 31, 36-8
Home-interest, 186
Horizon, 36
Horne, D, 215
Houghton, V P, 228
Houle, C O, 63, 65, 66, 68, 69
Housewives, higher education, 40
Houston (Clear Lake City) postgraduate programmes, 43
Hsinhua News Agency, 205, 206, 207
Hubbard, Geoffrey, 80-5, 314
Human development, 259
Humanistics, 34
Hungary:
  co-operative systems, 172
  rural areas, 173
  selectivity, 171

ILO (International Labour Office), 141, 155, 276
IMPACT, 214
ISOS (In-School Off-School), 214
ITBs (Industrial Training Boards), 232
ITN (Independent Television News), continuing education, 276
Ideas, exporting, 88
Ideological control, 177, 178
Illich, Ivan, 101
Illiteracy *see* Literacy
Imagination, creative, 35
Immigrant workers, 48, 169, 173
Incomes, real, lifetime, 90
Independent:
  learning systems, 253
  schools, 230
Independent Television, continuing education, 276
India, 211, 212
Indoctrination, 187
Indonesia, 211
Industrial change, 287
Industrial democracy, 22, 97-110
  see also Co-determination
  construction of knowledge, 108-9
  content, 104-8
  education for, 240
  links with permanent education, 54
  nexus with recurrent education, 221
  Scandinavia, 222
Industrial investment, 169
Industrial Training Act 1964, 232
Industrial Training Boards *see* ITBs
Industrial training schemes, 232
Inequality, 183
Informal tutoring, 129
Information:
  accessibility, 69
  computer-based, 31
  continuing education, 252
  manipulation, 32
  meta-, 42
  obtaining, 36
  organization, 36
  recycling, 31, 40-1
  revolution, 32-3
  Swedish recurrent education, 156-7
  techniques for obtaining, 42
  transfer across generations, 38
  use of, 42-3
L'Informatisation de la Societé, 33
In-School Off School *see* ISOS
Integrated circuits, 32
Interdisciplinarity, 41-2
Interests, exploitation, 41
International Labour Office *see* ILO
Inter-professional convention on vocational training, 1970, 129-30
Investment:
  education as, 32, 91
  industrial, 169
  policy, 107
  return on, post-compulsory education, 174
  training as, 91
Iran, 219
Irish, G H, 72
Italy:
  decentralization, 173
  rural areas, 173
  selectivity, 171
  workers' control, 172

Jacobs, E, 107
James, David, 270
Jamison, D T, 188

Japan, 210, 219, 222
Java, 211
Jefferson, Thomas, 113, 120, 126
Jencks, 183
Jensen, G, 72, 73
Job/s:
   see also Careers; Occupational:
   careers, instrumental values of education, 19
   changing, 261
   enrichment, 104
   future availability, 20
   rotation, 169, 172
   satisfaction, 104, 106
   -sharing, 19, 22, 26-7
   structures, 258
Johnson, E, 66
Johnson, Ron, 257-70, 314
Johnston, D F, 21
Johnstone, J W C, 57, 63, 69
Jones, H A, 235
Joyce, B, 65
'July 21' workers' colleges, 202-3

Kallen, Denis, 45-54, 174, 314-15
Kansu Peasant, 196
Karabel, J, 185
Keith, S, 187
Kemenade, J A Van, 237
Kerr, E, 231
Kessen, W, 201
Kidd, James Roby, 70, 113-27, 315
Kindergartens, 173
Klevins, C, 65
Knowledge:
   as an industry, 33
   construction, 108-9
   creation, 32
   definition, 41-2
   exploration, 41
   value, 184
   Volkshochschulen, 164
Knowles, M S, 63, 64, 66, 68, 72, 73
Knox, Alan B, 57-79, 315
Korea, industrialization, 210
Kotler, P, 69
Kozol, J, 189
Kuomintang, 194, 195, 204
Kurland, Norman D, 71, 121
Kutner, 115
Kuypers, J A, 61

LBER (Lifelong Basic Education Reform):
   Africa, 176-92
   capitalist exploitation, 177
   contradictory nature, 184-8
   critique, 181-4
   impoverishment of peasants, 186-8
   LENSLR, 188-91
   schooling, 179-80
   socialist revolution and reconstruction, 177
LEAs (Local Education Authorities), 230, 232, 271

LEE (Lifelong Educational Entitlement), 121
LENLSR (Lifelong Education for National Liberation and Socialist Revolution), 188-91
LO (Norwegian Federation of Trade Unions), 137, 138, 140
Labour:
   conflict of interests with capital, 99
   divisions, 167-9
   equalization with leisure, 27
   flexibility, 91-2
   market:
     implications of recurrent education, 52
   interplay between educational policy, 146
   relations with training, 296
   vocational education, 257, 261-2
   mobility, 92
   turnover, 106
   versatility, 33, 34
Lamb, William *see* Melbourne, 2nd Viscount
Land Reform Act 1950 (China), 199
Lappin, I M, 73
Law:
   company, 106
   continuous education, 258
   re-certification, 125
Lawson, K H, 239
Lawson, M, 108
Lawton, M P, 59, 61
Leadership, adult learning, 71
Learners:
   attitude and performance, 121-2
   motivation and social conditions, 173
Learning:
   ability, 61
   achievement, accreditation, 296
   adult *see* Adult learning
   cost-effectiveness of enjoyment, 36
   definition, 241
   eagerness, 52
   linkage with work, 114
   readiness, 60
   resources centres, 278, 279
   self-directed, 66, 114, 259
   society, 114, 120, 121, 126
   strategies, 62
   styles, 65, 259
Learning by Appointment Centres, 84
Learning to Be (UNESCO, Faure Commission), 51-4
Least-developed countries (LDCs), 211
Leave:
   see also Holidays, Sabbaticals, Vacations
   Australia, 217
   educational, 26-7, 50
   paid, 53, 217, 240, 253, 276, 290, 292-4; France, 128-36, 289, 293;
   Norway, 141
   Sweden, 154-6

INDEX 327

Leave (cont)
  West Germany, 162
  worker, 131
  long service, 217
  teaching, 131
Lecturers, peasant, 190
Lee, Jennie, 273
Legislation *see* Law
Leisure:
  see also Non-work time
  activities, working groups, 165
  constructive use, 35-6
  contribution of education, 81
  demands for education and leisure opportunities, 22
  distinguished from work, 23
  education alternating with work and, 19
  education for, 94
  effects on nature of the family, 95
  equalization with labour, 27
  increasing, 289
  life cycles, 17-30
  meaning, 27
  use of, 94
  women's preferences, 89
Lengrand, Paul, 115
Leninism, 203, 204
Lerner, D, 219
Lessing, 249
Levinson, D J, 61
Levitas, M, 182
Liberation, education for, 221
Libido Sciendi, 52
Libraries:
  role in lifelong education, 84
  support for, 120
Library archives, global, 37
Life:
  education for, 34
  expectancy, 24-5, 289
Life cycles:
  adult, 59-60
  economic and employment conditions, 26
  recurrent education, 100
  work/leisure/education, 17-30
Life-styles, 27-8
Lifelong Basic Education Reform *see* LBER
Lifelong education/learning, 51-2, 81-2
  counselling, 122-3
  definitions and distinctions, 45-54
  educational brokering, 122-3
  futurologists, 168
  motivation, 52
  non-traditional studies, 122-3
  Poland, 169
  USA, 113-27
  Western and Eastern Europe compared, 167-75
  West Germany, 160, 169
  Yugoslavia, 169
Lifelong Educational Entitlement *see* LEE

Lifelong Education for National Liberation and Socialist Revolution *see* LENLSR
Lifelong Learning Act (USA), 113, 115, 118-19
Lifelong Learning and Public Policy, 120
Li Mao-yuan, 196
Lin Yu-sheng, 204
Linder, S B, 23-4
Lindquist, J, 64
Literacy, 271-2, 279, 280, 289, 291
  adult, 235, 280, 290, 292
  China, 195-7
  humanistic, 34
  India, 212
  LENLSR, 188, 189
  rates, LBER, 186
  school leavers, 184
  technological, 34
  Thailand, 212
Liu Shao-chi, 195
Lloyd, A S, 72
Lloyd Jones, D E, 246
Local Education Authorities *see* LEAs
Location, Swedish recurrent education, 153-4
London, J, 63
Long, H B, 62
Looking Backward, 120
Lorenzetto, A, 189
Loring, Rosalind, 123
Lowe, J, 59, 75
Lowe, Robert, 294
Lowenthal, M F, 61

MSC (Manpower Services Commission), 234, 258, 260, 263, 293
Maas, H S, 61
McAnany, E G, 188
Mace, J, 46
McIntosh, Naomi E, 244-56, 315-16
McKie, 65
Maddi, S R, 61
Mahler, F, 172
Malraux, André, 199
Management:
  development, 258-9, 264
  training, 264
  working time, 24
Manning, 106
Manpower:
  needs, 113, 183
  schemes, 19
  training, 149
Manpower Services Commission *see* MSC
Manual workers, working time, 24
Mao Tsetung, 193-6, 198-200, 202, 205
Mao Tsetung Thought, 203, 204
Maoris, 215
Marketing, adult learning administration, 69
Market policies, 106
Marriage Law 1950 (China), 199
Marxism, 203, 204

Marxists, 207
Mass communication systems, literacy, 188
Mass media, control and use, 221
Material goods, as motivators, 21
Mathematics, computer-assisted learning, 37
Mature students, 40
Mauger, Peter, 193-208, 316
Maurice, M, 25
May 7 cadre schools, 203-4
Mbilinyi, Marjorie, 176-92, 316
Media:
  choice, 48
  control and use, 221
  role in continuing education, 253
Medicine, re-certification, 125
Medsker, L B, 61
Megarry, Jacquetta, 9-14, 316-17
Melbourne, 2nd Viscount (William Lamb), 98
Melo, A, 173
Men, working life, 89
Merriam, S, 72
Meta-information, 42
Meta-technology, 32
Metroplex Assembly, 66
Mezirow, J, 64, 68, 70
Microelectronics, impact, 80-2
Microprocessors, 32
Middle classes, LBER, 177
Migrant workers, 48, 169, 173
Miles, M B, 66
Miller, H L, 65, 69
Minimal education, 182
Mitrovic, L R, 172
Mobility:
  social, through education, 170
  upward, schooling system, 181
Mobilization:
  education for, 221
  mass, 189
  non-formal education, 214
Molyneux, Frank, 227-43, 317
Mondale, Walter, 113, 115
Monette, M L, 64
Money, importance, 28
Moore, D, 232
Moral education, China, 201
Motivation:
  adult education, 248, 252
  group, 296
  learners, 173
  non-academic factors, 174
  participation, 106
  self-, 42
  work effort, 21
Mulder, M, 103
Multi-national companies, 107
Multiple job holding, 25
Multiwork alternative, 21
Murray, Len, 99
Museums, support for, 121

NACEELF (National Advisory Council on Extension and Continuing Education), 117, 119-20
NAF (Norwegian Employers Confederation), 137, 138, 140
NCES (National Centres for Education Statistics), 117, 124
Nakamoto, J, 64
Nankai University, 206
Napier College of Technology, 84
National Advisory Council on Adult Education, 117
National Advisory Council on Career Education, 117
National Advisory Council on Community Education, 117
National Advisory Council on Extension and Continuing Education *see* NACEELF
National Advisory Council on Vocational Education, 117
National Board of Universities and Colleges (USA), 151
National Centres for Education Statistics *see* NCES
National Commission on Libraries and Information Sciences, 117
National Commission on Manpower Policy, 117
National Institute of Adult Education, 263, 292
National Institute of Education, 117
Nationalism, 34
Needs:
  adult education, 248
  adult learning, 64
  assessment, 249
  identification, 102
Neijs, A, 189
Nelson and Colne College of Further Education, 232
Nepal, 211, 213, 219
New Chiuchuan Daily, 196
New Zealand, 212, 215
Niemi, J A, 72, 73
Neugarten, B S, 61
Newcomb, T M, 61, 63
New School for Social Research, 40
Nigeria, schooling system, 179
Non-formal education (NFE), 114-15, 210-14, 221
Non-traditional studies, 122-3
Non-work time, trends and changes, 23-5 *see also* Leisure
Nora, Simon, 33
Nordic Council of Ministers, 53
Norfolk Federation of Women's Institutes, 282
Northern Ireland Department of Education, 230, 263
Norway:
  adult education, 137-45
  Basic Agreement, 137, 138, 140-3
  co-determination, 140-1

Norwegian Adult Education Act 1976, 102
Norwegian Employers' Confederation *see* NAF
Norwegian Federation of Trade Unions, 137, 138, 140
Norwegian Institute of Adult Education, 145
Numeracy, 279, 280, 291, 292
Nursery schools, 173

OECD (Organization for Economic Co-operation and Development), 168
  commenced work on recurrent education, 17-18
  Conference on Future Structures of Post-Secondary Education, Paris 1973, 238
  Conference on Policies for Educational Growth, 1970, 51
  Education Advisory Committee, 217
  integration, 171
  interdependence, 98
  leave of absence, 26-7
  living patterns, 28
  Pacific Circle, 209, 210
  profiles of the elderly, 28
  recurrent education, 47-50, 52-4, 114, 216, 228-9, 239, 290
  role, 46
  women in paid work, 25
Oakes, Gordon, 237, 247
Obedience, 187
Objectives:
  adult learning, 64-5, 74
  LBER, 182
Occupational:
  see also Careers; Job/s
  analysis, Open University, 236
  choice, postponement, 138
  role, adult life cycles, 60
  skills, 105-6
Office of Education, 117
Older people *see* Elderly people
Ombudsmen, 21
On the Move, 271
Open Broadcasting Authority (proposed), 276
Open-door schooling, 201
Open learning systems, 84, 268
Open University, 40, 84, 228, 234-5, 245, 250-2, 267-8, 271-84, 288, 290
  broadcasting, 278
  cable television, 36
  Committee on Continuing Education, 273-9
  Continuing Education Division, 278, 281
  course arrangement and design, 279-82
  credit transfers, 293
  employers' attitudes, 253
  fees, 276
  finances, 278-9, 292
  Interim Delegacy for Continuing Education, 281
  Learning Resources Centre, 278, 279
  objects, 273
  occupational analysis of applications, 236
  Planning Committee, 272, 273
  Post-Experience Unit, 277, 279
  Report on Adult Concern Courses and Materials, 280
  sponsorship, 281-2
  statistics, 274
Opportunity costs, 19
Oral communication, 291
Organizational skills, 34, 35
Organization for Economic Co-operation and Development *see* OECD
Orr, B, 60
Östlund, Hans-Erik, 146-58, 317
Outreach activities, 156-7
Over-production, education, 19
Overtime, 24
  reduction, 22
Owen, J D, 24
Oxenham, J, 182

PLA (People's Liberation Army), 193, 199, 201, 204-5
Palaces of culture, 206-7
Palme, Olof, 47, 146
Panorama, 36
Papua New Guinea, 220
Part-time:
  courses, 231, 251, 252
  programmes, 58
  students, 40
  study, 290; adult preferences, 250
  work, 22, 26; increases, 25
Part-work, part-study schools, 197, 200, 203
Participation:
  see also Industrial democracy
  adult learning, 69-70
  education for, 240
  educational management, 169
  non-formal education, 214
  pilot schemes, 53
Participatory research, 189-90
Participatory Research Approach in Africa, 190
Party schools, China, 204
Pasquier, B, 131
Pateman, C, 101
Peasants:
  impoverishment, 186-8
  lecturers, 190
Peasants' Vocabulary Textbook, 196
Pedagogy, 245
Peer teaching, 39, 41, 42
Penfield, K R, 72
Pennington, F, 63, 64
People's Daily, 200, 207
People's Liberation Army *see* PLA

INDEX

Performance:
    adult life cycles, 60
    interaction with self-concept, 60
    lifelong learning, 121-2
Permanent education, 46, 51-4
Perry, P J C, 264
Perry, Sir Walter, 273
Personal:
    characteristics, adult learning, 69
    development, 49; unrelated to work, 20
Personality:
    development, 60
    variables, 61
Peston, Maurice, 86-96, 317
Peterson, R E, 115-16, 118, 119
Pflüger, A, 174
Philippines:
    ISOS, 214
    non-formal education, 213
Physical skills, 35
Planning:
    company, 106
    responsibilities, Sweden, 153
    strategic, recurrent basis, 146-58
Play, importance to children, 38
Plays, 105
Pleasure, education for, 35-6
Poland:
    lifelong education, 169
    rural areas, 173
    rural *v* urban education, 173
Policy-making skills, 105
Political:
    competence, 105
    democracy, links with permanent education, 54
    education, 289; China, 201; WEA, 293
    studies, China, 204
Political Education, report, 160
Politicians, educational policies, 168
Polytechnics, 232
Poor, the, LBER in Africa, 176-92
Post-industrial economy, 32-43
Post Office, 36
Poverty, solutions, 35
Power, equalization, 97-8
Premises, 166
    adult education, 254
    self-help labour, 185
Pre-school education, 173
Pre-School Playgroups Association, 281
Presentational form, educational process, 83
Prestel, 36, 253
Pricing, 106
Primary education, universal, in Africa, 179
Prior knowledge, 259
Problem-solving, 62, 107
Procedural rules, 105
Procedural skills, 105
Proceedings of the Invitational Conference on Continuing Education, Manpower Policy and Lifelong Learning, 1977, 120
Production, integration with education, 172
Productivity, 49, 92, 106
    LBER, 177
Professional:
    development, 49
    education, 100-4
Professionals, working time, 24
Programme development, adult learning, 63-6
    activities, 65-6
    evaluation, 66, 74
    needs, 64
    objectives, 64-5
    setting, 64
Programme evaluation, adult learning, 74
Projects, team, 42
Propaganda, China, 200
Public hearings, simulated, 42
Publicity, 165, 252
Public relations, 165
Public service, demand for, 22
Public wishes, 21
Punctuality, 187
Purvis, J, 245

Qualifications, 171
    admission barrier, 252
    employment prospects, 19

RLS (Regional Learning Service), 123
ROEAO *see* UNESCO: Regional Office for Education in Asia
Radio:
    courses in China, 206
    electronic education, 36-7
    in place of literacy, 188
Rahnema, Majid, 217
Rate of return analysis, 183
Reading, 37-8
Reasoning, 291
Re-certification, 125-6
Recreation:
    see also Leisure
    Volkshochschulen, 164
Recruitment, 106
Recurrent education:
    compared with non-formal education, 210
    costs and benefits, 92
    definitions and distinctions, 45-54
    economic cost, 92
    evolution, 47-51
    financing, 86-96, 294
    nexus with industrial democracy, 221
    normal approach, 93
    not understood in USA, 114
    perceptions, 228-34
    social policy, 157-8
    terminology, 228-34
Recurrent Education — A Plea for Lifelong Learning, 228

INDEX

Red Army *see* PLA
Re-education, 91
   compulsory, 126
Regional colleges, 232
Regional Learning Service *see* RLS
Regione Toscana, 174
Relationships, within and between societies, 34
Relevant, 46
Re-licensing, 125
Remuneration systems, 50
Report of the Committee on Continuing Education, 228
Representations, *Volkshochschule* participants, 166
Research:
   adult learning, 71-2
   and development, 106; importance, 32; production of new wealth, 33-4
   integration with education, 172
Resources:
   adult learning, 70-1
   allocation, 70
   misallocation, 94
   natural, constraints, 82
Retirement:
   age at, 90
   changes, 239
   class structures, 25
   early, 26, 289
   higher education, 90
   policies, 20
Re-training, 18, 91
   vocational, 82
   West Germany, 159, 161
Reward:
   separation from work, 21
   system, 269
Richardson, K, 228
Richta, R, 173
Rivera, R J, 57, 63, 69
Robbins Committee Report, 271
Robbins Principle, 238
Robots, 32-4
Rodriguez, C, 234
Rogers, E M, 69
Role changes, 60
Romania, Council of State of the Socialist Republic of Romania, 174
Rules, learning, 104
Rural:
   areas, 173
   development, definition, 181
   impoverishment, 177
Russell Report on Adult Education, 232, 235, 245, 272

Sabbaticals, 22, 26-7
Safety, 141
Salary, minimum national guaranteed, 135
Salesmen, training, 264
Sanders, J R, 66
Sandwich courses, 231

Satisfaction, personal, 20
   see also Job/s: satisfaction
Scandinavia, industrial democracy, 222
Schaie, K W, 59, 61
Schein, E H, 69
Schoggen, P, 63
Schön, D A, 69
School-based education, 38-9
Schooling:
   reform needed for LENLSR, 188-90
   system, upward mobility, 181
School management, China, 199-200
Schools Commission (Australia), 217
Schramm, W, 219
Schuller, Tom, 97-110, 317
Science Conference, national, 1978 (China), 207
Sciences:
   computer games, 38
   interaction of technology and science, 41
Scottish Council for Educational Technology, 278
Scottish Education Department, 230, 263
   Conference on Recurrent Education, 237
   Higher Education in 1990s, 237, 244, 246-8, 280
   Seminar on Recurrent Education, Glasgow, 1977, 228
Scottish Health Education Unit, 282
Scottish Institute of Adult Education, 263
Secondary education, separation of streams, 169
Secondary Education Commission, Sweden, 1976, 149
Secondary schooling, Norway, 139-40
Secretary of State for Education and Science, 229
Secretary of State for Northern Ireland, 229
Secretary of State for Scotland, 229
Secretary of State for Wales, 229
Security, economic, 21
Seeger, Pete, 114
Selection, 171
   see also Admission
   adult education, 70, 169
   Chinese higher education, 201-2, 207
   post-elementary education, 189
   secondary education, 235
   system, LBER, 183
Self-concept, 60-1
Self-development, education for, 35
Self-directed learning, 66, 114, 259
Self-directedness, 60
Self-expression, 114
Self-help groups, 58
Self-management, Yugoslavia, 172
Self-motivation, 42
Self-paced work, 259
Self-reliance, 34

Self-service economy, 20
Self-understanding, 114
Seminar on Education and Training Alternatives in Education in African Countries, 1974, 185
Service:
  economy, 20, 33
  value of, 81
Sesame Street, 36
Setting, adult learning, 64
Shanas, E, 59
Shanghai, colleges, 206
Shanghai Machine Tools Plant, 202
Shanghai No 26 Wireless Radio Factory, 202
Sharp, R, 182
Sheffield Group on Mature Entry to Education, 240
Sheffield, J, 182
Shiftwork, increase in, 25
Shoemaker, F F, 69
Shop stewards:
  interpretation of financial information, 103
  training, 108
Short-term programmes, 58
Shulman, C H, 114, 121
Simkins, T, 182
Simmons, J, 183
Simulation games, 42
Situational characteristics, adult learning, 69
Sjogren, D D, 62, 69
Skard, Øyvind, 137-45, 317-18
Skills:
  artistic, 35
  committee, 105
  obsolescent, 177
  occupational, 105-6
  organizational, 34, 35
  policy-making, 105
  procedural, 105
  social, 35
Smith, R M, 64, 67
Smith, Ralph, 281
Smith-Hughes Act 1917 (USA), 118
Snow, Edgar, 204-5
Social:
  change, personal adjustment, 73-4
  class, struggles, 168
  condition, learners, 173
  democracy, education for, 240
  development, 35
  functions, place of work, 169
  groups: life expectancy, 25; retirement, 25; work and non-work time, 29; working time, 24
  opportunity, equality, 49
  policy, recurrent education, 157-8
  relationships, estrangement by, 61
  skills, 35
  system, relationship with educational system, 234
  values, 21

Socialist revolution and reconstruction, LBER, 177
Socialist Upsurge in China's Countryside, 196
Societal contexts, 73
Society, interaction of science and technology, 41
Society of Industrial Tutors, 292
Socio-economic constraints, emancipation, 50
Socio-educational values, non-formal education, 214
Socrates, 291
Solomon, D, 65-6
Sorge, A, 98
South East Asian Ministers of Education Organization Centre Innotech, 214
South Pacific, exchange of ideas with Australia, 209-23
Spare-time education, China, 205-7
Spear, G E, 68
Specialization, 41, 42
Sponsorship:
  continuing education, 253
  Open University, 279, 281-2
Staff:
  see also Teachers; Tutors
  adult learning, 70
  Volkshochschulen, 166
Stake, R E, 66
State Planning for Lifelong Learning: Improving Access for all Citizens, 120
Statistics:
  German continuing education, 163
  Open University, 274
  UK, 233
  USA, 124
Status:
  achievement, 20
  instrumental value of education, 19
Statute of Articifers 1563, 264
Stern, B, 20
Stonier, Tom, 31-44, 318
Stress, jobs, 28
Structural barriers, adult education, 251
Strukturplan für das Bildungswesen, 160
Stubblefield, H W, 65
Student-centred education, 102
Students:
  co-determination, 144
  course content, 102
  mode of operation, 83
Study groups, 164
Study trips, 164, 165
Sub-group activity, 259
Subject centred education, 102
Submissiveness, 187
Subsidies, employment in manufacture, 22
Suchodolski, B, 168
Supervision, obsolescence, 177
Swantz, M L, 190

INDEX

Sweden:
  Commission on Secondary Education 1976, 149
  counselling, 295
  Educational Commission 1968, 147
  educational reform, 228
  grants, 155
  paid educational leave, 293
  recurrent education, 146-58
  university admissions, 240

TAFE (Technical and Further Education Commission [Australia]), 216, 217
TOPS scheme, 264
TUC (Trades Union Congress):
  Conference on Continuing Education, 1978, 281, 282
  Counselling Advice and Information Group, 281
  needs assessment, 249
  Opportunity for Women Group, 281
  Priorities in Continuing Education, 245, 280-1
  Race Group, 281
  trade union education, 293
  vocational training, 264
Tanzania:
  grain storage, 190
  LBER, 187
  primary education, 179
Teachers:
  see also Staff; Tutors
  authoritarian relationships, 181
  education, 143
  on-the-job training, 189
  re-training, 269
Teaching-learning transaction, 65-6
Teaching leave, 131
Teaching style, 65
Technical and Further Education Commission, Australia see TAFE
Technical skills, 105-6
Technician and Business Education Councils, 293
Techniques, exporting, 88
Technocrats, educational policies, 168
Technological change, 258, 272, 287-8
  LBER, 177
  pace and direction, 21
Technological forecasting, 288
Technology:
  effects on labour demand, 87
  interaction of science and society, 41
  meta-, 32
Technology/consumption alternative, 21
Teleconference links, 278
Telephone teaching, continuing education, 253
Television:
  cable, 36
  college, Shanghai, 206
  continuing education, 276
  electronic education, 36-7
  home-based education, 31

recurrent education, 294
role in education, 95
Terminal education, 182
Thailand, 212, 213
Thames Television, 36
Third World, competition from, 88
Tientsin, Marxist-Leninist college, 206
Times Higher Education Supplement, 240
Times Newspaper Group, 228
Timiras, P S, 62
Toffler, Alvin, 43
Tough, Alan, 57, 66, 122
Tourism, education coupled with, 41
Toyne, Dr (Exeter University), 237
Trade Union Congress, 9th National (China), 207
Trade Union Research Unit, 103
Trade unions:
  accountancy, 101
  counselling, 295
  educational leave, 136; paid, 293; worker, 131
  education programmes, 172
  equalization of power, 98
  evening promotion courses, 129
  lifelong learning, 118
  rights, 130
  role, 99
  Swedish adult education, 153
  Swedish recurrent education, 155
  training programmes, 142
  vocational education, 264
  West and East Europe, 167
Trades Union Congress see TUC
Training, 106
  see also Re-training
  as an investment, 91
  compared with education, 91-2, 289
  co-ordination with education and employment, 295-6
  institutes, location, 94
  integration of initial and subsequent, 173
  interface with vocational education, 262
  on-the-job, 290
  plurality of responsibility, 257, 265-6
  relationship with education, 255
  services, UK, 263-4
Training Service Agency, 234
Training Services Division, 263
Transferability, continuing education, 252-3
Transistors, 32
Travel, in education, 40-1
Travers, R M W, 65
Trent, J W, 61
Trice, H M, 66
Truesdell, L R, 69
Trust, low/high-trust dynamic, 103
Tutor:
  informal, 129
  training, 277

INDEX

UIA, 174
UNDP, 184
UNESCO (United Nations Educational, Scientific and Cultural Organization):
  Asian office, Tehran, 219
  Asian region, 216, 218
  control and use of mass media, 221
  éducation permanente, 51-4, 113, 115
  Learning to Be, 51-4
  lifelong learning, 51-2
  non-formal education, 214
  Regional Consultation Meeting, 218
  Regional Meetings, 213
  Regional Office for Education, in Asia, Bangkok, 211
  role, 46
Ulster Polytechnic, 232
Uncertainty, problem-solving, 62
Under-privileged groups, recurrent education, 48
Unemployment, 19, 239
  see also Employment
  adult education, 144
  effects on education, 20
  future rises, 288
  impact of microelectronics, 82
  lifelong education as a counter to effects, 82
  permanent feature, 22, 25
  persistent large-scale, 94
United Kingdom:
  continuing education, statistics, 233
  industrial democracy, 172
  recurrent education, 227-43
United Nations Educational, Scientific and Cultural Organization *see* UNESCO
United States of America:
  credit systems, 40 *see also* Educredit
  financial entitlements, 290
  lifelong learning, 113-27
Universality, 173
Universal schooling, 188
Universities, 232
  admission rules, 140
  choice of, 35
  credit systems, 40
  extra-mural departments, 232
  UK, 230
  universalization, 188
University Council for Adult Education, 263
University Grants Committee, 263
University of the Air *see* Open University
University Without Walls, 288
Upper Secondary Schools, 148-50
Urban education, 173

VCRs, 253
Vacations, 20 *see also* Holidays; Leave
Vaillant, G, 61
Value added, 101
Value judgements, 157
Valves, 32
Van Straubenzee, W R, 245
Venables, Sir Peter, 267, 271-84, 318
Venables Report, 235
Verbal behaviour, social class differences, 62
Verner, C, 64
Veterans, educational support, 113
Video-tapes, home-based education, 38
Viklund, B, 108
Visalberghi, A, 172
Vocational education:
  access, 267-8
  adult needs, 260-2
  co-ordination, 257-70
  current provision, 262
  curriculum development, 266-7
  distinguished from non-vocational, 289
  employer's role, 253
  equality, 139-40
  interface with training, 262
  needs of client groups, 268
  purposes, 250
  responsibility for, 257, 265-6
  teaching staff, 174
Vocational Education Act 1963 (USA), 118
Vocational guidance, Sweden, 156
Vocationalism, 288
Vocationalization, 149
Vocational re-training, 82
Vocational training:
  integration with education, 249
  West Germany, 159, 161
Volkshochschulen, 159, 160, 162, 294
  functions, 164-6
  organization, 165-6
  position, 163
  programme of courses, 164-5
Voluntary educational associations, 153, 156
Vouchers, 121

WEA (Workers' Educational Association), 232, 264, 293
Wang Hsueh-lu, 196
Waniewicz, I, 122
Ward, Champion, 217
Weil, M, 65
Wensman Lodge Adult Education Centre, 282
White, R W, 61
White-collar work, proletarianization, 177
Whitlam, Gough, 216
Wilensky, H, 23
Williams, P, 182
Williams, R H, 61
Willmott, P, 27
Wilson, Harold, 273
Wirths, C G, 61
Wittgenstein, L, 108

For Product Safety Concerns and Information please contact our EU representative GPSR@taylorandfrancis.com
Taylor & Francis Verlag GmbH, Kaufingerstraße 24, 80331 München, Germany

www.ingramcontent.com/pod-product-compliance
Lightning Source LLC
Chambersburg PA
CBHW051628230426
43669CB00013B/2217